W9-DBW-163

THOUGHT AND EXPRESSION IN THE SIXTEENTH CENTURY

THOUGHT
AND
EXPRESSION
IN THE
SIXTEENTH CENTURY

HENRY OSBORN TAYLOR

Second Revised Edition

VOLUME I

FREDERICK UNGAR PUBLISHING CO.
NEW YORK

Second revised edition, published in 1930

Republished 1959

First edition 1920

Second Printing

Printed in the United States of America

Library of Congress Catalog Card Number 59-11670

TO

J. I. T.

PREFACE TO THE SECOND EDITION

Because of their many advances in civilization, the fifteenth and sixteenth centuries have been treated as periods of revival and have been dubbed The Renaissance. More essentially, however, they show the dynamic continuity of human growth. The concept Renaissance, with its implications, breaks in upon this continuity and, whether applied to the sixteenth century or the twelfth, seems to me inconsistent with a sound view of the mental and material development of western Europe.

In Italy and other countries the fifteenth and sixteenth centuries were a time of discovery. Commerce expanded, wealth increased, the arts flourished, knowledge grew and thought quickened. A livelier interest was taken in the direct investigation of nature including the human body. Indeed the term revival or Renaissance might least inappropriately be applied to the advance of natural science, which represented some revolt not merely from scholasticism but from the ancient Greek authorities. To be sure, the classic store was drawn upon even more largely than before. Copernicus made a new and prodigious use of the Ptolemaic observations, and Vesalius deeply studied Galen before denouncing his errors. But the essence of the scientific revival did not lie in any rediscovery or use of ancient knowledge. It lay in the rising spirit of independent and direct investigation. Those who wished to know the natural truth of man and the world about him turned to observation and experiment and dissection. By reason of its moving spirit this science was quick to dissent even from the authorities it used.

The present edition of this book is a reprint of the first with a few corrections and added references.

HENRY OSBORN TAYLOR.

New York, February, 1930.

PREFACE

My purpose is to give an intellectual survey of the sixteenth century. I would set forth the human susceptibilities and faculties of this alluring time, its tastes, opinions and appreciations, as they expressed themselves in scholarship and literature, in philosophy and science, and in religious reform. Italian painting is presented briefly as the supreme self-expression of the Italians.

The more typical intellectual interests of the fifteenth century also are discussed for their own sake, while those of the previous time are treated as introductory. I have tried to show the vital continuity between the prior mediaeval development and the period before us.

The mind must fetch a far compass if it would see the sixteenth century truly. Every stage in the life and thought of Europe represents a passing phase, which is endowed with faculties not begotten of itself, and brings forth much that is not exclusively its own. For good or ill, for patent progress, or apparent retrogression, its capacities, idiosyncrasies and productions belong, in large measure, to the whole, which is made up of past as well as present, the latter pregnant with the future. Yet, though fed upon the elements (sometimes the refuse) of the past, each time seems to develop according to its own nature. Waywardly, foolishly, or with wholesome originality, it evolves a novel temperament and novel thoughts.

We shall treat the fifteenth and sixteenth centuries as a final and objective present; and all that went before will be regarded as a past which entered into them. It included pagan Antiquity, Judaism and the Gospel, the influence of the fecund East, the contribution of the Christian Fathers,— this whole store of knowledge and emotion, not merely as it came into being, but in its changing progress through the Middle Ages, until it entered the thought of our period and became the stimulus or suggestion of its feeling. Distinctive mediaeval creations likewise must be included, seeing that they also entered formatively into the constitutions of later men. The Middle Ages helped antiquity to shape the faculties and furnish the tastes of the sixteenth century. These faculties and tastes were then applied to what the past seemed also to offer as from a distinct and separate platform. Only by realizing the action of these formative and contributive agencies, shall we perceive this period's true relationships, and appreciate its caused and causal being, begotten of the past, yet vital (as each period is) with its own spirit, and big with a modernity which was not yet.

Two pasts may be distinguished, the one remote, the other proximate. The former may be taken as consisting of the antique world as it became its greater self, and then as it crumbled, while its thought and mood were assuming those forms in which they passed into the Middle Ages. The proximate or immediate past was the mediaeval time, itself progressing century after century under the influence of whatever had entered into it, chiefly through those last solvent and transition centuries in which the remote past ended.

The Middle Ages and the fifteenth or sixteenth century bore the same fundamental relationship to this remote past. Each succeeding mediaeval century, besides inheriting what had become known in the time directly preceding it, endeavored to reach back to the remote past for further treasure. Thus the twelfth century sought to reach behind the eleventh, in order to learn more of the greater past, and the thirteenth reached behind the twelfth. So Petrarch, in the fourteenth, would reach behind the vociferously damned thirteenth century to antiquity itself; and the fifteenth century humanists endeavored to do likewise. That century, like Petrarch's time, drew from its immediate mediaeval past as copiously as each mediaeval century drew from its predecessor, and *willy nilly* resembled the mediaeval centuries in striving to reach back of them for treasures previously undisclosed.

One thinks of the transmitted influence of the past, whether remote or proximate, as knowledge and suggestion, as intellectual or emotional or social material to be appropriated and made further use of. It is well to think of it also as flowing on in modes of expression, which constitute the finished form of the matter, whether the form lie in language or in the figures of plastic art. Thoughts and emotions cannot pass from one time to another save in modes of their expression. And the more finished and perfect, the more taking, the more beautiful, the form of expression, the more enduring will be its influence and effect. The seemingly formless material which is transmitted orally or in manuscripts or printed books from age to age, had necessarily reached some mode of expression, however vile. And although much wretched matter has come down through time, we may not ascribe its survival to the shortcomings of its form, but rather to the fact that somehow in its wretchedness and intellectual squalor it suited the squalid ignorance of men.

So it is fruitful to think, for instance, of each mediaeval century, as well as of the great sixteenth, as drawing the language of its thinking from the past, and then building up its own forms of thinking and expression. Each province of discipline furnishes concepts and a vocabulary. As each century appropriates them and makes them its own, they become its modes of thought, and the forms of its self-expression. Thus not only thought, but the language of expression, is handed on with enhancements from generation to generation. Each generation uses the thought, and expresses itself in the forms and concepts, which it has made its own — has made into its self-expression. Yet there is some change, some increase, some advance. To the transformation of inherited thought and phrase into modes of self-expression, each century or generation brings a tone and temper of its own, perhaps some change of attitude toward life, and at all events the increment and teaching of the experience which has come to it through living.

Difficulties of arrangement confront a work like the present. Shall it cleave to racehood and nationality or follow topics? Topics ignore racial lines and geographical boundaries.

The plan must bend to the demands on it. Sometimes racial traits dominate an individual, and the conditions of his life and land shape his career, even a great career like Luther's. A national situation may point the substance of an issue, as, in England, in Wyclif's controversy with the papacy. For quite another illustration, one may observe how a diversity of interest and taste between Italians and Frenchmen impressed a different purpose and manner upon classical studies in Italy and France.

On the other hand such a story as that of the advance of the physical sciences in the fifteenth and sixteenth centuries has little to do with land or race; the votaries belong to every people, and pursue their investigations indifferently in their own countries or where foreign localities offer greater advantages. So a general survey should follow the course of the most dominant and vital elements.

A kindred question goes to the roots of the truth of phenomena: should one adhere to a temporal arrangement, century by century, or follow sequences of influence and effect across the imaginary boundaries of these arbitrary time divisions? While it is convenient to speak of "centuries," one is always pursuing the vital continuity of effect. The virtue of fruitful effort passes into future achievement. One seeks to follow facts in their progeny. Yet this is difficult, since the genealogical tree is infinitely ramified, and every event, every achievement, has as many forbears as a human being! The truthfulness of events lies in the process of *becoming,* rather than in the concrete phenomenon which catches our attention. It would be as foolish to end the consideration of Petrarch with his death as it would be to treat him as if he and his work and influence really began the day when he was born, or first read Cicero. Nothing begins or ends. We may even think of all that is, or ever was or will be, as one mighty self-evolving present, which holds the effective being, the becoming, of the past, and contains the future, of which this present is in turn the becoming.

HENRY OSBORN TAYLOR.

New York, May, 1920.

CONTENTS

BOOK I
THE HUMANISM OF ITALY

BOOK II

ERASMUS AND LUTHER

CONTENTS

BOOK I

THE HUMANISM OF ITALY

THOUGHT AND EXPRESSION IN THE SIXTEENTH CENTURY

CHAPTER I

THE LITTERAE HUMANIORES: PETRARCH AND BOCCACCIO

HUMANISM in a literary sense is usually thought of as referring to humane studies, the *litterae humaniores*. Their academic field has always been the literature and plastic arts of Greece and Rome. The conception seems just, as far as it reaches. For, in the main, the thought, the literature and the plastic arts of Greece and Rome are the record and expression of man living on the earth, and all things are conceived, reflected on, and felt in their relationships to humanity. Occasionally Greek thought and its expression soared beyond the sphere of man, as sometimes with Plato and his spiritual descendants. And the world of nature was embraced by Aristotle and those who preceded or followed him in physical researches. Among the Greeks there were wise physicians, great physicists, mathematicians and astronomers. Greek achievements in physical science are liable to be ignored because we have gone so far beyond them.

But in the sixteenth century, Greece still offered much physical science for profitable study by the learned world, which was only beginning a systematic investigation of the phenomena of nature. Interest in natural phenomena was as yet scarcely de-humanized, or accepted and pursued without regard to the assumed connection between the world of nature and the fortunes or designs of men. Nature bristled with portents. The science of Astrology observed the heavens for horoscopes and looked to celestial influences upon men. But Astronomy was Astrology de-humanized and set upon the basis of its own explanatory truth regarding the movements of the sun and moon and stars.

Such astronomy had been pursued by the astronomers of Alexandria, who still did not neglect its astrological bearings. With the Greeks, natural science generally was mindful of the connection between the apparent ends of nature and the welfare or miscarriages of men. Greek science was apt to be anthropomorphic, and Greek philosophy in its treatment of physical and metaphysical truth remained genially human. In all Greek thinking, man remained the πόλις, the city-state, whence thoughts as citizens went forth to return with sheaves of knowledge that were to be transformed to human wisdom.

So philosophy and natural science, as part of the Greek consideration of life, are not excluded from Greek humanism, which brought all intellectual interests into its web and kept them circling around man. This is why, although we no longer quite determine our thinking by what Plato said or Aristotle, we cherish their metaphysics as a beautiful and still moving human creation, closely knit into the intellectual needs of man. And the Greek and Latin literature, the poetry, the immortal stories of human fortunes, the profound and inclusive consideration of human life, all these have never ceased to charm the generations of men, nor have they ceased to be perennial fonts of human illumination and consideration of human life. They are a well which no one can exhaust, but from which every one may draw according to the capacities of his understanding.

Accordingly the literature of Rome and Greece, the Classics *par excellence,* have been called the humanities; the reading and study of them have been called humane studies, and their votaries have been known as humanists. Yet the proper humanist, whether belonging to the sixteenth century or to other times, is such not only in his pursuits, but in his mind. He must be as that which he reads and loves, interested and absorbed in man here on this earth, in his individuality and accordant or disaccordant fortunes, in his loves and hates, his fancies and desires, in all that makes the atmosphere of mortal life.

He will be not merely a reader of the classics, but an individual of definite temperament and taste, with which his favorite studies accord. His pursuits are the fruit of his desires and opinions, the fruit of his personality in fine. Consequently his humanism with its occupations, pre-occupations, and achievement, is an expression of himself. And when there are many humanists, living and reading and studying at the same time, delighting in the discussion and exploitation of their common pursuits, humanism becomes a phase of the time, a phase of its self-expression. Such humanism is not apt to flourish now, because our horizons are too large, and we have a different consciousness of a universe, in which man is a rather recent counter and one that possibly may also pass, as the creatures of prior geologic ages have had their aeons and have passed away. It is not that we constantly look beyond to another and immortal sphere, as most people did in the Middle Ages, and many humanists in the next centuries more perfunctorily. But natural science, physical science, biological science, all for their own sake, have their innings now, and the man-centered equilibrium of the old humanists is at least tipped, if not upset.

In the fifteenth and sixteenth centuries a large proportion of active-minded men devoted themselves to humane studies, possessed humanistic tempers, and took a humanistic view of life. They were absorbed in the mortal life of man, their own especially; in its conduct, deeds and passions, in its whims and desires and fancies, in its success or failures, and in the moral, philosophical, esthetic consideration of it all. They read and studied the great writings which were the universal and glorious exponents of these fascinating matters, and they were drawn by everything connected with that antique world of which these classic writers were the flower. So humanism may be deemed a phase of the self-expression of the fifteenth and sixteenth centuries and a characteristic feature of their entire mental progress.

I

The disparate humanity of the early Middle Ages required some centuries to develop a full complement of humane qualities. Only the antique Latin literature could be the guide, and furnish the means, of such development. Too constantly this literature of *litterae humaniores* was used wrongly and wilfully as the vehicle of what it did not contain. Men found in it instruction, set in allegory, touching the mysteries of all the worlds and man their denizen. Yet no century was completely lacking in humanists, who, perhaps in a hampered or uninstructed way, looked at the classics truly, and found in them solace and suggestion touching life.

The *litterae humaniores* were admirably cultivated by certain men in the twelfth century; [1] yet as it closed, the absorbing interest in Aristotelian scholasticism began to prove detrimental to letters, although it did not hamper the splendid advance in building and sculpture and glass painting, which is as great a glory of the thirteenth century as Thomas Aquinas himself. The main inspiration of that Gothic art was religious, even theological, rather than humane. Yet it embraced and seemed to carry heavenward humanity's daily round of tasks and interests, thus representing an ennobled or sublimated humanism. But while it lifted human nature, it did less to enlarge it or promote the capacity for mortal happiness and joy.

This was to be the office of the Latin and Greek Classics. Through the Middle Ages and afterwards, they were to expand and equip humanity upon the earth, and uplift it so far as might be without drawing it up to heaven. They were to enrich human life by humanizing all that made man's environment, transforming the world in which he found himself into objects of human perception, interest, sentiment. They also furnished their lovers with a variety of just reflections upon life, and fostered in them the habit of consideration.

[1] Cf. Taylor, *The Mediaeval Mind,* Chap. XXXI. My references to this work are to the paging and chapters of the second and third editions.

The vigorous literary use of the vernaculars had, by the fourteenth century, lowered the vitality and impaired the clarity of the Latin still employed by educated men. Especially, the Latin of scholastic philosophy and political controversy had become a dreadful example of how a language could be mishandled. While the learned of no one country held the monopoly of this abuse, still the obnoxious jargon of scholasticism was in the main a product of northern lands, where interest in theology had possessed so many minds. Men who were free from that obsession would naturally detest its lingo. But in distorting the Latin tongue, the treatises upon the civil law were not so far behind, and it happened that the strongest personal reaction against these logical and linguistic decadences arose in one who hated scholasticism and had no liking for the law, to which his father would have apprenticed him. This reaction proved a lasting irritant with Petrarch, although it was not a dominant influence in his life.

For such, one turns to his admiration for antiquity and his love of the classic Latin literature. Thousands of his countrymen had felt the like before him. One thinks not only of Dante himself, but of the Paduan Mussato, who cared for Latin letters and was crowned poet in Padua in 1314.[2] In Italy the cult of antiquity, with a dumb cultivation of the classics, had not been as sporadic, or as pressed upon by other intellectual interests, as in the north. It was always there, in more or less clear consciousness, working with more or less energy. In the fourteenth century it was natural that a love of classic letters should spring up in an Italian breast; and there were men in Italy ready to catch the fire — just as in England, when Wyclif's ideas were once started, there were men of kindred mind to carry them on.

But Petrarch was a great inaugurator. While young, he was recognized as *poeta,* a title dear to Italian ears and hearts. That gave him popular acclaim. He pos-

[2] Cf. Zardo, *Mussato,* (Padua 1884). He was particularly studious of Livy, Seneca and Ovid.

sessed a penetrating and sensitive intelligence. He had also a quality helpful to a successful man of letters, the faculty of pose,— in his case the faculty of posing for what he really was, with added pretensions to much that he was not. He never laid aside the pose of gifted poet, supreme man of letters: restorer of the glories of antiquity. If this was pose, it was also fact. But such a poet, scholar, restorer of a greater past, should be above personal vanities, free from envy, superior to greed. Petrarch posed as such a one, in his writings and before his world; and such he was not. For he was vain and envious, and if not inordinately greedy, he was not the *divitiarum contemptor eximius* that he calls himself in his *Letter to Posterity;* in which he otherwise elaborates his pose: " In others I perceived pride, not in myself, *et cum parvus fuerim, semper minor judicio meo fui.* Kings and princes cherished me, I know not why, and I was with some of them as if they rather were with me! " Even in writings devoted to searchings of himself, but which also safeguarded his pose, one sees that he was enormously self-satisfied.

If these traits give a certain smugness to his character, they helped to make him, in his lifetime and with posterity, the most successful of literary men: successful in leading his life as he wished and in accomplishing what he was capable of; successful in impressing himself upon contemporaries and posterity exactly as he would be taken. Although he thought himself unfortunate in the hour of his birth, he was most fortunate both in the hour and place. For his genius led him to those very pursuits to which Italy, and after her the north, were soon to turn with unprecedented ardor. While he lived, large and distinguished circles of like-minded admirers revered him as unique in his knowledge and virtuosity. It became an amiable convention among them to speak of him as equalling Cicero in eloquence and Virgil in poetry. Boccaccio says it, and Nelli writing thus: Te solum legens, Maronem Ciceronemque legam.[3] The same sweetly friendly

[3] *Lettres de Francesco Nelli à Pétrarque,* ed. H. Cochin (Champion 1892), Ep. 14 — Boccaccio in *Ep. Seniles,* XVII, 2.

Nelli begs to be numbered among his little slaves (servulos), and accounts himself happy to have lived in the same age with him. He describes the excitement over the supposed, and then assured, arrival of a letter from Petrarch: pulsat nuntius januam — a cry bursts forth, the servants run to usher in the bearer, who delivers to us "thy letters, nay rather, thy most precious pearls."[4] Who would have written this to Dante or Michelangelo? Or when did the great of this earth come to watch Dante composing his *Inferno,* as Pandolfo Malatesta, although sick, is brought supported by his servants to see Petrarch in his own chair, surrounded by his books? Petrarch was an excellent flatterer himself, especially of Kings from whom he sought emolument and honor. His praise of the epigrams of Robert, King of Naples, deserved much.[5]

In fine, before his death his fame was spread abroad, and afterwards grew mightier, because he had been in life a lovely poet in the *volgare,* and above that had been the lofty leader and achiever in what was becoming a dominating intellectual movement. He was thus the prototypal embodiment of the rising zeal for classical study, and of the best critical phases of it, for he saw the classics as clearly as any one with his available lights could see. He embodied also the ambition and misdirected effort of the coming period, in Italy at least, to compose works in Latin prose and metre, modelled upon classical standards of beauty. His attitude toward his own exquisite poems in the *volgare* was that which was held to be correct by later Italian humanists, who often professed to despise the vulgar tongue, including their own indiscretions in the same. Finally there was nothing in his career or character that the coming time could not admire. He had professed his contempt for wealth, and declared his freedom from such little weaknesses as envy and malice; and even if he were not quite taken at his word (like state-

[4] Ep. 11. *Lettres de Francesco Nelli à Pétrarque.*

[5] Sen. I, 6; Fam. IV, 3. Petrarch's letters — Familiares, Variae, Seniles — are usually thus cited: Fam., Var., Sen.

ments were to be humanist conventions), his foibles could not appear as blots to later men whose characters openly presented the same. For most of them were vain, self-conscious and affected, and addicted to envy, hatred, and malice and all unseemliness.

As touching Petrarch, we may say, for ourselves, that like Cicero, whom he adored, and like Erasmus after him, he was a great man of letters, and, like them, a man one must sympathize with in order to judge rightly, and "be to his faults a little blind." *"Libris satiari nequeo,"* he writes in a pleasant letter on books and reading (Fam. III, 17). Wherever there are books, some men are born with a sheer love of them, and it may be with that added impulse toward expression which makes a man of letters. In the fourteenth century what should a scholarly Italian read, when he disliked the law and detested scholasticism? — what indeed, except the Latin classics, especially when he was a poet, and born with a love of literary form? Despising his own age, foolishly wishing to have lived in some other time, he attached himself to the cult of antiquity: "Incubui unice inter multa ad notitiam vetustatis," he says in his *Letter to Posterity.* But he is glad to have been born in Italy and not in the Scythian north. He praises Roman Italy in comparison with Greece, and the Latin as compared with the Greek literature, of which he knew nothing save from report.

Naturally when Petrarch came to Rome, he felt a great sensation — how many pilgrim hearts had swelled at the sight of those towers, through all the Middle Ages! It was there that his heart's vainest wish was to be fulfilled, when he was given the laurel crown upon the Capitol. He was acquainted with that self-deceived arouser of enthusiasms, Rienzi — Tribune of the Roman People! — and writes to him in words as foolish as the shouts of the Roman populace: "Salve, noster Camille, noster Romule," (or by whatever name thou wouldst be called) — "salve Romanae libertatis, Romanae pacis, Romanae tranquillitatis auctor!" (Var. 48.)

Toward the Catholic faith Petrarch stood as a mediaeval man, but with some supervening waverings which, in our eyes, make his religious attitude more reasonable. He had read the Fathers, especially Augustine, whose *Confessions* he liked to have at hand; he took them with him in that ascent of Mt. Ventoux, which was suggested to him by reading in Livy how the King of Macedon ascended Mt. Haemas in Thrace, from which both the Euxine and the Adriatic could be seen (Fam. IV, 1). Petrarch, a poor climber, used the difficulties of the ascent to illustrate how hard is virtue to attain — the Middle Ages had always put mountains to this symbolic moral use! At the top Petrarch's thoughts run in the old channels of sin and concupiscence as he reads Augustine's *Confessions.* An odd place to worry over concupiscence and read Augustine!

Like any scholar, Petrarch was fond of quiet and solitude. Replying sympathetically (Fam. IX, 14) to an ecclesiastic's letter praising the solitary life, and speaking for himself, he declares it practically impossible to live or die well save in solitude —" natura dux nostra nos solitarios fecit." And he is capable of decrying carnal love and approving of monastic asceticism. (Fam. X, 3 and 5.) Yet it is easy to see that his reason for preferring the solitary life is the scholar's reason simply, just as he points out in his *De Vita Solitaria,* that the *occupatus* living in the world is exposed to more interruptions and annoyances than the *solitarius.* The imaginary dialogue with Augustine, which Petrarch named *Secretum Meum,*[6] seems to discuss how man may win his best tranquillity. Augustine searches into Petrarch's faults, reproves them gently, recognizes his freedom at least from the sin of envy, points out the incompatibility of carnal passion with man's best peace of mind, and shows the remedy in clarity of judgment, unity of aim, and strength of will to follow it. Petrarch sees the vanity of striving after many things, and has qualms as to the classic studies to which he is addicted — so had St. Jerome and many a mediaeval lover of the classics!

[6] Translated by W. H. Draper. *Petrarch's Secret,* &c. (London, 1911.)

Petrarch had solved the last difficult problem by leading the life of a man of letters. In this he had found his happiness and peace. And with the practical wisdom with which he had conducted his own life, he writes to his friend Boccaccio when both were grey. The latter, seized with compunctions, was proposing to abandon secular themes and studies, and prepare for death somewhat more exclusively than he had done. Petrarch views the situation fairly: an old scholar surely should not discard the studies which have been the occupation of his life, and are the best solace for old age. Without such needless sacrifice, he can still prepare for death (Sen. I, 5).

So Petrarch's attitude toward religion was that of the man of scholarly tastes, not deeply religious, who decorously recognized, and occasionally felt, religion's claims. Somewhat more firmly than a man of like temperament would have done a century before, he kept religion in its proper place. He would not have men think him either a Ciceronian or a Platonist, but of a surety a Christian. He was, however, always ready to attack the current scholasticism, though, of course, as a man of antique letters, he must be himself a follower of philosophy. "I love philosophy," he says, "not the loquacious, scholastic, windy brand . . . but the true, which lives in souls rather than in books." (Fam. XII, 3.) One suspects that he did not know much about what he was condemning or what he was praising. He took from Cicero or Augustine the idea of Plato's primacy, and in his *De Ignorantia*[7] conducts a moderate literary polemic against Aristotle. Yet he professed to respect that master, while he despised his hair-splitting so-called followers. *"Vir ardentis ingenii,"* he once called him. Nevertheless, much as he knew or did not know about it, Petrarch's acute intelligence perceived the emptiness of the current scholasticism. It was also characteristic of him that he should take a rational view of dreams (Fam. V, 7), see the falsity of astrology (Sen. III, 1) and note the quackery in the medicine then practiced. Nor would he accept

[7] Ed. Capelli (Champion, Paris, 1906).

Virgil as a magician, although Boccaccio was inclined to.[8]

As a scholar, Petrarch has rightly remained illustrious. He was not such incidentally, or in the midst of other occupations; but primarily and unremittingly with his whole bent of mind and purpose. Of course, he was an ardent assembler of manuscripts, the tools and means of his vocation. He passionately desired to collect and own them, and have the best and most correct. He was, perhaps had to be, a bibliophile as well as a scholar, the leader of that multitude of ardent lovers of the classics who loved to collect manuscripts, and had to be collectors in order to be students. Of course, one must not think of this as a new phenomenon in the world, although it was to manifest itself on an unprecedented scale. Through all the mediaeval centuries, scholars had been collectors of their precious books. " I am eagerly collecting a library; and as formerly at Rome and elsewhere in Italy, so likewise in Germany and Belgium, I have obtained copyists and manuscripts with a mass of money, and the help of friends in those parts. Permit me to beg of you also to promote this end. We will append at the end of this letter a list of those writers we wish copied." This extract is not from one of Petrarch's letters, though he wrote many like it; but from a letter of Gerbert who became Pope Sylvester II in the year 999.[9]

But undoubtedly Petrarch marks a new stage in the study and appreciation of the classics. And naturally. In a general way, if allowance be made for definite interruptions and catastrophes, and different fields of interest and effort, each mediaeval century shows an intellectual advance. Accordingly, a revival of classical study in the fourteenth century would start from a base of maturer intelligence than in the twelfth. On the other hand, being but the great pioneer of the movement, Petrarch's knowledge was less than that of the following generations of humanists who were stimulated and

[8] De Nolhac, *Pétrarque et l'humanisme,* pp. 126–7 (Paris, Champion, 1907).

[9] Ep. 44, Havet's Edition. Gerbert was not single in these tastes — see *The Mediaeval Mind,* chaps. XII and XIII.

assisted by his labors. The chief gap in his knowledge was his ignorance of Greek, which made his perspective faulty and left his ordering of classical authors still mediaeval. Says he with comical sententiousness: "Plato magnus vir, magnus Pythagoras, magnus Aristoteles, magnus Varro" (Fam. XVII, 1). The last had been a great figure in the Middle Ages.

Within the range of its knowledge, his acute mind discriminated justly. His idol in prose was Cicero; through long study and devotion he seemed to himself to have attained a personal intimacy with him. Yet, as it was only in middle life that he found a manuscript of Cicero's letters, he did not form his own epistolary style on them. In fact, Seneca influenced him as much as Cicero. One may remark that not only in the Middle Ages, but from Petrarch's time onward through the fifteenth and sixteenth centuries, humanists took kindly to the Latin writers of the silver and even the brass age, and when they came to know Greek, they preferred the later Greek authors. Some reasons for this are clear. Both the late Latin and late Greek writers were more cosmopolitan and easier to appreciate than their greater and often austere predecessors. The Romans themselves had not cared for Aeschylus and Aristophanes, who, like Plato, were distinguished by a sublime provincialism. More promiscuous and readily tangible human affinities were offered by the Hellenistic Plutarch. For analogous reasons, Seneca was the really popular moralist, and continued so through the fifteenth and sixteenth centuries. He was closer to the Christian mood, and at so many points touched the commonplace nature of man. Thus we may also see why Petrarch sought moral instruction from Ovid's *Elegies*, while he revered and imitated Virgil.

Following the examples of scholars before him, whether living in the fifth century or the thirteenth, Petrarch took the classic poets allegorically. One of his later letters (Sen. IV, 5) has much to say of the moral or allegorical interpretation of Virgil, and maintains that the end and subject — finis et subjectum — of the *Aeneid* is the perfect man, or man made perfect — *vir perfectus.* To discover an allegory in a narrative means commonly to moralize the narrative, generalize it from a moral point of view, or generalize a lesson from it. Allegory is a kind of generalization. And sometimes, as we follow an allegorical interpretation of a story, for example Petrarch's interpretation of the *Aeneid,* we perceive that much of it is but a pointing of its "lesson." Some such lesson, or revelation of the universal in the concrete, lies in every great story. And who shall say that the poet did not feel or mean it too, at least when he is so thoughtful, even contemplative, a writer as Virgil? Is it not possible also that the Greek critics, who held before Virgil's day that all great poetry should be taken allegorically — is it not possible that sometimes they may have meant little more than when we say such and such a narration carries a lesson?

The trouble was that some of those critics and interpreters overelaborated and specialized their allegorical interpretation, making it quite beside the probable intention of the author, pointing it, as in the case of the Old Testament, to apologetic uses, or making it silly and unlikely, as in the case of a great poem like the *Aeneid.*[10] Thus while Petrarch, in his letters just referred to, sometimes says little more than we ourselves might choose to fancy as the "lesson" of the tale, he is also, like his mediaeval forbears, or the grammarians of the transition centuries, quite capable of foolishness. The Virgilian picture (*Aen.* IV, 554) of Aeneas, when all was ready to set sail from Carthage, asleep on his ship, *celsa in puppi,* he interprets as *alta in mente certo proposito conquiescens* — or, so to speak, at peace in his high purpose. We do not think that Virgil meant this by *celsa in puppi.*

So for Petrarch all great poetry carries allegory. He intends his own Latin poetry to be taken in the same way. He sends his eclogue *Parthenias* to his brother, expounding it allegorically (Fam. X, 4). In fact, it is difficult to understand his eclogues without a key to the

[10] See *The Mediaeval Mind,* Chap. XXXI. (Vol. II, p. 141–2.)

symbolism of their language; in one of them, the *Bucolicum Carmen,* in the person of Silvius, he explains to his brother through allegories his need to write the *Africa.*[11] What shall one say of that supreme effort of Petrarch after immortal fame? Few human beings have read it![12] It seems to open with heavy notes of egotism and adulation; there is no epic plunge *in medias res!* As one proceeds, one finds classic involutions without the classic movement. It seems to go through the motions of the *Aeneid* stylistically; yet does not move. With its borrowed thoughts and borrowed phrases, not reproduced *in ipsissimis verbis,* it affects one as a sort of pseudo-copy.

One gathers from it the way in which Petrarch sought to form his style. He advises not to copy the words, but rather to master the classic thoughts. He would not slavishly imitate the phrasing of one writer, but avail of the excellences of many: nec huius stilum aut illius, sed unum nostrum conflatum ex pluribus habeamus. Not everyone can learn to write well by reading the classics; he must have, or gain through them, a serene and well equipped mind: he must be something, or have become something, in himself: "For speech is no slight index of the mind, nor the mind a slight director of speech; one depends on the other."[13]

Many a scholar in the generations and centuries before Petrarch had tried to write as well as possible, had striven for style and form. The vernacular poetry of the troubadours of Provence was mainly a thing of form; and often a mediaeval Latin writer in the twelfth or thirteenth century modelled his style quite consciously on the classics or on the approved writers of his time. With Petrarch, the effort for style has become portentously self-conscious. He is the forerunner of those genera-

[11] *Poemata minora Francisci Petrarcae,* ed. Rosetti, (Milan 1823); *Il Bucolicum Carmen,* ed. Avila (Padua 1906).

[12] The present writer has only read *at* it.

[13] Fam. I, 7 & 8; XXIII, 19. See his later remarks on style in a letter to Bruni. Sen. II, 3.

tions of Italian humanists who pursued "art for art's sake," and by striving utterly for form in writing, emptied themselves of substance. This forerunner, who himself was not always creative, tried so consciously for form, that most of his works have entered the company of those which are not read, but read about. His letters, carefully edited by him, are interesting as a record of his life. They may have done much to bring into vogue the *genre* of epistolary writing consisting of intimate short self-revealing letters or essays upon topics other than theology and politics. Beyond them, and perhaps his *Secretum,* who but a special student reads Petrarch's Latin works? In some of them the dullness of the Middle Ages seems clothed upon, as in the *De remediis utriusque fortunae,* where every conceivable good, and then every conceivable ill of human life is presented *seriatim,* with opposed or compensating considerations.

The *De viris illustribus,*[14] a work of greater rhetorical effort, is more alive by reason of its subject, the life histories of Roman worthies. Its substance was drawn from Livy, where that was possible, or again from Caesar's *Commentaries,* which Petrarch, in common with men before and also after him, ascribed to one Julius Celsus. Petrarch's principle of selection, as given in his preface, is to use only those matters which illustrate the virtues or their contraries; for the *fructuosus finis* of historians is to present that which the reader ought either to follow or avoid: — which is a way of writing history for the purpose of moral improvement, as more than one mediaeval compiler had done. The preface turns also to posterity, and expresses the author's wish to be dear to it. As the work warms up to the important people, it becomes good rhetorical exposition. Such is the story of Camillus; and a long, intelligently composed biography of Caesar is presented.

It is illuminating to compare Petrarch with Hildebert of Lavardin and John of Salisbury, noteworthy humanists

[14] Ed. Razzolini (Bologna 1874).

of the eleventh and twelfth centuries.[15] The former, who lived from about 1055 to 1130, ended his life as Archbishop of Tours. He was an enthusiastic lover of the classic Latin literature, and the spell of the antique lay on him. Visiting Rome, he wrote admirable elegies upon its ruined state, elegies in which the gods are made to marvel at the beauty of their own sculptured images. The prose of his letters was not disturbed by attempts at a pseudo-classic style; it has grace as well as force. His letters were studied as models after his death. John of Salisbury was born about 1115 and died as Bishop of Chartres in 1180. He was the friend both of Becket and of Henry II, and in his time had sat at the feet of many famous teachers, Abelard for instance, as well as Bernard of Chartres. He gives a charming picture of the latter's method of teaching. Always an advocate of a thorough classical education, John poured his sarcasms on those who "preferred to seem rather than be, philosophers and professors of the arts, engaging to impart the whole of philosophy in less than three years, or even two." He was quite at home with the classic authors, citing their lives as readily and as appositely as he cited Scripture. A student and clever historian of the antique philosophy, he knew as much of it as was possible for a man living before the unearthing of Aristotle. His writings as well as his personality were imbued with its spirit; he applied its teachings in his life and contemplation, and could look with even eye on all things. *Moderatrix omnium* was his favorite term for philosophy.

According to the present writer's taste, these men wrote Latin more agreeably than Petrarch. Since they were active in affairs of Church and State, they did not, like him, follow letters exclusively. Their writings do not disclose such absorbing curiosity as to everything connected with antiquity. It would indeed be hard to find anyone before Petrarch so completely devoted as himself to the study of the classics and so consciously

[15] See chapters XXXI and XXXII of *The Mediaeval Mind,* and Vol. II, pp. 403 sqq.

striving to be intimate with antiquity. Moreover, while these men had a just and true feeling for the classics, they lived when men knew less and had experienced less. One cannot expect to find them as mature as he. The clearest difference between them lay in their intellectual environment and in the immediate destinies of their respective epochs, with reference to the *litterae humaniores* of Rome and Greece. The twelfth century was the best period of mediaeval Latin writing, and also one when many scholars cared for the classics and read them diligently. But even then there were men of other minds, who looked on Latin letters merely as a means towards quite different pursuits. Before many decades, the dominant intellectual interests of the time moved away from the *litterae humaniores* somewhat more definitely. The period of the great and, on the whole, unliterary scholastic philosophers arrived — even as our time is the period of unliterary science; and although classical scholars may now know more than their predecessors of the eighteenth century, nevertheless interest in classical literature is on the wane, and the classics are less generally read and have less effect upon educated men than heretofore.

But Petrarch, in contrast with Hildebert of Lavardin and John of Salisbury, lived at the opening of an epoch which was to be intellectually characterized by a renewed, an enthusiastic, a fashionable, modish, almost universal, interest in the classics as veritable fonts of humanity. He and his labors and his fame were borne onwards upon the increasing currents of the coming time. Fate made him a precious pioneer. By reason of his happy timeliness, the fame of him and the effect of him and the inspiration of his example were not lost.

Thus in his Latin studies and Latin writings, Petrarch was a spokesman of the coming time. But beyond his classical virtuosity, through his sonnets and *Canzoni* in Italian, he devised modes of sentiment and the forms of their expression destined to royal fortunes. It was he more than any other who set the sonnet fashion for the following centuries, and within the sonnet form gave expression to those exquisite or precieuse sentiments which became conventions with the writers of love poetry of many nations. He was the main source and inspiration of an enormous sonnet literature in Italy, next in France, and ultimately in England. As the creator of these forms of expression one can find no definite limit to his influence.

II

Boccaccio was a slightly younger contemporary, a devoted friend, and an humble but gifted admirer of Petrarch. While his genius was drenched with his immediate mediaeval antecedents, he went beyond or behind them to grasp the fuller riches of the antique. Still more vitally he turned to the instincts and capacities of his own nature, and absorbed the living currents of his time. His personality and life and labors brilliantly represent his time and place, and with this advantage over Petrarch, that Boccaccio was less self-conscious and quite free from pose. He presents himself in his symbolical and mediaeval elements, in his enthusiastic study of the classics, and in the turning of his genius to life and to the expression of it in the vernacular.

The mediaeval centuries contained many kinds of men, though we justifiably choose to see mainly the more striking types. We are interested, for instance, in the type which created chivalry and the Arthurian romances, or again in those lines of spiritual energy which blended in the personalities of a St. Bernard, an Aquinas or a Dante. Yet one remembers that if the first part of the *Roman de la Rose* was written by the exquisite De Lorris, the clever and somewhat encyclopaedic second part had for its author that De Meung who has been likened to Voltaire, and may with equal justice be compared with Boccaccio. Both De Meung and Boccaccio employed the mediaeval machinery of presentation, the dream, the vision, the allegory, while both also saw human nature along the level of its actuality. Neither of them dwelt in the *machina,*— the vision or the allegory — which they conventionally used.

That the intellectual conventions and primary mental attitudes of this Florentine were those of the fourteenth century, and the centuries immediately behind it, is evident from his earlier works, which are mediaeval in substance and in the conventions of their construction. One notices the mediaevalism of that *Vita di Dante* in which Boccaccio expressed his admiration for the figure then dominating literary Italy. As Boccaccio was not mystically winged, but well equipped with human hands and feet and eyes, he does not cleave the empyrean with his poet, but makes him walk the earthy levels of the mediaeval meadows, and credits him with motives, romantic, pretty, by no means sublime. Boccaccio's own vocabulary was then full of the words and phrases of the *Commedia.*[16] And at the close of life, when his last labor was to deliver his lectures or *Commento* on it, he adopts scholastically what probably was Dante's own explanation of his purpose, when considering a commentary upon his own poem. The causes, says Boccaccio, of the *Commedia,* are the material, the formal, the efficient and the final. The first of these, which is to say the *subject* of the poem, is twofold, literal and allegorical. It is, " according to the literal sense, the state of souls after the body's death, taken simply . . . while, according to the allegorical sense, it is how man, mounting or falling through his free will, is bound to the justice which rewards and punishes." So he proceeds with the rest, saying at last that " the final cause is to help those who are living in the present life, to pass from a state of misery to one of felicity." [17] One may add, that this ardent admirer transferred to Dante himself the Dantesque and mediaeval appellative of Aristotle, calling him in the *Amorosa Visione,* " il signor d'ogni savere."

[16] E.g. the " infiniti guai," at the opening of the *Fiammetta,* and shortly after in the lover's words: " O donna, tu sola se' la beatudine nostra."

[17] *Commento,* Cap. I in Moutier's Ed. I, pp. 3–4.

That Boccaccio's way of handling the classics, and presenting their extracted substance in exhaustive compilations, was still mediaeval, may be seen in his *De Casibus Virorum Illustrium,* which shows the fatal turns of fortune through a line of ancient worthies, beginning with Adam; likewise in his *De claris Mulieribus,* a companion treatise; and finally in his vast *Genealogiae deorum gentilium,* in which he endeavors to satisfy his insatiate interest in mythology. No work of Petrarch shows such exhaustive learning. Yet it is clear that Petrarch appreciated the classics more intelligently than this younger man who equalled him in diligence of study and in zeal to extend the knowledge of them. There was no more eager searcher after manuscripts than Boccaccio.

Theoretically, Boccaccio joined with his friend in placing the writing of Latin above Italian composition. But, in fact, more genially and truly than Petrarch he recognized the value and dignity of the *volgare,* and accepted it as a worthy vehicle of narrative and thought, as Dante fortunately had done. Here lay the true progress of Boccaccio, wherein a realization that the classics also drew from life may have helped him on. Looking to life, drawing from life, Boccaccio knew that the *volgare* alone had the living power to depict it. In this he was not " mediaeval "; no man is when he goes straight to the life about him.

This great advance did not come suddenly, or in Boccaccio's early years, when he wrote his first poems in the *volgare.* They and their author were still entangled in the acceptance and conventional treatment of conventional subjects. It was not so much that the subjects were timeworn, as that his treatment of them still subscribed to the old notions; for there was life and beauty in the old story of Flore and Blanchfleur, of Troilus and Cressid, or of Palamon and Arcite. The poems made by Boccaccio from these tales, the *Filocolo, Filostrato,* and *Teseide,* have still too much rhetoric and convention, with too little of life's closer observation. Imitation and the old ideas enveloped him most appallingly in his *Amorosa Visione.* In form it copied, parodied rather, the *Divina Commedia,* and in contents was an encyclopaedic "Hall of Fame," in which the author beheld every imaginable person belonging to classical and biblical antiquity, or to the mediaeval time, and also the whole company of allegorical personifications. The enumerating habit followed him. Even in his prose *Fiammetta,* which so aptly delineated passion, he could not help letting Venus set before his heroine the tale of all the gods and demigods and heroes who had been overcome by love, as an argument why she should not resist it. Nor does she.

That Boccaccio at last should have emerged from these entanglements to write the *Decameron!* Its opening stories still carry conventional moralizings. But as the tales proceed, the author reaches an artistic freedom of his own, and, drawing upon universal life, gives pictures of manifold humanity. His cheerful and facile and abundantly carnal nature did not rise to those spiritual heights which may be just as veritable as the streets and gutters of human life. But, with this qualification, the wide actual world throngs through these tales, the world of men and women, resourceful lovers, clever rogues, shameless villains, caught hot in their doings. Many pretty stories, and stories unabashed, with author and audience ready to laugh at folly and applaud the successful ruse. Throughout, cleverness, quick faculty, *virtus* and *prudentia,* ἀρετή and πινυτή, to go back through Rome even to Homer, win life's prizes and applause. High principle, self-sacrifice, humility, gain scant attention, when not laughed out of court. Boccaccio's world has passion and desire, but not much heart or benevolence. It is not malevolent; but as the author does not let the wish to instruct or benefit deflect his story, or spoil his art, so no one in the tale is stayed from his desire by moral nicety.

Boccaccio did not invent many of the tales; he drew from books and on the cloud of homeless stories floating through the world. But his observation and his art made these stories the amusing things they have proved themselves to be for half a thousand years. The life about him and his quick selecting eye gave matter and form. And then his art,— that was a faculty which sprang from the whole Boccaccio and his entire training. Was he not courtier, man of the world, and lady's man and frequent lover? And was he not as well a careful writer, and a deep student of the Latin classics? If he felt that the *volgare* was the tool of life, did he not utterly admire Latin, and deem it better in itself? Could he not use the life which pulsed in the *volgare,* and yet mould that energy to seemliness, perhaps to the seemliness of the Latin period? This was what he did; nor did he fail to inject in it his own apt sense of fitness. So he built his style. And in that style, so apt if still rotund, and, in Boccaccio's faculty of composition, so disciplined, so slowly won, lay the best humanistic progress, the best which that time or any century after it could gain from the study of the classics: to wit, discipline, sense of form, knowledge of literary effectiveness, even a more excellently trained humanity directed toward self-expression.

Such were to be the results of a broader and more instructed study of the classics. Yet the Italians seem hampered by the constraint of the antique in their own natures, and by its survival in their customs and their environment. It was not the revival of classical studies that checked the Italian literary creativeness. Rather, the strength of the antique survival in the Italian nature through every mediaeval century, had checked creativeness. The revival of classical studies gave academic purpose to this hampering survival. Italian scholars, rather more than those of other lands, were touched with the ambition to write classic Latin. This absorbing purpose impeded the creative imagination. With such a darling of delight as Ariosto the fling of fancy would have its play; but many are the names of those Italian humanists, to whose zeal for the resurrection of the Greek as well as Latin classics we remain indebted, yet in whose own Latin compositions self-conscious purpose ill supplies the place of life. A mediaeval Latin writing might be more alive just because the author used Latin as of course, with little stylistic consciousness.

Through the thirteenth and fourteenth centuries, the Italian cities had advanced in wealth, and in human experience and capacity. Elsewhere, in England for example, such development of human faculty might take the form of sharpened political and theological insight, and address itself to religious reform. But, in Italy, it naturally directed itself to studies relating to the Roman past, which still was in the blood. As the prime Italian intellectual achievement of the twelfth and thirteenth centuries had been the revival of the Roman Law, so now in the fourteenth and fifteenth centuries the finer intellectual energies of the land wound themselves about the classics. If Petrarch was the hierarch of these studies, they were pursued by many other men, in cities less rude, more generally cultured, civilized, *urban,* than the towns across the Alps. Not without reason Petrarch contrasts his Italy with the Scythian barbarism of the north, of devastated France for instance, where nevertheless he found upon his journey groups of Latin scholars.

So, as of course, the great revival, the new florescence of classical studies began in Italy. There it presents itself as an original or indigenous movement, which had not come over the borders from another country; there, also, it was a direct study of the Latin and gradually the Greek authors, an acceptance of their influence unmixed with intrusions from neighboring contemporary peoples. This Italian humanism had thus the purity and originality belonging to priority. But in France, England, Germany, so many suggestions came from Italy that there was always a foreign contemporary flavor or suggestion mingling with the study of the classic writings. Whatever came from Italy, in the fourteenth and fifteenth centuries, was almost as that which was taken from the classic literature of Rome.

CHAPTER II

ITALIAN HUMANISTS OF THE EARLY FIFTEENTH CENTURY

UNDOUBTEDLY the general culture of the Middle Ages rested upon material conditions. The life of court and camp and town and castle, with the delectable productions of poets, church-builders, sculptors, artists in glass, was supported by the economic situation, if not part of it. Monks in monasteries and the student hordes thronging the universities were fed and clothed, and many of their intellectual needs ministered to, through the same supporting wealth. Nevertheless, the finest flowering of the mediaeval spirit ignored bodily well-being, even ascetically deprecated it. But in the coming time, the forms of intellectual achievement and the Protestant religious movement frankly made much of bodily well-being, and hung upon the increase of wealth and material civilization.

Starting with any mediaeval century, the twelfth for instance, one may observe how the factors in the increase of wealth were identical with the means or conditions of expansion of the human mind. Mental and material elements acted upon each other reciprocally, now appearing as result and again as cause. Intellectual development produced discoveries and alternately sprang from them: discoveries in knowledge, discoveries of mechanical contrivances like the compass; discoveries regarding building, sculpture, painting, the weaving of textile fabrics; relating to commerce and the routes of commerce, to the extension of the knowledge of the earth's surface through exploration of hitherto unknown lands and seas. All this had as much to do with the improvement of man's physical well-being as with the enlargement of his mind. The maritime discoveries afford the most picturesque illustration. From the time of the Scandinavian and Norman voyages, from the time of the Crusades, from the time of the Genoese and Portuguese explorations of the west coast of Africa, to that of the gradually led up to and grandly accomplished voyages of Columbus and Vasco da Gama, the course of maritime exploration is connected with the intellectual development of Europe, and on the other hand becomes the mightiest of factors in that increase in wealth which amounted to an economic revolution. During the sixteenth century, the money supply in Europe would seem to have been quadrupled; and the increase of gold and silver was matched by the expansion of the mental horizon.

A realization of the growth of wealth and luxury in Italy and Spain and France, not to mention England and Germany, is needed for any proper view of the intellectual progress of the fifteenth and sixteenth centuries. Humanism, the study of the classics, while not necessarily a thing of luxury and ease, will be seen to have advanced with the luxurious adornment of life, made possible through wealth. The prosperity of the Italian cities in the thirteenth and fourteenth centuries was the foundation of the brilliant life and culture of the fifteenth, and the necessary basis for the subsequent progress of humanism, science, and philosophy. Support from wealthy patrons, dynasts, tyrants, successful condottieri, enabled the humanists to prosecute their studies, or gave Leonardo da Vinci opportunity for observation and experiment. The famous arsenal at Venice, with its store of costly machines, proved full of teaching for him, as it did for Galileo.

One recalls the industrial growth of Florence. Her wars and treaties had been inspired by her industrial and commercial needs, the need, for instance, of a sea-port, which was not satisfied till Pisa was captured in 1406. A quick commercial expansion resulted. Before then, however, industrious and intriguing Florence traded vigorously with Bruges and the west of Europe, as well as with the near and further Orient. She had given attention to navigation, and to astronomy and other sciences useful in commerce and manufacture. The woolen industry was well developed. Two of her *Arti maggiori*, (the greater Guilds) were engaged in the finishing of foreign woolens and the making of the cloth itself. When English and Flemish competition impaired this lucrative business, the manufacture of silk was profitably taken up. Lawyers too, and money-changers who became great bankers, assisted in the ordering and extension of her industry and commerce. The city continued dominantly Guelf, and with reason, since great gain and the control of Italian finance came to the Florentines as Bankers to the Holy See.[1]

So, for the fifteenth and sixteenth centuries in western Europe, one sees how closely allied were the expansion of the mental vision and the increase of wealth and material civilization. But regarding this expansion of the mind and the varied advance of thought and knowledge, we meet again the question of the causal antecedence of one phase of intellectual progress, with respect to other phases possibly to be regarded as effects. The apparent stimulus came from the antique letters, including antique philosophy and political enlightenment. Yet in a way, these had been there always, and the palm of precedence might just as well be awarded to the advancing humanity which, with increasing intellectual capacity, turned to them for illumination.

Thus a questionable priority resolves itself into a more likely coöperation. Nevertheless, the intellectual progress of these centuries seems to begin with a renewed study of the classic literature. This led to a more varied philosophy, and even facilitated the advance of science. Hence a survey of the period's intellectual accomplishment properly begins with that revival of classic studies which has come to us as inaugurated by Petrarch and Boccaccio.

One need not retell the story of this revival of antique letters, which has been told so often, and with such

[1] Cf. P. Villari, *I primi due secoli della storia di Firenze,* chap. VI, (Revised Ed. Florence 1905).

charm and pleasurable excitement. Yet some of its more illustrative and personal incidents or phases may be given, and not too briefly, for the subject is beguiling. One passes quite naturally from Petrarch to the younger generation of his followers and admirers. These, with their pupils, included the majority of noted humanists flourishing in the first half of the fifteenth century. Petrarch had never made his home in Florence; but most of Boccaccio's life was passed either there or in the neighboring village of Certaldo. And, before long, Florence, chiefly through the energies and tastes of its citizens, became the centre of the classical revival, and one may say, of the new intellectual eagerness inspiring or accompanying it. The city's prosperity under the rule of an aristocracy of wealth, during the half century or more following Boccaccio's death, led to the same end. That the rich Florentines were keenly interested in the Latin classics, as well as in Christian scholarship and Italian literature, appears from an account, true enough if actually fictitious, of the conversation of a distinguished company assembled at the villa of the merchant prince, Antonio degli Alberti.[2] There is costly food and wine, there is music; stories are told, frequently ending in pleasant riddles; philosophy is discussed and Augustine; Ovid and Livy, and the origins of Florence and Prato; also Dante and Petrarch and Boccaccio; the greatness of these men and the richness and worth of the *volgare* find staunch supporters.

The finer Florentine spirits were constantly meeting for the serious pleasures of study and discussion before the fourteenth century had closed. Among them the name of Luigi de Marsigli should not be forgotten, nor will that of Coluccio Salutato. Both of them had "assisted" at the storied *conversazione*. The voluminous correspondence of the latter[3] brings the man and his thoughts before us, and affords an enlightening picture of a deeply respected Florentine official and meritorious hu-

[2] *Il Paradiso degli Alberti,* ed. A. Wesselofsky, 3 vols. (Bologna, 1867).
[3] *Epistolario di Coluccio Salutati,* Ed. Fr. Novati (4 vols., 1891 sqq.).

manist of the generation immediately following Petrarch.

Born in 1330, Salutato was some twenty-five years younger than his pole-star of a poet. Educated principally at Bologna, he fitted himself there for the business of a notary. He had even then heard of Petrarch, had sent him verses, and had received a little golden letter in return. Afterwards he moved about through various cities, and gained experience as a scribe in the papal Curia. He was forty years old when he came to Florence. For a while he acted as secretary to the Priori, and in 1375 was made Cancellarius, or, as one might say, Secretary of the Republic. Until his death thirty years later, he filled this office, enhancing both its dignity and his own repute through his abilities and uprightness. He was a man of presence, somewhat austere in manner, but of deep, controlled affections. All Italy regarded him highly; and his official papers, which everywhere were preserved as models, efficiently upheld the Republic's policy and fortunes in times of stress and conflict with the papacy. His honor never was impeached, and having trained a family of noble sons, he left them no ill gotten gains. He was given a public funeral, and crowned with laurel in his coffin as a poet. He had composed poems enough; yet their merits scarcely won for him this crown, but rather his public services and his reputation as a humanist.

One marks his boundless admiration for Petrarch, his *pietas* toward him. The poet was dead; the world of scholarly taste was agog to know about his *Africa* — had he destroyed it, as he had threatened, or had he left directions for its destruction, as Virgil had ordered the destruction of the *Aeneid?* No! the "divine *Africa*" still existed, for the joy and solace of mankind. After urgent efforts, it was copied and brought to Florence, where the new-made humanistic Cancellarius set himself reverently to expunge such harsh expressions as the poet himself would have remedied, had he lived to perfect his work.

At the news of Petrarch's death, Salutato had added

a postscript to a letter he was writing: "I have heard, woe is me! that our Petrarch has migrated to his stars." He soon begins to write more at length about him; for instance, to the Count of Battifolle, somewhat as follows: Since Petrarch lived enough for nature and glory, there was nothing more for him to enjoy among mortals, but only to say with the Doctor to the Gentiles, "I desire to be dissolved and be with Christ." He excelled all in wisdom and learning, and in his matchless *eloquentia,* the *eloquendi facultas,* "from which either prose melody (prosaica melodia) pours forth with loosened reins, or is constrained by the continuous straits of metres." Dividing prose into that which serves debate and that which serves instruction (*contentio* and *sermocinatio,* a division in mediaeval use), the letter maintains that Petrarch in his "Invective against a physician," surpassed the Philippics and Catiline orations of Cicero. "Believe me, though someone should contend that Cicero was his equal in oratorical power, yet in the adornment of speech and weight of meaning . . . without any doubt it would be admitted that the parent of Roman eloquence was conquered by this one of ours." Cicero excelled only in the one form of *eloquentia,* and Virgil in the other: Petrarch, who achieved so gloriously in both, is to be set before either of them. And if Greece should insolently compare herself with Latium, we still have Petrarch to set above them. Besides there are his poems in the *volgare,* in which it is acknowledged that he excelled Dante.[4] All hail! consummate man — summe vir, cui etiam se tota equare non potest antiquitas!"[5]

Such epistolary rhetoric reveals the writer's mentality. Salutato could worship many gods, though for the time one of them should fill his vision. Later he writes in praise of Virgil, saying: "Placet mihi stilus, quem hactenus nemo versibus adequavit, nec putem posse ad eius altitudinem atque dulcedinem humanis viribus pervenire."

[4] Probably this was not Salutato's more considered opinion. In Lib. XI, 10, he says at great length that there is nothing greater than the *Commedia.*

[5] *Epistolario,* Lib. III, Ep. 13 and 15.

Yet still later, in 1379, when Petrarch had been dead for five years, he argues, lengthily as was his wont, that Petrarch is superior to Virgil, and in prose the equal of Cicero.[6]

If Salutato appears stupid, Bruni and Poggio were among his protégés. The latter could not endure that his venerable friend and benefactor should put Petrarch above Cicero and Virgil; and the aged Salutato writes to defend his views. You seem to hold, says he, that no modern can be compared with the ancients. That is easy to answer. But first one should consider the Christians, Origen, Chrysostom, Jerome, and Augustine, the best of all. Would you set Plato or Aristotle or Cicero or Virgil above Augustine? And surely, the Latins were superior to the Greeks.[7]

Such crude comparisons, and the conviction of the superiority of Latin over Greek, of which Salutato knew next to nothing, were not common in the next generation. The letter last referred to is so long and tedious that one loses any likely thread of argument. In it Salutato distinguishes between *sapientia* and *eloquentia,* and argues that Aristotle, Plato, and all the Gentiles were necessarily inferior in *sapientia* to the Christians, and therefore inferior to Petrarch. And if they failed in *sapientia,* their *eloquentia* was vain. He expresses his agreement with Cicero that writing should progress from age to age, and correspond with speech and customs. And, returning to his comparisons, he intimates that in putting Petrarch before Cicero and Virgil, he really meant that Petrarch excelled Cicero in verse and Virgil in prose!

Through a small hole, the old man emerges to this ridiculous conclusion. Was he failing mentally, or just involved in stupid mental habits? He does not seem foolish when, in a still later letter, he says that we should not slavishly imitate the ancients. But his head is full of them; sometimes they mould his own mood or seem-

[6] Ep. Lib. IV, 15 and 20.
[7] Ep. Lib. XIV, 18. Dec. 1405.

ingly living thoughts, or again they are as names which he keeps waving in his letters. He can argue as to the authorship of the tragedies ascribed to Seneca, with better knowledge and acumen than could have been found, say, before Petrarch, and can show a real appreciation of Cicero's character drawn from his letters; and he wrote frequently upon questions of textual interpretation. But his critical knowledge was so incomplete that apparently he took no exception to the statements of " Dares " and " Dyctys," in their wretched Trojan forgeries, which the Middle Ages also had followed. Nor does he feel the absurdity of his long epistle combatting the charge that Aeneas was not the *legitimate* son of Venus.[8] He is ready with the string of names that so long had served as band-horses. He consoles a young Count for the death of a father whose writing and speech *redolebat* of the streams of Cicero, the pointedness of Quintilian, the vehemence of Demosthenes. He would have the young man lift up his heart; — how are our minds inflamed for virtue in thinking on the " Claudios, Fabricios, Curios, Catones, Fabios, Metellos, Scipiones, Decios, Lucullos et ceteros." And writing to a prominent citizen of Lucca, he finds him not inferior to Brutus in one respect, nor to Manlius in another, nor to Camillus in a third. Coluccio knew himself and the compass of his mind, when he wrote to Cardinal Orsini, urging the reading of the good old ancients; for we invent nothing new, and are but patchers of antique apparel.[9]

Though naturally maintaining that zeal for sacred studies did not call for the banishment of the pagan poets, Salutato was not a pagan, but a serious person, who liked to discuss free will and predestination. He was a man of piety, distinctly recognizing how fraught with dangers were the praise and glory of this world. It was natural that Greeks and Romans should have delighted " ardently in the extinguishable light of glory, and have found it dulcissimum pro gloria mori. But be it far

[8] Ib. V, 18; VIII, 7; X, 9 and 12; XII, 21.
[9] Ib. II, 18; III, 17; VI, 4.

from me, a Christian man, to glory in knowledge which puffeth up, or in anything save the Mediator of God and men." And in the following letter which is an argument for the use of *tu* instead of *vos* when addressing a single person, he says "we are born for glory, eternal glory, not the fragile and fleeting glory of the world." [10]

In sundry letters, written to console Andrea de Volterra for the death of his sons, the antique temper supports Christian sentiments and convictions. These letters were less completely pagan than one written in the early twelfth century by Bishop Hildebert to Henry I of England on the drowning of his son.[11] Salutato borrows thoughts which Scipio and Laelius might express concerning friendship, and blows them up to a thin flame. Yet, beneath these quasi-affectations, classic sentiment had entered and disciplined his nature.

Although this worthy man affected to set Latin above Greek, no one did more to bring to Florence the Greek language and literature, in the person of the excellent Chrysoloras,[12] a Byzantine of quite another class from the charlatans who had imposed on Boccaccio. He was ever quick and generous in aiding the cause of letters; and, in his old age, was like a father to Bruni and Poggio, who then enter his life and correspondence. The fifteenth epistle of Liber XIV (Aug. 1405) to Pope Innocent VII, is a hearty and ornate recommendation of Bruni for the post of Apostolic secretary; and the same Liber contains many letters to the young Poggio, affectionate and filled with good advice. Poggio as well as Bruni called him "father and teacher"; and a picture of the old man is given in Bruni's *"Libellus de Disputationum etc. usu,"* [13] written in 1401, when the author was about thirty.

This little book enlightens us as to the change which

[10] Ib. IV, 18; VII, 17; VIII, 10 and 11.

[11] VIII, 17, 18, 19, cf. XI, 8. See *The Mediaeval Mind,* II, p. 173. In Lib. IX, 9, Salutato mentions Hildebert, Abelard, St. Bernard and other mediaeval worthies, as good letter writers.

[12] Lib. IX, 14 (1406) formally invites him to Florence at a salary.

[13] Printed in T. Klette, *Beiträge zur Ges. und Lit. der Italienischen Gelehrtenrenaissance,* (Greifswald 1888).

had come over the younger generation of scholars. It opens with the friends, Bruni, Niccolo and de Rossi, going to see the venerable man, just as Scipio and Laelius go to see the aged Cato in Cicero's *de Senectute*. The nominal subject of their talk is the value of discussion of literary themes. Niccolo opens with a harsh note: "I fail to see, Coluccio, how in these dregs of time (in hac faece temporum, a common humanistic phrase) and in this great dearth of books, anyone can acquire the faculty of discussing." Our ancestors, he continued, preserved Cassiodorus, and suffered Cicero to perish. Then, assailing the ignorant present-day followers of Aristotle, he deplores the condition of philosophy, dialectic, grammar, and rhetoric.

Salutato is less pessimistic: if we have lost much, much is left; and consider the pre-excellence of Dante, Petrarch, and Boccaccio. Niccolo will not hear of praising them, whom the crowd praises. Dante showed his ignorance in giving a white beard to Cato, who died at the age of forty-eight; and his treatment of Brutus was very bad. He should be left out of any "concilium litteratorum." As for Petrarch, his long looked for *Africa* was born a "ridiculus mus"; his friends were sick of it; it was a poor performance. Enough could be said against Boccaccio too.

Smiling as was his wont, Salutato postpones the defense of these men to the next day, when the friends meet again at his house. The task of defense is laid on Bruni; but Niccolo says that he had spoken as he had only to hear what Salutato would say; in fact he admires them all, and he proceeds to praise each in turn, but stands to it that he does not care for the *Africa* or Petrarch's *Bucolics*.

These younger men had thrown off the Petrarch spell,[14] and had discarded certain of Salutato's stupid notions. They knew more; some of them knew Greek, and had

[14] After writing the lives of Dante and Petrarch, Bruni compares the two. He speaks of Petrarch's greater faculty of keeping the friendship of princes, and comments thus: "E certo il vivere in reputazione ed in vita onorato da tutti i Signori e Popoli, non fu senza gradissima virtù, e sapienza e costanza." This was written about 1436.

read Greek authors. They had thus gained a better perspective. They wrote easier Latin than Salutato or Boccaccio or Petrarch. They and their generation were eagerly engaged in the search for manuscripts, and their efforts were rewarded.[15]

Florence was still the hearth and home of humanists; and it was of lasting import for the cause of learning that Chrysoloras came there to lecture. We turn to Bruni's story of the call he felt to study Greek, told in his *History of his own times in Italy*.[16] The closing years of the fourteenth century are referred to:

"Then first came a knowledge of Greek, which had not been in use among us for seven hundred years. Chrysoloras the Byzantine, a man of noble birth and well versed in Greek letters, brought Greek learning to us. When his country was invaded by the Turks, he came by sea, first to Venice. The report of him soon spread, and he was cordially invited and besought and promised a public stipend, to come to Florence and open his store of riches to the youth. I was then studying Civil Law, but . . . I burned with love of academic studies, and had spent no little pains on dialectic and rhetoric. At the coming of Chrysoloras I was torn in mind, deeming it shameful to desert the law, and yet a crime to lose such a chance of studying Greek literature; and often with youthful impulse I would say to myself: 'Thou, when it is permitted thee to gaze on Homer, Plato and Demosthenes, and the other poets, philosophers, orators, of whom such glorious things are spread abroad, and speak with them and be instructed in their admirable teaching, wilt thou desert and rob thyself? Wilt thou neglect this opportunity so divinely offered? For seven hundred years, no one in Italy has possessed Greek letters; and yet we confess that all knowledge is derived from them. How great advantage to your knowledge, enhancement of your fame, increase of your pleasure, will come from an understanding of this tongue? There are doctors of civil law everywhere; and the chance of learning will not fail thee. But if this one and only doctor of Greek letters disappears, no one can be found to teach thee. Overcome at length by these reasons, I gave myself to Chrysoloras, with

[15] The exciting story of the search and rescue of manuscripts of the classics is told by J. A. Symonds in his "Revival of Learning," and more circumstantially in G. Voigt's *Wiederbelebung des Klassischen Alterthum's.*

[16] *Commentarius rerum suo tempore in Italia gestarum,* by Leonardus Aretinus (of Arezzo) called Bruni; Muratori, *Script.* T. 19, pp. 914 sqq. Bruni was born about 1370 and died in 1444. The passage quoted begins on page 920 of Muratori.

such zeal to learn, that what through the wakeful day I gathered, I followed after in the night, even when asleep."

Bruni gives the names of fellow students, who studied Greek with more or less pertinacity and success. Some of them were to be noted humanists; but none of them was as good a Greek scholar, or did as much with his knowledge of Greek, as Bruni himself. The fame of Greek, even the enthusiasm for it, was spreading among Italian students of the humanities; but its study presented more difficulties than opportunities; and through the first half of the fifteenth century, more humanists talked about Greek than seriously attempted to acquire it. Of those who did, not a few were discouraged by the difficulties of the script and language, and the lack of competent teachers and manuscripts. Bruni himself collected Greek manuscripts, as he had to in order to pursue his studies; but he never carried his search into the East. It was Giovanni Aurispa who returned from Constantinople to Venice in 1423, with a grand load of manuscripts; and a few years after him, Filelfo, of many-sided repute, brought not a few, and did much to advance the study of Greek literature in Italy. If the renewed study of the Latin Classics, with the unearthing of new manuscripts, proceeded with zeal and pleasurable excitement, and became the darling pursuit of many a man of wealth, one may imagine the expectation aroused at the prospect of a new and greater world of Greek literature; an expectation which was not to be disappointed.

So, in Bruni's time, an acquaintance with Greek was hardly more common in Italy than a knowledge of Sanscrit is at present in America. The difference was in the hope of enlightenment, which no one expects from Sanscrit, but which those men of the fifteenth century fervently looked for from the Greek gospel of knowledge. Of course, all knowledge of the language, even that possessed by the very facile Bruni, was imperfect, and his translations faulty. But his accomplishment was extraordinary, and the spirit of his labors admirable. He translated many of Plutarch's Lives, Plato's *Phaedo, Gorgias, Phaedrus, Crito,* and *Apologia;* ten books of Aristotle's *Ethics,* eight books of his *Politics,* two books of his *Economics;* then Aeschines against Ctesiphon and Demosthenes' *de Corona,* and something more from Demosthenes with bits from Aristophanes, and extracts from Xenophon. In a letter to his occasionally rasping friend, Niccolo Niccoli,[17] Bruni writes that his love for Plato grows as he advances with his translations; and he is grateful to " Coluccio patri ac praeceptori meo " for urging the work upon him.

" There is in Plato the utmost urbanity, the finest method of reasoning, and subtlety; while the abundant and divine opinions of the disputants are given with marvellous pleasantness and an incredible fluency of phrase. His is the utmost facility of speech, with an abundance of that admirable χάρις, as the Greeks call it. There is neither sweating nor violence; everything is said as by a man who holds words and their laws in his power. . . . Such a one indeed is Plato among the Greeks, and unless I show him such to the Latins, let them be sure that he is made worse through my fault, and not think they are reading Plato, but my ineptitudes. I promise to labor to keep that from happening; I do not promise to succeed, for I would not dare make any such promise. But unless I am mistaken, I will warrant you, that you shall read your Plato without annoyance, and, I will add, with the greatest pleasure; which I think neither Calcidius, nor the other [translator] who has carefully withheld his name, has enabled you to do. They perhaps set about it in one way, and I in another. For they, departing from Plato, have followed syllables and figures of speech; but I adhere to Plato, whom I imagine to myself as knowing Latin, so that he can judge, and be a witness to his translation; and I translate in such wise as I know will please him best. In the first place, I preserve all his ideas, so as not to depart from them in the least. Then if I can render him word for word, without impropriety or absurdity, I choose that way. But if that is impossible, I am not afraid of falling into the crime of lèse majesté, if, when I have kept the idea, I depart ever so little from the words, so as to avoid absurdity. For Plato himself presently orders me to do this, since he, who is most elegant of speech among the Greeks, does not wish, among the Latins, to appear absurd. Following these principles, unless I do as I promise, I do not object to being thrown into the oven."

[17] Lib. I, ep. 8, in L. Mehus's edition of Bruni's letters — *Leonardi Bruni Aretini Epistolarum Libri VIII,* Florence 1741, 2 vols. (There are in fact ten *libri* in this edition.)

In the next generation, Bruni's translations of Plato were to be superseded by Ficino's; and in his lifetime, he had many a battle to fight over his renderings of Aristotle. He vows that he never added one jot or tittle to Aristotle's meaning, and had differed from former translators only after deep consideration. Let his critics first understand Greek and know the force of its words, upon which he has spent more than eighteen years of study, and has overlooked no point of brilliancy in the Greek tongue. "Besides Aristotle, so much from Plato, Demosthenes, Plutarch, Xenophon, have we translated, that we have become veterans in that art, not tyros!" Bruni admired Aristotle even as a writer: "I do not see how anyone could write more suitably or pleasantly or fluently upon those matters which Aristotle treated. . . . Surely, if anyone should throw dirt on one of Giotto's pictures, I could not stand it. How then do you think it is with me, when I see Aristotle's works, more precious than any picture, defiled with such dirt of a translation!" [18]

Bruni's letters, though less brilliant than Poggio's, are pleasant reading. He wrote many books, among which he may have attached most value to his *History of Florence*. Innocent VII called him, while still little more than a protégé of Salutato's, to the post of papal secretary. The pope was taken aback at his youthful appearance, but was amply reassured by the first letters which he composed, as Bruni recounts to his old friend and master.[19] His clear and sprightly epistolary style attracts one now; the writer was very much awake. Passing over the Eastern Alps from Trent to the Council of Constance, this papal secretary was impressed with the asperities of the way: "Mountains so great and cliffs so high, such ridges, peaks and summits, such giants everywhere rise up, that one marvels exceedingly what that parent and framer of the world, Nature, was after when she made them. Horror, indeed, and awe held me as I gazed on those eternal and everlasting masses, and I cannot recall

[18] Lib. X, Ep. 26; IV, Ep. 22. cf. VII, 4 and 7.
[19] Lib. I, Ep. 1 and 2.

them now without a shudder." [20] Doubtless Bruni felt this; he is still close to the classic attitude toward mountains, for which the Middle Ages also had no love.

Bruni appreciated the humane influence to be gained from classic studies. "Let your application have a two-fold end," he writes to a youth, "the one the knowledge of letters, the other an understanding of those things which pertain to life and manners, which on that account are called *humanitatis studia,* because they perfect and equip the man." He was finely conscious of the inner significance of language, the meaning to be read between the lines: "Intent is grasped not only from words, which may be feigned, but from the expression in the face and eyes of the speaker. . . . I also seem to notice the same in the letters of a good writer . . . in which, besides words and sound, there is something behind, a tacit indication of the mind, which, as from the movement of a speaker's eyes, you may catch, in a writer, from the very vibration of his discourse." [21]

Bruni held his papal secretaryship under successive popes; but he closed his life as chancellor of Florence, as his master Coluccio before him; and, like Coluccio, as he lay in his coffin, "indutus sericam vestem calore ferrugineo," he was crowned with laurel by Mannetti, who gave a long oration upon his career and virtues; to which Poggio added a shorter and admirable one.[22]

The cleverest of all these early Latin-writing, Greek-studying scholars was this Poggio Bracciolini.[23] Although he spent most of his life in the service of the Curia at Rome, he belongs to the Florentine group, through birth in the neighborhood of Florence, through early education, and through life-long association. Born in 1380 of impoverished parents, he came when but a boy

[20] Lib. IV, Ep. 3.
[21] Lib. VI, Ep. 6; VII, Ep. 3.
[22] These orations are printed in Mehus's edition of Bruni's letters, Vol. I, pp. LXXXIX–CXXVI.
[23] There is a good monograph on Poggio, E. Walser, *Poggius Florentinus,* (Berlin 1914), which has been translated into English.

to the city, where Salutato became interested in him, and soon treated him as a son. He made friends, above all with that collector of friends as well as books, the excellent Latinist, Niccolo Niccoli, who lent him his countenance and books and money. He heard Chrysoloras lecture; but at that early age had still to devote himself to Latin and to earning a living by copying manuscripts. When twenty-three, he went to Rome to begin a long and wellpaid, though often interrupted, service of the Curia. But his mind clung to Florence, whether his body was at Rome, or in England, or at Constance, Baden or St. Gall. And afterwards in the Florentine *contado,* when he was rich, and the father of two families, he still would build his villa, and fill it with books and broken antique statues, coins and gems and other paraphernalia of a fifteenth century Italian lover of the classics. Florence in her turn honored him; sent him her citizenship when far away in Constance, recognized his quickness to use that pen of his in her defense, and at the end, when he was seventy-three, pressed the office of Chancellor upon him. He died six years after.

In the meanwhile, what a life of student energy had been his! how had he as a hound hunted out manuscripts, freeing them from their dungeons (ergastula) in German cloisters, and restoring more than one classic to actual life. In this hunt he was *facile princeps,* rescuing Quintilian's *Institutes* in St. Gall, and Valerius Flaccus' *Argonautica,* copying them with his own skilled hand. To his credit also should be placed Lucretius, Ammianus Marcellinus, and some of Cicero's orations. He also proved his scholar's intelligence in his ceaseless copying of ancient inscriptions from the monuments, which he recognized as a source of sure contemporary information. And à propos of Poggio, one may remark how naturally classical studies joined with an interest in antiquities of all kinds, with a love for old heads and broken statues, which were also beautiful; and so with the love of visible, sensual beauty, and all things ministering to it. Thus letters were at one with the love of beauty, luxury, and gorgeous living, which one associates with the Italian quattrocento and cinquecento.

Some of Poggio's letters strike us as rhetoric; but often they are delightful, and usually are written in bright, easy Latin, yet with the constant sufficient correctness of a great scholar and litterateur. Well known is his letter telling of the life of Baden, with men and women enjoying themselves socially in the baths. The next epistle is renowned for its narrative of the trial and defense and burning of Jerome of Prague at the Council of Constance, where the martyr heretic dies with the constancy of a Cato, an admirable sight. Again how colloquial Poggio can be — writing to his closest friend: "Quid mihi agendum fuisse existimas, mi Nicole? Constitue te in locum meum:"— put yourself in my place.[24] And what eagerness and impatience fill his page when he scents a new manuscript to be unearthed — in one case the supposed manuscript of Livy; hurry! hurry! pants the letter; get Cosimo to put up the money; get it quick! In this case, he was chasing an *ignis fatuus*. And so he writes and writes, about getting books and books and books, from this and that other German monk or monastery; and he can be sharp enough — why mince words with a friend? as he says to Niccolo: "De libris Germanis nil dicam amplius, nisi me non dormire more tuo, sed vigilare." [25]

Obviously these people, Poggio above all, gave themselves over utterly to collecting books and to classical studies, as men had not done in the Middle Ages. Poggio and Bruni were reputed to be pagans. Italy in their time had no objection to such, hating only heretics. Poggio and his friends do not play, as in the Middle Ages, at making all knowledge the handmaid of theology; yet he knows well the phrase, parens et regina scientiarum omnium. Even Poggio has not quite thrown over

[24] This is Ep. I, 11, of Vol. I of Tonelli's edition. The two others precede it.

[25] Ep. III, 1.

the Fathers, will at least read them in default of other occupation; in London, for example, whither he had gone, and had been disappointed in his hopes of emolument. There he reads Augustine, and the homilies of Chrysostom in translation. There also he had three months' leisure for Aristotle, turning over his works to see what was in each — reason enough for studying Greek (in which Poggio never was proficient), to know this man in his own tongue, who in another tongue is "elinguis et absurdus." For an expositor, he had Thomas Aquinas, "virum egregium et fecundum." But he returns quickly to Chrysostom and Augustine, wishing to read Augustine on Paul and Matthew: "nam, pace aliorum dixerim, hic vir longe humero supereminet omnes." "Hic vir" is Augustine, and this letter shows how that great Father could hold his own with Poggio, as he had half dominated Petrarch.[26]

Poggio says that the English monasteries had few books to interest him; he saw catalogues containing nothing "dignum studiis humanitatis." Curiously enough, in the same letter he evinces qualms: he cannot adjust his conduct with his principles; even his interests waver. "The sacred books which I have read, and daily read, have cooled my early studium humanitatis, to which, as you know, I have been devoted from boyhood. For the foundations of these studies are vain, partly false; — all vanity! But the foundation of sacred eloquence is truth, which lost, we can hold and do nothing good." He adds, "If you think I have mended my ways, they are worse than ever." But on his fiftieth birthday, he writes to Niccolo that he will seek *gradually* a better sort of life.[27]

One may smile! Poggio's morals were weak enough, though at the age of fifty-five he gave up his mistress, from whom he is said to have had fourteen children, to take a fresh young wife. He was true to his friends, and grateful; but a vile reviler of his enemies, as was the custom of his tribe. Likewise he hunted the emoluments of

[26] Ep. II, 16; I, 6 & 8.
[27] Ep. I, 13; IV, 5.

life and learning; and none equalled him in turning dedications of his writings into money. His *Facetiae* were more often foul than funny. But he was quite of his time, and a fine scholar, to whose zeal for rescuing manuscripts the world owes much.

One cannot speak at length of all the men composing this chief group of early humanists, whose hearth and home was Florence, and whose Maecenas was Cosmo dei Medici. One feels that they were very happy in their enthusiasms. The antique world was a sort of new world for them, newly discovered by them, as it seemed; for they had come to it with such a young new interest; and an interest which in the volume and diffusion and effect of its energy was new in fact. So they felt themselves happily exploring a land unexplored and full of fascinations, full of promise. Their way of life was also new. They did not live in monasteries, nor cluster around Cathedral schools, or hold chairs at universities. They were *literati,* secretaries to cities, to despots, to popes, court scribes, court poets. But among themselves they formed a band, not of brothers, often of hateful foes, but still of men united in their enthusiasms and pursuits. They helped each other enormously. No one of them could have done as much as he did to advance classical scholarship, had not the others aided him; each to each was a tap of information, a lending library, sometimes a source of cash. Those who did not produce much themselves, like Niccolo Niccoli and Ambrosio Traversari, were pivots around whom the others profitably circled. Niccolo Niccoli, a fat little man and autocratic Latinist, is spoken of by Cortesius of the next Florentine generation as one " who gained great glory through cultivating the friendships of the most learned men." He had the best library in Florence; of its eight hundred volumes, two hundred were in lending in 1437, when he expired devoutly, in the arms of his friend Traversari, the General of the Order of Camalduli. The voluminous collected correspondence of the latter, comprising his own and his friends' letters, serves to bring these men into a group.[28]

As monk and General of his Order, Traversari was a prelate active in ecclesiastical intrigues, and a pillar of conventional piety; but as a man and humanist, he was a vivacious companion, an eager student, and an aid to others. He was worried often by religious compunctions, as in his work at translating the heathen historian of heathen philosophy, Diogenes Laertius. In his own compositions he endeavored to avoid profane citations! He sends to Pope Eugenius IV St. Bernard's *De Consideratione,* as an apt book for a new pope; he is much interested in Greek, and in books, books, books. Also a great reader of the Church Fathers, with a predilection for Lactantius because of his Ciceronian style, and for Athanasius as the rock of orthodoxy. Admiration for that " eximius vir " so holds him, as he says, " ut ab eo divelli non possim." He will devote himself to that " igneo ac coelesti homini," when he can command time. The letters to his close friend Niccolo are generally interesting. A number of them are taken up with his delightful humanistic journey to Rome, and to Venice, Ferrara, Mantua, Ravenna. He stays at the monasteries of his Order and rummages them for manuscripts; he also looks at the antique curiosities of each town: at Ravenna he admires the churches (templa) and many-colored marble columns, and all the mosaics; at Venice, Ciriaco shows him his coins.[29]

The man last named, Ciriaco of Ancona, is known to fame as the tireless, fearless explorer of antique sites, and collector of gems and coins, statues and manuscripts, and all sorts of information from places far and difficult.[30] It were a long task to describe his journeys. He was a trader with a passion for exploration, and gained his knowledge and his education as he travelled, even his Latin and Greek. In Rome he visits antique tem-

[28] *Ambrosius Traversarius Camaldunensis,—Epistolae, Vita &c.,* ed. by L. Mehus (Florence 1749).

[29] Lib. VIII, ep. 12 and 42–54.

[30] See G. Voight, *Wiederbelebung &c.,* I, p. 269 sqq. (3rd Ed. 1891).

ples, theatres, palaces, baths, triumphal arches, aqueducts as well, and bridges; he makes drawings of columns, and copies inscriptions. He takes ship for Byzantium, and searches for antiquities in Chios, and collects Greek and Latin inscriptions. He visits Rhodes and then Beirut and Damascus, everywhere buying, both as connoisseur and trader, manuscripts and bronzes, coins and gems, any object of antiquarian interest. He visited Adrianople; and afterwards ranged Italy through and through, from Sicily to the northern bounds: he travelled in Dalmatia, Greece, Egypt, visited Crete: it were hard to say where his restless feet did not tread. He appears in humanistic circles, with antiquities to show or sell, and all manner of information (some of it wrong) to impart. His scholarship might be questioned,— that of the self-taught man is likely to be peccable; but he was a well-known and interesting personality. In spite of his faulty knowledge, his collections of inscriptions were of great value.

There was another and more important man, who wandered also, or at least often changed his abode, not from love of exploration, but from restlessness and the difficulties caused by his insolence. This was Filelfo,[31] a man of much learning for his time. He had lived and studied in Constantinople, and had married a Greek wife. In 1427, when not yet thirty years old, he returned from the East, landing at Venice. Well equipped with Greek, he taught there for a while, making a sensation, as he says. About two years afterwards, having tried various ruses to secure a high salary, he came to Florence, at the invitation of Niccolo and Traversari, and under the patronage of Cosimo and other great ones. Besides his Greek accomplishments, he was one of the best of Latin writers in prose and metre. He was to lecture on Livy and Cicero, and Terence, Thucydides, Xenophon and the

[31] On Filelfo, see Voight, *Wiederbelebung* etc., I, 348 sqq. (3rd Ed.); G. Benadduci, *Prose e poesie volgari di Francesco Filelfo* (Ancona 1901); E. Legrand, *Cent-dix lettres grecques de François Filelfe,* (Paris 1892); T. Klette, *Die griechische Briefe des Franciscus Philelphus,* (Greifswald 1890).

Iliad. His lectures drew great audiences, and he gave hours at home on the humanities, all most successfully. His friendship was sought by the best men. But his head began to strike the clouds a little overmuch; the earth could hardly hold him. He fell out with the temperamental Niccolo — a bad man to fall out with — and sundry others. Cosimo and his brother showed estrangement. In 1433 a revolt of the nobles brought Cosimo to prison. Filelfo spoke out, and urged his death. Cosimo was exiled, but recalled to power within the year, and Filelfo fled advisedly. Some months afterwards a bravo attempted his life in Sienna. The feud was on, the literary feud, with Poggio the chief gladiator on the other side: the weapons ink and filth. Foul as were the mutual accusations, they were not all calumnies. We will not take up this oft-told story. After many decades, when Cosimo had long been dead, Filelfo, reconciled and pardoned by the Medici, returned to Florence a man of eighty-three. It was in the summer; the heat and fatigue of the journey were too much for him. He died as the result. He had done much in Greek as well as Latin prose and verse, and in the *volgare* too.

It is necessary to speak more particularly of Lorentius Valla, unquestionably the hardest thinker and closest scholar that had so far appeared among the Italian humanists. Alfonso of Arragon had made good by force of arms his claim to the Kingdom of Sicily and Naples. He adopted the humanistic fashions of the time in Italy, by showing a constant interest in the classics, having them read to him in translations daily after dinner. He cultivated the society of the learned, and was a patron of those men whose writings should immortalize his deeds and enhance the glory of his reign. Lorentius Valla attached himself to the King in the midst of a campaign. He accompanied him to Naples, and for some years dwelt beneath his aegis, serving him in various literary capacities.

Valla loved to call himself a Roman, although he seems to have been born in Piacenza in 1407. But he passed his youth in Rome, and his early manhood, enjoying there the society and instruction of Bruni, Poggio, and the Greek scholar Aurispa, who had brought his fund of learning and his store of books from Constantinople. Valla was never at his best in Greek, but he possessed a close knowledge of classic Latin, a powerfully reasoning mind, and a temper none too sweetly combative, when he left Rome in 1431. He first taught in Pavia, there attacking both the dialecticians and the jurists. Then he stayed transiently in Milan and Genoa, Ferrara and Mantua, and at last more permanently in Naples, under Alfonso's protection, which he needed.

For Valla did not content himself with piling factitious scorn on rival humanists; he attacked long-held acceptances, and made himself a danger to papal pretensions, if not to Christian morals. With all his devotion to Latin letters, his mind was destructively and constructively critical, and recalcitrant against authority. Curiously enough, in part from an instinct to combat received opinion, Valla maintained the superiority of Quintilian as a rhetorician over Cicero; he later was to assert the superiority of Demosthenes over Cicero as an orator. He stands out among his fellows as an absolute classicist.[32]

The humanist theory, beginning with Petrarch, was to contemn the post-classical and mediaeval changes in Latin, and insist upon conformity to classical models. Yet the practice had been looser, and many current usages were accepted. Valla alone, with strenuous consistency and unique grammatical insight, insisted upon adherence to classical correctness in practice; and proceeded by grammatical analysis to distinguish between classical and all aberrant forms. He set forth these principles with ample illustration in his *Elegantiae* of the Latin tongue, a work occupying him for years, and containing the closest consideration of the meanings and proper use of words. No work of the period evinces such profound reverence

[32] The works of Valla, except the *Elegantiae,* are difficult to come by. I have gained much from Vahlen's excellent essay on him, in Almanach der Kaiserl. Akad. der Wissenschaften, Vienna, XIV Jahrg. 1864, pp. 183 sqq.

for the ancient language of the Romans, *nostrorum majorum,* an ancestorship which Valla held to as a faith. The *Praefatio* proclaims the benign conquest of Europe by the Latin tongue, when arms indeed had failed the Romans: Magnum ergo Latini sermonis sacramentum est:

"Great therefore is the saving power — the sacrament — of the Latin speech, great surely its divinity, which is preserved these many centuries among foreigners, among barbarians, among enemies, scrupulously and religiously, so that we Romans should not grieve, but rejoice, while the whole listening earth should glory. We have lost Rome, we have lost empire, we have lost dominion, not by the fault of us, but of the times; nevertheless, in virtue of this more splendid dominion, we reign until now in a large part of the world."

Rome is indeed captured by the Gauls, he continues, through the horrid decay of Latinity; which this book shall do its share in re-establishing. So far the preface to Book I.

The preface to the next book reviles the Latinity of those who came after Donatus, Servius and Priscian — "to whom I ascribe this much, that whoever after them wrote something of Latin (aliquid de Latinitate), would seem to stammer: of those untaught ones, the first and most arrogant is Isidore." The preface to Book III takes a grammarian's view of jurisprudence, agreeing with Quintilian, that "every legal right rests on the interpretation of words, or on the distinction of right and wrong." The preface to the next book turns against those who despise classical learning. Some years later, in 1455, Valla delivered an inaugural *Oratio* in Rome, at the opening of the academic year, taking for his theme the great value of the Latin tongue, which, universally diffused, spreads and preserves knowledge, and enables all men to build together the tower of knowledge understandingly, and not as at Babel.[33]

If Valla's *Elegantiae* laid the foundations of modern

[33] Text published by Vahlen, *L. Vallae tria opuscula,*— Sitz-ber. Phil. Hist. Classe, Vienna Acad. 1869, B'd 62 pp. 93 sqq.

classical philology, they also disclosed the quality of their author, his intellectual method, and the sequence of his intellectual activities. He was fundamentally a philologist and grammarian; and it is from the discipline of his analysis of the Latin language that he passes on to criticize the loose or empty thinking obfuscating the minds of contemporaries. In all branches of thought, it is his way to reach greater clarity by analyzing the meanings of words, or again by discovering the impossibilities hinging upon the inconsistencies of statement. So this incisive questing spirit, from the suggestions of a scientific philology, proceeded to attack grammarians, literati, jurists, dialecticians and philosophers, and monks. By sifting the exact from the loose, realities from falsities, he passes to broader criticism, historical or philosophical. Throughout, he shows himself as inconsiderate of other men's opinions as he was considerate of fact.

A true Valla note is struck in a letter touching his old friend Bruni: "I have read through his *Laudation of Florence,*— plenam levitatis et supinitatis. . . . He speaks as if he expected no one to reply to him and much less that anyone should not assent to his absurdities. He would have Florence the heir of the imperium of the Roman people, as if Rome herself were extinct! . . . The style is lax and fluid and enervated, lacking dignity and character, and in many places speaking unlatinly, not to say corruptly." [34]

This hard-headed Valla, so critical of Bruni's patriotic foolishness, can readily be imagined declaring that Hector and Aeneas, even Rinaldo, were imaginary persons; or we hear him entering upon a critical discussion of the Roman legends, and pointing out inconsistencies in Livy; as in his *Emendationes sex librorum T. Livii de secundo bello punico.* He proceeded more hardily in the interests of Alfonso, as well as truth, to show by lengthy analysis that "Constantine's Donation" was a later

[34] To Petrus Candidus (cir. 1435), taken from Barozzi e Sabbadini, *Studi sul Panormita e sul Valla* (Florence 1891).

forgery.[35] His patron's protection was needed when he was attacked in Naples by the Inquisition, on many grounds, and among others for impugning the accepted view that the Apostles successively enunciated the clauses of the "Apostles' Creed."

There were plenty of other grounds. Valla's quest of truth, and of solid reasons even to support alleged other-worldly thinking, rode rather roughshod over time-honored acceptances as well as interests. The sequence of his writings is not certain. But it was not far from 1447, and when the desire to see Rome again was strong in this Roman fosterling, that he produced his critical *In Novum Testamentum adnotationes,* in which he sought to hark back to the Greek original, and to criticize the Vulgate translation from the invidious vantage ground of a closer philological investigation. He also noted certain inconsistencies among the Gospels.[36]

Only a little less revered than the Vulgate, were the dialectic traditions of the universities; and by attacking these — even the Ten Categories! — Valla made himself obnoxious to the scholastics of his time, whose hate he also drew by the contempt he poured on them, in his book of *Dialecticorum Disputationum.* A veritable pruning of dialectic, *repastinatio* as his sub-title called it, was this writing, which should show how simple an affair was logic really; much simpler than grammar, if only hair-splitting dialecticians would let it stay so.

But before this book had appeared, indeed before he ever came to Naples, he had made himself suspect to serious people by his famous *De Voluptate,* in which, following Epicurus, he showed that man's highest good lay in a tranquil mind; or, rather, perhaps he did, for he seemed to let Christian teaching triumph in the end. Yet through the work, arguments setting sense-pleasure above all are given with enthusiasm, and may have been intended

[35] *De falso credita et ementita Constantini donatione Declamatio.*

[36] Erasmus was the first really to appreciate and indeed appropriate many of Valla's suggestions. See *post,* Chapter VII.

to prove a valid human truth.[37] At all events, Valla was a hardy reasoner in this book, as well as in his *De libero arbitrio;* and these works seem to have had their effect on the great Leibnitz.

None of these writings stirred such ecclesiastic hate as the dialogue *De Professione Religiosorum,*[38] against the monks. Valla, as one of the speakers, denies them the name of *religiosi,* since they do not make a *religio* but a *secta,* a word corresponding to the Greek αἵρεσις, and pregnant with the detestable innuendo of this derivation. The *Frater* answers. But the course of the argument invalidates his claims to a superior mode of life; an analysis of his statements shows them to prove nothing. Valla prefers to twist his opponent up in his own misused words, rather than put forward counter allegations. Naturally, the monk's side is feebly stated, and Valla's cleverly. Yet some years later, in an *Apologia* addressed to Eugene IV, Valla queries whether he did not, in the Dialogue concede too much in admitting that the monastic life, while not *melior,* might be *tutior.* "Etenim via a Christo tradita nulla est tutior, sicut nec melior, in qua nulla professio nobis injungitur." [39] However this may be, the Dialogue is an instance of the cold light of a new worldly reason, without faith, playing upon the monastic argument.

This *Apologia* did not make Rome livable for Valla till after Eugene had been succeeded by that lover of the humanists, Nicholas V. Then indeed Valla might return, to spend the last decade of his life in the city he loved best. Nicholas set him to work translating Thucydides, and other Greek works, it being this Pontiff's darling wish to possess the Greek literature in readable Latin. The huge income from the papal Jubilee of 1450 enabled him to subsidize the scholar world and set it to this task.

Yes, wealth and humanism went together; nor did these

[37] F. Gabotto has an article on L'epicureismo di L. Valla in *Rivista di filosofia scientifica* for 1889 (pp. 651–672).

[38] Published by Vahlen — *Laurentii Vallae opuscula tria.* Sitz-ber. Phil. Hist. Classe, Vienna Acad. 1869, B'd 62, pp. 99–134.

[39] Luther took a like position regarding monks' vows. See *post* chap. IX.

flattering humanists care for the glory of a threadbare coat. The *joi de vivre* and a more splendid life suitably accompanied the renewed delight in the classics, themselves exponents of a full round of human quality, and friendly to the glory of this world. Those ancients were nobly garbed and splendid gentlemen; and it will seem proper enough that the elderly and none too prosperous Machiavelli, living on his farm, after coming in from his daily rustic mire, should lay aside his dirty clothes, and put on *abiti regali e curiali,* before sitting down with those stately masters of the world. Moreover, a taste for letters and the love of luxury and art and splendor, naturally are found together in those lordly patrons, those proper amateurs, of the fifteenth and sixteenth centuries in Italy; and craft and letters often would work together in the creation of the work of art, as when Bruni was called in to advise upon the choice of subjects for Ghiberti's doors to the Baptistry.

If the other humanists had been, and were to be, artists in words, Valla was a man of science, whether as philologist or philosopher. His literary powers were not marked, and his instinct was at fault in his weeding out of current Latin usage, and his demand for a no longer possible adherence to the classic phrase and use of words. After all, the question of writing classical or unclassical Latin was becoming a battle of shades, in the face of the likewise academic strife between Latin and the *volgare,* and the actual literary triumph of the latter. One should realize that in Italy the study of the Latin humanities was a phase of human growth, leading on to a fuller expansion and expression of humanity not only in art but in the other living medium, to wit, the *volgare.* The humanists of the fifteenth century were not quite so dumb as to fail to see the worth of the Italian works of Dante, Petrarch and Boccaccio.

CHAPTER III

LORENZO, POLIZIANO, ARIOSTO, TASSO

TOUCHING the earlier humanists spoken of in the last chapter, one may ask, what advance of thought, what growth of human intelligence, what novelties of expression do they present? They drew inspiration from Petrarch and Boccaccio; and more unreservedly than had been possible in the Middle Ages, their minds were fixed upon the intellectual and artistic concerns of mortal life. They were disposed to love it all; only upon intrusive reminders would they doff their caps to the threats and promises of their religion.

Palpably and, as it were, externally, their education and progress hung upon devotion to the antique, its study and its imitation. They brought to the reading of the classics a renewed openness of mind, and perceived their significance more truly than mediaeval students. The early fifteenth century to which they belonged had profited from the increase of wealth and the accumulation of experience. The fields of knowledge were broadening. And if Petrarch was a better classical scholar than anyone before him, he was surpassed by his successors, who availed of his example and accomplishment. Many lost classics had been brought to light by eager searches through forgotten places; and a century of devotion to the classics bore its fruit.

The veritable progress of these men, so far as it existed, lay within themselves, although seemingly it issued from their studies. Those we have taken as examples were diligent and clever; and at least one among them showed an incisively critical intelligence. Yet intelligent and clever as were Valla, Filelfo, Poggio and Bruni, they do not appear to have evolved and compassed novel and interesting modes of expression, which are the sure proof and exponent of human progress. They were still students and assemblers; their self-expression lay in their ardent scholarship. Perfected and, as it were, classical forms of humanistic expression in Latin and Italian prose and verse were to arise from the finished humanistic genius of younger men, who likewise had absorbed the accomplishment of their immediate predecessors.

I

Some of these younger men were notable artist-scholars; one or two of them were extraordinary personalities. Not merely they surpassed their predecessors in knowledge of the classics; they had achieved a more intimate appropriation and transmutation of them into active faculty. They can do more with them, or with the knowledge and discipline acquired through their study. Beyond this, they can do more with the *volgare,* than the men nearer to Petrarch; they have attained, partly through their classic discipline, a better mastery over the proper forms of Italian compositions in prose and verse. They have reached the power to express artistically the fruits of their discipline and knowledge. Like their immediate forbears, they owe much to each other, much to the circumstance that there is an enthusiastic well-equipped group of them. They help each other in their education and their work. More particularly Lorenzo the Magnificent and Politian, whom we especially have in mind, were assisted by one of the last and most admirable of Cosimo's protégés, Ficino, who was born in 1433, and was to be the central luminary of the Platonic Academy in Florence. He will be considered in a future chapter, in connection with the philosophy of the period.

Cosimo's grandson, Lorenzo, merits the epithet of superman, from his qualities of temperament, his exceeding energy, and his notable and diverse powers. He was an Italian of his time. This most astute and unscrupulous politician sang ballads of his own making in the streets of his city, equally to please the people and himself. If he ruled his people, he belonged to them, and delighted in them, in their songs, in their fêtes and dances, and in the hot embraces of their daughters. He was reputed as licentious as he was intellectual. The splendid and unbridled festivals, with which he tamed and debauched the Florentines, gave him spontaneous joy. No mere politician, no merely voracious ruler, but only one who had, besides, another nature, could have written this verse from his *Trionfo di Bacco e Arianna:*

> Quant' e bella giovinezza,
> Chi si fugge tuttavia!
> Chi vuol esser lieto, sia:
> Di doman non c'è certezza.

The lines dance of themselves, as Lorenzo also danced from delight.

Educated in the classics, instructed in some sort of antique philosophy, he still loved his own Italian literature and his Italian tongue. He was a deep admirer of Dante, a devoted lover and imitator of Petrarch's *Canzoniere.* He defended the *volgare,* and with such success, or in such accord with life's insistence to express itself in the vernacular, that the *volgare* needed no advocate after him to maintain its complete supersession of Latin as the vehicle of living literature. Lorenzo gives his voice for the *volgare,* not only because it is in general use, but because it is "copiosa e abondante, ed atta a esprimer bene il senso e il concetto della mente," and because of its "dolcezza ed armonia," and because of its good repute and fame and the many noble things already written in it.[1]

Doubtless Lorenzo's most effective vindication of the *volgare* was his use of it in his ballads and other writings; — indeed it had already won the victory in the greatest of all literary creations of the Italian mind and mood, the *Divina Commedia.* One might as well realize

[1] See the great Florentine edition of the *Opere de Lorenzo de' Medici,* Vol. IV, p. 15, sqq.

the essential feebleness and sheer academic quality of whatever the humanists had said or done to re-classicize and maintain the literary vitality of Latin. One will still encounter misprisals of the *volgare*,[2] but they had no effect upon the period's real progress in thought and faculty.[3]

Cosimo was an able financier and politician, and an intelligent patron of arts and letters. With equal ability in politics and statecraft, Lorenzo had but casual taste for banking, and even in politics, with his enormous aptitude, and under the incessant need to guard his power and life, he shows the dilettante nature, which is amused by its task, rather than absorbed in it. Was not Lorenzo entertained by all the means he used to beguile and rule the Florentines? Must he not have enjoyed that possibly last cast of the die, when he went to Naples and put himself within the power of his enemy, King Ferdinand, and won a favorable peace from him by sheer virtuosity of argument?

Indeed in Lorenzo one has the superman as dilettante, a character which he shows more clearly in fields other than politics. A dilettante was he in things spiritual; he would try the charm of this and that — would turn from love-songs to Augustine and then again to music. What a connoisseur he was; and a collector, if not unrivalled, at least unequalled in Italy; and with what copiousness he spoke on painting, sculpture, philosophy, poetry and music! Lavish in his expense, lavish in his patronage of letters. And yet even as dilettante, he was still the man of more than human energy, always the superman: whether in his discourses or his revels, or his licentiousness, and so markedly in the mass of his vivid poetry. Political power came to him when he was twenty-one; and he was but forty-four when he died, leaving, as some

[2] For instance, L. Gyraldus, *De Poetis nostrorum temporum,* ed. by Wotke, (Berlin, 1894), p. 40 and p. 85.

[3] Yet such a considerable man as Pontano wrote altogether in Latin. Although born in Umbria, he was much more of a Neapolitan than a north Italian. See A. Gaspary, *Ges. der italienischen Literatur,* B'd II, pp. 301–321.

think, Italy to break in ruin after him for lack of his shrewd balancing mind.

Politian's often quoted letter to one Jacobus Antiquarius describing Lorenzo's pious death, is to be taken rather as a comment on the times than on Lorenzo individually, a comment on the times indeed, that toward the last gasp a famous doctor should arrive with a *medicamentum* compounded of pearls and all manner of gems. It was administered, and still the patient died. After his death, prodigies currently were reported.

A certain Benedetto of Montepulciano, which was in the Florentine territory, realizing that he was in danger of assassination from his wicked neighbors, recommended himself and his children to the protection of Piero, son of Cosimo, and father of Lorenzo, and was murdered some months after, as he had feared. His eldest child, Angelo, was sent to Florence. This was in 1464, when Angelo was ten years old. Apparently he lived and studied in poverty for several years, and attended lectures at the Florentine *Studium Generale* or University, which, having started in 1321, was re-inaugurated in the year of the great pestilence, 1348, according to Matteo Villani.

Probably the Medici knew of Angelo, and of his studying in the School. His precocity attracted the notice of Ficino, and the flowing translation of the second book of the *Iliad* which he sent to Lorenzo in 1470, apparently led Lorenzo himself, so young and newly come to power upon his father's death, to remove the " Homeric youth " from his poor lodgings to a Medici palace. From that time until his death twenty-four years later this Angelo, called Poliziano from his birth place, was praised and fostered as the paragon of poets and scholars. In the minds, or words, of some of his admirers such was the masterful excellence of his translation of those few books of the *Iliad,* that old Homer, but for his natural patriotism, would have wished himself a Latin. Nor has the name of Politian ever lost its glamor; his name and face, and the fame of Lorenzo's friendship for him, still touch the imaginations of men and women who love Florence.

One need not credit the myth of his having produced the *Giostra,* at the age of fourteen. He was over twenty when he composed that piece, and had written the "*Orfeo*" two years before. Soon he began to lecture in the rooms where he had been a learner, and men of twice his age came from near and far to listen to his fluent learning. For Florence it was the very golden time of letters and Platonism,— those short decades which were still to pass before Lorenzo's death in 1492. Then came revulsions and catastrophes. Politian died in 1494, at the age of forty, having seen the approach of evil days; and Ficino died, a much older man, in 1499; while the most astounding phoenix of them all, Pico, prince of Mirandula, had ascended to his star the same year with Politian, when but little over thirty.[4] Savonarola was left to reform the threatened city, and go to the stake in 1498.

Politian was a Greek scholar. He wrote Latin admirably. He excelled as a poet in the *volgare:* the bosom friend of Lorenzo could not pretend to despise the *volgare.* Indeed it triumphed distinctly in this humanist of humanists, in whom, as with Boccaccio, it reaped the benefit of the classical *disciplina.* Politian brought Latin metrical suavity to Italian verse, and his poems became veritably popular, and took root among the people. He also, like Lorenzo, often imitated Petrarch's sonnets. There was not very much originality in his Italian poetry. Yet through his skill, and because he could draw from nature as well as from books, his poems on love and springtime have a delightfulness which is their own.

From his youth, Politian studied and absorbed, and through his life never ceased to assimiliate, the classics. Although he lectured on many parts of the philosophy of Aristotle, and wrote whimsical *Praelectiones* to his courses, he insisted in one of these that he was not a philosopher, but an interpreter, having the equipment of

[4] On Pico see *post* Chapter XXX.

a *grammaticus,* according to the Greek word, or *literatus,* as one should say in Latin: " nec aliud inde mihi nomen postulo quam grammatici." [5] Politian was not a serious Aristotelian; nor was his knowledge of Plato always worthy of a pupil of Ficino; at least he makes an unaccountable slip in this same Praelectio, when he gives the Platonic fable of the shadow-seers in the cave, and ascribes it to Iamblichus, " whom the consensus of Ancient Greece called divinissimum." Altogether this is rather dreadful, seeing that " Ancient Greece " knew nothing of that fourth century hierophant, and we hope would not have regarded him highly. Yet if Politian cultivated Iamblichus more than the veritable Plato, he did but follow the tendency of his time really to read and enjoy the later Greek and Latin authors. His own *Giostra* reeks with Statius, and was modelled on those poems of eulogy which, with their mingled elements of myth and lyricism, are to be found in Latin literature from the time of Statius to its last decline.[6]

In the *Orfeo,* Politian did a stroke of genius, by applying the form of the Mystery-representation to the classic fable of Orpheus and Eurydice. He wrote this short and pleasant piece for a festival at the Mantuan Court of the Gonzagas in 1471; a lovely little pastoral play he made of it, a different and lesser *Comus,* less transforming, less transcendent, if one will.[7] With the borrowed fable

[5] Politian gave the title of "Lamia" to his Praelectio to the course on the *Prior Analytics.* It is printed in Del Lungo's *Florentia* (Florence 1897), pp. 133 sqq. The phrase quoted is from page 169–170.

[6] Carducci, p. xlviii, of the introduction to his edition of *Le Stanze, l'Orfeo e le Rime* (Florence 1863).

[7] The pastoral composition which was read far and wide, and influenced French and English literature, was the *Arcadia* of the valiant and worthy scholar, the Neapolitan, Sannazaro. The work belongs to the last decade of the fifteenth century. It was a pastoral romance in prose and verse. Its author had Virgil and Theocritus on his tongue's end, and knew the Greek romances. For Italian antecedents, the work harked back perhaps to Boccaccio's *Filocolo* and his *Ameto.* It was the cleverest of mosaics of borrowings and imitations, filled with the sentiments and phrases of the old bucolic poems, which the author used as naturally as if they were the current words of his language. It also incorporated long extracts from those poems. It is edited, with introduction and discussions by Scherillo (Turin, 1888). Tasso's *Aminta* (1573) and Guarini's *Pastor Fido* (1581) are more organic compositions than either the *Arcadia* or the *Orfeo.*

went many borrowings of classical phrase and sentiment quite naturally, and all so trippingly and lightly put together, fused into a melodious idyllic play.

Much the same may be said of the *Stanze per la Giostra,* a more difficult and slowly composed poem, descriptive, rather than dramatic. It was intended to immortalize the prowess of Giuliano de'Medici in the jousts, and his love for the gentle Simonetta, whose death followed not long after. Either that sad event, or the catastrophe of Giuliano's own assassination in 1478, discouraged the completion of a poem which may have proved tiresome to its author. For, as the subject of an elaborate composition, the matter was empty enough, though Politian made the most of

> Le gloriose pompe e' fieri ludi,

commanded by the great house who would thus show how they had turned from banking to the noble arts of chivalry. Reading the poem, one can hardly believe one's eyes, and the learned footnotes of Carducci's edition, to find its sonorous octaves built of reminiscence, sentiment and phrase taken from classic poetry; not " taken," perhaps, but rather imbibed, breathed in, appropriated, made the new poet's own, and breathed forth again, or at least reissued, in flowing and well molten verse. Lucretius, Virgil, Ovid, Statius, Claudian, with touches from the Greeks, are there. But in the *Orfeo* and the *Giostra,* as well as in Politian's love poems and ballads, not merely sentiments and phrases were borrowed from the antique; but more subtly the discipline and order of classic letters were drawn into Italian poetry.

So the classical literature yielded forms and phrases to these humanists, through which they gave expression to their tastes and their own natures, though in borrowed or imitated language, and, as it were, at second hand. The spirit of the *Orfeo* and the *Giostra* likewise reflects something of the spirit of the antique, as a summer pool, stirred by a sunny breeze, reflects, with a brightness of its own, the branches waving overhead.

Politian was not satisfied with merely studying, understanding, and enjoying the classics. He would follow and imitate their beauty, reproduce that in words of his own, whether in Latin or Italian. For he and others of his time were endeavoring to transform their knowledge of classic style and substance into a facility of their own in Latin composition. And then they would bring all this discipline to the aid of their Italian prose and verse. This meant to turn knowledge into art, and, in accordance with the Italian nature, into the art of producing that which was beautiful in form.

But the endeavor to imitate the phrases, and follow the patterns, of classic literature tended to make form the chief consideration, and to disregard substance. Yet these unoriginal composers were not so conscious of their emptiness; nor did they really intend to set mere empty form (were such conceivable) before them as their goal. An endeavor to be and express themselves is observable in the best among them, and, curiously enough, in this paragon of a Politian, who was in fact so unoriginal and for the most part indifferent to substance. More than once he reminded his pupils that their own talents and judgment should not be buried beneath other men's opinions. He also adjured them not to blunt the point of their discourses with overmuch verbosity, nor lose the thread of argument.[8] And again, when someone had said that his own letters were not Ciceronian, he had answered " in epistolari stilo silendum prorsus esse de Cicerone." But if another should accuse him of imitating Cicero, he might answer: " nihil mihi esse magis in votis quam ut vel umbram Ciceronis assequar." [9] So the propriety of following or ignoring Cicero depended on what one was writing; in letters there is a virtue in negligence. He blames his friend Paulus Cortesius, a great stickler for Ciceronian Latinity, for blind imitation: and if it be said:

[8] Cf. Del Lungo, *Florentia,* p. 131.

[9] *Omnia Opera Angeli Politiani* (Venice, Aldus 1498) Ep. 1 to Petrus Medici.

"Thou dost not speak like Cicero — non exprimis Ciceronem — what then! for I am not Cicero. Yet, as I opine, I express myself — me tamen exprimo." [10]

Politian, dead at forty, was also a wonderful scholar; one is tempted to call him an "elegant" scholar, but without using that term disparagingly. His sheer scholarship is shown in his *Miscellanea,* a work of the nature of Valla's *Elegantiae,* and composed of matter from the lectures given at the University. It discussed all sorts of questions affecting scholarship: the origins of classic institutions and ceremonies, the significance of fables, words and their uses, even spellings. His mind was clear and penetrating; his treatment pertinent to the matter; and he showed a true scholarly aversion to pretense and subterfuge. He was an admirable critic and restorer of better readings in corrupt texts. The *Miscellanea* met the needs of an advancing scholarship, just as, some centuries before, the needs of a scantier knowledge were met by orthographies and grammars. Politian was also a valiant translator from the Greek. Besides those early glorious translations from the *Iliad,* he rendered into Latin Herodian's *History,* the *Enchiridion* of Epictetus, and the *Problemata* of Alexander Aprodisias.

Whatever a man may say, the truth of him lies in what he does preponderantly. And preponderantly Politian was the ideal Italian humanist, wonderfully clever in his faculty of giving beauty, perhaps a new beauty, to his assimilation of classic sentiments and phrases; not deeply caring for the validity or seriousness of the substance, but beyond others clever in reaching the form which pleases, whatsoever be the content which is therein beautified.[11]

[10] In Lib. VIII of epistles, same edition.

[11] Francesco de Sanctis calls Politian "la piu spiccata espressione della letteratura in questo secolo. Ci è già l'immagine schietta del letterato, fuori di ogni participazione alla vita publica, vuoto di ogni coscienza religiosa o politica o morale. . . . Il Poliziano aveva uno squisito sentimento della forma nella piena indifferenza di ogni contenuto." From page 367 of *Storia della Letteratura italiana* (Naples, 1870) — whatever else one reads for information, De Sanctis always should be read for his impressive suggestiveness.

Withal one may appreciate his excellent judgment by contrasting the opinions of his young friend who disagreed with him.

Paulus Cortesius, to give his name in Latin form, as he would have preferred, was a younger member of the Florentine group of humanists. He had upbraided Politian for the lack of Ciceronian qualities in his letters, and had been taunted by him for his own ape-like imitative habits. He defended his implicit copying of Cicero, but added that he preferred to be called his *filius* or *alumnus,* rather than his *Simia!* In 1490 he dedicated to Lorenzo a *Dialogus de hominibus doctis,*[12] which spoke (rather rashly) of past and present Florentine notables. To the learned, says he, Dante, Petrarch and Boccaccio are already antiquated. The first is as an old picture with its colors gone, while its lines still please. His poem was wonderful — if he had only put his marvellous thoughts in Latin! As for Petrarch, a man, of course, greatly to be admired, his rough style is scarcely Latin; his matter was composed diligently, rather than elegantly. Naturally the "*ornamenta scribendi* were lacking to a man born *in faece omnium saeculorum.*"

Cortesius then censures Boccaccio's Latin and Coluccio's, which never laid aside *asperitas* and *maestitia.* Bruni was the "first to bring a certain rhythmic tone to that rough way of writing; and he certainly gave us something rather brilliant . . . weighty and judicious in everything, for those times he was not uncultivated." His *History* was better than his funeral orations because "there remained no funeral orations from the ancient authors for him to imitate." One may praise him as learned and eloquent, and the best in his time, "but you know the way of our men to approve of nothing unless it is refined, and elegant and polished and embellished." Incidentally, the Dialogue states that "Latin letters had suffered from the destruction of Greece (i.e. the "fall of Constantinople"), since much was brought by the Greeks

[12] Printed in a volume entitled *Philippi Villani liber de civitatis Florentiae famosis civibus etc.,* ed. by G. C. Galletti (Florence 1847).

to Italy, and our scholars were wont to go to Byzantium for study, as to the home of learning."

II

Among the literary productions of the late fifteenth and early sixteenth centuries, certainly one, perhaps two, and possibly three poems have proved a perennial source of entertainment. They made use of that facile and efficient Italian octave which the latest of the three authors perfected to the admiration of the world, in spite of a fool named Bembo, who advised him, Ariosto, to write the *Orlando Furioso* in Latin! This most delightful of Italian narrative poems was finally finished and revised the year before the author's death in 1533. It had been written in an Italy devastated by the lustful struggles of Spaniards, French and Germans. Boiardo, the noble count of Scandiano, had completed the *Orlando Innamorato* in 1494, ending his glad chivalric poem with a cry of sorrow: —

> Mentre che io canto, o Iddio redentore,
> Vedo la Italia tutta a ferro e a foco.

And Pulci had finished putting together the matter of *Il Morgante* in 1483, eleven years before the fatal French invasion.

Pulci was a Florentine, belonging to the Medici circle; and as the composition of his poem was suggested by Lucrezia, the mother of Lorenzo, so its successive parts appear to have been recited at Lorenzo's table, presumably before such intimates as Politian and Ficino. If these made an exceedingly clever literary circle, they were not a knightly company; nor was the Medici house either aristocratic or chivalric in its tastes and temper, any more than in its dealings with men and states. Luigi Pulci himself was a genial and comic soul, cast in no heroic mould; and one need not wonder that the martial and adventurous elements in his poem should be outweighed by the more jovial. The heroic note stirs indeed through his recital of the route of Roncevalles; but who could tell that unheroically? The half comic giant Morgante sways the poem, and the lesser but wholly comic and abandoned Margutte. Pulci used the matter of the French *Chansons de Geste,* as it had passed into Italian compositions in prose and verse. He also drew from the popular recitations of the same matter, which delighted the Italian folk of town and country; for the legends of Charlemagne and his paladins had long since won a new home and a new life with the Italian people. Pulci did not turn the heroic to burlesque with satirical intent; but the people's loud laughter pervaded the stuff he drew from, and he was no knightly prude, that he should suppress it. The poem is serious or comic to suit the episode; certain passages show a philosophic knowledge which has led the critics to find in them the hand of the author's friend, the famous Toscanelli. For its frequent classical allusions, one need not think of any special contribution from Politian. Pulci was scholar enough to supply them, and make Orlando apostrophize his friends already dead upon the field,— O terque, quaterque beati!

The chivalric epic was not to come to its true florescence in Medicean Florence, but around the more castellated and feudal court of the Este at Ferrara. Matteo Boiardo was the honored liegeman of that ducal house, from whom he held the governorships of Modena and of Reggio. The same house was to be the patron, niggardly and exacting as he thought, of Ariosto. Both had proved themselves men of achievement in Latin letters as well as in Italian poetry before setting out upon their great poems. These were to be the chief romantic creations of the time. The knowledge and attainment of the period entered into their composition, palpably appearing in their matter, but more vitally in the disciplined faculties of their authors.

As for antique allusions, personages, episodes, enough of them were taken into these poems, and romanticized by Boiardo, and by Ariosto made utterly his own. Then there was the mediaeval material, and the somewhat dishevelled and fantasticized mediaeval atmosphere. Charlemagne and his paladins, domesticated everywhere in Italy, pressed upon the poets. Those personages were too romantically real and insistent to be passed by, and too popular. They were fictile, plastic, ubiquitous in their gallopings and voyages, unheld by any land, unhindered by sea or mountain; as early as the twelfth century those paladins and their emperor had travelled through the East, encountering strange adventures in Constantinople! Then their stories, their progressively romanticizing chansons, went on along the usual way of mediaeval legend, passing from crusading and feudal war to giants and enchantments and wandering damsels, jousts, sword-encounters, and adventures everywhere occurring for their own delightful sakes. Boiardo and Ariosto were also steeped in the tales of Arthur's Knights, whose curvetting careers never had any real purpose or set aim, beyond the joy of adventure and romantic love. Boiardo first, and following him, Ariosto, wherever the Carolingian cycle had not become sufficiently romantic, could readily introduce Arthurian adventure, Arthurian love and exquisite Arthurian courtesy:

> Amore è quel che dona la vittoria
> E dona ardire al cavaliero armato.

This chivalric love which enveloped Arthur's court, furnished a leading motive in the composition of both the *Innamorato* and the *Furioso*. Boiardo was a leal-hearted gentleman, with whom love and courtesy were moving sentiments. The quiet humor, which was also his, occasionally broadened to laughter in his poem. That had a sufficiently insistent plot. Its whole matter, antique, mediaeval, or invented and well imagined by the poet, was made into an artful epic, congruous in tone and color. Borrowed strains were put together with a new art, and made to live again with a new life.

What that new art was, and whence that new life came,

is clearer in the *Orlando Furioso*. This was the last issue of the late antique and mediaeval love-and-adventure motive. It was also a harmony of all its elements, and a perfected work of art. If indeed its plot seems to take up with each new fancy, and wander over the fields of the imagination, it nevertheless passes very happily from field to forest, and over seas and mountains, and even through the entertaining and instructive regions of the moon. Every incident, every inwoven tale, is aptly placed and happily composed. The whole forms an ample canvas of delight; no mosaic either, but a well tempered picture, with values and perspectives, and flooded with the atmosphere of high romance. And what compass and inclusion! Its structure was of mediaeval legend; it carried easily old matter from classic Greece and Rome, from the early Christian ages too; chivalry was there, long since emerged from the dour actuality of feudalism, and moving in a spacious and joyful unreality, such as never was nor could ever be, yet satisfying to the whims of mortal fantasy. This still will hanker for a magic lance to overthrow foes so easily, for a horn to scare armies from their trenches, a ring to make invisible, a hippogriph to carry one to the moon; and for the chances too of draughts from fountains of quick love and rude aversion. Such fantasy would have youth and beauty everywhere, with love and wrath and courtesy, and delicious fighting, best joy of all.

Over all his scenes the poet smiles with an artist's sympathy, and with an irony free from bitterness. There is neither malice nor denunciation in his satire, but sheer fun, as when Michael searches the cloisters through for Silence, quite in vain, and readily finds Discord; or when Astolfo flies to the moon and journeys through it seeking the lost wits of Orlando, finding there most of his own as well! Forever famous stories!

Ariosto wrote his poem in a shattered Italy. How he must have taken refuge in it! It had the truth and validity of art, achieved through constantly revising labors. It was the creation of an untiring genius, which had grasped the virtue of all that his and the preceding Italian generation had been acquiring. That had passed into the strength and temperament and poetic faculty of Ariosto. Touching his subject-matter, how could he, the poet-child of his age, have treated it save with an artist's sympathy and with art's irony? There was in Italy no deep sentiment of chivalric honor, and little loyalty to anything, except the beauty of life and literature and art. The *Furioso* was no fierce epic of crusading faith, or of any faith at all. Its spirit was as the spirit of the time and land, playing with a past of chivalry which had never been Italian, transforming it into a poem. Irony was the means and method of this poet's art. Through it alone could the poem be true to the convictions and lack of convictions of the poet and his time. For the poem was the poet's truth; his aim, to make it fit, delightful, beautiful. Only through gentle plastic irony could he fashion the matter of his subject to the kind of epic which Ariosto in the first quarter of the sixteenth century, under the patronage of the court of Ferrara, could create.

Ariosto died in 1533. Tasso, born eleven years after, closed his unhappy eyes in 1595. But his work had been done years before. He had written his smoothest lyrics; the lovely pastoral drama, the *Aminta,* was given in July, 1573, on a luxurious island in the Po near Ferrara; and the *Gerusalemme liberata* was completed two years later. Ariosto's *Furioso* offered the still surviving truth of artistic excellence. Tasso, with a different temperament, was separated from Ariosto by an altered time. The moment was less favorable for the composition of a romantic epic. Italy, sombre beneath the Spanish pall, trembled before the Inquisition and the terror of the Turk, while dully stiffening her sinews with the revived and sharply defined Catholicism of the Council of Trent. Humane literature was critical, meticulous, empty. But a genius was there and would produce a poem, despite the stifling environment and the ligaments of criticism, which the poet's mind accepted too.

For Tasso was a self-conscious critic, and morbidly deferential to the criticism of others, as well as fearful of offending the Inquisition. But, at least in his young years, he was an unquenchable and incomparable poet. He was gifted with melody of language, and an imagination overflowing with delightful images. Reading had strengthened his mind with the discipline of classic literature, and had enriched it with the wealth of fable. Defining his purpose in his own critical prose, he said that he had set himself the task of composing an epic having its unity in the dominance of a single theme or "action," but diversified by chivalric and romantic episode, and with every incident so organically interwoven that to omit a single one or change its place would ruin all. The poet's blood was warm; he drew breath in the sentiments of love and passion; he delighted in the bewitchments of romance, which art might make convincing. He was a potent and very conscious artist.

The instant peril of the Turk in which the poet lived, gave him his theme, the First Crusade. His chivalric and romantic power rendered the theme in epically splendid verse, and festooned it with enchanting episodes. As conceived and written, the poem told the passions and subtler sentiments of love, and made romance and enchantments live for their own delightful sake. Afterwards compunctions seized the poet, and perhaps fears touching the opinions of Inquisitors. So he bethought him of allegory, which had not been within his first intention. He saved his enchanted woods and gardens, and the molten words uttered in them, by moralizing their significance. He even imagined a concurrent allegory as the spiritual double of his romantic epic.[13] Such invested meaning was not far to seek; for he could draw it from his own deeply moral and religious nature.

So the poem passed through many perils; from the critics to whom Tasso submitted it, from his own morbid

[13] See the "discorso proemiale" to Solerti's critical edition of the *Gerusalemme liberata,* vol. I, pp. 37 sqq., and extracts from Tasso's statements given there.

fears and the qualms of rather friendly Inquisitors. But it was saved, and was to live for the world in its undestroyed charm and beauty. Too seriously religious for a chivalric romance, too flowering with romantic episode for an epic, it still shaped its variety to the unity of a pervading nobility of statement and an unfailing music of diction. A gentle element of elegy preserved its hardiest episodes from baseness. The result was something as uniquely beautiful in Italian poetry as the *Faerie Queen* in English.

CHAPTER IV

MACHIAVELLI AND GUICCIARDINI AND THEIR FORERUNNERS

THE disillusionments and civic deterioration which, to some extent, were both the cause and the result of the stricken state of Italy could not fail to impress certain scholars who had share in the renewed and larger intimacy with the classics, which we have been following. Such would naturally consider the fortunes of their cities in the light of their classic reading. Ever since the revival of Justinian's *Digest* in the twelfth century by the Bologna School, imperial and royal statecraft had looked to the principles of the Civil Law; and since the time of Aquinas the *Politics* of Aristotle had become part of the political consciousness of Europe. Why not now apply the lessons of the actual political experience of the ancients, as well as their civic wisdom more formally expressed? So it seemed at least to Niccolo Machiavelli, whose practically instructed yet generalizing genius set itself to draw from Roman history the closer teaching of the actual courses of affairs at Rome, and to deduce from them the imperative logic of facts — the *forza delle cose*. Such lessons and examples of political consequences this Florentine gathered in his *Discourses* upon the histories of Livy, and brought to sharper, but more questionable, expression in his *Prince*.

I

There had been bold, if less instructed, forerunners in the field of political observation and theorizing. The boldest had been Nogaret, a Provençal of heretical extraction; then Pierre Dubois, a Frenchman and international theorist; there had been the Englishman Occam, and the important pair of co-workers, John of Jandun and Marsiglio of Padua.

The relation of the Church to secular government was *par excellence* the political controversy of the Middle Ages. In the course of it, the claims of the Papacy were extended to a universal absolutism, while Emperors and Kings sought to maintain their co-ordinate if not superior authority. Unity was always dear to mediaeval thinking, and thought moved in allegories as readily as in facts. Mankind was conceived as a great organism; from which idea flowed endless allegory. Disputants in the controversy between Pope and Emperor argued from mankind as a mystical body whereof the head was Christ. Should this body have one head or two, the papacy alone, or papacy and Empire? Or could a single head be found above the two in Christ? Thereupon the body-analogy was carried out into the imagined details of physiological function. Curiously enough the most elaborate construction of the allegory comes at last from Nicholas of Cusa, whose life does not fall within the Middle Ages, and whose thoughts presaged much that came to expression in the years following his death.[1]

But the men who seem more like Machiavelli's predecessors cared little for the arguments of allegory; and as against the authority of the Canon Law set up the imperial law of Rome. They were actors or pleaders in two notable political conflicts which marked the passing of mediaeval politics. In the first, the national French monarchy under Philip the Fair broke the power of the universal papal monarchy under Boniface VIII: the second was that noisy battle between the Avignonese Pope, John XXII, and the would-be Emperor, Louis of Bavaria.

It was in 1302 that Philip summoned the States General in order to assure himself that the French nation stood behind him in his struggle with the indomitable and raging octogenarian Boniface. Assured of his subjects,

[1] Cf. *post*, Chapter XXX.

he won the victory through his lawyer ministers, who upheld the royal claims with the authority of the civil law. Among them was Guillaume de Nogaret, learned, astute, and daring beyond the thoughts of others. Armed with a letter of credit and some royal vague authority, Nogaret went with one or two confidential aids to Italy. His purpose was to kidnap the Pope and carry him to Lyons. He enlisted Sciarra Colonna and other desperate characters in the plot, and in September, 1303, made the famous attempt at Anagni, the Pope's natal town, where the aged despot was staying at the papal palace, and was just about to launch against Philip a final bull of excommunication and dethronement. It was never launched. Nogaret and his fellows broke in, seized and insulted and made a prisoner of Boniface. To carry him off to Lyons was absurdly beyond their power, and they were soon fleeing for life; but his authority was broken, and within a fortnight he died in senile rage. Nogaret and the King afterwards forced this pope's successor to anathematize his memory, and free from his excommunications the desecrators of the papacy.[2]

No literal dare-devil like Nogaret, another legist, Pierre Dubois, devised a rather far-off scheme, in which the rights of kings should be exalted, peace assured among Christian peoples, the papacy be put in its right place, and the Holy Land recovered from the infidels. He called his work *De Recuperatione Terre Sancte*.[3] It advocated peace among Christian princes as the first step toward the recovery of the Holy Land, the nominal object of the book. There should be a council of the princes and the pope, to adjust all differences. Whoever breaks the peace by war with brother Catholics shall be punished by the pope, but not excommunicated, since that

[2] The whole story of Nogaret is told with consummate skill by Renan in his contribution to the *Histoire littéraire de la France,* Tome XXVII; republished in *Études sur la politique religieuse de Philippe le Bel* (Paris 1899).

[3] Written probably in 1306; edited in *Collection de Textes,* etc., by Langlois (Paris 1891). See also Renan, *Pierre Dubois,* in the same volume with his Nogaret. In his youth, Dubois heard both Aquinas and his Averroist opponent Siger at Paris. He mentions Roger Bacon.

is merely to augment the number of damned souls, and is less efficacious than temporal punishments. In the case of disputes between potentates who acknowledge no superior, the Council shall appoint arbitrators to hear and determine.[4]

The work proceeds, devising reforms and remedies for political ills. For example: Since the possession and government of the patrimony of St. Peter has caused so many wars, the pope should hand it over to some secular potentate in return for a fixed charge payable to him in some place he shall select; the revenues of the Cardinals, which are far beyond their needs, should in part be applied to the recovery of the Holy Land; the temporalities of bishops and other secular clergy, as well as of the regular orders, should be turned over to lay management, in return for a suitable fixed income; the celibacy of the clergy is undesirable; schools for the instruction of girls should be established, and the present revenues of the nunneries applied to their support. Dubois did not balk at the thought of tearing down and building anew: "It is scarcely possible to discover anything in this world that will prove good and desirable in every time and place and for all people. So the laws should vary with places, times and people. Many philosophers have taught the expediency of this, and the Lord and Master of all sciences, and of the Holy Fathers and the philosophers, has not feared to proclaim it, since many things which He appointed in the Old Testament He changed in the New."[5]

The victory of Philip and the fatal migration to Avignon marked the beginning of the end of the papacy's spiritual headship of western Europe. Its prestige was

[4] In these days of a League of Peace the passage is of interest: . . . quod concilium statuat arbitros religiosos aut alios eligendos, viros prudentes et expertos ac fideles, qui jurati tres judices prelatos et tres alios pro utraque parte, locupletes, et tales quod sit verisimile ipsos non posse corrumpi amore, odio, timore, concupiscentia, vel alias, qui convenientes in loco ad hoc aptiori, jurati strictissime, datis antequam conveniant articulis petitionum et defensionum singularum, summarie et de plano, rejectis primo superfluis et ineptis, testes et instrumenta recipiant, diligentissime examinent. *De Recup.* § 12. If one of the parties rejects the award the matter may be sent to the Pope.

[5] *De Recup.* § 48, p. 39 of Langlois' edition; also cited by Renan.

impaired forever; legitimate reasons for its universal authority could not continue in a predominantly French city, with no tradition behind it. There was danger lest the papacy become a French appanage. Its revenues decreased, and the means to which the Avignon popes resorted to recruit their finances strengthened the opposition to their claims. The Minorite Order was estranged by a bitter polemic concerning the poverty of Christ and all true Christians. Moreover, the growing force of nationality was inimical to church unity; while the revivified antique conception of the State countered the papal authority in men's minds. There seemed no longer any need for the universal papal tutelage, maintained so usefully through the Middle Ages. The Great Schism which broke out upon the return of Urban VI to Rome, and lasted from 1378 to 1417, was not merely the adventitious and deplorable result of an angry clash of tempers and interests between that intemperate pope and his worldly Cardinals, who were mostly French. It sprang from the stay at Avignon, and from all the forces and conditions which had compelled that sojourn. Indeed as one reflects upon the energies of national growth which were to break this pope-dominated Church unity, one comes to view the whole Avignon episode, with the dependence of the popes on France, their hostility to the Empire, their weakness, the Great Schism, and all that it brought forth, as necessitated under peculiarly obvious compulsion.

The conflict which those partisans of France, John XXII (1316–1334), Benedict XII (1334–1342), and Clement VI (1342–1352), waged against the German Empire, under Louis of Bavaria, was a noisy battle. Although Louis's unsteady nature brought upon him disgrace and defeat, victory proved pernicious to the papacy, by aggravating its French bias, and by stiffening its secularization to the detriment of its spiritual authority. The papal victory was a victory only over "the Empire," an idea to which no actual might of arms and loyalty responded. But there were powerful German princes, German cities, and a German people, all becoming alienated from the papacy.

In this last lost battle of "the Empire," the champions of the State set forth arguments which anticipated later thinking. Occam, a fearless scholastic destroyer and initiator, took his stand against the papacy's worldly lordship and the pope's supremacy in matters of the faith. More effective enemies of the papacy were Marsiglio of Padua and John of Jandun. Something is known of each of them. John of Jandun was clever, a learned Aristotelian, and withal a sensitive soul, as appears from his appreciation of the charms of Senlis, where he lived for a time; and then from his vivid sketch of the impression made on his provincial eye by Paris, with its motley street-life, its overwhelming cathedral — *terribilissima,* and yet such that the soul knows no satiety in gazing — and above all with its glorious university. Paris then, as now, was the city of the mind, as this scholar realized.[6] But with his eye fixed also on advancement, he did not refrain from fulsome praise of Charles le Bel, whose deafness to his by no means mute appeal turned John eventually to the service of the German monarch.

This was in 1323, and within a year John had helped his greater friend Marsiglio to achieve that veritable hammer of the papacy, the *Defensor Pacis.* Marsiglio, in quest of emolument and fame, had reached Paris more than ten years before, and had been honored with the post of rector of the University. From a poem by his friend, the Paduan Mussato, he seems to have been trained in medicine and physics, and exceedingly bent on self-advancement. He also made the trip to Avignon, and both he and John obtained favors from John XXII, before they composed their book. There is no means of determining the share of each in the work, though one may surmise that John supplied the Aristotelian learning, and Marsiglio the constructive plan and the envenomed

[6] What is known of John of Jandun (and of his *De Laudibus Parisius*) as well as of Marsiglio, is skillfully put together in Tome XXXIII (1906) of the *Histoire littéraire de la France,* pp. 528–623.

thought that the papacy was in its very nature the chief disturber of that peace of the world which it was the aim of the *Defensor Pacis* to establish. As the decades wore on after their deaths, fame ascribed the leading rôle to Marsiglio.[7]

Divided into three parts, the work sets forth in logical continuity the authors' conception of the State, then their ideas of the Church and its relations to the State, and finally the conclusions from their argument. Peace is society's sovereign boon: the chief disturber is the papacy. The Church should be made into a properly subordinated department or function of the State. This is the burden of the argument of this lengthy book.[8]

[7] As to the critical insight of our authors, the worst that can be said is that neither perceived that the "Donation of Constantine," which they discussed and sought to minimize, was a forgery.

[8] The usual, though unsatisfactory, edition is in Goldast's *De Monarchia,* II, folio 154–312. Some of the points of the argument are as follows; According to Scripture as well as Aristotle, the maker or primary effective cause of law is the people or its duly chosen better part (pars valentior). Def. Pacis I, 12. The people may express its will directly or through representatives; it appoints the executive, that is, the Ruler, and may depose him. The ruler is a part of the greater whole,—*pars principans;* he is bound by the laws, and his government will be best as it best conforms to the will and consent *subditorum suorum.* Marsiglio thought that the whole multitude, because comprising the more intelligent part, was as capable of wise legislation as the intelligent part acting alone. It is for the ruler to appoint and direct all public functionaries according to law. For the preservation of order he should have at his disposal a moderate military force, but not enough to make him a tyrant. Marsiglio advocates an elective monarchy, and his arguments lead on to the final conclusion of Part One, that political disturbances are due to the improper claims and actions of the papacy, striving for control, instead of permitting the Church to subordinate itself to the State of which it is a part. He sets forth the successive papal usurpations. He doubts whether Peter ever was in Rome, and argues that in any case he had no greater authority than the other apostles. The constitution of the papal hierarchy is examined and its secular authority disproved. This is the second part of the *Defensor.* The last part states conclusions: The People are the ultimate human sovereign. They legislate through their chosen representatives; unanimity being an impractical demand, a majority vote is valid; the ruler is the people's executive, answerable to the laws; the priesthood has only spiritual authority; it is subject to human laws; priests and bishops should be chosen by the people; the Church should own nothing, and have the use only of necessities; the primacy of the Popes can properly rest only on the delegation of power by a Council; the Bible is the foundation of the Christian faith, and Councils, not popes, should decide points of doctrine; only the community or the Council can excommunicate; heretics should be punished only when they transgress human laws: no one should be forced in his belief; (Def. Pac. II, 9) men

A year or two after the composition of the *Defensor Pacis,* its authors presented themselves with their book at the Court of Louis of Bavaria. They were his counsellors during his descent into Italy. His coronation at Rome, where he received from the hands of a Colonna the crown bestowed by the Roman People, his creation of an anti-pope, and other acts of his in Italy, carried out the principles of the *Defensor Pacis.* Apparently the Emperor made John of Jandun, bishop of Ferrara, and Marsiglio, archbishop of Milan; but whether they actually enjoyed these princely offices is doubtful. Turmoil and trouble resulted from Louis's Italian expedition, till that weak personage was driven to make his peace with the pope, and vow to punish these heretics, John and Marsiglio. This was in 1336; but John had in fact died long before; and Marsiglio seems to have continued in Louis's service as late as 1342.

The *Defensor Pacis* did not die with its authors. To the popes it was a stumbling block and scandal, worthy of repeated condemnation; while to men who opposed the papacy it remained a store of living arguments. A papal bull of 1377 declared that Wyclif took his heresies from it. Through the Great Schism and the Conciliar movement, men drew on it. Nicholas of Cusa used it in his *De Concordantia Catholica* (1431); Matthew Döring drew from it in his *Confutatio Primatus Papae* (1443). Later still, Luther apparently used it and other Protestant leaders, possibly even Calvin.[9]

II

Marsiglio and these other fourteenth century publicists were students of antiquity and observers of affairs. To them the papacy was an obstacle to the peace and welfare of the world. Keenest of Italian haters of the papacy,

should not be held to the Mosaic law, but only to the precepts of the New Testament. Cf. Riezler, Die literarischen Widersächer der Päpste, p. 225 *sqq.* (Leipsic 1874).

[9] See James Sullivan in *American Hist. Review,* Vol. II, (1896–97); also *Hist. lit. de la France,* T. XXXIII, p. 622.

Machiavelli also gained his knowledge of politics from his experience of affairs and a constant study of antiquity. The writings of the ancients furnished him with ideas, and suggestions for their expression. With matter from his own genius, he still largely expresses himself through the thoughts of the old writers, and conforms his argument to the events of ancient history. In his dedication of *The Prince,* he presents to Lorenzo, grandson of the Magnificent, this most precious "cognizione delle azioni degli uomini grandi, imparata da me con una lunga sperienza delle cose moderne, ed una continova lezione delle antiche."

Born in Florence in 1469, he received the usual education of the son of a respectable family. The first real news of him is from a letter written in his thirtieth year, maintaining the rights of his family to the patronage of a certain church. Savonarola was burned in the piazza on the twenty-third of May, 1498, and soon afterwards, the Republic of Florence, being engaged in the long struggle to reconquer Pisa, employed Machiavelli as secretary to the *Ten.* He was briskly occupied in the Pisan war, as appears by his *Discorso sopra le cose di Pisa.* Next, the Republic sent him with another on a mission to placate the temper of Louis XII of France, ruffled at the lack of progress of the war, in which his mercenary Swiss had played no glorious rôle. Their conduct, apparently, convinced Machiavelli that a State's only sure defence is its own citizen soldiery — if such soldiery would only fight!

He was sent the next year to Duke Valentino, commonly called Cesare Borgia, whose doings were causing anxiety to Florence. After this, in 1502, the people of the Val di Chiana, and more especially the townsfolk of Arezzo, rebelling, this thoughtful secretary sought to apply the lessons of Roman experience, in his paper on *How to treat the rebel peoples of the Val di Chiana.* "Lucius Furius Camillus," he began, "having conquered the rebellious peoples of Latium, entered the Senate and said: I have done what is possible through war; it is now for you, Conscript Fathers, to ensure the quiet of these rebels in the future." And the Senate generously pardoned the conquered, making an exception only " of two cities, one of which they demolished, and in the other replaced the inhabitants with men faithful to Rome." With such an effective policy as this, Machiavelli contrasts the folly of half-measures, especially making the point that while the Florentines had done so much to persecute and anger the people of Arezzo, they had left the city intact, and a source of danger to Florence.

In the latter part of 1502, Machiavelli was again sent to Duke Valentino in the Romagna, to watch his movements and report, a delicate and perilous task. He came to admire this fearless and unscrupulous man, and took many lessons to himself from his acts and bold successes, and at last from his downfall through the unexpected conjunction of two facts, the death of his father, Pope Alexander VI, and his own desperate illness at the time. From these missions, and others to Pope Julius II, Machiavelli gained knowledge of political affairs; and in 1506 and 1507 he realized his darling project of a Florentine citizen militia; but what it would accomplish was still hidden! There were yet more missions before him, to the Emperor Maximilian, and to France; and he was otherwise kept busy in the affairs of the Republic.

Things were confused and violent in Italy; with leagues and breakings of them, as well as fighting, among Imperialists and French, and Pope Julius II, protagonist in the restless strife. Machiavelli proved himself an apt diplomat, appearing at his best in his letters and reports. His acuteness of intellect exceeded his powers of action, and even his skill in devising efficient measures. Like Italy herself, he was a mind, understanding much, seemingly unprejudiced and clear-seeing. His own Florence was involved in politics beyond the control of a rather impotent Republic honey-combed with Medicean influences. The Spaniards were approaching; Prato was sacked, Florence came to terms; she was in fact in the power of the Medici before their palpable restoration.

The heads of the house were Cardinal Giovanni (afterwards Pope Leo X) and his brother Giuliano, sons of the Magnificent. As for Machiavelli, if he entertained hopes of a Republic under the Medici, with himself an active official in the same, he was to be disappointed. Just what he did and said in those trying times is not as clear as what was done to him; for in November, 1512, he was stripped of all his offices, constrained in his liberty, and the next year, being in some way compromised by a conspiracy against the Medici, he was imprisoned and examined under torture. He was soon released, but write and speak and flatter as he might, he was not taken into their confidence nor given employment. It was only many years afterwards, in 1526 and 1527, when his life was closing, and the affairs of Italy were hopeless, that Machiavelli, with busy patriotism, again circulated among the men and things he could not influence. Shortly after the sack of Rome, he died broken-hearted over the misfortunes of the land and the realization that his Florence did not desire his services, although the Medici had been again expelled. It was in the intervening years of rustication and straitened inactivity at his villa in the Florentine contado, that this man who never was of great importance in affairs, produced the works which assured him a permanent position among the world's publicists.

From the days of Rome, the quick Italian mind had never been unoccupied with politics. Italian cities were the homes of political discussion, as well as conflict. What politicians were the Medici and many of the Popes! And that great reforming Friar, Savonarola, who looked through shows and shams to sheer reality, which might be clothed for him in the mystic light of holiness, had a shrewd mind for practical measures of government. The constitution adopted by Florence in 1494–5, so largely following the recommendations of Savonarola, was excellent, and his tax reforms became the enduring basis of a system tolerable for centuries. He looked to the Venetian Constitution as a model. Its stability and

another arising." It is impossible to adjust matters satisfactorily once for all. " Human affairs being in motion, and unable to rest as they are, they must either rise or fall; and necessity leads you to measures to which reason would not have led you."

Machiavelli's purpose in the *Discorsi* was to elicit the working verities of Roman history applicable in the construction of rules of political action for the princes and statesmen of his day. He sought its political rather than moral teaching; and there may have been an intellectual blunder in his not realizing that the " political " and the " moral " are but different sides of the complex of social well-being. Possibly there were inconsistencies in his view of the State and human welfare, attributable to the weakness of his will and purpose,— an individual weakness analogous to the impotence of an Italy equipped with intelligence and knowledge, possessed of physical strength and material resources, and yet crushed by brutal forces from without, which in some way drove on with a will to grasp and get. Machiavelli, without the strength of purpose which unifies a man's thinking, was impelled to seek the rule of action seemingly applying to the case in hand, and valid for all other similar cases. His furthest intellectual end and practical object all in one, was validity, pragmatic truth, *verità effettuale,* the rule that may be acted on successfully. Such a rule must, of course, recognize facts, and the forces of events, the physical logic of a situation. It must be built out of such logic, be a true reflex or recognition of force in action, that is of all the forces making and controlling the situation. Possibly Machiavelli's intellectual pragmatism, which of course took no thought of absolute truth or underlying being, was to find its counterpart in those sixteenth century philosophies and systems of physics, which were substituting force for matter as their fundamental conception.[11] In this way, also, his consideration of politics and the rise and fall of states, had in it something that is represented in all modern thought.

[11] Post, chapter XXXIV.

Through the *Discorsi,* through *The Prince* as well, Machiavelli's personal or temperamental convictions affect the logic with which he construes a situation and its necessary consequences. His underlying conviction, readily to be gathered from antiquity, is that the state — *patria,* his Italian heart loves to call it — is of first importance and utterly supreme above all its citizens: its ends, its mere advantage, overrides individual interest and private morality. Religion, a Church, is well; may even be necessary; but it should be in all respects subordinate to the *patria,* and promote its well-being. He is also convinced, or at least feels, that a republic where men are in some way free and equal, is better than a kingdom or tyranny. Italy is the *patria* of his mind; would it were united in patriotism! The cause of its disunion, of its weakness, of much of its corruption is, and through the centuries has been, the papacy.

The essence of Italy's impotence and corruption is the selfishness of individuals, their lack of corporate patriotism, whereby a citizen forgets private gain and private hate, and is quick to risk life and fortune for the common weal. There could be no mutual dependence in an Italy where there was no common bravery, which is strength. He had proved again and again that the strength of a land does not lie in its fortresses, nor in its material resources and money, with which to hire mercenaries; it lies in the patriotic valor of its people.[12] Such patriotic valor is good, since it is the means by which the *patria* attains its ends, or maintains them. So with great individuals, kindness and humanity are good qualities, which

[12] See *Discorsi* II., 24. In Chap. 36 of B'k III of the *Discorsi* Machiavelli speaks of three kinds of armies, the first and best possessing valor (furore) and discipline (ordine), by which valor is made firm; the second has valor, like the French, and must win at the first rush; the third kind has neither valor nor discipline, like the Italian, and wins only by accident. In his *Arte della Guerra* the pith of his argument is that the strength of a state lies in the armed people, fighting chiefly on foot, and to that end military discipline should be ordained. "It has proved a fatal error in Italy to have separated the military from the civil life, making of the former a trade, such as is followed by the mercenary companies. Thus the soldier becomes violent, threatening, corrupt, and an enemy to all civil life." From the dedicatory letter to Lorenzo Strozzi.

enable the possessor to attain his ends, just as in the proper place severity and cruelty may also gain them. And in so far as justice and the like good qualities attain the ends of the *patria*, they are desirable. It is always a matter of attaining ends. Humanity revolts at the thought that the means, in themselves, are indifferent; yet they stand or fall by their efficacy; by that they must be judged; therein lies their justification; there is no other.

Machiavelli was of his own Italian time, part of its weakness and corruption, of its mind — one of the very best of its minds. But well he knew, both for himself and Italy, how impotent is the intellect without strength of purpose. Lacking that, men are the prey of chance, of fortune: "For when men are weak, Fortune shows herself strong; and because she changes, states and governments change with her; and will continue to change, until someone arise, who, following reverently the example of the ancients, shall so control her, that she shall not have opportunity with every revolution of the sun to display anew the greatness of her power." [13]

A man weak in character may write books of different flavor, as he bends to the matter of his composition and the end in view. In the *Discorsi* Machiavelli would show the rules of action by which a Republic might attain power and maintain it. He will apply his same reasoning to a despot, who, privately viewed, may be an evil man. He too, good or evil, would maintain his rule and aggrandize his power; he too must employ means suited to that end — and again it is the end that justifies.

Moreover, if the end be good, that is, if it embrace the welfare of many people, it will seem to ennoble the means, as the aggrandizement of a tyrannous individual cannot ennoble them. Many of the notorious doctrines of *The Prince* appear in the *Discorsi*, wherein the welfare of the *patria* is made to justify the murderous act: "Where the welfare of the *patria* is at stake, you should

[13] *Discorsi*, Bk. II, ch. 30, Thompson's translation.

not consider whether a measure be just or unjust, merciful or cruel, praiseworthy or ignominious; rather, all else laid aside, you should do what will ensure the safety of the *patria* and maintain its liberty."[14] This may be an indecorous amplification of the old motto — *salus populi suprema lex.* But when the end in view is the strengthening of a tyrant in his tyranny, the evil end will seem to us to aggravate the villainy of the means. So it did not seem to Machiavelli, who looked solely to the efficacy of the means with respect to the end desired by the doer. He admired success and the abilities which win it, and not the least among the latter was the faculty of using relentlessly and logically whatever means were best suited to the end. It is the old worship of ἀρετή, virtus, virtù, which is faculty, or better, superfaculty. Machiavelli admires and somewhat idealizes *Cesare Borgia* as the virtuoso, who unhesitatingly uses any apt means. He would never have been guilty of the fault of Giovanpagolo Baglioni, whose scruples kept him from seizing Julius II in Perugia in 1505 when he had the chance.[15]

There is a chapter on Conspiracies in the *Discorsi,*[16] which is an expansion of passages in *The Prince.* It is a masterly examination of the odds and chances and the psychological phenomena of conspiracies. The employment of men who have already had experience in assassinations, is recommended because even brave men who are used to arms and death under different circumstances, may prove uncertain instruments of assassination Public sentiment has commonly applauded the tyrannicide. But Machiavelli's professional consideration of the best methods for conspirators would not have been affected by the circumstance that their object was the overthrow of a free government.

In reading *The Prince,* one should beware of thinking of the prince as a mere individual. He is also the symbol of the State he rules; and therefore, as touching the

[14] *Discorsi,* III, 41. Passage quoted in Villari's *Machiavelli.*
[15] *Dis.* I, 27.
[16] *Dis.* III, 6.

justice or atrocity of his measures, one should remember that the principle of *salus populi* applies to him, the sovereign. And at the end of the book, the fading light of Italian patriotism casts its gleam backward over the work of the sinister personality of its protagonist, till one beholds, in hope at least, this ideal Prince as the instrument of Italian strength and unity. The author closes with his grand appeal to the Medici to assume the rôle which some centuries later was fulfilled by the House of Savoy.

Machiavelli's famous work suffers from too much logic and the unqualified application of general principles to human affairs. One may doubt whether it carries as large a consideration of human nature, with its gusts of feeling and its waves of unpredictable conduct, as the *Discorsi*. The latter was the slower fruit of years of thought, and had the unliterary advantage of being more desultory. It is especially clear in *The Prince* that one weakness of Machiavelli's reasoning lies in itself — that it is sheer reasoning, and will not fit the unexpected turns of human life. A writer who sets forth, not what men should do, but how they will necessarily act, may fool himself as readily as one who takes into account the irrational and generous conduct of men struggling for ideals or uplifted by a situation. The author of *The Prince* never could have foreseen or imagined that which has been the greatest fact in the experience of our own generation, the mighty awakening of America's enthusiasm and resolve for a war of righteousness and the ideals of man.

It is indeed a general characteristic of Machiavelli that his statements are but half-truths: every statement a half-truth, and usually the dirty side. Possibly no man ever speaks a whole one, since the human mind cannot formulate more than one phase of life at a time. Machiavelli at least might have corrected some of his half-truths from Plato! It is clear that one devilish fallacy pervades his reasoning. He never realizes the evil effect of the evil act upon the doer, be the doer an individual or a government or a partly responsible people. Again to refer to our own time, as modern Germany has shown herself the most Titanic example of Machiavellianism that the world has seen, so has she calamitously exemplified the specific Machiavellian fallacy which ignores the degeneration entering the nature of the evil-doer.

III

Like Machiavelli, another Florentine, fourteen years his junior, harboured the thought of Italy, and hated the French, the Spaniards, the Germans and the Swiss; but unlike Machiavelli, Francesco Guicciardini brooded and hated without hope. He was no theorist, but the hard-headed man of an Italy politically disillusioned and obviously lacking in those qualities which once had driven the small city by the Tiber on to greatness. Machiavelli had unmasked that Italy in his *Florentine History,* giving the story of those wars in which no warriors fell! Wars that might be entered on without fear, waged without danger, ended without loss — if one had the wit! Such was the war between Florence and Venice, which he narrates in his fifth and sixth books: Duke Filippo Maria Visconti of Milan with Francesco Sforza on the one side, and skillful Piccinino on the other; safe marauding, bloodless battles, till the war ends when the Duke has married his much promised daughter to Sforza, after lies and double dealing, tedious, but curious to relate.

This was before the middle of the fifteenth century; and Machiavelli ends his History with the death of Lorenzo de' Medici in 1492. Guicciardini takes up the tale in his *Storia d'Italia,* beginning with the descent of the French, that dire event of 1494, a year apparently marked by prodigies which the historian does not care to discredit. Charles VIII wavered to the last, ready to abandon the enterprise, when he was caught again by the argument of Cardinal della Rovere (destined to be Pope Julius II) that "fatale instrumento e allora e prime e poi de' mali d'Italia." Besides the excellent artillery of the French, Guicciardini gives further reasons for their military superiority over Italians; the men at arms were subjects of the King, and gentlemen, and paid by his ministers, having the best of horses and arms, and, above all, the sense of honor, with the fair chance of promotion. So their captains, all of noble blood, even barons and lords, and subject to the King, eager to merit his praises, and without other chance of betterment. This was quite different from the Italian armies, in which were peasants and plebs, and subjects of other princes, dependent for pay on their captains, who were rarely the subjects of the cities or princes whom they served, but had interests of their own, with envy and hatred of each other; avaricious, unstable, these captains were the mere *padroni* of their companies.

The *Storia d'Italia* passes on through rapine, villainy, and perfidy, the sack of cities and the ruin of liberty. Years are consumed, till the mingled tide of impotence and wickedness, for want of some brave and able man to stop it, nears the Eternal City, with no barrier except the knavery and poltroonery of Pope Clement VII! Who cared? Who should stop it? So the vile army of Spaniards and German Lutherans presses on for plunder,— fate helping, no one impeding — to the sack of Rome. That was in 1527, and in two or three years there is accord between the royal scoundrels, and Italy is pacified, enslaved as she deserved (Ah! if we all should get our deserts); and abandoned Florence is fighting helplessly for her liberties, till she too is taken in the besieger's net.

Assuredly Guicciardini was the successful Italian diplomat and statesman of his time — successful, that is to say, in his own advancement. He loved Italy and hated the priests, but above all else he loved himself, and was ready to bend his sentiments to serve his purposes. Advantageously born and advantageously married in Florence, he was sent as Ambassador to the king of Spain, at the age of twenty-eight. This was in 1511. After his return, he progressed in favor with the Medici and the popes. In his city he occupied one important position after another. Then, in the service of Leo X, Adrian VI, and Clement VII, he was governor of various cities, commissary-general, president of the Romagna, and held the rank of lieutenant-general in that papal army which did not prevent the sack of Rome. Nor did he afterwards lack papal employment.

During all the years while he served his papal masters — shall we say "faithfully"? — his own opinions, and such feelings as he had, were as he expressed them in his *Ricordi:*

> "I know none more disgusted than myself by the ambition, the avarice, and the effeminacy of the priests; each of these vices is odious, and ill-fitting those who profess the life which depends on God. . . . Yet my relations with the popes have compelled me to love their grandeur *per il particulare mio* — for the sake of my own interest; and if it were not for this, I should have loved Martin Luther as myself, not for freeing me from the laws of the Christian religion as it is universally interpreted and understood, but to see this troop of scoundrels put in their right place, where they should remain either without vices or without authority." Again: "Three things I wish to see before my death, but doubt, even though I live long, of seeing any one of them: — a well ordered republic in our city; Italy freed from all the barbarians; and the world freed from the tyranny of these vile priests." [17]

Guicciardini passes for a man without illusions — unless to be such be the great delusion! Yet, as with most men, several souls dwelt in his breast; and no single expression reflects his whole nature. He could at least appreciate moral qualities, speaking of his own father as a man of "large judgment, and good conscience, a lover of the welfare of the city and of the poor; nor did he ever do the least wrong to anyone." He even speaks of his own endeavor to keep a good name, and repeats that he had ever loved "la patria." He can consider life "as a Christian, as a philosopher, as a man of the world.[18]

[17] *Ricordi politici,* XXVIII and CCXXXVI.
[18] *Ricordi Autobiografici, Opere inedite,* X, pp. 90, 103, 132.

Nevertheless, he appears predominantly as a man of insight and clever faculty, pursuing the interests of his employers, and certainly his own. His thoughts usually discredit or ignore the more general human motives, and place little reliance upon such general principles as Machiavelli constructed from his study of Roman history. To him, Machiavelli was a theorist, with his head wrapt in dreams of what could not come to pass. Guicciardini viewed facts as they were. The contrast between the two appears in his *Considerazione* of Machiavelli's *Discorsi* upon Livy; in which the younger man quickly sees such holes as there might be in the arguments of his friend, pointing out, for instance, the fallacy of regarding the disunion between Patricians and Plebs as the cause of Roman liberty. Sometimes he approves points in the *Discorsi,* but again he finds expositions in them suitable to books and to the imagination, rather than agreeing with the way things actually take place. This critic rightly felt that he had the larger knowledge of affairs. Of course, with Machiavelli, he regarded fraud and violence as praiseworthy or foolish according to circumstances. He was not himself an unqualified admirer of antiquity, thinking it had been over-praised, and that his own time in some respects was preferable. He thought less highly of the Roman civil constitution than of their military system. Machiavelli had laid the ills of Italy, and its disunion, upon the papacy, which had been always so ready to call in the barbarians. Guicciardini points out that the barbarians had begun their invasions in the times of the Roman Empire. It was true that the papacy had hindered Italy from becoming a single State; but it were hard to say whether that was an ill thing or a good. A single republic might have made the name of Italy glorious, but it would have ruined the other Italian states. This view was correct with regard to such Italian republics as these men had known, since their way was to exploit the towns and territories conquered by them, without extending the privileges of their citizenship to the conquered.

The tenor of Guicciardini's opinions may be gathered from his *Storia d'Italia.* But his thoughts are put in nugget-form in his commonplace book, which goes by the name of *Ricordi politici e civili.* There his penetrating consideration of humanity appears, and his distrust of theory. "It is a great mistake to speak of mundane affairs without distinguishing and qualifying, and as it were, by rule; for they all involve distinctions and exceptions due to circumstances, and the same measure will not fit; these variations are not in the books, and discretion must instruct us" (vi). Precedents (esempli) are fallacious guides; since they do not serve us unless they agree in every particular, and the least variation in the case may lead to great variation in effect, and those little differences are so hard to see (cxvii). Still, the same proverbs are found with every people,— for they are born of like experiences (xii). And while it is said that one cannot judge well without knowing all the particulars, nevertheless I have often noticed with people of mediocre judgment, that they do better with only a general knowledge, than when all the particulars are laid before them, through which they are confused, while upon the general idea a good resolution may be based (clv).

"These *Ricordi* are rules such as one may write in a book; but the particular cases, which for various reasons call for other decisions, are difficult to write down save in the *libro della discrezione*" (cclvii). Guicciardini's Italian has been occasionally condensed in the following examples of his sentiments:

If you must insult another, be careful to say what will offend him alone, and not many other people (viii). Do everything to appear good, which helps infinitely; but, as false opinions do not endure, you will hardly succeed in seeming good in the long run, unless you are in truth (xliv). States cannot be ruled according to conscience, for their origins were in violence. The Empire is no exception, and as for the priests, their violence is enforced by spiritual as well as temporal weapons (xlviii). Neutrality in a war between others is a safe policy for that state which is so powerful as to be unconcerned which of the belligerents is victorious. The weak neutral will be the victor's prey. But the worst policy for a neutral is to be drawn through vacillation to a course which his judgment disapproves, and he pleases neither belligerent. This happens more frequently with republics than with despots, because the people are divided, and counsel this and that (lxviii). "I observed while I was Ambassador in Spain, that the Catholic King, Ferdinand of Aragon, when he wished to undertake some new enterprise, or make an important decision, managed so that the Court and people were clamoring for it, before he made known his mind" (lxxvii). Do not start a revolution in the hope of being followed by the people; for the people may show no mind to follow you, and may have ideas quite different from what you think (cxxi). "Who speaks of a *people,* speaks of a fool animal, filled with a thousand errors, a thousand disorders (confusioni), without taste, without joy, without stability" (cxl). No wonder there is ignorance of the things past or remote, when so little is known of the present, or even of what is going on in the same city, where often between the palace and the piazza there is a cloud so dense and a wall so high, that the eye cannot penetrate it — so much the people know of what their rulers do, or of their reasons (cxli).

The same mood, or strain of opinion, is not always represented in these *Ricordi;* slowly and carefully the author says: "He errs who thinks that the success of enterprises turns on their being just or unjust; for one sees the contrary every day; that not the just cause, but prudence, force, and good fortune bring the victory. It is true that in him who has justice with him is born a certain confidence based on the opinion that God gives victory to just undertakings, which makes men keen and obstinate; and sometimes victory springs from such conditions. A just cause may thus help indirectly; it does not help directly" (cxlvii).

But again: " I do not blame fasting, prayer and such like works, which are ordained by the Church or advised by the Friars; but the best of all, in comparison with which the rest are slight affairs, is not to injure another, and to help everyone as you may be able " (clix). Following close upon the last, this excellent sentiment takes one's breath away. In the very next note, the mood is not quite the same. Everyone knows he has to die, and yet lives as if he was to live forever. " I believe this comes because nature wills that we should live as the body requires and the true disposition of this mundane machine; for not wishing us to stay dead and senseless, nature has given us the property of not thinking on death, which if we thought about, the world would be full of sloth and torpor " (clx).

And finally: " It has been truly said that too much religion spoils the world, because it enfeebles the minds, envelops men in a thousand errors, and turns them from many noble and manly undertakings,— nor do I wish through this to disparage the Christian faith."

CHAPTER V

ITALIAN SELF-EXPRESSION IN PAINTING

VOLUBLE as were the Italian people, loving talk and song, and possessing a melodious language, they were a seeing, rather than a reading or listening, folk. Their minds ran to visible images, painted in color. Not only did they think, they felt in images; which thronged in their emotion as well as in their thought. Leonardo was constant to the instincts of his race in his impassioned arguments that painting is a nobler and more potent art than poetry.

All Italians, from the unlettered rustic to the much lettered prince or condottièro, looked naturally to painted forms and decorations not merely for their pleasure but for their ideas. The visualizing faculty, the need of forms to fill it, was part of their Graeco-Roman heritage of mental habit. Those who were conversant with antique letters, *saw* the figures of the old gods and heroes, and the forms of antique personifications. And all the people, lettered and unlettered, *saw* the saints and angels, the Virgin, Christ, and even God Almighty, whom the mightiest of Italian geniuses painted on the ceiling of the Sistine Chapel.

Books were for priests and scholars. The people loved painted forms, appreciated them, and could criticise them too. Painting was for interior embellishment, and for the exemplification of the people's faith upon the walls of churches and over the high altars. For the outside, there was carving in stone and marble, or better, in the warmer and more salient tones of bronze. Color was a delight, whether within or without the church or palace or civic structure. No building should lack its raiment, pictorial or sculpturesque, decorative and beautiful, of course; but also illuminative, speaking. The colors, lights and shades, the expressive figures, addressed themselves both to the outer and to the inwardly speaking eye of this Italian people, whose thoughts were forms and images, and rarely disembodied or unclothed themselves in colorless ratiocination. Naturally again, this same people, high and low, delighted in the passing gorgeousness, the living, entrancing figures of civic pageants, or those through which princely despots displayed their power and magnificence.

The Italian passion for the delights of vision might becloud the intelligent appreciation of other factors of expression, which might be equally clever and pleasurable and even more to the point. The Elizabethan drama culminating in Shakespeare was immeasurably greater than the Italian drama of the sixteenth century; it was given naked, with no more setting than the needs of its action positively required. But when a play, whether by Terence or by Ariosto, was given at Urbino, Ferrara, Mantua or Milan, it was an occasion for display. Its trappings, its mechanical contrivances and fantasies, its magnificence of tapestry and painting, not to mention the interjection of scenic masking and dancing, tended to distract attention from the play. All eyes were fastened pleasurably upon the gorgeous pictures that enframed it, and bore such stately and delectable testimony to the wealth and taste of the Magnifico who had set the festival.

The plays themselves might be weakened in their composition by the Italian passion for pictures; their dialogue might become word-painting, as in the *Orfeo* or the *Stanze* of Politian. Though an Ariosto or a Machiavelli might write clever comedy, great drama could no more come into existence in sixteenth century Italy than a great era of painting could arise in Elizabethan England. The achievement in either case sprang from the genius of Italian painters or English playwrights, supported by the enthusiasm of the people.

Springing thus from the demands and appreciations of a people, painting and sculpture utterly surpassed the literature, whether prose or poetry, of the fifteenth and sixteenth centuries in Italy. However scholars and poets might esteem themselves, and grace the tables of the rich, the painters and sculptors, with now and then an architect, were the best men of the period. It was no accident, but due to the nature of the time and people, that Leonardo, Michelangelo and Raphael are the true representatives and indeed the greatest Italians of their era.

Who should rival them? In sheer scholarship the Italians were not destined to equal the energy and insight of the Flemings and the French. Poetry, in its finer modes, was clogged with classical conventions and the weight of antique phrase; it was, moreover, of rather courtly and parasitic growth; it fed or starved at the courts of the Medici or the Gonzagas or the Este. The mightier energies of Italian painting were instructed, but not hampered, by the antique; while a far stronger popular demand supported them along a broader way of growth. And if sculpture carried on the antique tradition more markedly than painting, that tradition was as a guiding form within an organism which was unfolding its own living powers.

Nor until Galileo came, might one look to science for rivals of these great painters, who were sculptors, architects, engineers, as well. The best physical science in the fifteenth and earlier sixteenth centuries still consorted with the arts of construction and design. Alberti and Leonardo proved and glorified this union. While Leonardo lived, no other investigator of the properties of things might touch the hem of Leonardo's cloak.

Among the rulers were men of finesse and subtlety, and one at least, Lorenzo the Magnificent, possessed astounding faculties. The rule of these picturesque despots did not lack gracious elements. The Medici, the Sforzas, the Gonzagas, the house of Este, did much to adorn and render prosperous their states. They were enlightened patrons of the arts, taking pleasure in them and recognizing that it was the political function of the plastic arts to spread the fame and establish the ruler's power in the very eyes of men. Nor were these rulers beyond measure evil. Doubtless they exemplified in their various personalities, and in their methods of aggrandizement and political self-preservation, the principles set out by Machiavelli and the clever Venetian diplomats. Commonly they used even truth but to deceive. Yet it was only in their rather personally directed employment of poison, strangulation, and the dagger, that they seem more vicious than apparently greater men of other times who have directed the destinies of larger states. The largest Machiavellian criminality in all history has gone on through the decades in which we ourselves have lived, and has come to its own in war and overthrow. So with Italian rulers of the fifteenth and sixteenth centuries. They scarcely reached the redeeming goal of stable success and lasting prosperity for their houses and their people. Their policies seem afflicted with some sort of impotence: — were not inspired by an efficient, and potentially self-sacrificing, national sentiment; were too internecine; too deeply affected with the cormorant individualism of the men who devised them. So these men, with all their subtlety and deceit and knowledge, will scarcely impress us as great statesmen who might overtop the greatness of Leonardo and Mantegna, Michelangelo and Raphael.

In considering the origins of Italian painting, it is best not to draw distinctions between substance and form. One may assume that the sculptor, mosaicist, or fresco painter, who worked at his art in the fourth century or the fourteenth possessed the current knowledge of the Christian story: that he was acquainted with the more popular Old Testament incidents, with the life of Christ and the Virgin, and the lives of the Saints, beginning with the Virgin's parents, Joachim and Anna. Yet that which filled and shaped his work would always be the representation of these salient incidents in the mosaics, frescoes, or carvings of earlier artists. Their presentation of the same matter which it was his task to present gave him at once the form and method and the theme. In these compositions in stone and color, the theme or content of the work had no separate existence from the form or method of its presentation. One and the other made a single whole, coming to him as a theme expressed, even as his task was to express the same, possibly with modification or improvement. The finished execution or expression of the theme had been given him; and not on the one hand, forms or method or technique, and on the other the substance of the theme which he must render. The theme was composed, rendered, expressed, even in such form of expression as he should use with such development or improvement as his mind might aspire to, and his faculties achieve.

The expression of these Christian themes in modes of painting and sculpture begins in the Catacombs of Rome, where scenes from the Old Testament and the New are crudely rendered: Adam and Eve, Noah in the Ark, Moses smiting the Rock, Daniel among the Lions, and the story of Jonas. From the New Testament are taken the Adoration of the Magi, the Miracle of the Loaves, the Raising of Lazarus. Most frequent of all is the figure of Christ as the Good Shepherd, carrying a sheep, a figure directly copied from a type of Hermes. There were also mythological figures and decoration taken from the current pagan painting, and Christian symbols, like the fish, the dove or the lamb. These frescoes range from the first to the middle of the fourth century, when the Catacombs ceased to be used for burial. The style is that of the poorer contemporary pagan work. Practically the same subjects are rendered in the figures carved in high relief upon the Christian sarcophagi of the fourth and fifth centuries.

The themes will be found to enlarge in the decoration of the great Christian basilicas erected after the official conversion of the Empire. Upon their walls the lessons of the Christian faith were to be set forth, as it were, prophetically in the prefigurative types and incidents of the Old Testament; then, in the miraculous and saving scenes of the life of Christ; and triumphantly in the final victory of the Cross and the visions of the Apocalypse. Mosaic was the chief means through which the Christian artists sought to decorate and glorify the walls of the new-built churches with these impressive Christian themes, — which Christian preaching had made familiar to the people. The selection was not left to the artist, but prescribed by custom or authority. These fourth and fifth century mosaicists followed the traditional conceptions of the scenes and personages which they now sought to depict in stately compositions. The subjects were not limited to the canon of the Old and New Testaments; but were drawn as well from the Old Testament apocrypha and from the apocryphal Gospels. The series grew from century to century until they included the whole story of the Virgin's life and parentage, and many a theme from the great company of angels, saints, and martyrs. Yet tradition and authority guided the compositions. The nave of the church was assigned to scenes from the Old Testament and the earthly life of Christ; while the apse and triumphal arch presented the glory of the apocalypse or a Christ enthroned in majesty.

These compositions were an enormous advance over their childlike beginnings in the Catacombs. Instead of the rudest, they represented the best craftsmanship of the time. The dignity of Rome had entered them; the ceremony of Byzantium is approaching. The leading figures have reached a typical individuality. The subjects are no longer given through crude outline suggestions, but are adequately treated, with a larger historical rendering, and a stricter dogmatism. Yet the effort of the artist seems exhausted in presenting his subject with dignity and correctness. Emotional qualities are lacking.

These stately compositions were to be as type-patterns through the following centuries. They were carried on in countless repetitions, while undergoing modification, deterioration, or development; they might even change with the changing spirit and capacity of later times. Just as the matter of a tale may be retold in sagas, and resung in epic and ballad forms; and yet continue fundamentally the same story, though modified and perhaps made perfect, and imbued with a feeling which its first rude telling scarcely held.

At all events, however the style might change, whatever modification there might be of incidents or figures, whatever increment of feeling might enter, the sacred themes were carried on and delivered from generation to generation of artists in modes of pictorial or sculpturesque expression. In this expression, form and composition and technique blended with theme or substance. Meaning and significance, as well as esthetic value, were held in this blended result, this finished whole.

Style, pattern, composition, and the theme thus embodied and expressed, passed through deterioration or development, and varied change of manner, in the centuries between the fifth and the thirteenth. There was the fundamental Graeco-Roman style, invigorated and re-inspired by Christian energy and the need to express these novel sacred themes. Then followed general deterioration or barbarizing. This was countered by the influence of the developing Byzantine style, making for dignity and balance, but stiffening into a ceremonial manner. The Byzantine style dominates the stately mosaics of Ravenna from the fifth to the eighth century. It had likewise much effect upon the contemporary art at Rome. In the eleventh century, Byzantine artists were brought to Monte Cassino by its Abbot Desiderius; and in the twelfth, in the Norman kingdom of Sicily, the final glories of Byzantine mosaic color and composition made beautiful the churches of Palermo and Cefalù. The remarkable reign of the Emperor Frederic II in the next century effected a great revival of palace and cathedral building in Apulia and Campania, with a clear return to the antique style of sculpture, as in the still surviving portrait-busts executed at Capua to adorn the palace of this admirer of antiquity.[1]

The imitation of the antique, which made the conscious note of the revival of sculpture under Frederic, was but a clearer emphasizing of what had always formed the basis of Italian art. Italy itself was a constant alteration and effacement, with an equally constant renewal, of the Rome of Trajan. The face of the land to-day might still be Roman, had not Italy so industriously preyed upon her antique heritage, constantly rebuilding herself from the old structures. It is the land-wide extension of the story of the lime kilns of the Forum, of the travertine blocks of the Colosseum taken for St. Peter's, of the columns of palaces and temples taken for the naves of churches. Not the devastation of war, but the industrial demolition of the antique buildings, has partially transformed the land. But for this, one might still see the Forum and the Colosseum, and the Appian Way, and the whole land indeed, very much as it was in the days of Constantine.

Allowing for changed purposes, even the mediaeval buildings constructed from such demolitions or from new cut marble, still were as antique as they might be. If the Pisan Cathedral (begun in 1069), with the Baptistry and Leaning Tower, represent some development of a new Romanesque architecture, they also represent renewed skill and replenished resources still following the methods and the forms which Italy never had departed from.

So much for building, antique in modelling and method, Christian merely in purpose. In painting or mosaic and in sculpture, not only did style and method derive from the antique, and constantly hark back to its source; but decorative motives also were antique, and the great mass of subsidiary figures, which in the later times of the fif-

[1] See Emile Bertaux, *L'Art dans l'Italie méridionale,* Tome I. These busts have also been thought real antiques. The Byzantine style tends to Italianize in the mosaics in St. Mark's and the Florence Baptistry.

teenth and sixteenth centuries were to reassert their independent interest, and their right to be depicted and reexpressed for their own sake. A fund of antique motives and figures, allegorical or otherwise, had carried clear across from the pagan era to all times of Christian art — a limitless number of graphic and plastic conceptions of such clarity and distinction that Italian sculpture and painting should never even wish to discard them. As personifications or personal realities they included Sun and Moon and Ocean, the Seasons and the Hours, the Winds and Rivers, Victories and Liberal Arts, the Virtues and the Vices, Sibyls, Muses, Sirens, Psyche, Cupid, Orpheus, not to mention Alexander, Caesar and Trajan; all in patterns and compositions, completed forms of pictorial and plastic expression.

In the time of the great inception of truly Italian sculpture and painting — the time of the Pisani for the one, of Duccio and Giotto for the other — these pervasive pagan elements of expression were made use of as of course. The consciously presented theme was Christian, as suited the pulpits of baptistries and cathedrals, and the resting places for the dead who looked to Christ. Yet though the theme was Christian, the very thought of expressing any religious theme in carved or painted forms was pagan, that is, Graeco-Roman, or indeed Hellenic. Left to themselves, Jewish followers of Jesus, like the ancient Hebrews from whose loins they sprang, would have held pictorial representations of sacred personages as rank idolatry — as the racially kindred sects of Mahometans still hold. It was the Graeco-Roman world that, turning to Christianity, required images of its new faith, just as its habit had always been to worship its gods and goddesses in plastic forms. So the sacred art of the Christian faith is pagan in the original demand for it and in its consequent inception.

Looking at the sculpture of Niccola Pisano (cir. 1206–1280) and his son Giovanni, one may realize what blends of stylistic method and patterning, and what intricacy of cultural and religious sentiment and conception entered their work, to be appropriated by them, and made their own. Niccola accepts the topics of his Christian theme — the Annunciation and the Birth of Christ, the offerings of the Magi, the Crucifixion, the Last Judgment — from his predecessors; their methods and schemes of composition were also part of his equipment. Since apparently he came from Apulia, he may have felt the influence of almost any style used before his day in Italy. Most obviously his own early work, the pulpit of the Pisan Baptistry, (completed by 1260) imitates the relief carvings of certain Roman sarcophagi, which may still be seen in Pisa. Toward the end of his career, as when working with his son upon the pulpit of the Sienna Cathedral, he had progressed toward a freer and more natural manipulation of his figures, and had availed of the lessons of contemporary French Gothic sculpture, as one may plainly see in the figure of the Madonna holding the Child at one of the angles of the Sienna pulpit. His sculpture has become more expressive and more beautiful. The son Giovanni likewise shows the French influence; but his admirable reliefs, as upon his pulpits in Pistoia and in the Pisan Cathedral (finished respectively about 1301 and 1311), mark energetic progress toward a natural beauty in his figures; pointing onward to the beautiful bronze door of Andrea Pisano designed for the baptistry at Florence, and to the painting of Giotto.[2] It was doubtless by reason of the presence of so many antique models, that the progress of sculpture under Niccola Pisano and his son preceded Giotto's grand uplifting of the art of painting: a phenomenon which repeats itself in the next century, when Ghiberti and Donatello are the predecessors of Masaccio, Fra Lippo Lippi and Mantegna.

In the work of these great artists of the thirteenth and fourteenth centuries is seen the growth of a veritable

[2] The door was completed and installed by 1336. Giotto, born some thirty years before Andrea, died in 1337. He aided Andrea with counsel. Vasari says that he furnished the designs.

Italian style, which was progressing through the constant rendering and re-rendering of the same themes, and the modifying and perfecting of them, incited by comparison with former renderings and by contemporary living competition. Each artist who does not merely copy some previous rendering, but makes the theme his own and endeavors to improve the rendering, uses his own imagination, and follows his idea of improvement or perfection. He is thus expressing himself: his work is his self-expression. And when a succession of great artists, Niccola and Giovanni and Andrea, perfects, each of them, the rendering of his master, his work, which is his self-expression, becomes part of a larger self-expression, which may be called that of the race or time or people.

This remains true even when we turn to so great a creator of living and dramatic composition as this tremendous Giotto. He too had accepted from convention and authority, and from his predecessors in pictorial and plastic presentation, the round of sacred topics hitherto expressed. It was not for him to seek beyond this circle for novel subjects. Remaining well within it in his early work in the Arena Chapel at Padua, he re-expressed and again presented the story of the life of the Virgin and the story of the life of Christ, but with a power of living and speaking composition which never had been given them before. Herein certainly was an expression of Giotto's faculties and of his realizations of life and the power of painting to represent it, of his nature in fine, whereof his work was a disclosure, an *actualization* in the old scholastic sense, and assuredly an expression.

Yet providentially — for all things that happen fitly happen providentially — there had been a wonderful life which passed to its apotheosis a generation before Giotto's birth; and this wonderful life of Francis of Assisi, with the religious experience of the generation so stirred by it, supplied this inventive or creative painter with a new series of topics, almost a new gospel story.

Giotto did not have to seek for this; it flooded his consciousness, and insisted upon presentation. It was so telling, so dramatic, and, above all, so pictorial. Painters before Giotto had but feebly rendered its episodes. Now he would take it, transform it somewhat in his potent nature, and give it new dignity and stateliness in frescoes which should present Francis as canonized by the Church and beatified in the adoration of the Italian people.[3] The frescoes which present Francis in allegory and beatification, on the ceiling of the lower Assisi Church; those later ones which gave the great scenes of his life and death, in the Bardi chapel in Santa Croce; — are likewise expressions of Giotto's artistic tastes and faculties and composition, of his supreme artistic balance and self-control; they are a self-expression of the man.

Giotto's career held many elements of progressing greatness. Summing up the past's attainment, it incorporated riches of its own, and altogether was a prefigurement of the culmination of Italian painting in the Cinquecento. It was, first of all, a great advance toward naturalness, toward life. Possibly in the imitative representation of living forms, it hardly equalled the sculpture of Giovanni Pisano, not to mention Andrea. The technique of painting was not abreast of sculpture. But Giotto made a giant stride in composition, a wonderful stride onward toward the representation of life, its action, its aspirations and attainments, its deflections, its constraints and sufferings: and all as exemplified by noble beings in significant situations. In this way his painting follows life, seizes upon telling acts, presents significant groupings, with the figures of the tableau naturally participating. In becoming natural in this large sense, Giotto's compositions have become dramatic and endowed with the power of narrative. Perhaps the story of the Virgin and the story of her Son were never painted as tellingly as Giotto painted them on the walls of the Arena

[3] Giotto was no painful biographer or portrait painter. Individualized conscientious portraiture had not yet entered painting. Giotto's St. Francis is idealized, more excellent in physical form and feature, than the early Lives would justify. St. Bonaventura had in like fashion transformed the Legend in his, as it were, official life of Francis.

Chapel. Painting and sculpture in Giotto's time had to tell the sacred story which people did not read so readily in books. They should also tell the story truly, rendering its incidents as they occurred. None could be more earnest than Giotto in his endeavor to represent the holy scenes truthfully.

In this dramatic naturalism, this trenchant following of life, nothing is more marked than the advance which has been made in the expression of emotion; — of emotion which, whether expressed or visibly subdued, makes part of every human event. Failure to realize and express this most natural element in the incidents of the Gospel had been the great shortcoming of the frescoes and mosaics which illuminated the walls of Christian basilicas in the fifth century. As the truths of salvation and condemnation were pondered on and lived with from generation to generation, men saw them through a gathering emotion, which, for a while, a decadent and barbarized art could not express. In Italy, with some slight advance in technical skill, the endeavor to express the feeling of these moving scenes appears in the thirteenth century. With Cavallini at Rome,[4] with Cimabue at Assisi, with Niccola and Giovanni Pisano, and then with Giotto, whose frescoes belong to the fourteenth, comes a new capacity to realize the feeling or emotion proper and natural to these scenes, and technical ability to express it.

One may also think that the life of St. Francis had renewed men's religious sentiments, stirred their emotions; and that because of Francis and his legend, sculptors and painters had become more sensitive. At all events an hitherto pictorially unexpressed intensity of emotion is rendered by Giotto on the walls of the Arena Chapel, culminating in the scenes of the Crucifixion and the Deposition from the Cross. The expression of emotion in the faces and the gestures of the Mother and the disciples and the angelic host is unexampled in previous painting or sculpture. These may have been completed

[4] In his mosaics in S. Maria in Trastevere and his frescoes in S. Cecilia in Trastevere executed in the last part of the thirteenth century.

by the year 1306, when Giotto was about forty. His later work, depicting allegorically the glorified St. Francis on the ceiling of the lower church at Assisi, shows a larger balance entering his composition; a balance which is well fitted to the dignity of saintly grief, visibly restrained, shown in the still later fresco of the death of Francis, in the Bardi Chapel in Santa Croce. Although the life and death of this most loving and beloved of saints were the theme of his mature work, Giotto's genius for large and balanced composition and his sense of seemliness control the final self-expression of this painter. In the next generation the combination of feeling and naturalness with composition in the grand style, is carried on by Orcagna, Giotto's greatest and most independent follower. The many other disciples of Giotto, copyists of their master, tend to retrograde in style and composition.

One feels that the tradition of antique sculpture was dominant in the work of Niccola Pisano and his son, and in the work of Andrea. Antique personifications, decorative patterns and the lessons of antique sculpture, either directly or through the Pisani, entered the art of Giotto. The result appears, for example, in the beautiful figure of Hope, draped in antique fashion, which he painted as a Christian virtue on the Arena Chapel. At the same time these sculptors and this great painter were striving for fidelity to nature. These two intentions are not inconsistent, and may promote each other, when the artist is no mere copyist of antique statues or the antique manner; but is more vitally appropriating that antique idealizing fidelity to nature which seeks to ennoble the type by following the pointing of nature's best suggestions.

Since much antique statuary survived, and very little painting,[5] sculptors were more strongly drawn than painters to follow the antique in the thirteenth and succeeding centuries. Yet from Niccola Pisano to Michelangelo the imitation of the antique by Italian sculptors was

[5] Pompeian frescoes had not yet been unearthed.

usually but part of that idealizing imitation of nature, which likewise characterized the sculpture of the Greeks. There was no such servile copying as might have kept their work from being an expression of their own faculties and tastes, instincts and judgment.

Although the scanty remains of antique painting do not permit a sure comparison, it is probable that the painting of the ancients as an independent art was inferior to their sculpture, which might, however, use color or rich materials like gold and ivory to enhance its beauty. Sculpture had the closer affinity with the Hellenic genius, and would seem to have been more highly prized by the composite Graeco-Roman taste.

The opposite was to prove true of Christian Italy. From the fourth century, mosaic, rather than sculpture, was employed to tell the sacred story, express the Christian faith.[6] Mosaic continued the chief vehicle of expression in the Greek Christian, or Byzantine, art, whether practiced in Constantinople, Sicily or Italy. In Italy, with the revival of civilization, sculpture was the first to blossom in the thirteenth century, and was to continue as a chosen vessel for the self-expression of the Italian genius. Yet painting overtook it, surrounded and enveloped it with quickly budding myriad energies, answering to the universal Italian love of painted forms. And if it was the nature of the Italians to see their ideas, or find them, in forms and images, then painting was the most facile means of expressing those pictorial ideas on church walls and palaces. Yet the fact that painting could perform this function more quickly and at less expense than sculpture scarcely explains why painting became, and never ceased to be, the supreme expression of Italy. The Italian genius unfolded itself most completely in painting, found in it scope for the study of

[6] Was mosaic better adapted than sculpture to give such ample expression of the Christian matter as was demanded? Possibly. Yet where the national genius ran to sculpture rather than painting, sculpture was the chief means employed, as on French Gothic cathedrals; and who shall say that it did not do its office as effectively and as beautifully as mosaic, or fresco painting?

human beings and of the circumambient world; found in it scope and satisfaction for its love of the gorgeous and the visibly delightful, and for its love of ideal, harmonious, even formal beauty, by which its continuance of the Greek spirit was made clear.

Notwithstanding this affinity with Greek art and the many lessons which Italian painting drew from it, along with its adoption of antique patterns and figures, the course of Italian painting was one of organic growth, a clear and free self-expression of the Italian people. Painters and those who wrote about them, and the people who delighted in their works, regarded the progress of painting as progress in the imitation or portrayal of nature, until the painters should achieve its perfect rendering in their pictures. This view of the matter, which seems to be the view of Leonardo as well as Vasari, must be taken with all the observations and explanations in which Leonardo enwrapped it, and the qualifications which he made and illustrated in his practice. First of all, the many ways of "imitating" nature should be remembered, and the vast and varied range of the objects of imitation. Beyond the visages and forms of man in infinite variety, "nature" includes animals and trees, herbs, grass and rocks, all the natural objects in a landscape, and such works of man as buildings. To paint all these as they are, it is necessary to observe linear and aerial perspective, and paint, or "imitate," the atmosphere, its light and shade and color, clouds, sunsets, rainbows, darkness, and all the phenomena of the air.

Moreover, in order to imitate these matters truly, which include the facts of human life and the actions of human beings, the "imitation" must embrace congruous grouping and arrangement, composition. And if the painter is to rise to the portrayal of beauty, that is, to the idealizing of the objects of his art, he must have mastered their particular realities, before he can advance to perfection, which is beauty, along the lines of nature's truth. To this end, besides the idealizing choice of types and elements, he must attain to principles of inclusion and exclusion, to the high notes of unity in composition, that he may present his theme consonantly and perfectly, with the fewest possible detractions or distractions. It is in the presentation of forms and colors pleasing to the eye, as well as consonant with the spirit of his theme, that he will be likely to reach principles and realizations of pictorial composition, which will bring his painting into agreement with those modes of Greek art which also had passed onward, through somewhat analogous stages, to a like attainment. For example, when the purpose of a composition is to present a significant event, the interest and action would increase toward the centre of the design, and decline to quietude at the extremities. Leonardo da Vinci never saw the eastern pediment of the Parthenon; but in his Last Supper, in Milan, from the comparative quiescence of the disciple at either end of the table, the eye is led on through the excited action of the other disciples to the contrasted and momentous calm of the Christ at the centre who has spoken. All this presents a spiritual analogy to the pedimental grouping of the figures which set forth the birth of Athene: wherein the action and interest culminate at the centre, and literally slope down to quietude and contemplation in the figures toward the extremities of the triangle.

Leonardo's exhaustive notes, or treatise, upon the study of nature for the purposes of painting indicate what painting as an imitation of nature might signify and include. The complete and perfect imitation of all natural phenomena is inculcated and elaborately illustrated from such penetrating observation of natural appearances as perhaps none other ever made. "Darkness, light, body and color, form and position, distance and nearness, movement and rest,— this little work of mine will be a tissue of these attributes, recording for the painter the rule and method by which his art should imitate all these things, the works of Nature and ornament of the world." [7] So he investigates perspective "the best guide to painting,"

[7] J. P. Richter, *Literary Works of Leonardo da Vinci,* § 23.

perspective both linear and aerial; then light and shade and color, the appearance of trees and other natural objects, the proportions and movements of the human figure, and all of this with wonderful care and minuteness, and accompanied with such drawings as may not be found elsewhere. There is no detail so slight as not to be worthy of the painter's study, whether in the muscles of the human body, in the modulations of shadows or of the lustre and transparency of a leaf.[8] It is fundamental in painting that the objects shall stand out, appear in relief, show natural modelling; and that the backgrounds and distances be shown in true perspective. In judging a picture, the first thing to consider is whether the figures have the relief required by their position and the light which falls on them; next the distribution of the figures, and whether they are arranged to meet the needs of the story, and thirdly, whether each is doing its part.[9]

Obviously excellence of grouping, with each feature of the picture performing its function, is part of a truthful imitation of nature, and leads on to that idealizing and ennobling imitation, which selects and combines that which is most beautiful or effective.[10]

At this point one touches Leonardo's virtual qualifications to his general principle of fidelity to nature, qualifications which his own painting tacitly exemplified. The painter argues and vies with nature — disputa e gareggia — says he.[11] He will try to improve upon her, excel her if he can, in his endeavor to paint what is significant, noble, and beautiful. This Leonardo did, and Raphael, and Michelangelo, and Titian. In order to make his painting effective, the painter will even, literally and meticulously speaking, falsify nature, by altering or omitting such details of appearance as actually may be seen in nature, but which blunt the effectiveness of his painting, obscure the form or contour of his conception or of the chief

[8] Ib. §§ 148 *sqq.*, 363, 365, 423 *sqq.*
[9] Ib. §§ 17, 554.
[10] See e.g. Ib. §§ 587, 588, 592, 593.
[11] Ib. § 662.

objects by which he designs to present it. Leonardo says this substantially; and this he also did, and Raphael and Michelangelo and Titian.

Nevertheless that the principle of fidelity, or the higher fidelity, to nature must in general obtain, Leonardo shows in a pregnant paragraph upon the course of Italian painting: The painter's work will have little merit if he merely copies another artist; but only if he studies from nature. The painters after the Romans imitated each other, and art declined. "Then came Giotto the Florentine who was not content to imitate the works of his master Cimabue . . . but began to draw on the rocks the actions of the goats he kept." He drew all the animals in the country till after much study he surpassed the masters of his time and of many centuries before him. After him, art declined again by copying what had been done, until Masaccio, a Florentine, "showed by his perfect work how those who take any guide but nature, mistress of masters, weary themselves in vain." [12]

So Leonardo brings us to this remarkable Masaccio, who looked into the face of nature and saw more perfectly than anyone before him how painting should imitate. Vasari says that he painted things as they are, and was the first to make his figures stand firmly on their feet. He individualized his people, making them look real; and greatly improved his perspective, giving his pictures atmospheric depth. Every figure has its place where there is room for it, not merely for the part which shows, but for the rest of the figure remaining invisible behind another form. Light and shadow have become important in his painting, as they are in every actual scene. So this young genius expressed his understanding of the face of nature, and died, not much over twenty-seven, about the year 1428, leaving those frescoes in the Carmine at Florence to be studied by all Italian painters of his own time and long after him.

Masaccio marks a stage in the progress of painting toward that complete and perfect modelling which Leon-

[12] Ib. § 660.

ardo held to be the "soul of painting," and exemplified in his Mona Lisa. After Masaccio, or in his time, others worked diligently, bringing out their understanding of how things looked, and endeavoring to arrange and paint them beautifully, decoratively; sometimes raising their types, and even trying to educe the soul. Such a one was Fra Angelico, born before Masaccio and long outliving him. Of a truth he was a saintly soul, and one whose constant study and subtle skill invested with loveliness and saintliness the forms he painted. All his long life (1387–1455) he observed and studied. Starting from idyllic sweetness, he progressed year by year, improving the shading of his backgrounds, thus beautifying them with truth. He raises the ordered composition of his pictures, as in the Uffizi *Coronation of the Virgin* and the *Last Judgment* in the Academy at Florence. He advances in the individualizing of figures and the rendering of expression, and in the naturalness of his grouping, even reaching that impressive and beautifully composed grouping which may still harmonize with the natural. Having impressed the walls of his Convent, San Marco, with an intensive and hitherto unpainted saintliness, he put his very last pictorial attainment into the Preaching of St. Stephen and the Saint's Martyrdom, in Pope Nicholas's Chapel in the Vatican.[13] Thus through his art, and as it were progressively, Fra Angelico expresses his own lovely nature, which was a painter's also, and imbued with the instinct of beauty and the passion to see and paint appearances.

After Masaccio, in Florence, a realistic and more analytical study of things went on with Paolo Uccello and the Pollajuoli. Then painting turns toward a full expression of the vivid life of Florence in the quattrocento, which shall be painted in its whole pageantry and individual delightfulness. Upon this alluring actuality of street life about him, as well as upon Masaccio's frescoes, is turned the gifted though over-greedy eye of the Carmelite, Fra Lippo Lippi. He is delightful in his

[13] See generally Langton Douglas, *Fra Angelico* (London, 1900).

cheerful human rendering of sacred themes; a portrait painter always, yet executing many lovely altar pieces filled with pleasing women, he approached great composition in his decoration of the Prato Duomo, even attaining it, and with a more refined beauty, in the *Annunciation* in the Duomo at Spoleto. A little younger than Fra Lippo, was Benozzo Gozzoli, who put life's cheerful pageantry into the anything but sacred scenes of the Riccardi chapel. Still younger were Ghirlandajo and Botticelli. Both were students of Fra Lippo as well as of Masaccio's frescoes, and both were to become famous and significant painters. No painter has rendered on so ample a scale the complete life of quattrocento Florence as Ghirlandajo (1449–1498), a man of extraordinary aptness and facility in composition, who, with his pupils, covered a goodly acreage of surface, and sometimes with admirable pictures. His *Calling of Peter and Andrew* on the wall of the Sistine Chapel is scarcely surpassed by any of those compositions over which arches Michelangelo's ceiling. His best known, and most amply illustrative work fills the choir of S. Maria Novella. Among those quite delightful pictures, *The Birth of the Virgin* excels in deftness of general composition and in the beauty of the figures. Yet Ghirlandajo's pleasing rendering of the detail and incident of life, which made him a great painter of *genre,* scantily covers the incongruity between his gaiety and the sacred themes. In spite of his cheerful attractiveness, the thoughtful mind may be disturbed by a certain pervasive irrationality, or at least by the incomplete rationalizing of his composition. He does not object to irrelevancy of detail and corner incident, an irrelevancy which will serve as contrast to the more strictly drawn principles of composition and mightier harmony of design already showing in Leonardo, and to attain more obvious splendor in Raphael. Yet Ghirlandajo offers a brilliant expression of himself and of his quattrocento Florence.

A very different painter and human being was Sandro Botticelli (1444–1510), to whom Ghirlandajo's successful and rather superficial art may have been a spiritual thorn. Yet he was a cheerful soul, beneath his rather sad and pregnant painting. The charmed study of the classics, pervading a Florence ruled by Lorenzo dei Medici, and by Politian in the humanities, affected Botticelli as a new and high romance. He was touched by the joyful-sad vibrations of their poetry, by Politian's *Orfeo* and his "Ben venga Maggio," and why not by Lorenzo's "Triumph of Bacchus and Ariadne," beginning:

> Quant' é bella giovinezza,
> Che si fugge tuttavia.

His later life was as deeply moved by the strident eloquence, and then the fate, of Savonarola. Yet Botticelli, in some saddened sense, remained Botticelli, and still felt and thought either in allegories or in images which were living symbols. His *Judith* seems as much a symbol as his *Fortezza*. Pallas crushing the Centaur, but not with physical force, whether it signified Lorenzo's victory over the Pazzi (1478), at least symbolized much that then was pressing to expression in the painter's phantasy. A puzzled sense of life's loveliness and pathos speaks unspoken from the face and form of Venus — newly born? one doubts it. The *Spring* is sheer allegory, classical in its provenance, romantic in its quality; and the *Calumny* is allegory so completely veiled that men have felt impelled to link it with the unjust destruction of Savonarola. But Botticelli was a splendid draughtsman too, having early learned his lesson from Antonio Pollajuolo; and he showed the resources of his composition in those scenes from the life of Moses, painted by him in the Sistine Chapel. Leonardo reproved him for belittling landscape, and thinking it a thing that might be done offhand. Botticelli did not set himself to that as he did to his Madonnas, and to his boys or angels, and to his Venus which allures as through some subtler sense-fascination working within the veil of flesh. His phantasy which pervades his apprehension of the antique, his very personal imagination and indwelling mood, find expression in these forms through this painter's mastery of a significant and speaking line.

A different reflection of the antique was brought to masterful expression in the painting of another man, Mantegna (1430–1506), the Paduan who worked so long at Mantua. His painting drew lessons from the sculpture of Donatello who came to Padua in 1443, and executed his equestrian statue of Gattamalata. This universal Donatello was a gluttonous observer of nature, and here Mantegna gained from him; but the antique had not failed to work upon the sculptor and his fellows: Alberti says that " the spirit of the ancients passed into the frames of Ghiberti, Brunelleschi, Donatello and Masaccio, and fitted them for the most honorable enterprises." [14]

Mantegna absorbed the plastic qualities of Donatello and of the antique sculpture, showing them even in his early frescoes in the Eremitani chapel in Padua, executed before he went in 1459 to serve the Gonzagas at Mantua. He could paint action naturally, and was a great portrayer of individualities when the task was set him, for example, to paint Lodovico Gonzaga and his family. But he had always been, and more and more became a student of ancient monuments and a signal lover of the antique and its qualities. No painter before him had so masterfully brought the lines and motives and emblems of antique art into effective union with his own, one might say, classic genius. He is the great quattrocento painter who advances to that beauty which rises above the charms of the individual and above the so humanly attractive painting which delights in them. Mantegna rises above such actual or imagined portraiture, as Leonardo will rise, and Raphael and Michelangelo. He has likewise made his own advances toward their greater art in the high unity of his composition and the discarding of distracting incident. Such classic self-expression of Mantegna may be seen in the historical composition of the

[14] Quoted by Crowe and Cavalcaselle.

Triumph of Caesar, what there is left of it, in Hampton Court, and in the mythological *Parnassus* in the Louvre.

Art is the best criticism of art; and never was so great criticism passed on the previous manner and achievement of painting as that contained in the work of those three great men whose names have just been set together. Two of them (not Raphael, who was altogether a painter) were capable of criticism in words; a more final judgment lay in their painting, and the manner in which it lifted itself above much that had been and still was popular. So lofty and so ideal became the painting and sculpture of these three great artists and certain of their fellows, that it indirectly compels attention to the character of the society in which they had their being, and the effect of it in promoting or hindering their attainment.

There are different phases of personality within that mysterious form which cloaks a so-called individual — as may be seen, outside of Italy, amply illustrated in many an English Elizabethan. The same is true of a people, or of what we call the genius of a race. If its phases are indeed parts of an unity, at least they appear separable and distinct one from another. The virtues of mind and disposition, all the positive and exemplary elements of human being, rarely work together either in an individual or a people. Some of them may exist in marked degree, while others, which might seem their normal concomitants, are as noticeably wanting. One might ideally hope to find intellectual power accompanying a correspondingly large benevolence; one might expect the religious sense of reverence and dependence on the divine to be associated with the social virtues, for which it sometimes is a substitute; and still more reasonably might one look for a close association between beauty of character and a delight in the beauty of visible things and their representations. But we know that these wished for conjunctions fail quite as often as they greet us in the records.

The universal Italian delight in all the delightful things of form and color which may be created, fashioned, or put together by human craft, bore slight relationship to civic virtue. It was connected with Italian religious feeling, because that demanded images, delighted in them, functioned by means of them. It was akin to the Italian critical sense, or reason, in so far as that employed itself upon the pleasure-giving qualities of the products of human art.

Another point of comparison: in a large way Elizabethan plays accorded with the popular taste and the approvals and disapprovals issuing from the English mind and character. But many of the plays, especially those which were *Italianate,* did not represent the ethics of the audience. The audience, listening to Webster's *White Devil* or *Duchess of Malfey,* might enjoy upon the stage what it neither was nor approved of. Likewise Italian painting assuredly corresponded with Italian taste, and yet its themes and the beauty and loveliness of their presentation might bear no obvious resemblance to the characters of the men who ordered the paintings and took pleasure in them. These paintings were what they liked, agreeing with their tastes rather than their morals. Pietro Aretino (1492–1557), the blackmailing litterateur who plied his vile trade from the tolerant security of Venice, was an intimate of Titian and an excellent critic of painting; he was very sensitive to the beauties of Venetian sunsets, and could describe them charmingly.

Nor were Italian paintings necessarily a reflection of the moral natures of the painters themselves. One may fall back on the Aristotelian-scholastic thought, as given by Aquinas: Ars est recta ratio factibilium — the right reason, or way, of making things that are makeable. In itself *ars* is innocent — the *locus innocentiae* — in the sense that the making of a thing, the building of a house or the painting of a picture, is not an act of ethical import; is neither moral nor immoral, righteous or wicked.

It was not the moral natures of the Italians, or their truthfulness, their civic loyalty and patriotism (which were conspicuously lacking) that painted their beautiful pictures. It was Italian love and genius for painting.

The genius, the heaven bestowed grace of form, was theirs. They succeeded more splendidly in painting than in their poetry and belles lettres, where form seems won at the expense of substance. Indeed in their writing, form stands out plastically. In Castiglione's famous book, the qualities, the equipment, the manners of a perfect Courtier appear as forms visible and pleasing to the eye.

Painting and sculpture naturally change their style and manner, and incidentally their aims, as they move on to a culmination. The painters of the quattrocento had shown individual differences in conception, method, and achievement, according to their faculties and temperaments. Their painting had been an expression of themselves, and withal an image of the tastes and fancies of the time. Italy had been growing richer; had been constantly increasing the assets of her civilization. There was ampler means to indulge the taste for painting and remunerate the painters. Little had occurred to check life's happy effervescence. The last decade of the century opened as a glad climacteric, at Florence especially; but was to end in perturbation. Lorenzo dei Medici died in 1492, and his great scholars soon followed him to the tomb. The French invasion came, with its easy overthrow of states, to demonstrate insultingly Italian weaknesses. With their Medici for the time expelled, the Florentines, scared by the demonstrations of Savonarola, rather calamitously abandoned art for goodness; then they burned the prophet, as they had burned their finery, and returned to earth and art. In Milan quite as rude events took place a little later, and the Moro (Lodovico Sforza) passed to a dungeon at Loches, with the shame of Italy's invasion on his head. Cesare Borgia too, after his baleful meteor course, had flitted to a prison in Spain. Such object lessons might damp the Italian mood. Perhaps sobering Spanish manners were entering the high society, which possibly looked for a more sedate decoration of its habitation. Perhaps some influence flowed from the new study of Plato.

It is hard to bring such events or changes, local or

general, to bear upon the progress and mounting style of Italian painting. Rather, we see the advance taking to itself the previous attainment, and as from its *milieu* rising to its culmination. It even re-asserts its affinity with the earlier achievements of Giotto and of Masaccio, which Leonardo recognized as epoch-making. But most assuredly this supreme advance was due to the genius of three men, and to the significant work of contemporary craftsmen. The careers of these three began, indeed that of Leonardo reached its meridian, in the quattrocento. Born in 1452, Leonardo's *Last Supper* was painted before the century closed. Michelangelo, born in 1475, passed the susceptible and pregnant years of youth at work among the art treasures of Lorenzo, associating with his great Platonists, before Lorenzo died in 1492. Raphael was born in 1483; he also had much to learn before the sixteenth century ushered in his eighteenth year. His feet were planted in the quattrocento; schooled in its art, he took its lessons with him even to his fresco-painting in the Vatican.

The creations of these men of genius — their self-expression — can neither be detached from their enabling antecedents nor accounted for by them. Their work passed onward from what had been done; it asserted its affinity with what was most significant in the past: at the same time it was distinct creation. Their art opened new depths of truthfulness in the modeling of natural objects invested with the verities of light and shadow. Their genius realized the beauty and the profound representative significance of the human form, which their art rendered with intrinsic dignity and lofty graciousness. They intensified the import of its movements and postures. They grouped human forms and other matter of their compositions beautifully, so as to give pleasure to the eye, and functionally, so as to contribute to the action of the piece. They avoided irrelevance and distraction, and kept all things true to the master motive of their composition.

The mind of Leonardo, analytic, curious as to all things

visible and their effective relationships, the mind to which there was nothing negligible or unimportant; the eye to which likewise there was nothing insignificant or unimpressive, an eye that discerned more subtleties in the appearance of things than ever had been imagined; the artist temper delighting in the import and beauty of appearances, eager to fix their fleeting loveliness; the deft finesse of hand which could execute, change, or retract whatever might be supplied by eye or mind; and then the re-composing, intensifying, creative faculty which could present the inclusive and enduring verities of the human personality, and the moment of supreme import in the human drama — such may have been the qualities of this, in all respects wonderful, Leonardo, through which he brought painting to a perfection never before realized, and in its intimate intent and execution not to be surpassed.

Leonardo was a true Italian, to whom vision, the function of the corporeal eye, the sense of sight, was the chief purveyor both of pleasure and of knowledge of the world. Under its instigation worked the investigating, re-producing and constructive hand; both eye and hand reporting the data of their visual and tactile inquiry to the common sense which dwells behind the other senses, and judges and compares the testimony of its five instruments.[15] Painting is the means and art *par excellence* which captures and preserves the phenomena of the visible world — le opere di natura — for future pleasure and enlightenment, and presents them as they are in reality.

"He who disparages painting, the sole imitator of all the visible works of nature, of a surety disparages a subtle invention, which with philosophy and subtle speculation, considers all the qualities of forms, backgrounds and settings (arie e siti), plants, animals, herbs and flowers, which are enveloped in shadow and light. And

[15] . . . l'occhio riceve le spezie overo similitudini delli obbietti, e dàlli alla imprensiva, e da essa imprensiva al senso commune, e lì é giudicata. E. Solmi, *Leonardo-Frammenti* (Florence, Barbera, 1904) p. 241. L'occhio, che si dice finestra dell'anima, è la principale via, donde il comune senso può più copiosamente e magnificamente considerare le infinite opere di natura. ib. p. 235.

truly this is the science and legitimate daughter of nature, because painting is born from Nature. Or, more correctly, we should call it Nature's grandchild, because all visible things have been born from Nature, from which things born from Nature painting is born. So we rightly call it grandchild of nature and kin to God." [16]

But the painter is no sheer copyist, for he argues and vies with nature. He shall even have a conception in his imagination, an idea, a composition, and bring out its design, and build it up so that it may express his idea; but with all his figures drawn and placed in true perspective, and executed according to reason and natural effects.[17]

Such statements indicate why painting was one of Leonardo's dominant passions, and through what courses of reasoning he justified his profound interest in it, connecting it with other branches of his scientific inquiry into the kinetic values and relationships of things.

It was impossible that Leonardo should not have set painting above the descriptions and narrations of poetry, being an Italian man to whom all things addressed themselves in images,— to the eye and tactile hand, rather than in words. He constantly emphasizes the greater power, directness, and instantaneity of the impressions of sight, as compared with the infiltration of the meaning of words through the ear to the *senso commune*. Painting presents the essence of its matter in a single instant, and all at once gives the impression of the natural objects in the harmony and proportion of the parts and the whole which they compose.[18]

Leonardo follows again the genius of his people in judging painting to be superior to sculpture; — through its " larger mental discourse," and more universal powers of representation; through its means of linear and aerial perspective and power of bringing the remote and the near into the same composition; and because of its beauty of color and its marvels of *nuance* and *finesse*.[19]

[16] Solmi, *Leonardo* o. c. p. 276.
[17] Solmi, o. c. p. 278.
[18] Solmi, o. c. pp. 233–251.
[19] Solmi, o. c. pp. 289–297.

His own painting and his own work in sculpture never satisfied Leonardo's passion for fidelity to nature and for the effective presentation of the modifying conception in his mind. His love of beauty might omit distracting incidents in order to enhance the impressiveness of the painted reality. He had always realized that the truthful apprehension and representation of the outward appearance of an object depends upon knowledge of its inner structure and organic *rationale,* whether the object be living or inanimate. Never did his mind cease to impel his eye and hand to the investigation of the structural or causal relationships which produced the outer appearance. If he was a painter, he was just as integrally a man of science, and indeed one whose curiosity and passion for knowledge constantly checked the painter's productivity. In the end, the man of science mastered the artist.[20] The painting and the sculpture of Leonardo da Vinci were but a partial self-expression of this man of insatiable intellectual curiosity and utterly astounding intellectual insight.

Leonardo, painter and man of science, lived in a world of nature's works (which include man), as well as in his own modifying conceptions of these natural creations. But he who is not half withdrawn from his art through following after knowledge infinite, and is altogether painter, may build a world more completely in accord with his creative sense of beauty and other factors of his plastic genius. There had been a Giotto world, made of personages whom we quickly recognize as belonging to it. There was a Fra Angelico world of blessed saints: — who would have the heart to exile a single one even of his somewhat less blessed damned to any region of hard actuality! There was a cheerful human world of Fra Filippo, another more daintily fashionable of Ghirlandajo, and a strange world of Botticelli. There was a world of Perugino, with its admirably composed array of regularly beautiful balanced figures, where one might feel scanted of spiritual or vital sustenance. And now there was to be

[20] See post, Chap. XXXI.

a world of Raphael, indeed, more than one of them. First an idyllic world like Perugino's, only with a bit more soul; then a world of perfect groupings, mother and child and often the young John, the world of altogether lovely Granduca and Del Sedia Madonnas and Belles Jardinières; and then a finally ennobled world, composed and patterned in beauty, and peopled with beings perfected in new grace. Compared with these final compositions, those of other painters seemed to lack life's complete harmony; in the presence of the beings who filled them, the figures of previous painters might seem to lack something of the fullness of life's comeliness. This world had no meticulous realistic insistences, as that all things in it should submit to compass and yard stick. In that great cartoon of the *Miraculous Draught of Fishes,* had the two boats been drawn large enough to hold the Apostolic fishers, the dramatic greatness of these human figures would have been sacrificed. Yet such was the visual validity and appeal of this final pictorial world of Raphael that it carried no suggestion of unreality. Raphael's historical personages in their portraits, a Julius II, a Castiglione, fit in to this same world.

Perhaps nothing lent more beauty to this final world of Raphael than the position of each figure in it: the pleasing relative position as well as posture of every figure in the *School of Athens,* for example. That was part of the nobility of the whole design, the visual effect. The eye draws as great pleasure from the whole picture as from the beautiful figures that fill it so adequately, and neither crowd nor impede or jar upon each other. Thus Raphael's supreme faculty of pictorial composition found expression, and the efficient harmonies of his nature. He felt no craving for novelty; his painting sought no drastic innovation. He accepted his subjects easily, as from tradition. He presents them with more potent and more beautiful unison of composition than had been reached before. Even the so beautiful and so telling contrast of gesture between the arm of Plato pointing aloft in the *School of Athens,* and that of Aristotle horizontally covering the field of nature's works, was traditional in literature, though it might never have been so shown in fresco.

In Raphael artistic interest and creative faculty direct themselves to this perfected unison of composition, this harmony of lovely forms, which admits neither discord nor irrelevance. He conceives the composition as a whole throughout its parts; he represents it as a whole, and as a whole will the spectator see it. It is simplified through exclusion of the impertinent, and yet is intensified and given dramatic energy through the presentation of well directed contrasts and the ennoblement of all participating forms. The drapery will drape and render speaking, but neither overload nor obscure, the action of the figures; while the action of each will fit so perfectly into the action of the others, that no detail can be altered without disturbance of the whole.

In all these qualities the compositions of Raphael are approaching the noblest manner of antique sculpture, but without direct or conscious imitation.[21] His painting, and with greater emphasis, the sculpture and painting of Michelangelo, are rising to the level of the work of Scopas or Praxiteles, even to that of the masters of the Parthenon. The great art of Raphael and Michelangelo ascends to the peak of excellence reached by the ancient masters, not necessarily by following in their footsteps, but by climbing, it may be, the opposite side of the mountain.

Of a surety Italian painting had never been ignorant of the antique, had never been slow to borrow whatever figures or patterns or ideas it felt impelled to use; some-

[21] Of course, Raphael borrowed scores of antique decorative patterns, frankly enough: as one may see abundantly in the Loggia of the Vatican. And sometimes he manifestly imitates the ancient sculpture, as in the nude figure of Apollo (?) in the niche to the left of the centre in the *School of Athens*. But in the grand manner of his composition there would seem to have been no conscious copying of the antique. Doubtless he had drawn the symmetry of his compositions from Perugino or Fra Bartolommeo, even as for energy in action he drew upon Michelangelo and Leonardo.

times it would appear mindful of the antique lessons, and again quite disregardful of them. Whatever detail might be borrowed, the painting of Ghirlandajo, in general motive, form, and composition, was as unantique as possible. With the same antique background behind them, Raphael and Michelangelo in the clear development and progress of their Italian arts of painting and sculpture approach the classical. They have adopted, and made vitally their own, principles of composition, conceptions of beauty, realistic idealizing methods of compassing artistic excellence, all intimately related to the ways of ancient sculptors. But if, for instance, Michelangelo had any direct forbear, it was Signorelli and no antique statue; and, passing over the disputes as to details of his early instruction, we know that Raphael first imitated Perugino, then availed himself of what he could learn from Florentine painting, and took his last lessons from Michelangelo.

It was through mastering all these lessons, and the vital absorption into his own artistic faculty of the influences composing his physical and spiritual environment, that Raphael, prince of painters, brought to expression the last possibilities of his genius — of himself; the last possibilities which he might realize before dying at the age of thirty-seven in the year 1520, to the grief of Italy.

We have nothing of Raphael that reveals him except his painting. There we stop. Leonardo and Michelangelo have left much besides,— Leonardo some thousands of pages of manuscript which disclose the workings of his mind. Besides Michelangelo's poems, there are hundreds of his letters, many to his father and brothers disclosing his devoted and querulous affection, and his habit of living miserably and complaining of it. He writes to his father from Rome in 1512: "I live in a miserable fashion, caring neither for life nor for honors . . . and I suffer excessive hardships assailed by a thousand anxieties. It is now about fifteen years since I had an hour's repose, and all that I have ever done has been to help you; and you have never . . . believed it. God pardon us all." [22]

To his brother Buonarroti: "I live here surrounded by the greatest anxieties, suffering the greatest bodily fatigues. I have not a friend of any sort, and I do not want one; I have not so much time as suffices for me to eat the necessary food. However, I trust I may have no additional worries, for I could not bear another ounce." [23]

Michelangelo did live miserably at Rome and elsewhere. While working on Pope Julius's statue at Bologna, he did not take off his clothes or boots for weeks at a time, and slept in the same bed with his three workmen. On removing his boots the skin might peel off with them. His letters show how wretchedly he kept himself, complaining always. He was difficult and violent in temper, suspicious, thinking that people were cheating him. He was nervous and timid. When about twenty, he cleared out of Florence with a man who had had bad dreams of the coming downfall of Piero dei Medici.[24] Thirty-five years later, while directing the fortifications of his city during the fatal siege, he fled again, suddenly, to Venice; a letter of his tells about it.[25] He could also be very prudent politically, avoiding speech with the Florentine exiles at Rome, lest it compromise him.[26]

Such apparent weakness of character may be only indirectly relevant. But the man's virtues were touched with weakness, at least with lack of judgment. Michelangelo was generous, the main support of a father as complaining as himself; he was always helping his brothers and a nephew whom he eventually made his heir, and wrote quantities of letters to, the following among them: "As I was quite unable to decipher thy last letter, I put it in

[22] Trans. from R. W. Carden, *Michelangelo, a Record of his life as told by his letters*, p. 84.

[23] Ib. p. 63, Rome 1509.

[24] Condivi, *Life of Michelangelo Buonarroti*, § XIV. This *Vita* speaks from a close intimacy with Michelangelo, and was published some years before he died.

[25] Carden, o. c. p. 168 (Letter dated Sept. 25, 1529).

[26] See letter of March, 1548, o. c. p. 232.

the fire." [27] He was comically obstructive touching this nephew's marriage, objected, for example, to a wife who was near-sighted; altogether he was fearful of the ways of women. Besides his family, Michelangelo was generous and affectionate toward Urbino, his trusted servant. He would show impulsive love for those he liked, whether or not they were worthy of his regard. His praise was apt to be as extreme as his anger or irritation. He could debase himself before mediocrity, and was over-grateful to Vasari, who, of course, worshipped him. Yet he can write with very noble modesty, as to one Martelli who had sent him a sonnet in his praise: "I perceive that you have imagined me to be as God wished me to be. I am a simple man and of little worth, spending my time in striving to give expression to the art God gave me." [28]

Michelangelo had deep affection for Sebastian del Piombo, and praised him prodigiously,[29] as well he might; but he ascribed Raphael's success to his great diligence. The passionate devotion expressed for Tommaso Cavalieri, a cultivated Roman gentleman of great personal beauty, falls in the same category with the love for Victoria Colonna, soon to be referred to in connection with the sonnets.

The mention of these paltry incidents of character is pardonable if they prove not quite irrelevant to the self-expression of this complete and prodigious artist personality. Michelangelo adored beauty, and, above all, the beauty which might be rendered through the human form, which he glorifies in his painting and sculpture as Pindar glorified it in his Odes. Not altogether painter, but altogether artist, he seems to us. His temperament, his impulses and devotion, his imagination, his intellect and faculty, the complete efficient nature of the man, drew the whole compass of his life,— knowledge, opportunity, experience and incidental passion,— into the creation of beauty through the media of poetry, sculpture, painting,

[27] Carden, o. c. p. 248 (1548).
[28] Carden, o. c. p. 185 (Jan'y, 1542).
[29] Carden, o. c. p. 154, letter of May, 1525.

and architecture. He was an artist, and he lived no other life, save casually, distractedly, impertinently, under the passing jar of insignificant irritations, fears, and small infatuations.

With soft human spots in his soul, he might be hungry for affection, or, rather, might feel the need of feeling affection and expressing it. He cast his pearls before objects worthy or unworthy. His need was to cast his pearl, but not that the pearl should be taken into some warm and sympathetic bosom. Such an artist's love is like the first love of a youth, whose need is to love, and feel and think it out to its full reaches, imagine its relations with the eternal stars, express it in hidden or fearfully revealed adoration. This love is most fortunate when not returned. For responsive affection from the object of it would check the youth's imagination, and might clog the expansion of his nature and faculties.

So with the love of an artist, an artist in his whole nature and through all his years, like Michelangelo. The youthful lover is or should be a poet. This artist was always young, loving imaginatively, seeking to clothe his affection in beauty. Michelangelo's love, as we find it in his poems, was Petrarchian, expressional and creative. It was the artist's love for the thing of beauty which he creates, while likewise uplifting to the spheres his conception of devotion to it. Unwise Pygmalion, to wish to have his statue come to life, in response to the love which had created it! The love expressed in Michelangelo's sonnets looked for no more return than did the ardor which he put into his painting and his sculpture. An equivalent return from the object of these impassioned expressions would have perplexed him; he could not have recognized himself as a fitting altar for such worship. He might even have been in a predicament; as if those creatures of his brush upon the Sistine ceiling, or, horror upon horror, those in the Last Judgment, had come to life and were thronging to clasp the knees of their creator and cover him with their Titanic affection!

We may not err in finding the sonnets of Michelangelo

and the passionately sublime thought contained in them, to be sheer art. In them thought and imagination and emotion fuse and press with energy to artistic utterance; while the upper reaches of human passion are forced along the tortuosities of a hyper-poetic imagination. Were the sonnets an expression of a real passion? Assuredly; but it was a passion for beauty, perhaps rather for the expression or the creation of beauty; and not for the possession of the body and soul of another human being. They were the self-expression of the poet who composed them, and incidentally accepted the suggestions of certain actual relationships or experiences. The suggestions sprang from actuality; and the sonnets in which they were uplifted and finally enshrined were as true as art could make them. Theirs was the truth of valid and beautiful conceptions set in fitting words.

As befitted a sixteenth century Italian, this artist was less great as poet than as painter and sculptor. He seems to have composed verses through most of his life, certainly throughout the latter portion of it. He did not fling them off casually and carelessly; but corrected and rewrote them, and permitted a collection of them to be made for circulation among chosen spirits who could understand. The latest editor of these difficult poems [30] believes that he has succeeded in printing them in their proper temporal sequence; though often he has felt less certain of the individuals to whom they were sent, or addressed in the poet's mind. A number were addressed to a man, Cavalieri,[31] and these gave rise to the same questionings which have attached to some of Shakespeare's sonnets. In both cases the answers lie in the poet's impulse to express himself, already commented on. A more interesting analogy may be found in the way each of these poets has used the literary conventions in the air

[30] *Die Dichtungen des Michelagniolo Buonarroti,* herausgegeben etc., by Carl Frey (Berlin 1897). The first critical edition, that of C. Guasti, (Florence 1863), contains helpful prose renderings of the contents of each poem. J. A. Symonds's translations of the Sonnets must suffice for the English reader. They are not always the equivalent of the Italian; but represent a brave attempt at the impossible.

[31] E.g. Sonnet 50 (Frey's edition), beginning *Se nel volto.*

about him, and made of them vehicles for his own powerful and significant self-expression.

From the affinities of his own nature, Michelangelo revered Dante and felt the power of Dante's meaning. Occasionally he uses the metre of the *Commedia,* and his verse becomes Dantesque in phrase. But Petrarch afforded the chief store of conventional conceits and images. Michelangelo's thought also reflects the current Platonism of the Medici circles, as well as the sinuous far off rivulets of seeming Platonism which had percolated through Italian lyrics. Whether he read Plato for himself has been much disputed.

A number of these sonnets and madrigals are Petrarchian in sentiment and phrase. The query, for example, whether the beauty seen by the lover in his mistress is verily in her or in his own soul, is an echo of Petrarch as well as Dante.[32] But all such apparently borrowed notes have been revitalized in Michelangelo's deeply emotional as well as deeply intellectual nature, and reemerge in the sonnets as elements of his own rending self-expression.

Power, rather than facility, marks the work of Michelangelo, whether in marble or pigment or in verse. There is neither ease nor clarity in his sonnets. One feels in them first the difficulty of the thought, and then the power which compels the words to do the master's utterance. No other sonnets, Italian, French or English, evince such strainings. Yet the mind breaks through and conquers. And, when love is the burden of the sonnet, though the lines may not keep their significance sweetly and surely human, love is the more sublimely lifted to its eternal goal of beauty; and the love of beauty in mortal form unites with the love of the beauty and goodness of God.

Some of the sonnets move with the feeling of an individual or reciprocal situation. Surely those do which express the grieving thought of Michelangelo on the death of Victoria Colonna. But still he is an artist and a poet, obeying the compulsions of his conception of eternal

[32] No. 32 (Frey) — Dimmi di gratia. See Frey's notes.

love and beauty. The personal feeling or situation of the writer seems to inspire and guide the poems giving utterance to sorrow and contrition over the caducity and vain waste of life, when at the end the soul must cast itself on the piteous saving sacrifice of Christ. Alas! when it knows itself near death, but far from God! —

presso a morte e si lontan da Dio.[33]

Michelangelo wrote a number of sonnets and fragments of sonnets having this theme in the last years of his life, and among them the most famous of all his poems:

Giunto è gia 'l corso della vita mia. . . .

Now that his life has reached the port where account of every unhappy or good deed must be given, alas for the life-long passion, the *affectuosa fantasia,* which has made art for him *idol' e monarcha!* Death is near and certain, and the second death, the everlasting, menaces. Neither painting nor carving can calm the soul now turned to that love divine which to receive us opens his arms upon the cross.[34]

If the poems of Michelangelo were to be for the world the least important exponent of his genius, they illuminate the passionate tension of his sculpture and his painting. Also they show the manifold completeness of this man of four natures, as he was called, or of four gifts or faculties, which unfolded themselves in his four arts of poetry, sculpture, painting and architecture. These four arts were the expressions of his nature which was one in its manifold striving to create the beauty which it yearned to realize. The poems gave their harnessed utterance to the same endeavor which the mightier plastic genius of the man was embodying in sculpture and painting. St. Peter's dome was its last realization. Through all his arts, though in architecture least articulately, he sought to express the forms of visible beauty. Its high-

[33] No. 48 (Frey), and see 49.
[34] No. 147 (Frey).

est type was the human form, the veritable human body stripped of obscuring accessories and distractions.

The instincts of his dynamic nature turned to the masculine rather than the feminine form; and in the masculine achieved its grandest triumphs: the *Adam* of the Sistine ceiling is incomparably more beautiful than the *Eve:* though one may stand astounded before the feminine figure of *Night* in the Medici Chapel. But the sheer decorative idealized athletic figures on the painted beams of the Sistine ceiling are all male. No man before or since ever drew forth such import and beauty from the trunk and limbs of man. Yet when the figure and situation warranted, he gave proportionate emphasis to the human visage, as the crowning and most complex and subtle feature of the human form.

None had ever shown such knowledge of the human form; and no man's work approached such miracles of expressive tension and repose. Michelangelo studied and followed nature, the natural body; and then along the principles of its organic structure he passed beyond his source, surpassed his teacher. He is the grand exponent of Leonardo's pregnant words, the artist disputes and vies with nature, that his work may present further beauties and perfections through following the principles and suggestions of the natural world.

The work of no other artist has ever represented such enormous effort; and one may doubt whether the work of any other artist has surpassed it in achievement. The vocabularies of critics have been drained bare in describing these stupendous creations of sculpture and painting, or in criticising their alleged exaggerations and possibly baneful effect upon the following time. The effect may be condoned for the sake of the achievement! There is no call here to go beyond the works themselves or add to the discussion of them. The *Pietà,* the Sistine Ceiling, those recumbent demi-gods of pain on the Medici tombs, the statues in the niches over them, the Slaves in the Louvre, the *Moses* in S. Pietro in Vincoli, are exhaustless in beauty and import. They are like the Bible, like Shakespeare, like the Phidian Parthenon or the Cathedral of Chartres. Each thoughtful person shall appreciate and draw from them according to his understanding; and a residue will still be there! They were the self-expression of a daemonic artist.

It seems absurd to end this chapter without any reference to Venetian painting, which was so utterly expressive of the whole esthetic soul of Venice. The Venetian soul cast itself upon painting and color. Painting, colored decoration, was their art, their art *par excellence,* almost their sole and single art. Was this due to their affinity with the Byzantine East, where art was color rather than salient modelling? Was it due to their own atmosphere and sea and sunset? Who knows? The fact remained: Venice was all for painting. Her sculpture was insignificant, her poetry a blank.

But the field becomes too vast. Venetian painting is better to look at, and surrender one's self to, than to read and write about. All painting is primarily to be seen; but Venetian painting is somewhat more altogether to be seen rather than reflected on. Is not this true of Titian? He loved the naked body quite as dearly as did Michelangelo, and painted its flesh, its feminine color far more exquisitely. But Michelangelo's bodies, not Titian's, are meet for thought and reflection. The glories of the Venetian master's color surpassed all the coloring of Florence and of Rome; while the blander harmonies of his composition equalled Raphael's achievement. And he was a grand inaugurator of landscape painting.

And what like things might be said of *his* master Giorgione? And of Veronese? And what more like things, and other things besides, of that last Venetian Titan of a painter, Tintoretto, who seems to hurl his compositions on the canvas, miracles of light and dark. Nevertheless, there is too much to write about, or it is all better to be seen.

BOOK II

ERASMUS AND LUTHER

CHAPTER VI

SCHOLARSHIP IN GERMANY AND THE NETHERLANDS

WHETHER in her times of mental squalor or her times of brilliancy, Italy was reminiscent of her past and sensitive to its influence. Classic literature and art were for her an expression of a greater pagan manhood, once hers and still having silent part in whatever her people might achieve. It was natural that a renewed and broader reading of the Classics and a more facile imitation of the ancient buildings and the ancient sculptures should be the chief element in her intellectual and catholic progress in the fourteenth and following centuries.

But the Roman past was not the source of all intellectual elements in the North. The northern peoples had their own potent antecedents. They were not the direct descendants of the Romans, but, at most, spiritual collaterals with other strains of blood. Their past had been monastic and feudal, rather than secular and urban. Monasticism had scant sympathy for the classics, and feudalism had developed a taste for turbulent epics and adventurous romance. The North had looked on the classics as a store of knowledge; and northern intellectual energies, focussing at last in the University of Paris, devoted themselves to a most unhumanistic exploitation of ancient philosophy in scholasticism and mediaeval science, false or true. Christianity itself as understood and developed or corrupted in the North had but loose kinship with the Latin paganism which underlay the religiousness of Italy. The northern religion held Celtic and Teutonic heathen elements, unhumanistic and unmalleable. It proved more unyielding to the influence of pagan humanism than the Christianity of Italy.

Nevertheless, the Latin language and the great works composed in it had been the vehicle of educational discipline in France and Germany and England. And in those countries as well as in Italy, the classics offered human wisdom and a broad consideration of life to whoever might read and partially understand them.

Accordingly when, under suggestions from the passionate classical revival in Italy, the peoples of the north turned to the classics with a renewed and deeper zeal, their purpose was not confined to improvement in education and Latinity. The intentions and desires of the northern humanists were as broad as their own natures, and their natures were developing with the study of this humanizing literature. Their pursuits were an expression of their wish for a more humane, a more rational and reasonable, treatment of life. Clearly the growing interest in the classics and the broadening of the purpose of their study was part of the general intellectual and social development, and a moving factor in the same.

The whole matter is illustrated by the career and function and effect of the northern apostle of humanism and reasonableness, Desiderius Erasmus. Since all classes in the north were keenly interested in their religion, the labors of Erasmus were naturally directed to the scholarly study of the New Testament and the Church Fathers as well as to a better understanding of the pagan classics. What is true of the great Erasmus is true of northern scholars before him as well as those who felt his influence. And with them, as with their leader, classical studies were part of a more instructed appreciation of what was rational, and of what was irrational, absurd or intolerable, not merely in social life but in religious doctrine and practice. Humanism became an early factor in the coming religious revolution, from which it was destined later to part company in Germany and France and England.

In the Low Countries, where Erasmus was a native, as well as in the Germany educationally affiliated with them, there had been educational and intellectual progress in the fourteenth century. Stimulus usually would come, or seem to come, from some person gifted with energy, vision, or initiative, above his fellows. Toward the close of the century an influence making for the diffusion of a better education sprang from Gerard Groot, founder of the *Brothers of the Common Life* at his home city of Deventer, in the northeastern part of what now is Holland. He had been a vigorous preacher against the lusts of the clergy; and it was a simple teaching and preaching fraternity that he founded, composed of men who inclined toward evangelical piety, yet were obedient to the Church, and had no revolutionary aims. They were not bound by monastic vows; they taught the poor *gratis,* and preached in the vernacular, urging those who could not read Latin to read the Bible in their own tongue. On the other hand, they advocated frequent reference to the original texts in order to correct errors in the Vulgate. They spoke little of dogmas in their sermons.

One senses a certain freedom of the spirit among these Brethren, with a perception of the religious and educational elements which soon were to be recognized as cardinal. One also sees in them a tendency toward a purer Gospel faith, and an effort to better the lives of clergy and laity. Groot died in 1384, still in the prime of life. Able coadjutors remained; and Deventer became the home of pious and sensible education. The Brethren extended their labors, and opened schools at many places in the Low Countries, the influence of which reached the neighboring parts of Germany. These schools attracted capable teachers and pupils, and seemed to develop the talents both of those who taught and those who studied in them. The numbers were great, and the list of names is impressive. Thomas à Kempis, born near Cologne, was one of the Brethren; and Nicholas of Cusa, whose intellectual power was unequalled in his time, studied at Deventer.

Rudolf Agricola touched this circle, and Hegius was very part of it. The former, a Frisian, born in 1442, studied at Deventer and Louvain, and then spent several years in Italy completing his classical equipment. Returning to Germany, he devoted himself to translating the old German chronicles and diffusing a knowledge of the classics. He did not fail in Christian piety, and held to the idea that all learning should serve the Faith. He died in 1485.

Of about the same age as Agricola was the Westphalian Hegius, who chose to call himself his pupil and became Deventer's greatest schoolmaster. He had been a pupil with the Brethren, and in middle life fixed himself at Deventer, where he taught from 1475 until his death in 1498. A man of unquestioned piety, he was also a scholar and knew Greek. He improved the methods of teaching, replaced the old text books by better ones, and made a study of the classics the centre of his curriculum. Pupils came to him from near and far, till his school numbered above two thousand. His crown of praise lay in the names of those who called him master. Erasmus was among them.

We turn from the Brethren and their pupils to a famous German educator who in no way belonged to them, the Alsatian Wimpheling. Born in 1450, he first studied at Freiburg, where the old *Doctrinale* was his grammar. Next at Erfurt, where he touched the new humanism, but only to be drawn back to Heidelberg, whose university was still threshing the old scholastic straw and little else. Disgusted with the Canon Law, to which he had been destined, he felt various currents drawing him to *belles lettres* and versemaking, to public questions, and to religion, for he too was looking for salvation. He became a bachelor of Theology in 1483; but instead of following that vocation, turned to teaching the sadly needed humanities at Heidelberg. The futility of the dispute as to universals became with him a favorite topic of discourse. Later in life, he went to Strassburg, and there rather vainly undertook to establish better schools. He did not die till 1528. His life and somewhat confused labors at least evince serious endeavors for a better scheme of education, for the diffusion of liberal knowledge, and a reform of the morals of the clergy. The writings of this occasionally bitter disputant were effective and popular. They laid bare the absurdities of current ways of education, and presented rational methods of teaching the ancient languages, and training the intelligence and character of pupils.

The lives of these men covered the period of the invention of printing, or more specifically speaking, of the art of casting metal type. Wimpheling said truthfully that the Germans could so justly pride themselves over no other invention of the mind. From the year 1462, when the secret process was divulged at Maintz, presses were established rapidly through Germany, and in Italy and France. Printing was hailed as a portentous event, for good or evil. It was indeed the main title of the Germans to intellectual fame. They might respect themselves for the improvement of their education and their progress in classical studies; yet so far there was small matter in one or the other to attract the praise or attention of other peoples, Italians, French, English or Lowlanders. The historian who is not a German will trace without enthusiism the advent and progress of the new waves of humanism. "Educators of Germany," arose, a title given to Rabanus Maurus in the ninth century, and now to be shared by Wimpheling with the younger man, Melanchthon, and perhaps others. But these educators of Germany were not like the Italian humanists, educators of the world. The one man who rightly won a towering fame was not a German, but Erasmus of Rotterdam.

The classics had not been left unread in mediaeval Germany, but the taste of the thirteenth and fourteenth centuries turned to a scholastic exploitation of Aristotelian logic and metaphysics, with some incursions into the antique field of physical science. The renewed interest in the classics, appearing here and there in the fifteenth century, usually carried a lively detestation of the methods and topics of scholasticism, which still occupied the universities. But this reaction did not spring from any such natural disposition toward antique humanism as marked the Italian mind. There had been no substratum of antique civilization in Germany, a land never subjected to the transforming discipline of the imperial Roman order.

The German past had been that of Teutonic barbarism, with its hard heathen religion. Next, Germany became feudal and monastic, still unsuited to the urban antique humanism. What city life there was remained dull and uninstructed far into the fifteenth century. Moreover, although the Germans showed few signs of becoming a nation, they had attained a stubborn racial character, which would hardly yield itself to alien moulds. They had, to be sure, been ready to accept literary and social fashions, for example from the French side of the Rhine; but they had sturdily remained Germans; and now were to prove again in the fifteenth and sixteenth centuries that they could take up the study of Latin and Greek literature, and interest themselves in the Italian humanism, without imperilling their German natures. It held true as a corollary that they would use the new knowledge according to their own convictions and abiding interests. German scholars did not become humanists after the Italian fashion, bent solely upon absorbing the classics; but rather they sought to apply the new knowledge to the conditions of life in Germany and the problems of the approaching religious upheaval. Least of all, did German scholarship attempt an artistic or creative imitation of the classics, as the Italians did; but earnestly studied the Greek and Latin languages and endeavored to obtain a solid understanding of their literatures.

Stimulus and suggestion came from Italy. For example, the chancellor of the Emperor Karl IV, Johann von Neumarkt, who flourished between 1350 and 1375, drew an inflated inspiration from Petrarch. In the next generation, another German thinks Salutato the wonder of scholars, and seeks his acquaintance in Florence. Soon the Emperor Sigismund was to feel a lively interest in the literature, the history, the ruins of antiquity, and become a patron of Italian humanists. Then incitement to antique studies came from Italy in the person of Aeneas Silvius, ardent humanist, clever diplomat, future cardinal, and at last Pope.[1] He did his best to infuse a love of

[1] Aeneas Silvius Piccolomini was born near Sienna in 1405. He went

letters into these northern swine, as he deemed them; but the result fell short of his wishes. His race and personality roused distrust in the German bosom. We see the antipathy toward him concentrate in Gregor Heimburg, jurist and statesman, and most emphatic German, whom Aeneas by no blandishment could win either to his policy or his friendship. This able speaker professed to despise the artifices of rhetoric and all Italianate imitation of the ancients.

Study of the classics did not shake the piety of German students in the fifteenth century, whose names and particular accomplishments need not be catalogued. An earlier generation was succeeded by those born in decades when the German people were entering a period of religious and political conflict. These younger men were affected by the controversies of the time, and some of them caught by its whirlwinds. Naturally they used their faculties and inclined the fruit of their studies to timely ends.

One may make one's approach to the years of larger conflict through the achievements and troubles of the most distinguished German scholar of his time, Johann Reuchlin.[2] Born in Pforzheim, the gate of the Black Forest, in 1455, he studied for a while at Freiburg, and then made his way to Paris, where he learned some Greek. He went next to Basel and then to Paris again, to learn more Greek. But having chosen jurisprudence as his profession, he turned his steps to Orleans. He had become a teacher now, of Latin and Greek, and as such went to Tübingen at the close of the year 1481. There the patronage of the great came upon him, and within a few months he was taken to Italy by the Count of Würtemberg. So he made the acquaintance of Italian humanists, and impressed them with his Greek. It was, however, on a later Italian journey that he met Pico della Miran-

to the Council of Basel in 1432; and afterwards was much at Vienna and elsewhere in Germany. He became Pope Pius II in 1458, and died in 1464.

[2] See L. Geiger, *Johann Reuchlin,* (Leipsic 1871).

dola. This may have inspired him to take up the study of Hebrew and the Cabbala, as he did under the guidance of learned Jews. Reuchlin moved with people of station: as a man, as a publicist, as a scholar, he was honored by all. The list of his writings opens with a brief Latin Dictionary, produced at the age of twenty. In course of time, he wrote Latin verses and comedies, some of the last apparently in imitation of a French model. He made Latin translations from the Greek; Homer's *Battle of the Frogs and Mice* and some treatises of Athanasius were among them, and denote his range.

All this was respectable. But Reuchlin's service to scholarship was his work in Hebrew. His *Rudamenta hebraica* laid the foundations of its study among the Germans. He did not stop, however, with scholarly and unquestionably meritorious work upon the languages; but chose to follow the venturesome Pico into the caves of the Cabbala, which held nostrums of blessedness not found so clearly in the Old Testament. Like Pico he took from it according to his taste. Rejecting its sorcery and astrology, he made his own its equally wonderful wisdom, which linked man with his beatitude. The "wonder working word" he made the title of his book, *De Verbo mirifico*. This was followed by further seductive exposition in his *De Arte Cabalistica;* which appeared in 1517, when Luther was already holding forth other matters!

Troubles fell on Reuchlin. The Vulgate was the authoritative sacred vehicle of truth; and to many churchmen Hebrew and Greek scholarship, with its appeal to the original texts, was irritating and disturbing. So Erasmus learned when he had edited the Greek New Testament, and so Reuchlin might learn from the fortunes of his Hebrew grammar. Some people likewise looked askance on his ponderous flirtation with the Cabbala. Such were the suspect fringes of his great repute, when partly through the force of circumstances, and partly through his self-respect, he became the centre of a struggle for the freedom of scholarship. A preposterous converted Jew named Pfeffercorn, with malignant eagerness to convert his stiffnecked people, obtained a decree from the Emperor Maximilian authorizing him to find and destroy those Jewish books which were hostile to the Christian faith. He was supported by the Dominicans of the Cologne university. A bitter and most elaborate and complicated controversy followed. The universities gave their opinions. Reuchlin was drawn in, and showed himself the champion of the Jewish books; for he held the cause of scholarship, as well as true religion, to be involved. The Dominicans brought charges of heresy against him and his writings. The cause, tried once and again in Germany, was decided there in Reuchlin's favor; and the Dominicans appealed to Rome, where, after years, a halting decision was rendered. That did not end it. The matter was still fought out in Germany, and even in other lands. The scholar humanists were Reuchlin's partisans, with many a good reactionary on the other side. A few years before Reuchlin's death, his grandnephew Philip Melanchthon, a prodigy of precocious scholarship, was called to Wittenberg, and the great uncle sent him with his blessing. The Lutheran revolt was already moving briskly with great noise. The venerable Reuchlin, like many another humanist of his generation, drew back from it and died within the bosom of the church.

If Reuchlin's cause was won, it was won by wit and laughter, quite as much as by more solemn means. Wit's best contribution to the fray was from the humanists of Erfurt, aided by the redoubtable Ulrich von Hutten. It was a vicious kind of confetti, these *Epistolae Obscurorum Virorum,* written in the funniest hog-Latin. The fun carries sheer across the centuries, and stirs to laughter yet. The Cologne Dominicans could never pick these burrs out of their hides.[3]

A leader of the Erfurt humanists was one Konrad Mut, called Mutianus Rufus, or, less euphoniously, the redhaired. Though not shown to have contributed to the *Letters of the Obscure,* he wrote many of his own,

[3] There is an admirable edition of the *Epistolae Obscurorum Virorum,* with introduction and English translation by F. G. Stokes (London 1909).

through which he remains noticeable, if not notable. He will answer for a closing example of the German humanist of Erasmus's generation.

Born at Homberg in 1471, he too studied under Hegius at Deventer. He came to Erfurt in 1486 and is found teaching there in 1492. Three years later he set out for Italy, travelled through its cities and listened to the humanists, Pico and Ficino among others. He did not return to Germany till 1502. He tried official life, abandoned it, and built himself a little house in Gotha, near the Cathedral. Inscribing *Beata Tranquillitas* upon the door in golden letters, he settled himself within, and lived there till his death in 1526.

Mutianus was a cultivated man, devoted to carrying out his tastes. The classics were his chief love, as scholasticism, according to the humanistic convention, was his abomination. He had a good knowledge of the Civil Law, and held, with the new school of jurists, that one should study the *Corpus Juris* itself, and not the commentators. He was not unread in medicine and Pliny; had a mild belief in astrology, but rejected magic.

Naturally he was a partisan of Reuchlin. But Erasmus was his idol, in scholarship and in attitude toward life. He saw in him the restorer of theology and the font from which Œcolampadius, Luther, and Melanchthon drew.[4] This was the view of many. As a follower of Erasmus, Mutianus took a rational or rationalistic view of religion, going a little further than his model, or at all events expressing thoughts which Erasmus would have disavowed. Indeed he strikes us as one of those paganizers whom Erasmus disapproved in his *Ciceronianus*.[5] One God or Goddess, *Natura,* he would adore under many names or manifestations — *nomina* or *numina.* They included the old Pantheon, to which Moses and Christ should be added. "When I say Jupiter, I mean Christ and the true God." Of course, Muti-

[4] As in Epistle to Lang, (1520) printed p. 641 of C. Krause, *Briefwechsel des Mutianus Rufus* (Kassel, 1885): with a full introduction.
[5] See post, chap. VII.

anus finds a Christianity before Christ, whose humanity he regarded merely as a semblance. "The true Christ is soul and spirit, not to be handled with the hands." So he interpreted Christianity loosely and easily, discarding, for example, the resurrection of the body. His wit hovered on the edge of irreverence.

This man of scholarly habit, who disliked tumult as much as Erasmus did, drew back from Luther, of whom at first he approved. He preferred books and a rational life; and like Erasmus, he found himself rather solitary in his closing years, having declined the conflict in which his countrymen were engaged. Yet he held himself a good German, read books in his native tongue and professed a high regard for at least the possibilities of German culture.

So we are brought back to the fact that the German humanists were emphatically Germans; they held themselves as German patriots, and evinced not infrequently an active interest in the history and literature of Germany. Kaiser Max set the fashion, and German princes imitated his patronage of studies, which threw light on the German past and enhanced the Fatherland's repute. Here humanist patricians, leaders in their cities, like Wilibald Pirckheimer of Nuremberg or Conrad Peutinger of Augsburg, vied with scholars of private station, like Celtis or Beatus Rhenanus. Or one may name Trithemius, abbot of Sponheim near Kreuznach, reformer of his Order, and founder of something like a learned Academy. He was perhaps the first to outline a history of German literature. A different and more tempestuous German patriot will be found in Ulrich von Hutten, who will cry aloud for mention when we come to speak of the German hatred of the Italian papacy.

Before leaving Germany proper, one notes the hostility of Cologne and other universities to the newer better learning. This fact was by no means peculiar to Germany. The hostility of the established faculties at Louvain will drive Erasmus to abandon his attempt to establish there a college for the study of Greek, Hebrew and

Latin. In France, the attitude of the Sorbonne, that is, the theological faculty of the University of Paris, was even more malignantly reactionary. As the fifteenth century passes into the sixteenth, the Sorbonne became suspicious of the slightest change in institution or opinion, and was quick to crush any attempt for the reform of education or the advancement of learning. Rightly they felt that light from any side might imperil their position. Many a French scholar sought a freer air in the large provincial cities like Lyons, or found it at the court of Margaret of Navarre.[6] Likewise in Germany learning was cultivated by individual scholars apart from universities, or in liberal minded circles in the great commercial cities of Strassburg, Augsburg or Nuremberg. The routes of commerce brought the good things of the spirit too, and the wealth of the leading burghers was turned to the patronage of art and letters.

Looking now more particularly to the Netherlands, one notes the general establishment of printing presses between the years 1473 and 1491. As in Germany so in the Netherlands, the diffusion of knowledge, and especially of the new humanism, was facilitated and encouraged through the new art of printing. Deventer was among the first to have its press (1476). And with Deventer and the Brethren of the Common Life one recalls that the currents of school education overran political boundaries.

Yet there was a difference between German and Netherland scholars, and between the purposes to which they applied their culture. The Germans, as remarked, were enthusiastic, sometimes rampant, Germans; the scholars of the Low Countries had no corresponding passion. Theirs was not a great self-conscious country, feeling its racehood perhaps the more acutely through despair of political union. The Netherlands had no such hope. This little country had been a battle ground for rival potentates whose homes were elsewhere; politically it

[6] See post, chaps. XII and XVI.

seemed doomed to be an appanage of Burgundy, of Austria, of Spain. It had no national tongue; but hung divided between Dutch, Flemish and French. Territorial pride and intellectual energy did not unite in the creation of a national literature. The country was too small; its people too few. It was a highway of commerce and ideas; the people had industrial and commercial aptitude; their cities were as factories and marts, open to the traffic of the world. Thought and scholarship were not impressed with local aims or national ambitions, nor provincialized through patriotism. Till persecution came, there was nothing to prevent acceptance of whatever might present universal human interest and validity.[7]

It may be remarked that an advance in sacred studies usually accompanied the progress of classical scholarship. There were efforts in the Middle Ages to reach a closer understanding of the Scriptures than could be had from the Vulgate, which a few scholars dared to say was sometimes faulty in its renderings. To this end at Cambridge in the thirteenth century, Robert Grosseteste and Roger Bacon planned and labored to revive a knowledge of Hebrew and of Greek.[8] The result of their labors did not perish, but continued, trickling in hidden currents, which now and then rose to the surface in the work of some man we know. Such a one was Nicholas of Lyra in the diocese of Evreux, where he was born toward the close of the thirteenth century. He became a Franciscan monk, and died about the middle of the next century. He acquired a considerable knowledge of both Greek and Hebrew and was a good Biblical scholar, writing brief commentaries upon the Scriptures, and a much needed work distinguishing the canonical from the Apocryphal books. As a commentator his chief and rather individual merit was that he tried to ascertain the actual meaning of the text, and did not abandon himself to the conventional allegorical interpretations.[9]

[7] Cf. H. Pirenne, *Histoire de Belgique,* t. III. pp. 285 sqq. (1907).
[8] See *The Mediaeval Mind,* chap. XXXI.
[9] See Altmeyer, *Les Précurseurs de la Réforme aux Pays-Bas,* vol. I.

In Italy the fifteenth century brought a reviving interest in Christian letters, especially in the works of the great fourth and fifth century doctors. Even earlier Christian writings occasionally appear in the large libraries, as that of Pope Nicholas V. (1447–55) and that of Niccolo Niccoli, the Florentine, who died in 1437. Christian letters owed much to the labors of Niccolo's friend, Ambrogio Traversari, both as a collector of manuscripts, and as a painful translator from the Greek.[10] Lorenzo Valla, most critical of Italian scholars, exposer of the forgery of the "Donation of Constantine," was a younger contemporary of these men. In the next generation comes the Florentine, Ficino, who lectured upon Paul as well as Plato, and whose influence may have suggested the famous lectures which were given at Oxford about the year 1500 by Colet, Dean of St. Paul's, a liberal and intelligent Christian scholar, a friend of Thomas More and Erasmus. All three were bent upon applying the resources of the new scholarship to the interpretation of Christian documents, and their best intelligence to an understanding of the faith. Their friends and admirers, especially those of Erasmus, were so great in number and so conspicuous in attainments and influence, as to constitute a party in favor of a rational and considerably reformed Catholic religion. Colet and More will come before us hereafter. We turn now to Erasmus who presents the culmination of this revival of Christian scholarship in the North, and a good deal besides.

pp. 99–101 (The Hague, 1886). I wish to express my indebtedness to the admirable chapter entitled "The Christian Renaissance" by M. R. James, in vol. I. of *The Cambridge Modern History*. Cf. also P. Wernle, *Die Renaissance des Christentums im 16. Jahrhundert* (1904).

[10] Cf. ante chap. II.

CHAPTER VII

DESIDERIUS ERASMUS, THE NORTHERN APOSTLE OF LETTERS AND REASONABLENESS

ERASMUS was the most influential man of letters of his time and the most catholic in the scope of his pursuits. He was the universal humanist, not merely following the profession of humane letters but inculcating their lessons of reasonableness in his writings and his life. And as he exemplified the northern tendency toward erudition and at the same time cultivated the elegances of composition as aptly as any Italian, he combined the intellectual characteristics noticeable on opposite sides of the Alps.

He happened to be born in Holland,[1] which was one reason why he was an unattached citizen of the world — the world of letters. Many of his later years were passed at Basel, where he died in 1536. Basel was a chief city in a small country divided in race and language, religion and politics. Erasmus was attracted by the absence of national obsessions, as well as by the facilities afforded there for the printing of his books. But he felt at home wherever he was comfortable, had the food and wine which suited him, found congenial friends, was let alone to work, and left unmolested by religious strife. Of uncertain health and delicate physique, he required a considerable income for his comfort; and was importunate and industrious in obtaining it. He insisted upon freedom of movement and occupation; ties and obligations,

[1] The year was 1466. The facts of Erasmus's life as far as known, and a little further, may be left to the numerous biographies, and introductions to his various works. P. S. Allen's *Age of Erasmus* is a summary by one whose knowledge of Erasmus's life and letters is unequalled. Several volumes of Allen's edition of the letters have appeared. I should also refer to F. M. Nichol's *Epistles of Erasmus,* 2 vols. in translations (Longmans 1901) and E. Emerton's *Life of Erasmus,* (New York, Putnams, 1899).

such as regular teaching at a university, were intolerable to him. He belonged to no country, was untouched by national prejudices, hates, or aspirations, social, political, or religious. Void of racial sympathy and antipathy, detesting partisanship, except that making for intellectual enlightenment, he would link himself to no revolutionary movement nor to the reactionary powers seeking to suppress it. The one or the other might imperil the advance of letters and true piety. Reckoning wrongly with the power, even the power of advance, which lies in passionate rejection, he held to the futile hope of purifying and rationalizing Catholicism, without breaking its unity. Yet his efforts to incorporate in religion the spirit and certified results of the best scholarship, bore fruit. Of course he did not realize that the will to remake the Church represented the most intense phase of the northern desire for truth, a desire heated by antagonism to Rome and empassioned with yearning for unmediated union with the saving grace of God.

The moving sincerities of Erasmus, and the motives of his conduct, appear in the very things in which he was thought a dissembler. His was a rational and penetrating intelligence; a strong and educated common sense. He had the gift of seeing the point, the veritable principle: for example, that virtue lies in good intent and corresponding conduct, and not in the letter of the indifferent and superstitious observance. He saw the lack of essential connection between such observance and spiritual betterment. If this had been perceived by men before him, from the time when Isaiah reported that Jehovah would have righteousness and not sacrifice, nevertheless Erasmus saw for himself, with a renewed and timely insight, the silliness and brutishness of the current religious and social life. He would apply an informed intelligence to the improvement of education, the betterment of society, the purification of religion. As the fanatic impulse was not his, he had no wish to destroy whatever might be harmlessly retained in the established order of religion, government, or daily living. Enlightenment based on scholarship was his aim for himself and for society. In religion, as in secular culture, this pious, but not extravagantly religious, man loved the truth that was definite and tangible, and had no taste for the mystic or metaphysical. The ethical element appealed to him more than the theological. He wished to establish and publish the most authentic Christian record, which for him set forth the surest religious truth. Hence he spent a good part of his life and strength in editing the texts of Holy Scripture and the accredited Fathers of the Church.

At the same time Erasmus was always a wit, a litterateur, a professional author of prodigious facility and artistic temperament. He was drawn to the artistically admirable in life as well as literature. He could not complacently endure physical discomforts, or the incongruous or disagreeable in his relations with other men. With him the pressing trouble was apt to give shape and color to a situation, which he might then set forth plausibly and even self-deceptively, so as to accredit himself, dispel his annoyance, or present a means of escape. Not infrequently he sees his relations to other men as he would have them, and as he thought they should be. His supple epistolary faculty lent itself to the subconscious, or sometimes conscious, manipulation of fact. Just as in his youth he had been addicted to the over-expression of friendship; which is one way of idealizing actual relationships and apprehending them as they should preciously be, but not quite as they are, and certainly not as they endure.

This scholar-artist passed three years in Italy when Leonardo, Michelangelo, and Raphael were at their zenith; his own portrait was painted many times by the greatest of German painters. He was himself an observer of *moeurs*. Yet as with many supremely bookish people, his writings show small interest in art outside of literature. Even in literature, he had little taste for poetry. He was not gifted with the emotionally impelled imagination of the poetic faculty. His imagination was entirely rational. Even in religion he apprehended rationally, not with quick intuitions; and entertained no feelings, experiences, convictions, which he could not rationally explain and justify.

There is no need to worry because the letters of Erasmus show flaws of character, shared with many other humanists: readiness to flatter for money, querulous fault-finding, a tendency to abuse those whom he had unsuccessfully adulated. Why insist upon staunchness of character in a man of letters, who is a lover of learning and rational enlightenment, and a sincere commender of sensible and pious conduct? Erasmus's strength lay in the genius which responded to these desires, and boldly enough displayed itself in the witty and purposeful presentation of the ridiculous and the rational, the degraded and the intelligent, and from a like point of view, the evil and the good. There was enough strength of character in his will, which kept him free to pursue his scholar-quest of knowledge, even truth, and through a long life, set it forth in books.

One may say that the central purpose of the life and labors of Erasmus was to get an education, and enable others to obtain one. To this end, the first step, taken or forced upon him in his youth, was an acquaintance with the current methods and knowledge included in the curriculum of elementary and university teaching. He absorbed this discipline with a conscious acceptance of some of its principles, and an irritated rejection of others. Those processes of acceptance and rejection included religious as well as secular education. They extended through Erasmus's long apprentice years, and, in the nature of things, never were concluded. On such foundations he built the higher stages of his education, which led on through improving the educational apparatus of his early years, through acquiring further knowledge, and through presenting with novel insight whatever he had learned.

Judged by Erasmus's standards, the schools of the closing fifteenth century were backward in methods and textbooks. The barbarous *Graecismus* of the twelfth century was dictated to Erasmus at Deventer. A rather better grammar, likewise metrical, the *Doctrinale* of Alexander de Ville-Dieu, was still in universal use. The scholarly bent of the masters of Deventer seems not to have affected the routine of the school. Erasmus studied under them from his eleventh to his eighteenth year. He next spent two years at the school of the Brethren of the Common Life at Bois-le-Duc; and then, impelled by circumstances, he entered as a novice the house of the Augustinian canons at Stein, near Gouda, where he remained for seven or eight years, and took the vows. Later, he inveighed against the barbarous and monkish education of this period of his life. Yet at Stein he studied the Latin classics and occupied himself fruitfully with the *Elegantiae* of Valla, making an epitome of it. He could have found no better compend of the newer classical scholarship.

Erasmus had progressed notably in learning by the year 1493, when at the age of twenty-seven he was taken from Stein by the Bishop of Cambrai, and two years afterwards sent to study theology at Paris, where he was entered in the malodorous College of Montaigu. His contempt deepened for the "Scotists," and for scholastic philosophy which they seemed to symbolize. So he cultivated the classics as best he might, and also taught. He thus fell in with a number of Englishmen, among them his pupil-patron, Lord Mountjoy, whom he accompanied to England in 1499, where he became the friend of Thomas More and John Colet, to the lasting pleasure and advantage of the three. At Oxford, Colet suggested lectures on the Old Testament, to supplement those novel discourses on the Epistles of Paul with which he was then stirring the University.[2] Erasmus's antipathy to current scholastic ways of treating Scripture needed no goad. But he became acutely conscious of the need of Greek for one who would be a New Testament scholar. As Oxford possessed little Greek, he returned to Paris to resume its study.

[2] Post, chapter XVIII.

Greek concluded the predominantly acquisitive stage of Erasmus's education. He studied it without instructors or the modern apparatus of dictionary and grammar. By the year 1506, when he was no longer young, he had made such progress as to embolden him afterwards to assert that he learned nothing from his sojourn in Italy, which extended from that year to 1509. There was a Frenchman, named Budé, who could still have taught him, and doubtless did, since the two became frequent correspondents, if not friends. As the years increased Erasmus's fame, he did not evince a genial spirit towards his great rival for the primacy of European scholarship.

The education of Erasmus, as with all intelligent people, continued through his life. The acquisitive phases were always interwoven with his critical development and conscious rejection of much that he had previously been taught. To these educational processes of learning, criticism and rejection, were joined his more productive activities, which also were to be educational for himself as for the student world. These extended back into his acquisitive period, and on through his entire life.

This most effective educator of northern Europe spent little time teaching in universities. In consequence his influence, his effect, was tenfold greater. Unhampered and undulled, he gave his entire strength to scholarship and the making of books which were of enormous educational effect. In them one can follow — if one has sufficient leisure! — the cumulative self-expression of the author. They are of endless bulk, ten large folios in the Leyden edition. Had Erasmus written less, he might be more read today. But that would signify little. His writings are not needed now; they tell us mostly things we either know or have forgotten to our advantage. But they were needed in their time, and were found neither too many nor too long. They were serviceable to the people of Germany and France and England in the sixteenth century, and contained much matter which it was well at that time to bring to men's attention.

Among the formal educational treatises of Erasmus, the *De Ratione Studii,*[3] written in 1511 at Colet's request, presents a plan for imparting to the pupil something of the wisdom of the Ancients, which embraced all knowledge: " omnis fere rerum scientia a Graecis auctoribus petenda est "; — one need not be surprised at mediaeval echoes in Erasmus's writings.[4] The teacher, says he, should learn the contents of the classics and arrange their matter in his note books, that he may impart it methodically. If he lacks a full library, he will find Pliny most rich in information, and next to him Macrobius, Aulus Gellius and Athenaeus. But he must " seek the *fontes ipsos,* to wit, the old Greeks. Plato best teaches philosophy, and Aristotle, and his disciple Theophrastus, and Plotinus, made up of them both. In Christian theology none is better than Origen, none more subtil than Chrysostom, none holier than Basil." The Latin Fathers Ambrose and Jerome are recommended, and other authors for various reasons.

Erasmus was well on in his sixties when he wrote an educational tract which laid intelligent stress on the need of beginning the boy's education very early, and under the most competent masters, who should employ methods of gentleness and understanding, rather than those of violence and fear. This was the *De pueris ad virtutem ac literas liberaliter instituendis idque protinus a nativitate.*[5]

[3] Leyden edition of Erasmus's *Opera,* Tome I, fo. 521–530. I have used to advantage W. H. Woodward's *Desiderius Erasmus concerning the aim and method of Education* (Cambridge 1904), which also gives a translation of this treatise and the *De Pueris Instituendis.* I cannot but think that Prof. Woodward might have made his translations somewhat closer to Erasmus's language, and have been less free in the use of modern educational phrases, which represent concepts not current in the sixteenth century.

[4] Sometimes he uses exactly the mediaeval phrase, as in his letter dedicating the first edition of the *Adagia* to Lord Mountjoy: "Accordingly, laying aside all serious labors, and indulging in a more dainty kind of study, I strolled through the gardens provided by various authors, culling as I went the adages most remarkable for their antiquity and excellence, like so many flowers of various sorts, of which I have made a nosegay." F. M. Nichol's translation.

[5] Published in 1529,—Leyden Ed. I, fo. 489–516. Translated by Woodward.

One notes the last words of the title — "from their very birth." An uneducated man is not a *man; institutio* or training is more important than *natura.* Here man differs from the dumb animals,

"whose protection nature has set in their inborn faculties; but since divine providence has bestowed the power of reason on man alone, it has left the chief share to training (Efficax res est natura, sed hanc vincit efficacior institutio). When nature gave thee a son, she delivered nothing but a *rudem massam.* It is for thee to impress the best character upon this submissive plastic material. If thou art remiss, thou wilt have a wild beast, but if vigilant, a divinity."

This treatise is not all wisdom. Erasmus gives, apparently from his favorite Pliny, plenty of absurd examples of what man may learn from brutes. And he says that boyhood's proneness to depravity, which so puzzled the ancients, is due to Adam's sin. But one will not ignore the fault of bad early training, he adds, perhaps with a submerged smile. He is clear as to the abomination of spoiling a child by indulgence and bad example; and shows how foolish it is to leave youth to acquire by experience such practical knowledge as might properly be taught.

For the rest, the treatise intelligently anticipates many of the demands of modern enlightenment touching juvenile education; for example the need to consider the disposition and faculties of each child. As a parent should instil in his child reverence and love, rather than fear, so in the boy's education, intelligent kindness and encouragement, not flogging, are the means to be employed. The very best and most scholarly men should be selected for schoolmasters. There is no more important function. A teacher should not be too old; indeed he should become a boy again, that he may be loved by the boy. If he understands boy nature he will not treat his pupil like an uneducated little old man.

Erasmus speaks of suitable primary studies. Among them is language, which may be taught through pleasant fables, and by bringing the boy up among good talkers.

There are hints for modern kindergartens, summed up in the recognition of the need to adapt the teaching to the child's nature. The closing paragraphs criticise the methods then pursued, and deride the still more wretched instruction of Erasmus's boyhood, when he learned Latin grammar through the repetition of absurd distiches, and wasted precious time in the labyrinth of dialectic. So, through ignorant teachers, the critical years of life are thrown away! His words echo the endless wail over the teaching of children; — teaching by rote, learning by rote; not easy to avoid even by enlightened modernity, and perhaps having some disciplinary value.

Erasmus descended more nearly to the needs of pupils in his *De Copia,*[6] a book to assist young people to acquire a Latin style. Admirable are its generalities: when and how to enrich, or condense, the expression of one's thoughts, while avoiding repetition in the one case, or an inept bareness in the other. The need of something to say is pointed out, as well as the need of a scholarly command of Latin to clothe one's thought. Erasmus proceeds, usefully and drearily, to a mass of detail and example which make the work a store of varied classical phrase and circumlocution. At Colet's solicitation weighted with coin, Erasmus dedicated it to the use of his friend's foundation, St. Paul's school. It proved a wonderful schoolbook and was republished sixty times in Erasmus's lifetime, and afterwards indefinitely reprinted and epitomized. Our author's *De conscribendis epistolis,* written ten years later (1521) makes more attractive reading, and was very useful, judging from the great number of editions. It is an excellent treatise on the epistolary art by a past-master of the same.[7]

[6] *De duplici copia verborum ac rerum,* Leyden ed. T. I. fo. 3–110.

[7] Leyden Ed. T. I. fo. 345–484. The excellent Spaniard, Juan Luis Vives (1492–1540), an admirer of Erasmus, merits more than a short note for the excellence and influence of his educational works. He was a man of broad intelligence and moral purpose, an industrious scholar and writer. Living and studying for many years at Louvain, Paris and Bruges, he achieved a cosmopolitan education, while retaining some of his Spanish instincts. He became the educational adviser of Catharine

By the side of this treatise upon Latin composition may be placed the polemic *Ciceronianus*.[8] It was a dialogue upon the best form of literary expression, directed against those pedant humanists who recognized Cicero as their only model, and were becoming indecently pagan in thought and expression. The controversy was not new. Intelligent men had fought it out before against the "apes of Cicero." [9] Yet the latter never received a more elaborate drubbing than from this dialogue, in which Erasmus displays his magnificent and enlightened common sense, though at such length as to make a modern reader cry, How long, O Lord!

To us the one side of the argument seems so plain, the opposite so foolish. The Erasmian position, substantially that of Politian, Pico della Mirandola and many others, is that Latin still is a living language, to be adapted to present needs, and to the faculties and characters of the living individuals who use it. Cicero also was a living man, as well as a great writer. The whole Cicero, "totus Cicero," is only in himself. Since you are yourself, with your own surroundings, and your own exigencies of conception and expression, you cannot be Cicero, nor think or express yourself through his phrases. In attempting to be his mirror, you make a fool of yourself. We should not strive specifically to imitate Cicero, but to imitate or attain to that true art of oratory and writing, which we find in him, and in others also. Some change of forms, some novelties of expression are demanded by novel subjects and novel thoughts. Christian

of Aragon and the tutor of the princess Mary. He was more interested than Erasmus in instruction in the vernacular, and equalled him in his intelligent ideas upon juvenile education. His voluminous works have been published, and selections from them translated from the Latin into various languages: into English, for example, by Foster Watson in his *Tudor School-boy Life* (1908) and *Vives and the Renascence Education of Women* (1912). The benevolent intelligence of Vives is shown in his letter to the Senate of Bruges *Concerning the relief of the Poor, etc.*, translated by Margaret M. Sherwood in *Studies of Social Work*, No. 11 (New York, 1917). There is a good article on Vives in Library Supplement of the London *Times*, Nov. 25, 1920. Vol. 1, p. 164.

[8] Leyden Ed. T. I. fo. 973–1026, translated by Miss I. Scott (N. Y. 1908).

[9] Cf. e.g. ante Chapter III.

thoughts, for example, will not altogether fit the language of Cicero. Every phrase, every word, once had its inception. If novelty were always barbarism, every word was once a barbarism.

Erasmus shows all this through the convincing satire of his Dialogue. His own theory and practice recognized the rightfully constraining power of the genius of a language upon everyone using it in speech or writing. Within that broad conformity, there was scope for individual genius to express itself, as it did in fact in his own writings. Theirs was a pure Latinity, a formal Latin grace; yet they were pervaded and enlivened by a personal variety of style adapted to the subject and the situation.

The evil pedantry which eschewed all words and phrases not found in Cicero, had led, argues the Dialogue, to a paganization of Christian concepts in a classical nomenclature; it was part and parcel of the paganism which was pervading conduct, ethics, religion, till it threatened not merely to color, but to vitiate the Christian life. "We are Christian in name only," says the right-minded interlocutor. The opposite should be striven for; all our studies should have the effect of making us better Christians; they should be pursued to the glory of Christ: "His est totius eruditionis et eloquentiae scopus."

If the last words seem an echo of pious convention, Erasmus nevertheless believed that all scholarship should make for a better understanding of Christianity. Before tracing the proof of this in his religious writings and sacred studies, let us notice his *Adagia* which were so effective in spreading the humanizing influence of the classics. Like Montaigne after him, he had a genius for modernizing their lessons, and making them live again in the life of the present. In him humane studies produced their perfect fruit in the dissemination of human enlightenment. His whole life was educational for himself and for his age. There was instruction in everything he wrote, in his educational tracts which we have noticed, in his religious writing, in his editings and translations, in his imaginative *Colloquies* and symbolic Satire, and nowhere more diffusely than in his huge volume of *Adagia.*[10]

Most genially this great work adapted the wisdom of the Greeks and Romans to the tempers and understanding of sixteenth century Europeans. It became the commonplace book, *par excellence,* from which everyone, including Luther himself, drew his classical quotations. Year by year, Erasmus enlarged the collection for successive editions, until they became " Thousands four of Adages," as published the year he died. The name included what one would, in the way of proverbs, pithy sayings, admirable phrases, taken from the Ancients. They were all full of vitality, pregnant with meaning, charged with consideration of life.

The scholastic spirit, the need to classify and present through classification, worked in the author while he was writing his prolegomena and was setting forth the many uses of the wisdom packed in these old sayings. Yet their charm and usefulness were but academically suggested by the statement that the knowledge of proverbs conduces to many ends, and most potently to four, to wit: ad philosophiam, ad persuadendum, ad decus et gratiam orationis, ad intelligendos optimos quosque auctores.

Having got the prolegomena off his mind, Erasmus begins auspiciously with pleasant comment on his first proverb, τὰ τῶν φίλων κοινά, id est, Amicorum communia sunt omnia. He speaks of the early forms of this thought, and then of its later applications, as among the Romans, and so makes clear its general human value. He usually gives the original Greek saying first, and then its Latin equivalent, with the Greek and then the Latin examples of its use. The first proverb of the " first century " of the " Second thousand " is again an apt instance —" Σπεῦδε βραδέως, i.e., festina lente," and he expands the matter of its wisdom through several folios. The third thousand opens with the Ἡράκλειοι πόνοι, i.e., Herculei labores. This is, as it were, a topic become proverbial,

[10] The *Adages* fill Tome II of the Leyden edition, fo. 1–1212.

and Erasmus elucidates it with abundant comment, as he does also the more cryptic Sileni Alcibiadis.

Occasionally his treatment of a proverb expands into an essay. A noted instance is the *Dulce bellum inexperto,* which opens the Fourth Thousand, and has been frequently published and translated separately.[11] Erasmus hated war, as well might one whose life had been surrounded by its fruitless ravages. Tellingly he gives the adverse arguments, which applied so obviously to the Franco-Italian-Spanish struggles, with which he was familiar, as he was writing this pacifist tract about the year 1514. His arguments do not quite reach the case of a state or people protecting its freedom from a foreign foe or a domestic tyrant. It is easy to point out the wickedness of dynastic wars, and the folly of Xerxes invading Greece; but the armory of the stoutest pacifist would be taxed to find a valid argument against resistance on the part of the victors of Marathon and Salamis.

The lengthy disquisition is exceptional in the *Adagia,* where the vast majority of proverbs and phrases are treated shortly. In 1532 Erasmus published a not entirely dissimilar work, his eight books of *Apophthegmata,* which were sayings and incidents carrying a lesson, collected from the Ancients and adapted to the use of youthful princes. In them the brave Lacedaemonians pass before us, Socrates and the philosophers, Philip of Macedon, his great son, and many other valiant worthies and wise men. Quite pleasantly the lengthy work [12] followed the *Adages* in adapting the experience of the ancients to contemporary needs and tastes.

The religious writings and sacred studies of Erasmus, capped by his edition of the New Testament in Greek, would have been more palpably epoch-making had not the tumultuous genius of Luther merged all things gentler in a vast explosion. In Erasmus the love of letters fed the desire to let the light of reason fall temperately

[11] The old English translation is printed — *Erasmus against War* — in the Humanist Library (Boston 1907).

[12] Leyden Ed. T. IV fo. 93–379.

upon the profane and sacred follies of mankind. The same love of letters and of reasonableness held him back from Luther's paths of violence, an abstention destined to embitter his later years.

When about thirty-five years old, his temper still unwarped by controversy, he wrote, nominally for a carnal-minded friend,— the *Enchiridion Militis Christiani.*[13] It was an outline of Erasmian piety, and quickly became a popular manual. The friend, or his godfearing wife, apparently had asked Erasmus to prescribe a "vivendi rationem" or system of living, by which he might attain a mind worthy of Christ. Erasmus's title means either Manual or Dagger of the Christian soldier; and he begins with the assertion that the Christian life is warfare. Rites and professions will not help, unless we fight verily and spiritually against evil. This is the constant Erasmian ethical religious note. The *Enchiridion* will lay stress upon the heart set right and striving valiantly for Christ, and will minimize the value of ceremonies, vows, outward acts, and even the dogmatic theological element. The worthlessness of the outer act, when unaccompanied by any change of heart, had been recognized by good men and even by the Church before Erasmus. Yet he perceived this spiritual principle with ethical intelligence. There was a more portentous spiritual originality in his subconscious depreciation of dogmatic theology. Definitude, elaborate exactness of orthodoxy, he made little of. His reason and his humane studies thus led him into what many of his contemporaries deemed rationalism in a bad sense, but to which modernity will attach no evil imputation.

Yet the rationality of Erasmus was not quite freed from its intellectual environment. The second chapter of the *Enchiridion* indicates that he had not disembarrassed himself of the conventional allegorical interpretation of Scripture.[14] He and his fellow humanists of Italy and elsewhere commonly applied the same fancy to the

[13] Leyden Ed. T. V fo. 1–66. Written in 1501, published in 1503.
[14] See *Enchiridion,* Cap. II and Cap. VIII, Canon V.

interpretation of the classic poets. "As divine Scripture has little fruit for him who sticks to the letter, so the Homeric and Virgilian poetry will be found helpful if one remembers that it is all allegorical — eam totam esse allegoricam — which none denies whose lips have so much as tasted the learning of the ancients."

Chapter third of the *Enchiridion* had for its topic the wisdom which is self-knowledge, and the distinction between the false knowledge of the world and the true wisdom of Christ which the world thinks folly.[15] A manual of the Christian life could not omit these topics. Hence this chapter and several following, in which with little novelty Erasmus shows man to be *corpus* and *mens:* without the first, he were a deity; without the second he were a swine. There is also the usual teaching concerning the outer and the inner man; and the threefold man, anima, spiritus, carnis, is spoken of with little novel insight. Erasmus does better in his practical applications, for instance in pointing out that man may love Christ in his own wife, when he cherishes Christlike qualities in her.

His eighth chapter sets forth, without much novelty, the rules of Christian living: the point is the moral purpose of the act, the end for which it is done. This determines the religious worth of fasting and prayer, of letters and learning, and likewise the worship of the saints. "Deem Christ to be no empty word, but nothing else than love, simplicity, patience, purity; in fine, whatever he taught. Understand the devil to be nothing else than that which draws one from these." Taken by itself this is sheer morality, emptied of dogma. But Erasmus trims the course of his argument to navigate the open sea, if not the tortuous bays, of the accepted faith. He had no fancy to cast down whatever might be upheld with rational decency.

So he continues through this treatise, sensible and intelligent, pointing always to the intent and moral pur-

[15] Fo. 11. Using phrases from Paul, Erasmus here adumbrates some of the meanings which he will attach to this word *stultitia* in his "Praise of Folly."

pose, keeping means distinct from ends; showing how the spiritual life does not lie in observances, but in the love of neighbor; and how monks, even those reputed holy, may walk not in the spirit, but in the very flesh, with fasts and vigils. In this full sense, Christ is the end of the Law; one shall change his heart, rather than his garment; follow the spiritual lesson and imitate the Virgin and the saints, to whom one prays. Erasmus would not sanction reliance on the sacraments, without spiritual conformity to their import. For the still carnal-minded Christian, worship may be no better than the sacrifice of bulls to heathen gods. Yet he does not condemn rites performed as outer manifestations of the spirit, or as an aid to such as need them. He who does not feel this need, should still follow the observances that he may not cause his weaker brother to stumble.[16]

The years 1511 to 1514 were passed by Erasmus chiefly at Cambridge. During portions of this period he taught Greek grammar and lectured on the Letters of Jerome. But the best of his time seems to have been put upon his forthcoming editions of Jerome's *Opera* and the Greek New Testament, on both of which he had long been working. From Cambridge he proceeded to Basel to arrange for their publication with Froben. Scholars and printers connected with the great printing-house of Amorbach and Froben were already preparing an edition of Jerome; and Erasmus joined his work to theirs. By 1516 the complete edition appeared. Erasmus gave his time also to editions of Augustine and other Church Fathers. But that spent on Jerome, especially upon his epistles, was a labor of love; for above all the other fathers, he admired Jerome, who, he says in a letter to Leo X, delights by his eloquence, teaches by his erudition, ravishes by his holiness. He is tempted to place Jerome's style above Cicero's; this was rhetorical exaggeration. But the writings of this admirable scholar

[16] The rational qualities of the *Enchiridion* reappear in the *Institutio Principis Christiana,* written for Charles V. Leyden Ed. T. IV fo. 560–612.

and letter-writer appealed most sympathetically to Erasmus.

Reasons for going behind the Vulgate to the Greek text of the New Testament appealed to few. For what strikes us as the only sure method, that of always looking beyond popular versions to the original document, was then accepted only by the most advanced scholarship; and when applied to Scripture it seemed subversive of authority and faith. The theology of the early sixteenth century, like that of the fifteenth or the twelfth, in so far as it rested upon Scripture and its interpretation, rested on the Vulgate. To suggest that there was a more certain text might impugn the authority of the Church, not to mention the Holy Ghost who always had inspired the Church's dictates and beliefs.

So one realizes how profoundly educational was the publication of the Greek New Testament, with annotations upon its meanings and a revised Latin version; also what suspicion and disapproval were aroused. An example may be given from the well-meaning pen of his correspondent Dorphius, who sought by expostulation and lengthy argument to turn Erasmus from his undertaking: "You are proposing to correct the Latin copies by the Greek. But if I show you that the Latin version has no mixture of falsehood or mistake, will you not admit that such a work is unnecessary? But this is what I claim for the Vulgate, since it is unreasonable to suppose that the Universal Church has been in error for so many generations in her use of this edition, nor is it probable that so many holy Fathers have been mistaken, who in reliance upon it have defined the most arduous questions in General Councils, which, it is admitted by most theologians as well as lawyers, are not subject to error in matters of faith."[17]

Besides such decent arguments, there was abuse from the more violent. But Erasmus cut the wind from many hostile sails by obtaining the approval of Pope Leo X,

[17] Trans. from Nichols, *Epist. of Erasmus,* II, p. 169.

and dedicating the work to him. He laid stress upon his reverence and conservatism.

"The New Testament in Greek and Latin," he writes to Leo in August, 1516, "revised by us, together with our annotations, has been published for some time, under the safeguard of your auspicious name. I do not know whether the work pleases everyone, but I find that up to this time, it has certainly been approved by the principal theologians. . . . By this labour we do not intend to tear up the old and commonly accepted edition, but to emend it in some places where it is corrupt, and to make it clear where it is obscure; and this is not by the dreams of my own mind, nor as they say, with unwashed hands, but partly by the evidence of the earliest manuscripts, and partly by the opinion of those whose learning and sanctity have been confirmed by the authority of the Church, I mean Jerome, Hilary, Ambrose, Augustine, Chrysostom, and Cyril. Meantime we are always prepared to give our reasons, without presumption, for anything which we have rightly taught, or to correct, without grudging, any passage where, as men, we have unwittingly fallen into error." [18]

In the preface to the later edition of 1524, Erasmus says: Habemus fontes Salvatoris — what but salvation can we draw from them? It is safer to go to them than read the theologians. It is proper to draw from the sources this philosophy — hanc philosophiam — from which we are called Christians. Whoever would be called such, should not be ignorant of the *dogmata* of his King. Who could be a Franciscan and not know the *regula* of Francis; so one should know the *regula* of Christ.

For the editing of the text, Erasmus had not the apparatus, or the knowledge, or the painstaking habit of modern scholarship. Yet he perceived the problems and difficulties which he had not the patience and equipment to solve. Incited perhaps by Colet's way of viewing Paul's epistles in their historical setting, Erasmus weighed the human knowledge, or ignorance, possessed by the inspired writers of the New Testament, and sought to elucidate their meanings from a consideration of the his-

[18] Trans. from Nichols o. c. II, p. 316. See also Erasmus to Bullock, Nichols, o. c. II, pp. 324 sqq.

torical conditions under which they wrote. He was brave as a scholar. If ingenuousness did not mark his relations with friends and patrons, and if the dilemmas of a distasteful religious conflict drove him to tergiversation, he never lacked courage when defending the freedom of intelligent thinking and the sort of truth he understood and cared for. It was the bravery of a man defending his own home.

Erasmus effectively defended his Greek Testament, as well as his Latin version and his separately published Paraphrase, in an *Apologia Argumentum* "against certain unlearned and evil men." A passage not of a polemic nature may be given to show how he expressed the views of sundry of his mediaeval predecessors in open-mindedness. More than one of them had found foreshadowings of Christian truth in the heathen philosophers; and it was also a usual conviction, picturesquely set forth by Hugo of St. Victor,[19] that the Old Testament was the *umbra* of the New. Erasmus expresses the same opinions:

> "Since the Old Testament was the shadow and preparatory discipline for the Evangelical Philosophy, and since the Evangelical teaching is at once the restoration and perfection of nature, as first created in purity, it should not seem surprising if it were given to certain gentile philosophers, by the force of nature to discern some matters which agree with the doctrine of Christ. Paul bears witness that, from the visible fabric of the world, they gathered what the eye could not see, but the mind could comprehend, even the eternal power and divinity of God. It was especially congruous that Christ should bring nothing save that of which the shadow or scintilla had gone before in the books of the Old Testament, by which the faith of all would be the more inclined toward a thing not altogether sudden and unexpected. Therefore, whatever Christ set forth, was first promised in the oracles of the holy prophets, shadowed in figures, and even fragmentarily expressed."[20]

This passage presents the fact of spiritual evolution or development, as many passages had done in the works of

[19] See *The Mediaeval Mind,* Vol. II, p. 100.

[20] Erasmus, *Epistola de Phil. Evangelica,* printed in T. VI of the Leyden Ed. before the New Testament.

mediaeval doctors. But in the Middle Ages, and still in the time of Erasmus, men saw more definitely than to-day the preordainment of God and his providential direction of the entire process.

Two works remain to be spoken of, perhaps the most constantly read of all Erasmus's writings, both in his life-time and since his death: The *Praise of Folly* and the *Colloquies*.[21] Though differing in form, they agree in substance; and together express the opinions of the author upon those matters of contemporary life, belief, and superstition, which roused his interest, elicited his approval, or drew his criticism and contempt.

The *Praise of Folly* is called a *declamatio* by its author, a term carrying the idea of something entertaining. That the composition was a jeux d'esprit is abundantly stated in a letter of dedication to Thomas More,[22] in whose house the book was written. Its scheme had been the writer's diversion when returning from Italy; and now he wished the protection of More's name "For wranglers perhaps will not be wanting, who may assail it, on the score that these trifles are sometimes more frivolous than becomes a theologian, and again more biting than accords with Christian moderation; or will exclaim that we are bringing back the Old Comedy or the pen of Lucian, and seizing everything with the teeth." Yet study should have its relaxations, especially when they are such as may bring suggestion to the reader who is not dull. "Others will pass judgment on me; and yet, unless I am egregiously deceived by self-conceit, we have praised Folly not altogether foolishly." It is not too biting, seeing that he has mentioned no names, and has impartially satirized the vices of all sorts and conditions of men.

So then the *Praise of Folly* is a satire, meant to amuse,

[21] Μωρίας Ἐγκώμιον id est *Stultitiae Laus, declamatio,* Leyden Ed. IV fo. 402–504, first published in 1511; *Colloquia familiaria,* Leyden Ed. I, 627–890; first published in 1516, and added to in the innumerable subsequent editions.

[22] Printed and usually translated with the work; also by Nichols, *Epist. of Erasmus,* II, p. 1 sqq.

but also, as gradually becomes evident, intended to instruct and improve. The writer does not bind himself to any single idea of his protagonist. Folly has many shades of meaning. At the first it appears as life's hilarious and impulsive energy of desire, a child of Plutus.[23] Folly is impulse, childish or mature, innocent or debased, at all events not disillusioned. For illusion is a part of desire and action; who is without it is a dried and hamstrung Stoic!

At first the book makes kindly and approving fun of the ways of action and the foibles and weaknesses of mankind. It is not mordant, only amused. But gradually from fools innocent and natural and undebased, it passes to those whose illusions are vicious in their setting and results. Such are stultified grammarians, scribblers, sophisters; such are passionate dicers; and then those addicted to the marvellous and incredible, gaping fools, greedy of strange tales, who ascribe virtue to shrines and images, and to vows made to saints. Worse than such are they who rely on rotten pardons, and think to measure, as by clepsydras, the ages, years, months, days, which they have knocked off from Purgatory. Priests promote these evil follies, and reap gain from them. Now the satire becomes mordant: it ridicules, it lashes the fool-vices, their panders and their votaries; the fool-sophisters, Scotists, dabblers in split hairs and things incomprehensible, and the like-minded theologians, with their impossible fool-questions; and then the Monks! These are well scourged. As to kings, allowance is made for the blinding effect of their exalted station; but their courtiers are handled roughly. The discourse pounces upon Popes and Cardinals and bishops; the lashing becomes merciless. Luther might lay on more violently, but not more deftly.

After this, the satirical element is genially dispersed; the bitterness is past. Citing first the sayings of gentile authors and then the teaching of Christ, Folly finds the

[23] One may compare it with that all-embracing animal desire symbolized by Rabelais in his "Gaster." See post, Chapter XIII.

earth full of fools, and none to be called good or wise save God alone. Folly is part of man, and may even be his better part, more excellent than his wisdom. St. Paul speaks "as a fool." Christ bids his followers consider the lilies of the field; bids them take no thought of what they shall say when delivered up. Woe unto the wise! he cries, and gives thanks to his Father for having hidden the Kingdom of heaven from them and revealed it unto babes. Seeing that "the foolishness of God is wiser than man," let us be "fools for Christ's sake," for the sake of Him who crowned his life by the "foolishness of the Cross." In fine, concludes the author, "the Christian religion seems to have some relationship with folly, and is not in accord with wisdom." The true Christian will scorn the crowd which relies on the ceremonial of the flesh, and address himself utterly to the spirit. The crowd will think this insanity. And truly the life which is in the spirit and has foretaste of eternal beatitude, partakes of madness, like the madness of lovers praised by Plato.

The *Colloquies*, the Familiar Talks or Dialogues, of Erasmus passed through sixty editions in the author's life-time. Condemned by the Sorbonne, also denounced by Luther, they only became more widely read; they were used in schools as texts of Latinity and of enlightenment. They had been written and brought together by the author in the course of the twenty-five years or so beginning about 1500. More voluminous, more multifarious, than the Praise of Folly, they are withal simpler. No elusively doubling thread of meaning runs through them; they are just what they are, a series of familiar dialogues, between various fictitious persons, upon almost any topic of daily life or current practice and opinion. Opening in formulae of polite conversation; they quickly turn to chat of plays and pastimes; of horse-cheats and the tricks of common beggars; of the villainies of a soldier's life; of the contemptible lots of benefice-hunters; of early rising and temperate living; of marriages and funerals; of convivial feasts and those at which there is more serious flow of soul. They discuss common superstitions, rash vows, and the deceits practised on would-be nuns; the vain pilgrimages made to St. James of Compostella and across the sea; they hold up to view the heathen follies, the ceremonials and corruptions, which marked the conduct of the Church. The speakers are shown in all manner of situations: in shipwrecks, funerals, on silly pilgrimages, fooled by astrologers and alchemists, grovelling in superstition or practising upon the superstitious. Through them runs the most uncommon common sense of the writer; his intelligent apprehension of the real point; his rational consideration of it. One sees his tolerance of whatever is not positively false and harmful; his respect for honest and respectable opinion, qualities conducing to a recognition of the worth of honest scholarship and the desirableness of intellectual freedom, within the bounds of decency. The book itself is brave and free in its ridicule of abuses which still reposed on the authority of the Church, and from which came part of the Church's revenue.

Erasmus maintained that he attacked the abuse and not the ecclesiastical institution. But attacks on the one are apt to smirch the other. Men do not notice such distinctions. An attack on indulgences goes to the heart of much, although one may insist that nothing has been said against absolution following upon repentance and atonement. Who shall draw the line between abuse and institution? And in Christianity, when has the line been drawn between true faith and piety, and the superstitions wrapping the hearts of ignorant believers? Assuredly the worship of the Virgin and the saints is a Roman Catholic tenet. But "The Shipwreck" [24] ridicules calling on the saints and on the Virgin by flattering titles. What had she to do with the Sea? Note the utterly disintegrating answer: "In ancient times, Venus took care of mariners, because she was believed to be born of the sea; and because she has left off to take care of them, the Vir-

[24] Vol. I, p. 275 sqq. of Bailey's translation, 2 vols. (London, 1878). It is the *Naufragium,* Leyden Ed. I. fo. 712 sqq.

gin Mother was put in the place of her that was a mother, but not a Virgin." This quite indelibly connects the worship of the Virgin with the heathen cult of Venus.

In the *Religious Pilgrimage*,[25] more ridicule is put upon the Virgin and the saints and upon pilgrimages. At the end, the sensible speaker tells how he, who never saw Rome, performs *his* Roman Stations: "After that manner I walk about my house, I go to my study, and take care of my daughter's chastity; thence I go into my shop, and see what my servants are doing; then into the kitchen, and see if anything be amiss there; and so from one place to another, to observe what my wife, and what my children are doing, taking care that everyone is at his business. These are my Roman Stations." Such excellent sense may be rather solvent of religious observance.

But the *Colloquies* give utterance to a piety which is direct, sincere, ethical, pregnant with the religion of the spirit. Examples are "An Enquiry concerning Faith," "The Religious Treat," and "A Child's Piety."[26] In the last the excellent youth, stating his own creed, comes near to stating that of Erasmus: "I believe firmly what I read in the Holy Scriptures, and the Creed called the Apostles, and I don't trouble my head any farther; I leave the rest to be disputed and defined by the clergy, if they please; and if anything is in common use with Christians that is not repugnant to the Holy Scriptures, I observe it for this reason, that I may not offend other people."

His friend asks, "What Thales taught you that philosophy?"

"When I was a boy, and very young, I happened to live in the house of that honestest of men, John Colet."

In this way Erasmus testifies to the pious and reasonable influence exerted on him by that balanced and penetrating English mind.

The purposes, the opinions, the qualities of Erasmus reveal themselves in his works. These reflect his en-

[25] Bailey, o. c. II, 1; Leyden Ed., fo. 774 sqq.

[26] This is the *Confabulatio pia*, Leyden Ed. fo. 648 sqq. The two former are fo. 728 sqq.; and 672 sqq. They are all in Vol. I of Bailey's Trans.

vironment and his nature, making a very adequate self-expression of the man Erasmus; and the self-expression of a man is always true. Had Erasmus possessed the Titan nature of a Luther, convulsed with convictions as violent as they were trenchant, his self-expression would have appealed to us more pointedly than it does from out the compass of those huge ten folios of the Leyden edition. His innumerable writings did their work in their time, and still interest us historically. They spread the Erasmian personality before us. He who may bring himself to read them will note everywhere facility of presentation, broad, proportioning scholarship, not too exact, nor always profound; balanced common sense and clear intelligence which grasp the veritable point; interest in well authenticated fact, linguistic, historical and rational, which is the scholar's truth; care for what is truly ethical, dependent on motive and interest, and not bound up in ceremony and observance; insistence on unhampered study, on the rights of scholarship, on freedom to reach the most rationally verified result; recognition also of mutually tolerating differences of sensible opinion, but no patience for wilful ignorance and stubbornness; a cherishing of piety and rational religion, but with no taste for dogma or metaphysics, and as little for the transports of religious rapture.

Erasmus followed earthly, rather than heavenly light. He cared for the religion of Christ, and he loved scholarship. From some of his expressions one or the other might seem his chief care. But, with him, both belonged to the same quest of rational truth. He followed letters; as a scholar also he studied Scripture, still seeking to establish the surest record of the Faith. He was the scholar, not the sceptic, in religion; and never doubted of the salvation brought by Christ, as evidenced by Scripture. Thus he was evangelical, but tolerantly, without a wish to tear down whatever had been recognized or built up by the Church, so far as it did not counter either the Gospel or a rational morality.

One can foresee the attitude of such a nature toward

the Lutheran Reformation. As was generally said, no one had done as much to open men's eyes to the follies, abuses and corruptions, infecting the Roman Catholic religion. His writings had had universal currency and corresponding influence. The number of editions printed of them one and all is almost incredible.[27] Never was a scholar so widely read; and never was a scholar's word more potent. It seems safe to say that no man had done as much to prepare the mind of Europe for religious reformation as Erasmus of Rotterdam.[28]

Yet when it came through Luther, he could not go along with it. It was to be national; this universal Latinist had no appreciation of nationality. It was to be passionate, violent, intolerant, proceeding with fixed ideas. There was little here to gain his sympathy. Still less could he sympathize with the Catholic Church, which was more corrupt and quite as violent. With his mind set on enlightened scholarship, both sacred and profane, how could Erasmus not oppose whatever threatened either? How he hated this mutual intolerance and wrath, which might extinguish letters and intellectual freedom!

There had been a conflict into which he could throw himself with all his mind, because there, as it seemed to him, one side stood for piety and the full light of scholarship, while the other's strength lay in ignorance and prejudice. It was the struggle of Johann Reuchlin, against those who fought to suppress the study of Hebrew and with it the freedom of letters. Erasmus was on Reuchlin's side. He felt himself defending everything he cherished, while Reuchlin's persecutors were the kind of men he detested and despised.[29]

[27] The stupendous lists are modestly and succinctly given in *Biblioteca Erasmiana, Repertoire des oeuvres d'Erasme,* published in 1893 at Ghent, and distributed gratis and graciously to promote the study of Erasmus.

[28] By the year 1517, Erasmus's religious influence had been recognized: "me Christum sapere docuisti," writes one correspondent, (Allen o. c. II; p. 341 (1516), and another hails him: "Salve Erasme vas electionis et secunde post Paulum doctor gentium." Allen o. c. II, p. 505.

[29] See Nichols, *Epist. of Erasmus,* Vol. II, pp. 189, 193, and ante, Chapter VI. Later, under stress of the Lutheran conflict, Erasmus was inclined to

Erasmus's later years were made unhappy by the parting of the ways between the humanism of the North and the Reform which at first it had seemed to carry in its train. He recognized no hostile rivalry between secular and religious truth. It was monstrous that the truth which came by faith should not respect the aid of letters and cherish the truth which came through scholarship. Toward the end he wrote bitterly to Pirckheimer: "Wherever Lutheranism reigns, there is an end to letters. Yet these men have been chiefly (maxime) nourished on letters."[30] His life had been an unhampered progress in scholarship and fame till the Lutheran controversy reached such importance as to compel men to take sides. Incapable of this, Erasmus became suspect to both and was driven to subterfuge. His discomfort and unhappiness appear in his correspondence from this time to the close of his life.[31]

Erasmus never could have joined with Luther. The opposite tempers of the two would have held them apart. And before many years, Erasmus thought he saw the Reform throwing the world into a spiritual and political anarchy. But he could not go along with the Church in its measures to suppress the Reform; for he detested persecution, and deemed force worse than useless in matters of the Faith. The Church should conquer only through its reasonableness and its persuasion, and its imitation of Christ. Alas! neither side seemed to hold a brief for scholarship and the simple truth and freedom of the Gospel. In the end, Erasmus elected to adhere to the Church; and it was as touching the point of veritable freedom, free-will indeed, on which he first formally took his stand against the teaching of Luther. His *de libero Arbitrio* (1524) evinced his common sense in the matter and showed him on the side of freedom, to which he felt free-will to be essential.

minimize his interest in Reuchlin. See Ep. to Wolsey (1519), Allen, o. c. III, p. 589.

[30] Leyden Ed. T. III, Ep. 1006, fo. 1139.

[31] The letter to Wolsey, 1519, Allen o. c. III, p. 587 sqq., is typical. See ib. III, pp. 527 and 540.

At all events he was *facile princeps* among the men of letters of the North. He enumerates his works in the *Catalogus* addressed to Botzheim in 1523.[32] Touching upon reflections made upon him by Luther's friends, he says:

"they have nothing that they can bring against me, except that I would not profess at the peril of my head, what either I did not accept, or held as doubtful, or did not approve, or should have professed to no purpose. For the rest, who has written more against faith in ceremonies, against the superstition of fasts, of cult and vows, against those who ascribe more to the commentaries of men than to the divine Scriptures, who set human edicts above God's precepts, and rely for aid upon the saints more than on Christ himself; against the scholastic theology corrupted by philosophic and sophistic subtleties, against the rashness of defining what you will; against the absurd opinions of the crowd? . . . These and much besides, which I have taught according to the measure of grace given me, I have taught steadfastly, not clamoring against anyone who could teach something better. And Erasmus has taught nothing but rhetoric (eloquentiam)! Would that they could persuade my silly friends of this, who continually boast that whatever Luther has taught he has drawn from my writings! . . . The sum of my crimes is that I am more moderate; and for this I hear ill things from both sides, because I exhort both to gentler counsels. I do not condemn liberty founded on love."

Erasmus was not always quite so sweet as in the last phrase.

[32] Allen, o. c. I, pp. 1–46. The passage I have translated is on p. 29. Compare it with the letter to Gacchus, Leyden Ed. T. III, col. 1724–1730.

CHAPTER VIII

THE SPIRITUAL AND POLITICAL PREPARATION FOR LUTHER

IF ever a man expressed himself and his people, it was Martin Luther. Yet he spoke mainly in the language of the past. His doctrines won their acceptance through their religious strength, their timely pertinency to the German social and political situation, and through their emphatic statement. Luther's power of expression drove his teachings into the German mind. The rugged phrases of the *Address to the German Nobility* and *The Freedom of the Christian man* worked themselves into the German blood. Yet still they spoke in the language of the past. If Luther violently rejected such of its formularies as shocked his intelligence and countered his convictions, he continued to express himself and his people through old and well-tried forms. But he brought to his expression his own spiritual experiences and his understanding of the world about him.

Expression in language is not merely the symbol of thought, but its completion, its finished form. Sometimes, however, as these symbols, these phrases or formulations, pass from one generation to another, they fall out of accord with other thoughts and convictions, fruits of further experience and knowledge, which may be seeking expression in the later time. To some more zealously advancing minds, old symbols and formulations will seem to have become outworn, used up, fit only for discarding and the new time's intellectual scrap-heap; and even more patient souls may dumbly feel that their time-honored thoughts fail to bring comfort or conviction. In fine as the old symbols cease to correspond with the current consideration of life, they cease to express vitally the later generation.

Moreover, when concepts or symbols, and the institutions in which they may have been incorporated, cease to correspond with the thinking of a later time, and for that reason are no longer instinct with life, then, like sickly human bodies, they become open to corruption, prone to disease. This is seen most clearly when the conception has worked itself out in customs, pilgrimages for example, or the granting of indulgences for sins; or when it is embodied in an institution, monasticism, if one will, or a priesthood, or a universal church. Let us note some incidents of the course through which concepts or symbols conceived in the patristic period, or before it, and accepted in the Middle Ages, were developed into dogmas, expanded in beliefs, and incorporated in institutions. Then how some of them began to lose their validity, and became husks.

The Gospel symbolized divine strength, virtue, love, in the life and words and acts, the personality in fine, of Christ. The vitality of that symbol Christ has not passed away, because it has not ceased to correspond with human thoughts and yearnings. But in the centuries following the Crucifixion, Christ was elaborated, sublimated, rendered metaphysical in dogma, fixed in the larger symbol of the Trinity. This formulation obliterated some of the qualities which had been very living in the Gospel Christ. Thereupon the needy human mind, as it were, out of the lost bits of Christ, made other symbols. Chief among them was the Virgin Mary, symbol of refuge, preserving the divine qualities of love and pity and forgiveness that they might not be entombed in the metaphysics of the Triune God. Mary and the saints and angels were symbols made by the plastic mind in answer to its longings; symbols of realized assurance, they were held in the imagination, seen in visions, even touched in states of rapture. Yet with all their loveliness and comfort, they tended to lose vitality as the sixteenth century approached. For they no longer corresponded with men's larger thoughts of the workings of the divine. They had even taken on corruption, in that they had been brought to pander to what the keener moral perceptions of the time recognized as immoralities.[1] Soon they would be numbered among superstitions by large sections of Europe.

Monasticism was the expression of another Christian ideal. The celibate ascetic life for men and woman represented the fear of the devil, the horror of sin, the anxious detestation of the world and the flesh; also a yearning for purity, utter devotion to the Crucified. Through monastic living and mortification of the flesh, and abject penitence, ardent men and women had reached assurance and consolation, even had attained to union with God. Monasticism had had a great rôle in Christianity; had been instituted and developed, had fallen from its high estate, and had been time and again reformed. Its reformers and reinstitutors — Benedict, Damiani, Bernard, Guigo, Francis,— presented phases of its ideals: their lives also had become symbols. There was abundant monastic slackness and corruption in the sixteenth century. If that had resulted from the sheer weakness of human nature unable to adhere to an ideal, it might have been remedied again by strenuous reformers. But now monasticism was countered by a new ideal of living. Not human weakness, but a new and rationally supported attitude toward religion and toward life opposed its principles and prepared to demonstrate their invalidity. If the monastic ideal could not keep its throne in the human mind, its practice might become hypocrisy and its pretensions be laughed out of court. That also came to pass in parts of Europe.

The faith of Christ was dogmatized in creeds; first in the simple Apostolic creed, and then in the Nicene elaboration. Both creeds were symbols, the first representing the youthful still impressionable body of Christian belief; the second presenting its rock-ribbed metaphysical conciliar formulation. The Nicene symbol became the citadel of dogmatic Christianity, with subsidiary dogmas supporting it as buttresses. The power of patristic

[1] See, for example, the *Colloquies* of Erasmus, passim, ante, Chap. VII.

Christian thought had built it. Through the Middle Ages it stood sublime, intact, the Faith's foregone conclusion. To bulwark this citadel was the chief end of scholastic philosophy. In the fifteenth century the citadel showed no open signs of weakening. In the sixteenth, Protestants as well as Catholics professed to lock themselves within it. Yet it had long stood peak-like above Christian emotion, and now no longer held or symbolized the vital currents of Christian thinking. The religious storm swept by it, apparently.

Yet the storm shattered the transubstantiation of bread and wine, one sacramental buttress, and even disturbed the " real presence " in the Eucharist. Such dogmas were not yet emptied symbols, and were fiercely maintained and contested.

There was a paramount symbol of the unity and totality of the Christian salvation, which the storm conspicuously struck, and broke in twain. That was the imperial Roman Catholic Church, visible, tangible, august; sacerdotal mediator between God and men; sole vehicle and ministrant of salvation. Not that the thought, the symbol itself, seemed to have weakened or to have ceased to correspond with living ideals. Indeed the shattered reality continued to furnish an ideal to those men who in fact had broken it. Lutherans and Calvinists professed to belong to the one true Church composed of all true believers.

But the concept of the Church had never been quite settled and at one with itself. At any given moment, it had a different form in different minds, and it was always changing. The papal Curia and its priestly supporters did not hold the same idea as the laity, who paid church tithes throughout the world, and the secular rulers who might be hostile to the pope. Unlike the symbol of the Trinity or that of the Virgin birth, the Church idea was inextricably involved in practice and politics, bound up in things temporal, in the world, the flesh, and the devil. The Church was flesh as well as spirit. Its otherworldly functions might not have been contested, had they not needed to support themselves on temporal power and material emoluments. The concept of the Church had necessarily to embody itself in an institution; and institutions are of this world, part of its dragging needs and lowering practices.

In its temporal and material flesh the Church never could be free from shortcoming and corruption; or fail to be involved in practices inconsistent with its otherworldly purpose. Hence it never could be void of offense; and would always be attacked by saints as well as sinners.

Moreover, its material corruptions were always lowering its doctrines to correspond with its practices, and de-spiritualizing its teachings. Doubtless, even from Apostolic times unspiritual superstitions had been accepted, like the notion, for example, that the physical thing, the relic or the bread blessed by the priest, might have a magic or miraculous effect, in no way germane to its actual properties. Priests and laity could free themselves from such ideas only by perceiving more clearly that a thing cannot produce something else of an entirely different nature. Cause and effect must lie in the same categories: a physical thing cannot work spiritual miracles; a corporeal act cannot in itself produce a higher spiritual state. Both Erasmus and Luther (not to mention Wyclif) perceived this as touching gifts and pilgrimages and mortifications of the flesh. Possibly some such rational principle might before their time have been accepted by the Church, had not the needs of the Church as a temporal institution proved an obstacle. Instead, irrational unspiritual notions, which may have had their root in paganism, were retained through this degrading influence, and sometimes were aggravated. It was the plainly corrupt and material abuse of these derelict notions that aroused men's indignation; otherwise the doctrines themselves would have quietly fallen away or remained as negligible anachronisms. Luther's attack upon Indulgences and its immense results afford the most obvious illustration, while the futility of the reforming purposes of Erasmus was partly due to their primarily intellectual character. They demonstrated the absurdity of prevalent irrationalities in doctrines and practices, instead of attacking directly the corruptions which made those irrationalities abominable, and were the real reasons for overthrowing them. His labors helped to prepare men's minds. The explosion came otherwise.

The preparation for the revolt of Luther from the Roman Catholic Church is not to be sought in specific antecedents which happen to agree in form with some of the reformer's thoughts. Such merely mark the milestones on the way. Luther's revolt was led up to by the intellectual, economic and political progress of Europe and, especially, of the German people. As the mentality of Europe advanced in the fourteenth and fifteenth centuries, disturbing glances were directed toward the Church and the kinds of salvation which it furnished. The differences between peoples became more marked, and the consciousness of nationality stronger. Europe was progressing from homogeneity to diversity. One form of Christianity, one Catholic Church, possibly might no longer answer the spiritual and economic needs of all the nations. At all events, the deepening of the national consciousness of Englishmen and Germans carried some distrust of a church seemingly rooted in an Italian papacy which was always draining other peoples of their gold. Such conditions moved the revolt of Wyclif and led to the Hussite wars.

Religiously the Lutheran revolt and reformation was an announcement of man's dependence upon God for his salvation, to the necessary exclusion of sacerdotal mediation; intellectually it implied insistence upon a revised kind of mental freedom; politically it broke the unity of ecclesiastical authority.

The Church was the Catholic exponent of Christianity. Luther issued from the Church. Doctrinally, he shook himself free only just so far as he was compelled to by the need to establish his salvation immediately in Jesus

Christ. Catholic church doctrine was exceedingly inclusive; suited, in its various aspects or phases to different minds and different tempers. It was an *omnium gatherum* of saving means and doctrines. Luther's rejection of certain of its teachings was grounded in his more absolute acceptance of what it also taught. Salvation by faith had always been proclaimed; yet the Church, as a Catholic result of centuries of accretion, proffered other means of grace for such as needed other disciplines. There were different kinds of Christianity or quasi-Christianity within the Church, with opportunities for religious conviction and practices ranging from the sublime to the abject. Luther, more intense, more consistent, more individual, and more narrow, committed himself to certain Christian doctrines so absolutely and exclusively that others were thereby rejected, many of them make-shift teachings and practices which human weakness demanded, and the Catholic nature of the Church not only tolerated but, as it were, personally felt the need of.

Before Luther, there were men who accepted the same vital doctrines in such a way as to lead them also to reject much that he rejected. There was one Johann von Goch, a Low German or Netherlander, who died in 1475, having made little stir, and leaving writings which were not read by Luther, but were unearthed in later times. Goch held with inchoate pre-Lutheran insistence, upon certain of the doctrines which the Church so catholicly gathered together, along with some ill-sorted practices. He emphasized justification by faith, and held that the Faith should be based upon Scripture, and that the Sacrament did not save when taken by the unrepentant. He also held that the Church might err, which the church knew well enough, but could not formally admit. Another Johann, Joannes de Vesalia, or Wesel, wrote against the papal indulgences issued at the pope's Jubilee of 1450. He maintained that the pope could not absolve from divine punishment, and other things besides, which Luther was to hold.

A more notable figure is still another Johann, this time

a Johann Wessel spelled with double s, and if possible not to be confused with his older contemporary, Wesel. Wessel, who lived from 1420 to 1490, had been taught by Thomas à Kempis, his senior by forty years, and is even thought to have influenced his teacher. He early inclined toward Plato, and may have known a little Greek. He studied for many years in Paris, and spent some time in Rome. When sixty years old, he settled down at Heidelberg three years before Luther was born.

Wessel held so many of the doctrines which Luther was to hold, that the latter's enemies reproached him with wholesale borrowing. Luther recognized him as a forerunner, and Erasmus also spoke well of him. He sought to base his theology directly on the Bible, and endeavored to hold to the real meaning of its words. He stated the principle of justification by faith alone, and developed the idea of faith as the source of man's communion with God. Then he followed St. John in the conception of *love,* of God's love of man and man's answering love of God. Love nourishes love, and without it there is no life. Love is perfected in us through the spirit of God, till we are brought where man and angel pass away, and we become a new creature in Christ. The Church is the communion of all the Saints, living and dead. Its bond is love. We have faith in the Gospel through God; and faith in the Church through the Gospel. The reverse is untrue.

Wessel approaches Luther's conception of the priesthood. For him the pope is not infallible; his headship is an accident. The saving effect of the Sacrament depends on the spiritual state of the recipient. Wessel's conception of the Eucharist was less conservative than Luther's; it was like that of Zwingli, and appears to have influenced the radical Carlstadt. He questioned the Catholic doctrines of penance and priestly remission of sins. Christ did not entrust the power to remit sins to any one person, but to the *unity.*—" non uni sed unitati donavit." The pope cannot exclude man from the grace and love of God, nor enhance the believer's spiritual benefits. Wessel argued against indulgences, advancing, as it were, from the position of Wesel even beyond the points taken by Luther's Theses. Consistently with these ideas, he treats Purgatory as a stage of purification midway between human sinfulness and heavenly perfection. The purgatorial fire is spiritual; it is God himself, and Christ and the Gospel, working in love — an element not absent from Dante's Purgatory.[2]

In spite of the correspondence of their thoughts with Luther's own, these men affected him less than certain contemplative pietists, mystics as they commonly are called, whose ways of thinking were part of Luther's very German religious nature. They also were Germans or Lowlanders by birth. Meister Eckhart was the most creative genius among them, indeed, the creative type of much that was German and of much that became Luther. For this reason a few pages must be devoted to his profound obscurity.

Mysticism is a vague name for much that is amorphous. Along the Rhine and in the Low Countries, a directly yearning and contemplative piety had marked the Brothers of the Free Spirit and the partly kindred evangelical Beghards and Beguines, societies of men and women who had never been high in the Church's favor and were eventually to be treated as heretics. But Mary of Ognies, Elizabeth of Schönau, Hildegarde of Bingen, had been saints of the Church in the twelfth century, and, in the next, with Mechthilde of Magdeburg, the religious impulse had become a personally addressed symbolic and sense passion.[3] In their religious experience there had been scant admixture of justifying reason; but warm had been their zeal for the honor of God and for the purification of His Church. Then had come Meister Eckhart, who was born in Thuringia in 1260 and died in 1327.[4] His learning and genius made a frame for his religious

[2] On Wessel, see Ullmann, *Reformatoren vor der Reformation,* II, pp. 486–514 (Gotha, 1866).

[3] See *The Mediaeval Mind,* Chapter XX.

[4] On Eckhart, see Delacroix, *Mysticisme speculatif en Allemagne au 14. siècle* (Paris, 1900).

impulses, and brought the difficult content of his thought to striking expression in vital paradox and symbolism.

He was a Dominican and held high office in his Order. He was likewise a Doctor of Theology, versed in the teachings of Aquinas, and in the writings of the Arab commentators of Aristotle. He also had studied Augustine , but seemingly knew best of all the pseudo-Dionysius, the "Areopagite." There can be no doubt of Eckhart's full scholastic equipment, which is evinced by his Latin treatises and to a less degree by his German utterances.

These sermons and other German tracts of Eckhart disclose a vigorous ethical nature and tense thought, which they must also have demanded of their auditors. The Master was a severe thinker. Further, he was a speculative spirit, whose whole being drew toward God, one might even say toward the ultimate universal reality. Rather than a scholastic, he was a masterful personality moulding what he had received into what he was and would be and attain to. Wherein lay the chief emphasis of his thought and mood may not be easy for other men to state.

At all events Eckhart's teaching had to do with God and the Soul, or with the ultimate reality whereinsoever that be found. One may also be sure that its rational structure was but a vehicle of the man's desire and intent, at least if allowance be made for the necessary attachment of a Dominican Doctor to the scholasticism represented by his Order. Shall we say, the goal both of desire and of the thought which justifies it is the soul's oneness with God? The soul is of the divine essence; may the completed soul, conscious of its nature and overnature, so perfect this union as to convert the Divine from object to an inner experience? Even God brings his being to its full actuality and consciousness through coming to expression in the beings He creates and remains the essence of. Conversely, the true life of the soul lies in its turning, or perhaps returning, utterly to God, abandoning its worse than worthless distractions, comforts, pleasures. It may profitably exercise this ascetic rejection and mortal humiliation in order to attain its true homing in That which is its source and final blessedness. God, by passing out into His veriest actuality, becomes the true reality of that which He creates; and by knowing this, and living in accord with it, the human creature helps God to fulfil His realization of Himself, till God be All in All. In this perfected absorption which is re-absorption, the Soul attains its heights of love and inner contemplation, which is its bliss and its salvation.

Of this, Christ was and is the absolute example and realization.

"Says our Lord, 'I am gone forth from the Father and am come into the world. Again I leave the world and return to the Father.' Here he means that his coming forth is his entry into the soul. But the soul's entry is her coming forth: she must pass out of her outermost into her innermost, out of her own into the Son's own. Thereupon she is drawn into the Father as the Son leaves the world and returns to the Father with the Soul." But the Son is God, and his coming forth is very God: "His coming forth is his entry. Even as he comes forth from the Father, in the same way he enters the Soul. *His coming forth is God Himself.*" [5]

So creation is God's pouring forth of Himself. This is the old *Emanatio* of Gnostic and Neo-platonist, dear forever to the German mind. One may try to follow Eckhart as he brings similar thoughts to expression in another discourse — on seeing and contemplating God through the "wurckende vernunft," creative reason, the *νοῦς ποιητικός* of the "Areopagite" and of Aristotle too. "King David said, Lord in thy light shall we see light. . . . Man has within him a light, that is the creative reason; in this light shall he see God in blessedness. Man is created so imperfect that he cannot through his nature know God as creator and as type and form. For this a power above his nature is needed, the light of grace. Now mark my meaning. Saint Paul says, through the grace of God I am that I am. He does not say that he

[5] From a sermon on John XVI, 28 (Pfeiffer, *Deutsche Mystiker,* 2, 181. Printed in Vetter, *Lehrhafte Litteratur des 14 u. 15 Jahrhundert,* p. 159).

exists through grace. The difference is between being by grace and being [the true] self by grace. The masters say that true form gives being to matter. Now there is much talk among them as to what grace is. I say that grace is nothing else than a light flowing[6] immediately out of the nature of God into the Soul, and it is an over-natural form of the soul that gives it an over-natural being." [7]

So grace imparts a being to the soul exceeding the soul's nature. Without it the soul cannot, beyond her own nature, understand and love. "When the soul is steadfast in an overcoming of herself and passes into a not-herself[8] then is she through grace. . . . This is the highest office of grace that it brings the soul to the true self (das sie die sele bringet in das sie selb [not *ir*-selb] ist). Grace robs the soul of her own works (ir eygen werck), grace robs the soul of her own existence. . . ."

"The worthy Dionysius [the "Areopagite"] says: 'when God is not in the soul, the eternal image is not in the soul, which is her eternal source." God keeps this eternal image in the soul through his grace, or light, or "wurckende vernunft." In this the soul is raised out of her natural being, which had kept her subject to her own desires that draw away from God. And in this transforming of the soul, God is very God: "In my eternal *bild* is God God." [9]

The structural thought of German mysticism is due to Eckhart. As has been often said, this German mysticism was a very inward business. It was a power within each man and woman which might exert itself individually and Germanically, in the end most separatistically, one may say. One seems also to perceive in this German mysti-

[6] With Eckhart's "ein fliessendes liecht," we are back with Mechthilde of Magdeburg and her "fliessendes liecht der Gottheit"—see *The Mediaeval Mind,* Chap. XX.

[7] Observe how Eckhart uses the concepts of the dominant Aristotelianism of his Order.

[8] . . . stet in einem uberschwang ir selbers und in ein nicht ir selbers geit. . . .

[9] The above is translated from the "Traktat von dem Schauen Gottes durch die wirkende Vernunft" in H. Hildebrand's *Didaktik aus der Zeit der Kreuzzüge,* pp. 38 sqq. (*Deutsche Nat. Lit.*).

cism, as in other things Germanic, the absence of the original discipline, subjection, if one will, to form and order, which the Roman domination imposed upon the peoples of the "Latin" countries.

Eckhart was followed by Ruysbroeck, Suso, Tauler, excellent contemplators all, diffusers and preachers of his thoughts. There is no need to investigate Luther's particular indebtedness to each; for the thoughts of one and all seem to converge in a small pregnant volume, composed toward the close of the fourteenth century, which Luther published and named *Theologia Deutsch.*[10] Deutsch it was unquestionably, and adapted altogether to the German temperament, and not to French reformers, who never liked it. Luther said in his preface that he had not learned more about God, Christ, man and all things, from any other book except the Bible and St. Augustine. *Theologia Deutsch* at all events discloses the contemplative religious elements directly entering the German Reformation.

It opens with Paul's "when that which is perfect is come, that which is in part shall be done away." The perfect is God; the "in part" (geteilte) is the self, the creature; and the perfect comes as the creature puts itself away. Sin is nothing else than the turning of the creature from the unchanging good to the changeable, that is, to the imperfect and "in part," and worst of all to itself. This is what the devil did when he would be something. Adam's fall was a turning from God.

How shall there be a restoration? Man can do nothing without God, and God would do nothing without man. So God took on manhood and was made man, and man thereby was made divine (vergottet). Hence I, that is, each one of us, can do nothing without God, and God will do nothing without me. God must be made man (vermenscht) in me, so that He may take on himself all that is in me, until there is nothing of me left

[10] Luther found the book in 1516, and published it; but gave it this name only in his completed edition of 1518. It has frequently been edited. I have used the edition of Mandel, in *Quellenschriften zur Ges. des Protestantismus* (Leipzig 1908).

that strives against Him. The Incarnation would not help me unless God became man in me. All good and righteousness, yea God himself, cannot help me while remaining without my soul. Eternal blessedness lies in our own soul alone.[11]

And in this renewal and bettering of myself, I do nothing but suffer it to be done. God works it all; I merely suffer His will to be done in me. I hinder God by willing what is me and mine. Yet we do not become loveless, will-less, and without knowledge or perception. Rather these faculties in us become divine, and part of the eternal will and knowledge. The more we make surrender of them, the more perfect they become in us. As Christ's soul went into hell before rising to heaven, so must the soul of man. By realizing its own vileness, it makes the more complete surrender to God.

There is purification, by repentance and renunciation; there is enlightenment, and then union with God. If one could renounce oneself and perfectly obey, he would be free from sin as Christ was. Man is good, better, or best, or the reverse, as he is obedient or disobedient. So the more there is of self-ness and me-ness, the more sin; and the less of me, the more of God.[12]

Further on it is said: "Let no one think he can attain true knowledge, or reach the life of Christ, through many questions, or by hearing or reading or study; nor through great skill and cunning, nor through the highest natural reason." Follow Christ in poorness and meekness of spirit. In the union of God, the inner man abides moveless, while the outer man may be tossed hither and thither.[13]

Our extracts have brought us to the middle of the book, which here enters upon a metaphysical discussion of the Absolute Godhead and the conscious working

[11] I have changed the position of the last sentence. These and the following passages have much that became part of Luther. One recalls that in the old pagan Mysteries the votary becomes one with the god.

[12] Here Luther wrote on the margin: Quanto decrescit ego hominis, tanto crescit in eis Ego divinum.

[13] These sentences, as most of the rest when not in quotation marks, are condensed, rather than literally translated.

God, recalling the metaphysical side of Eckhart. After beating this upper air for a while, the *Theologia Deutsch* returns to our level with the statement that God does not compel anyone to do or refrain, but suffers each man to act after his will, be it good or bad. God will withstand no one, as Christ bade Peter put up his sword. " Moreover one shall note that God's commands and His enlightenment are addressed to the inner man united with God. And when that takes place, the outer man is taught and directed by the inner man, and needs no outer law or teaching."

The book lays stress upon the distinction, dear to these German contemplators, between the two lights, the false and the true, the divine and the natural.

" The true light is God or divine, the false light is nature or natural. It belongs to God to be neither this or that, nor to will this or that, nor to seek what is particular and individual in the man that is made divine, but only the good as such. So it is with the true light. But it pertains to the creature and to nature to be something particular, and to signify and desire this and that, and not simply to desire what is good, and desire it for the sake of the good, but for the sake of something that is this or that. And as God and the true light are without me-ness and self-ness, and seek not their own, so what is me and mine, and seeks itself and its own in all things, rather than the good as good, belongs to nature and to the false natural light."

It is false, and belongs to the false light, for man to think to be as the Godhead, unmoved, suffering nothing and possessing all. He must not think to transcend the *incarnate* life of Christ on earth. So it pertains to the false light to lift human action above the sphere of the moral conscience, and think whatever it may do is well. The false light curses everything that goes against nature and is hard for man to do. " In fine, where the true light is, there is a true and righteous life, that is pleasing and dear to God. And if it is not the Christlife utterly, it still is patterned on the Christlife and holds it dear. To the Christlife belong honesty, order and all the virtues; it seeks not its own, but only the good, and for goodness's sake. But where the false light is, man is careless of Christ and all the virtues, and cares only for what is pleasing to nature." The false light loves to know too much and too many things, and glories in its knowledge.

So one shall not love himself, but the good. Even God does not love himself as self, and would have greater love for something better, did it exist. All self-love and self-will is sin. He who knows the Christlife, knows Christ; he believes in Christ who believes his life is the best; so much of the Christlife as there is in man, so much Christ is in him. Where the Christlife is, there is Christ; and where it is not, Christ is not.

Reason and will are the noblest in man; but let him know that they are not from himself. The eternal will in its origin and essence is in God; moveless and unworking in Him, it works and wills in the creature's created will. Let the creature not will as of himself, but as if his will were part of God's will. The devil came and Adam, who is nature, and sought to turn the divine will in man into self-will. The noble freedom of the will is to work as God's will; whatever makes it self-will, robs it of this noble freedom. And the freer the will is in this divine freedom, the more repugnant is evil to it, as it was utterly repugnant to Christ. In the Kingdom of heaven, there is no *own;* and anyone there seeking his own would go to hell, and anyone in hell who is without self-will rises to heaven. Man on earth is between heaven and hell, and may turn to the one or the other. By giving up self-will, one comes to Christ, and through Christ to the Father, that is, to the perfect single Good which is all in all, and in which there is no creaturehood or this and that. Disclosure of the perfect good draws the soul to it; and thus the Father draws men to Christ. And no one comes to the Father save through Christ, which is through his life, as has been shown. Thus more than once the book brings human life and thinking back to Christ and to the Christ pattern.

The *Theologia Deutsch* contains much that passed into

Luther, much also that devout souls have clung to even to our day. It says nothing about indulgences, or popes or the sacerdotal functions of the priesthood. Yet it annihilated them all. For it presented a religion in which they had no place.

The greatest of all Luther's forerunners, John Wyclif, has not yet been mentioned. He was universally recognized as an arch-heretic, which he certainly was from any Roman Catholic point of view. There is no reason to suppose that Luther read any of his writings, either in the formative period preceding the posting of the Theses against Indulgences or afterwards. John Huss, however, drew his doctrines from the Englishman. Luther appears to have read nothing of Huss, likewise a universally recognized heretic, before the time of his Leipzig disputation with Eck, in the summer of 1519, when he was accused of holding certain views of that schismatical and heretical Bohemian. Soon afterwards he received warm letters from Bohemia, with a book written by Huss;[14] and not long after he declared in an argumentative letter to Eck, that he found himself holding more tenets of Huss than he had held to at Leipzig.[15] Indeed he had "unconsciously held and taught all the doctrines of John Huss. . . . We are all Hussites without knowing it."

If Luther was a Hussite without having been taught of Huss directly, he was a Wyclifite by the same token. Wyclif did not seize upon the Pauline justification by faith, and make it the all in all of Christianity, as Luther did. But in other respects the doctrines of the two men ran parallel, and also the circumstances of their lives. They both were nationalists or patriots, revolting against the abuses of a foreign papal church; and both of them as champions of their people won such popular support that they could defy papal bulls launched against them. Both took the same stand as to papal excommunications

[14] Letter to Staupitz, Oct., 1530, De Wette's edition of Luther's letters, I. p. 341.

[15] Nov., 1530, De Wette, I. p. 356.

and interdicts; both assailed the pope as Anti-Christ and both held (though Luther only for a time) a conception of the Church as the Community of all the saints of God alive and dead. They were both active in affairs, working under a dominant impulse to destroy religious abuses; and both had the power of wrath as well as the power of speech. They both attacked papal indulgences and absolution, pilgrimages and the worship of relics; they both denounced the notion of the funded supererogatory merits of the saints making a treasury from which popes drew and distributed for value received. Both were hostile to the monks, and deemed their vows unsanctioned by Scripture; both thought that priests should marry. Both assaulted the doctrine of transubstantiation, Wyclif being the less conservative of the two; but on the other hand, Luther threw off the scholastic form in his writings more completely than Wyclif, who never rid himself of it when writing in Latin, but only when writing English. Both of them translated the Bible, or parts of it, into their native tongue, held Scripture to be the sole authority in religion, and denounced whatever went beyond it as unsanctioned and erroneous.[16] In expounding Scripture, both sought the actual meaning, and made temperate use of allegorical interpretation. With both of them, their religious doctrines were of gradual growth: they were progressive in their "heresies." But unwarranted application of their teachings and peasant wars tended to make them conservative socially and politically in the end.[17]

Regarded from the standpoint of Church politics, the sixteenth century followed the period of the complete defeat of the so-called Conciliar Movement. The fifteenth

[16] Wyclif's older contemporary Occam declares that popes and councils may err, and that Scripture only is infallible: ergo Christianus de necessitate salutis non tenetur ad credendum nec credere quod nec in Biblia continetur nec ex solis contentis in Biblia potest consequentia necessaria et manifesta inferri. See Seeberg, in *Protestantische Encyclopaedie,* article on Occam, p. 271.

[17] Wyclif will be spoken of more particularly in Chap. XIX.

had opened with the Church and papacy struggling out of the Great Schism, consequent upon the return of the popes from Avignon. Distinguished statesmen of the Church, the Frenchmen Gerson and D'Ailly, and after them the German Nicholas of Cusa, not to mention Gregor Heimburg, sought to subject the pope to the control of councils representative of the catholic nations. It was a time when councils deposed popes and attempted Church reforms. There was the Council of Pisa in 1409, and the great Council of Constance from 1414 to 1418. Finally came the Council of Basel, which dragged out its existence from 1431 to 1449. Its preposterous conduct, corruption, and palpable impotence abashed Nicholas of Cusa and other honest supporters of conciliar authority. Aided by international jealousy and the impossibility of concord among the churchmen of Spain, England, France and Germany, papal diplomacy triumphed. It had played off interest against interest, order against order, nation against nation. The threat of a general council might still be used to worry popes; but the politico-ecclesiastical incompetence of councils had been demonstrated. The Church was again a monarchy, governed by a papal Curia which was becoming completely Italian.

Never had the papacy been so glaringly and flauntingly secular as under an Alexander VI., a Julius II., or a Leo X. The effect of their reigns was to aggravate the mammon in the Church at large. The Church smacked always of this world; had at least its feet of clay. It existed on the fruits of the earth, and was at any epoch an exponent and expression of the time — in the fourth century, or in the twelfth, as well as in the fifteenth. In the early Middle Ages it became part of the feudal system so far as concerned its tenor and occupancy of land and the performance of its landed functions. Abbots and bishops held feudal rank, and usually were scions of noble or princely houses. This general condition of the Church did not pass with the Middle Ages. In Germany at the close of the fifteenth century, the higher ranks of the German clergy were filled with the sons of the nobility and the great benefices were held by princes.[18] Such a condition might prove fuel for peasant uprisings, but could not, like papal exactions, incite Germans to revolt against a foreign papal Church.

Before men revolt, they must distinguish and separate from themselves what they would revolt against. Everywhere the mediaeval clergy, with their practices and privileges, made part of the social structure of the country. If they enjoyed exemptions and exclusive rights, so did the nobles, so did the burghers of the towns. Law applying to all men was of slow and jealous growth. Special rights of a locality or an order, or even of individuals, existed everywhere, and when contested were contested by some other special right. Hence the peculiar privileges of the clergy did not seem to separate them from other classes of society, whose rights were likewise privileges. Some monarch or potentate, the king of France for instance, or the king of England, might have his quarrel with the pope, and yet the various orders of his realm might not feel themselves concerned as partisans. Such an affair was out of their sphere, went on above their heads.

In Germany, however, the conflict over the investiture of the clergy with their lands and offices was long and bitter. It seemed to center in a struggle between Emperors and popes, and tended to rouse national antipathy. The German clergy took one side or the other. But the struggle produced in the minds of the nobility and princes and their followers, a sense of antagonism to the papacy. That seemed a foreign foe, and not the less so when it intervened in German politics, in favor of one royal candidate as against another. From the thirteenth century, German antipathy to Rome is voiced by those great German voices, Walter von der Vogelweide and Freidank, whoever the latter was.[19] The current comes down the centuries, till it finds expression in the effective violence of an Ulrich von Hutten.

[18] Jansen, *Ges. des deutschen Volkes.*, Vol. I, p. 681 sqq. (seventeenth edition).

[19] Cf. *The Mediaeval Mind,* Vol. I, Chapter XXVII.

He was a knight; a thorny sprig of the German nobility. A hater of Rome, he became a truculent partisan of Luther on realizing that the latter had defied the pope. He cared not a whit for dogma or doctrine; but hated the papal power and the papal abominations imposed upon his fatherland. He fought with his pen, though he would have preferred fighting with the sword against the Italian usurper and extortioner.

If ever a book had struck hard against the temporal pretensions of the papacy, it was the book of Lorenzo Valla against the forged "Donation of Constantine." Erasmus's admiration for Valla, and the political situation, had brought this seventy-year-old writing to men's attention; and Hutten published it in 1517, with a preface of his own addressed to Leo X.[20] He never surpassed the insolent satire and mock adulation of this dedication. It had nothing to do with doctrine, and everything with false papal usurpations; and the same may be said of all Hutten's attacks upon the papacy. He speaks as a patriot, as a liberty-loving German, opposing alien tyranny. Thus for example in his *Vadiscus,* or his *Bulla vel Bullacida,* two violent invectives in the form of dialogues, belonging to the year 1520.[21] Likewise in his fierce diatribes against Caracciolo and Aleander, the papal legates at the Diet of Worms, Hutten's invective has nothing to do with doctrine: "You," he cries, "all you Roman legates are robbers of our people, betrayers of Germany, destroyers of law and justice."[22] He inveighs as well against the higher German clergy: "Out with ye, unclean swine, out from the holy place, ye trucksters; do ye not see that the air of freedom blows?" He attacks even the Emperor Charles for bowing down before the priests.

A somewhat more definite statement may be made of the papal abuses which bore intolerably upon Germany

[20] *Hutteni Opera,* ed. Boecking, Vol. I, pp. 155–161.
[21] Both printed in Vol. IV. of Boecking's edition of Hutten: *Vadiscus dialogus qui et Trias Romana inscribitur,* pp. 145–268; *Bulla* &c., pp. 309–331.
[22] *Opera Hutteni,* Ed. Boecking, Vol. II, pp. 12–21.

at this time. It will be recalled how enormous was the Church's share in the landed property of Europe. The Church is reported to have owned a quarter of all the land; its revenues vastly exceeded those of any king; it offered riches and power to its bishops, abbots, and the rest of the higher clergy, making a huge army, and all exempt from the jurisdiction of any court except the ecclesiastical. Limitations upon the papal prerogative were uncertain and contested. As watchful as it was elastic, that prerogative was prompt to take advantage of weakness on the part of princes. In 1511, Julius II. excommunicated the King and Queen of Navarre, and offered their little Kingdom to whoever would seize it. The popes had always claimed the right to grant kingdoms and territories, to deprive rulers of their domains and annul their subjects' allegiance. The exercise of papal prerogatives forms a large part of mediaeval political history. The Church held a monopoly of salvation; and the popes found that the keys of heaven and hell were mighty levers to move the kingdoms of the earth. Diligently they worked them. Through the century preceding the revolt of Luther, the need felt by the popes to regain their power after the Great Schism and the attacks of councils, combining with the tendencies of life and thought in Italy, went far toward making the papacy a sheer political institution. Its story for that century is one of effort to maintain and aggrandize its power, and prevent those ecclesiastical reforms which would have weakened its temporal resources and influence.

In the later Middle Ages, on through the fourteenth and the fifteenth centuries, into the sixteenth as well, the papacy put forth systematic claims to control the patronage of the universal Church. Popular protests and royal statutes were uncertain barriers to this sleepless encroachment upon the rights of local or national churches and of states. The papacy had abundant use for the enormously lucrative proceeds of this patronage. The expenses of the Holy See were great. In the time before us, the lavishness of Leo X. led to that indiscreet and indecent sale of indulgences which drew out Luther's Theses. The papacy's extravagance made it a universal vendor of privileges and offices within its granting, of indulgences and marriage dispensations, of bishoprics and cardinalships.

Tithes and annates from the clergy were important sources of papal revenue. The annates, consisting of about half the annual value of a benefice, were exacted upon a change of the incumbent. They attached to every ecclesiastical holding, from a parish living of twenty-five florins value to the most opulent archbishoprics. It may be added that a good part of these revenues were absorbed in their collection. As fiscal agents of the papacy, the banking house of the Fuggers, at Augsburg, is said to have retained one half.

Germany was a convenient mine for the papacy. German kings and emperors had interposed so-called Pragmatic Sanctions and Concordats; but they could not, like the French or English kings, enforce the observance of them. And while the German princes could prevent abuses in their own dominions, they failed to unite in a protective antipapal policy. Hence the resistance from great personages, or from combinations of the clergy and laity could be effective only for the time and the occasion. The German grounds of complaint against the papacy, as set forth by public men or formulated by synods of the clergy or diets of the realm, have been termed *gravamina*. The so-called *Centum gravamina*, drawn up by the diet of Worms in 1521, are a *summa* of what had been stated from time to time through the preceding centuries. In substance they embrace: (1) Complaints over papal interference with elections to bishoprics and other church offices; over the bestowal of benefices on foreigners or on unfit Germans; and over the burdens placed upon the administration of the same. (2) Complaints over the grievous exactions for the papal revenue: annates and tithes and other matters. (3) Complaints over the papal judicial procedure, in that causes which should be decided in Germany were withdrawn to Rome, and there decided arbitrarily; also over exemptions granted by the Curia from the jurisdiction of German courts, both lay and spiritual, and over other abuses of ecclesiastical procedure.[23]

[23] See B. Gebhardt, *Die gravamina der deutschen Nation gegen den römischen Hof.* (Breslau 1895) passim, and especially pp. 103–113, and pp. 126 sqq.

CHAPTER IX

MARTIN LUTHER

I. Ferment and Explosion
II. Luther's Freeing of his Spirit
III. The Further Expression of the Man

I

The *Centum Gravamina,* spoken of at the close of the last chapter, summed up the German protests against the papal church. They reflected Luther's palpable attitude toward the ecclesiastical, social, and political situation. Pointedly they corresponded with Luther's address *To the Christian nobility of the German nation,* which had appeared six months before.[1] It was one of Luther's most effective writings, and if so, one of the most immediately effective ever written by any man. Incisively, explicitly, constructively, it set forth the ecclesiastical situation, and expressed the convictions, prejudices and antipathies of the nation. It brought sound doctrine and the truth of God to bear upon conditions grasped and presented by genius. A résumé of it will disclose those conditions and abuses which had already directed the yearnings and anxieties of Luther's religious nature into a torrent of revolt from Rome.

Having premised the necessity compelling so poor an individual to address their High Mightinesses, Luther opens with a warning not to rely on one's own power or wisdom, but on God. The Romanists have reared three walls around them, defenses against reform. They are these: First that the temporal power has no authority over the spiritual, but just the contrary; secondly, that no one except the pope may interpret the Scriptures; thirdly, that only the pope can call a council.

[1] Some of Luther's points touched other grievances and in a style unsuited to a state paper. See Gebhardt, *Gravamina* &c., pp. 126–133.

The first wall is overthrown by proof that the spiritual order is not composed of the pope alone, with his monks and bishops, but by all of us; for we are all a royal priesthood through baptism. Oil and tonsure make puppet idols; only baptism can make a Christian or a priest. Humanly the choice of priests lies with the Christian community. " For no one may take upon himself that which is common, without the mandate of the community. A priest is priest while he holds the office; he may be deposed, and then becomes peasant or burgher again. It follows that there is no distinction save that of office or function between laity and priests, between princes and bishops, between ' spiritual ' and ' temporal ' or worldly, as they are called. For all are members of the spiritual order, and really bishops, priests and popes, though they have not the same function; but neither has every priest and monk."

Now just as the " spiritual " are worthier than other Christians only because of their ministry, " so the temporal magistrates hold the sword and the rods that they may punish the wicked and protect the just. A shoemaker, a smith, a peasant, has the office of his handiwork; yet they are consecrated priests and bishops; and everyone should be useful and serviceable to the other, with his work or office, as all kinds of works are directed to serve the needs of one community, body and soul." It is for the temporal authorities to aid and punish priests, just as much as it is for shoemakers to make their shoes. Beyond their office, the alleged greater worth of the spiritual order is a human invention.

Think for yourselves, he bids his auditors, and recognize how preposterous is the notion that only the wicked pope may interpret Scripture, or call a council. The absurdity of the last idea grows as we consider the matters which councils properly may handle: to wit, the worldly pride of the pope with his three crowns, when the greatest king is content with one; the plundering of Germany and other countries, to find benefices for the cardinals, through which the land is wasted and the flock of Christ deprived of its pastors; the monstrous papal court which Germany helps to support by sending three hundred thousand gulden annually to Rome, and gets nothing in return — no wonder we are poor, but rather that we have not starved! "Here my complaint is not that God's command and Christian right is despised in Rome, for all is not so well in the rest of Christendom that we may make this high accusation. Neither do I complain that natural or temporal law and reason are made of no effect. The trouble lies deeper. I complain that Rome does not observe her own cunningly devised canon law, which in itself is tyranny, avarice, pride, rather than law."

The complaints thus far set forth were not novel. Other men had stated one or more of them before Luther, who now passes to more specific grievances. He begins with the Annates, and then points to one abusive exaction after another through which the pope and his cardinals plunder Germany. "How long will ye, ye noble princes and lords, leave your land open to such ravening wolves? . . . If Rome is not a brothel above all other brothels imaginable, I know not what a brothel is." There all things conceivable and inconceivable are done for gold. He refers briefly to other impositions — indulgences, permission to eat meat in Lent; and then proceeds to the remedies which the temporal power or a general council should prescribe. It will be enlightening to follow his points:

1. Let every prince, nobleman, and city forbid and abolish the annates.

2. Let them also see that no more benefices pass to the use of Rome.

3. Let an imperial edict prohibit bishops and other dignitaries from going to Rome for their installation; and forbid appeals to Rome in controversies: for now bishops and archbishops have no real power, but only the pope.

4. Prohibit the carrying of civil suits to Rome. What touches the temporalities of the clergy may be decided before a consistory of German prelates; only let them not sell justice as it is sold at Rome.

5. Abolish the papal reservation of benefices upon the death of the incumbent; and if Rome send an unrighteous ban, let it be despised, as from a thief.

6. Abolish *casus reservati,* i.e. sins reserved for the pope to absolve from.

7. Let the Roman Curia abolish its useless offices and reduce its pomp.

8. Let the bishop no longer take those oaths that bind them to the Curia, and let the Kaiser resume the right of investiture.

9. Let the Kaiser cease to abase himself by kissing the pope's toe; and let the pope have only the authority over the Kaiser of a bishop who crowns and anoints him.

10. Let the pope surrender his claim to the Kingdom of Naples and Sicily and other principalities which do not belong to him.

11. Have done with kissing his feet; let him ride or walk and not be borne by men, and no longer receive the sacrament seated, from a kneeling cardinal offering it on a golden salver.

12. Let pilgrimages to Rome be abolished, not as evil in themselves, but because it is not well for pilgrims to see the wickedness of Rome. Pilgrimages after all are questionable; it is better for a man to attend to his duties at home.

13. Build no more cloisters for the Mendicants; let them stop their begging, preaching, and confessing.

14. The marriage of the clergy was not forbidden in apostolic times. "I advise that it again be made free and left to the discretion of each to marry or not." Especially the parish priests should be allowed to marry their housekeepers, with whom they live, and legitimatize their children.

15. Let the rules of confession for the wretched cloisters be changed, so that monks and nuns more freely may confess their secret sins.

16. Give up the masses and fixed prayers for the souls of the dead; which are done without love. "It is im-

possible that a work should be pleasing to God which is not done freely in love."

17. Abolish various ecclesiastical penalties, including the interdict.

18. Give up all saints' days, with their carousing, except Sundays.

19. Change the degrees within which marriage is forbidden; abolish fasts.

20. Tear down the forest chapels, where miracles occur for gold; give up pilgrim jaunts, and let God exalt the saints.

21. Forbid begging through Christendom; let each town care for its poor.

22. Abolish the new foundations for prayers and masses for departed souls.

23. Have done with papal dispensations and indulgences — a measure which Luther urges with telling invective against the pope, and a call on Christ to descend and destroy the devil's nest in Rome.

24. Come to an accord with the Bohemians, and recognize whatever truth and justice there may be in their convictions.

25. Reform the universities, where there is too much Aristotle and too little Christ. Throw out Aristotle's *Physics, Metaphysics,* and the rest of him, except his *Logic, Rhetoric,* and *Poetics,* which, in condensed form might be kept for elementary discipline. Maintain Latin, Greek and Hebrew, with mathematics and history. I leave it to the physicians to reform their faculty; but with regard to jurisprudence it were well to omit the Canon Law, especially the Decretals. There is enough in the Bible. As for our secular law, God help us, it is a jumble of territorial law and custom and imperial law. For the theologians, I say, let them give up the Sentences [of the Lombard] for the Bible, and reduce the number of treatises. Let the Bible be read in the schools.

26. The papacy professes to have taken the Empire from the Greeks, and to have handed it over to the Ger-

mans. But the pope has our goods and honor, our bodies, lives and souls! Nevertheless, though the papacy took the Empire dishonestly, we have honestly received it: let us rule and manage it in freedom, not as slaves of the pope. Let the German Emperor be emperor indeed, in right and freedom.

27. For ourselves, we are luxurious and extravagant. We should be as well off with less trade and commerce. It were better to have more agriculture. And alas for our excesses in eating and drinking, for which we Germans have such ill repute abroad. Finally, alas for the houses of ill-fame among us! and alas also for their complement, the mistaken vows of chastity, on the part of monks and nuns and priests, which so few can keep! I have spoken boldly; perhaps too sharply. But it is better to anger the world than God!

In the power of its wrathful reason, the address to the German nobility is Luther truly, and yet Luther speaking as a German. It shows him as an element in a situation, and serves to introduce us to him through his participation in the convictions and detestations of his people. It is far from an expression of his innermost self, or of the needs, anxieties, and impulses which first drove him into a convent and then drove him out from that bounden way of living which brought no rest to his soul. His nature was religious fundamentally; its anxieties and impulses hung on his soul's relationship to God. To all this he gave convincing utterance in his tract upon *The Freedom of a Christian,* the pronunciamento of his very self. But before examining that writing, it were well to remember the lines of antecedents which drew together into this burning nature, and then observe the youthful fermentation preceding the explosion.

The inner verity (or falsity!) and outward facts of Luther's life — themes of whole libraries! Of outward facts it will be recalled that he was born at Eisleben in 1483 of well-to-do peasant stock. While he was a baby, his parents moved to the neighboring town of Mansfield, where mining was the chief industry. His father became a miner, a work for which the boy Martin showed himself unfit; the mines impressed him as murky places where devils bewitch and fool men with pockets of false ore, which were not so easy in the light of day. From his childhood to his dying day Luther believed in devils present and perceptible, perplexing men and hindering them, filling them with wicked doubts and devilish fears. One remembers his circumstantial story of devils throwing hazel nuts at him in bed in his chamber at the Wartburg.

In due course he was sent away from home to schools (of which he has little good to say) at Magdeburg, and then at Eisenach, where his pleasing boy's voice, singing in the street for his supper, won him the affection of Frau Cotta, wife of a prosperous merchant. When seventeen he entered the flourishing university of Erfurt. There he pursued philosophy of the scholastic type, adhering to the popular and progressive nominalism of Occam. A band of youthful humanists were gathering there at Erfurt. But Luther was never tempted toward classicism of style, though his earliest letters are not free from current humanistic phrases. He read the usual Latin authors, and became as ready with that tongue as he was with his mother German. It is not recorded that he was addicted to reading the Bible, or noticeably affected by religion. At the end of a year he received his Bachelor's degree, and three years later was made a magister with some éclat. He entered now upon the study of law, for which his father intended him.

But something happened to him, or perhaps had already happened, or been prepared, within him. In July, 1505, near Erfurt, he was caught in a heavy thunderstorm, and cried out: "Help, good St. Anna, I will become a monk." Something within him, beyond physical terror, must have responded to the thunder. It was the moment, or occasion, of his conversion. He announced his purpose, bade formal farewell to his friends, and entered the Augustinian convent there at Erfurt. The town had seven other monasteries, and he chose well; for the

Augustinian convent was pious and orderly, given to preaching and clean living; and had the admirable Staupitz for its head. Luther found there nothing to make him waver. He had fifteen months to consider his decision before taking the final vows. In the year following that event he was ordained priest (1507).

Luther's convent life passed in study and strenuous observance. He devoted himself to scholastic theology and philosophy, still following Occam, in whose system lay much disintegrating criticism of the whole scholastic structure. He also studied the works of Peter D'Ailly, a broadminded churchman, who favored the authority of Councils, and those of Gabriel Biel, an influential German scholastic who had recently died. He began a close reading of the Bible, which was not as yet to bring him certitude or peace. What was taking place in his mind? It was tortured with anxieties and fears beyond the understanding of his fellows. But one should not think of him as on the verge of religious melancholia; for a mental condition which might to-day denote weak reason and a neurotic temperament, had no such significance in the early sixteenth century, when the most intelligent were still justified by their intellectual environment in entertaining a lively fear of hell. In Luther's personality a powerfully reasoning faculty and an immense rational perception were united with emotional energy and that religious or self-depreciating temperament which contemplates human destinies as dependent on a mightiest being, and deems its salvation to lie in obedient union with that Being. Thus Luther's mind was held in dilemmas of its general education and doctrinal instruction, and its furthest spiritual intuitions. It was tormented by its sinfulness and inability to attain a righteousness that should unite him with the Being in whom was its salvation. The young Luther was endeavoring punctiliously to fulfil the righteousness of a monk; but his life, exemplary to others' eyes, seemed to him infected with shortcomings and frustration. Deep spasms of unhappiness came over him. One may also remember that he was twenty-five years old, and of a temper that might be prone to the ardors of the flesh.

In 1508 the watchful Staupitz procured Luther's call to Wittenberg, to teach logic and ethics of the Aristotelian brand in the Saxon Elector's new university. But before many months elapsed he returned to the Erfurt convent in order to teach or study theology. In 1511 Staupitz sent him with a brother monk on an errand to Rome. There his heart filled with reverence for the Eternal City with its myriad tombs and relics of the martyred saints; but he was shocked, as any earnest inexperienced German would have been, by the worldliness and immorality of the clergy. After his return in 1512 he settled permanently in the Augustinian convent at Wittenberg, to teach theology and philosophy at the university, which now made him a doctor of theology. He called himself Professor of Holy Scripture. Preaching was soon added to his duties; he had the gift for this, though at first he spoke with trepidation. In 1515 he was made district vicar of his Order, an office which put eleven monasteries under his care. His life had ceased to be that of a recluse monk; he had become a man of varied duties among men, with a huge correspondence, and the beginnings of a prodigious literary activity. No greater preacher had appeared in Germany; and never was there so great a pamphleteer as Luther became. His occupations freed him from the danger of morbidity, and with his studies and lecturing, promoted the growth of all his faculties.

Luther's first lecture course was upon the Psalms. The next year he took up Paul's Epistle to the Romans, and in expounding it, learned much for himself, as he says, " saw the light." He continued with a course on Galatians. According to the traditional interpretation concurred in by Erasmus, Paul's " works of the law " referred to Jewish ceremonies. Luther maintained that Paul meant the whole moral law included in the Decalogue. [2] It mattered little if man could not fulfil the minutiae of a ceremonial abrogated by Christ; but it was quite a differ-

[2] Letter to Spalatin of Oct. 19, 1516 — De Wette's Edition, I, p. 39. My references to Luther's letters are to this edition.

ent affair to become convinced that no man could fulfil the unabrogated moral law of God. This conviction appears to have driven Luther to take refuge with Paul in salvation through faith.

As Luther had little knowledge of Greek or Hebrew, he was obliged to use the Vulgate. He sought guidance in the works of the Church Fathers, especially Augustine; and also studied the commentary of Nicholas of Lyra, and the very recent work of Lefévre of Étaples.[3] Besides which, he read Tauler and the *Theologia Deutsch.* In 1516 appeared Erasmus' edition of the Greek New Testament, and Luther set himself to master that tongue. His mind always pressed for the best scholarship on the subjects holding his interest; before this, he had spoken out boldly for Reuchlin, against the bigots of Cologne. He cared little for Aquinas and his school; and began to abjure their pagan master, Aristotle. His influence was already felt by his friends at Wittenberg, among whom was Carlstadt, whose later radical views were to prove such a thorn in Luther's side. By May, 1517, he speaks of " our theology " as progressing, while Aristotle is declining to defeat.

Naturally Luther's keen mind perceived the follies of sundry religious practices, while his increasing knowledge of men and affairs acquainted him with the corruption in the priesthood and the monastic orders. He began to think pilgrimages foolish, and to say so in his sermons. While not as yet condemning in principle the worship of the saints, he protested vigorously, as Erasmus did, against the preposterous prayers which they were asked to grant; and he showed the silliness of some of their legends. He was painfully impressed with the dearth of true Gospel preaching in the Church.

Through the crying corruption of an institution, one may be led to denounce the institution itself on principle. It was thus with Luther in regard to indulgences. As early as July, 1516, he spoke with some uncertainty against abuses of the practice. And in later sermons through

[3] Cf. ante p. 153 and post p. 384 sqq.

that year and the first half of the next, he continued his attack upon their pernicious effects, while still recognizing their legitimate basis in the merits of Christ and the saints. Indulgences indeed were very old, and, within limits, justified by good church doctrine. It had long been held that sins committed after baptism could be blotted out only through the sacrament of penance. Repentance, confession to a priest, and acts in atonement were required. The priest pronounced absolution from eternal punishment, yet the satisfaction of penitential acts must be rendered, to relieve the sinner from punishment in purgatory. Various forms of penance were allowed: one could go on a crusade, or undertake less dangerous pilgrimages; then there were fasts and scourgings, and at last the payment of money. The souls of the dead might be released from purgatory by money payments. In the popular mind, and often by the connivance of the clergy, such payments freed the sinner from all the evil consequences of his sins.

This system appeals to many instincts, and, considering the level of intelligence through the Middle Ages, one realizes that the Church could not have maintained moral discipline by any more spiritual means. The old *wergeld* was in the blood; men understood penance and absolution upon atonement, payment — the painful costly act, or the money handed to the priest. Righteousness through faith alone would have been intangible.

By the sixteenth century, men had become more intelligent, and the abuses of the penitential system appeared grosser, and, in fact, had become more pronounced and demoralizing. In the famous instance before us, Pope Leo X., needing money to complete St. Peter's, proclaimed a "plenary indulgence" offering sweeping benefits to purchasers; and the impecunious Hohenzollern Albrecht, Archbishop of Mainz, bargained with the pope to manage the sale of indulgences in Germany on shares. Tetzel, a Dominican, was his agent. Now be it marked that the campaign of Tetzel, whose approach to Wittenberg roused Luther to post those famous Theses, had already led Duke George of Saxony, stanchest of Catholics, to forbid the sale within his territory. The great Elector too, Luther's Elector Frederic, had forbidden Tetzel to enter his part of Saxony. But without crossing the Saxon border, Tetzel had come near enough to draw many good Wittenbergers to his sale.

Luther devoted some months of study and reflection to the whole matter of penance and indulgences; and on the last day of October, 1517, he posted on the door of the Castle church the notice of a disputation together with the ninety-five propositions, or theses, which he proposed to maintain.

These began with a statement that when Christ commanded repentance he meant that the entire life of the believer should be a state of penitence. Passing on from this broad premise, the Theses, point by point, or rather blow on blow, demonstrated the futility of the sale and purchase of indulgences, and attacked the heart of the papal, or Catholic, penitential system. For example: the pope can remit only those punishments which he has prescribed in accord with sound doctrine: when the coin clinks in the box, though avarice may gain, forgiveness still depends on God; whoever thinks that the Indulgence makes his salvation sure, is damned eternally with those who taught him so; every Christian who lives in true repentance has complete remission of his sins, without any letter of indulgence; true penitence loves punishment, the indulgence marks its rejection; he does better who gives his money to the poor; the indulgences issuing from the so-called treasury of the Church makes the last first; Christ's gospel is the true treasure of the church, and makes the first last.

The doctrinal details of this controversy are no longer of interest. But the conflict was important for the world, being the obvious occasion of Luther's rupture with the papal church; for himself it was important as a stage in the attainment of his spiritual freedom; a fact of which he seems to have been conscious, since he now took to signing himself in letters to his friends, Martin Eleutherius, or Martin the Free. There is no need to speak of the storm of enthusiasm as well as condemnation, which the Theses roused, loosed, one might say. Germany was stirred; so were the indulgence sellers and papal advocates, and in time the papacy itself. Thousands of books have told the story, not always quite in the same words! The course of the dispute educed the steadfast intrepidity of Luther's nature, and served to show him where he stood and perforce must stand. Thus his defense before the papal legate Cajetan at Augsburg, his argument with the more deft and understanding Miltitz, the formal disputation with Doctor Eck at Leipzig, the lowering and certain papal excommunication, and at last its fall, all helped to evoke the man and propel him onward to the final freeing of his spirit. Friends and adherents anxiously upheld his hands, and the protection of his prince prevented his bodily snuffing out by papal legates.

II

A man whom the papal catholic church sought to annihilate, and who on his side was preparing to cast loose from it, would feel the need to justify and strengthen his steps. Luther felt as well the deeper need to make firm his convictions touching his new assurance of salvation, which was grounded, and had its height and depth, in faith, and had freed his soul not only from the salvation which the papal church claimed to monopolize, hierarchically and sacerdotally as it were, but also from the bondage of the works which the Church held needful for every one that should be saved. Thus, both within his soul and for the edification of the world, Luther had to establish a justification of his severance from the papal church, and the grounds of his saving faith.

Since the papal ban was about to fall on him, his first task was to demonstrate its nullity. Shortly after posting his Theses he had spoken on this, but by no means finally. Afterwards, returning to the subject (1519), he wrote a sermon on the Holy Sacrament of the Communion, as preparatory to the examination of the obviously connected *excommunicatio* which he considered in his weighty "Sermon on the Ban," written in 1519, and published early in the next year. He argues thus: As the Sacrament is both sign and significance, so is the Communion twofold. Priest or pope cannot sever the believer from the spiritual communion which rests in faith, though he may be excluded from outer participation in the Sacrament. This was the lesser excommunication. When extended to the prohibition of all intercourse as well as Christian burial, it became the greater excommunication. Later it carried with it fire and sword, thus going beyond Scripture, which leaves the sword to the secular authorities. An excommunicated person may be forbidden the Sacrament and even deprived of burial, and yet be safe and blessed in the Communion of Christ. Conversely, many who are admitted to the Sacrament may be in a state of spiritual separation. No excommunication has the effect of delivering the soul into hell, though, when deserved, it may be a sign that the faithless soul has given itself over to the devil through its sins. The object of the excommunication is to bring the damned soul back. Christians should honor and love it as the warning punishment of motherly love. So the sermon showed that even a rightful excommunication should not be regarded as an object of terror; while an unjust ban was a spiritual nullity. After Luther's excommunication, the latter point received adequate treatment in his polemic, *Against the Bull of the Antichrist.*

With his mind settled as to the spiritual impotence of papal bulls, the ills which might happen to his body could safely be left with God and the secular powers. He was a fearless man. But now while his opponent Dr. Eck was publishing the Bull in Saxony, Luther launched a mighty blow at the papal edifice, from which he had just emerged, or been ejected. At the close of his *Address to the German Nobility,* he had announced another little song about Rome and about his enemies who would accept no peace from him, and loud would he sing it. If the *Address* had breached those three walls with which Rome had bulwarked her corruption, he would now shatter her inner defenses and the armory where she forged her weapons and the chains in which she held the Church. In fine, it was the papal sacramental system that he sought to destroy by this *Prelude upon the Babylonian Captivity of the Church*. As his argument dealt largely with dogma, he chose to write the piece in Latin.

" I learn more every day, as I must, since so many clever masters push me on," — says Luther, mockingly. " And now would that what I have written on indulgences might be burnt, so that I might simply declare: indulgences are a vain invention of the Roman Flatterer. Eck and his like have taught me such things of the pope's high mightiness, that I could also throw away whatever I have written on that matter; for now I see that the papacy is Babylon, the dominion of the mighty hunter, the sheer dumping ground of the bishop of Rome."

The sacraments are not seven, but three, Baptism, Penance, and the Eucharist; and indeed Penance should be excluded if a sacrament is a promise coupled with a sign. The Eucharist is held captive first through the pope's godless withholding of the cup from the laity, whose conscience craves it; secondly through the doctrine of transubstantiation; thirdly, by the teaching that the mass is a sacrifice and a good work. But neither the pope nor even a general council can make new articles of belief. In the celebration of the mass, only faith is needed, faith in Christ promising forgiveness of sins to those who believe that his body and blood were given for them.

Through baptism, he who believes and is baptized will be saved: the belief is everything; the act is but the outer sign, carrying no saving virtue. But the freedom of our baptism is led captive by the pope through set prayers and fasts and gifts. And as for further vows, would that all those of monks and nuns and pilgrimages could be swept away; for they impugn the freedom of baptism, wherein indeed we undertook more than we ever shall fulfil! All rash vows, and vows of the young should be held void.

The pope alone can dispense vows! Absurd! Everyone may, for his neighbor or himself. But neither the pope nor another can dispense from the holy vows of marriage. Divorce is such an abomination that bigamy were better. Nor has the pope authority to invent artificial impediments, for the breach of which, unless he dispense them, the marriage may be dissolved. Yet marriage is not a sacrament, since it carries no promise and exacts no faith. Neither is confirmation, ordination, or extreme unction. As for penance (whether it be a sacrament or not), its virtue which lies in the divine promise and our faith, has been made null by prescribed works of repentance, confession and atonement. Whereupon Luther returns to his attack upon indulgences.

The "Babylonian Captivity of the Church" was for Luther himself, and for all the world, a sufficiently emphatic declaration of the Christian's independence of the papacy and its sacramental monopoly. But it did not contain the demonstration of that fuller freedom of the human spirit which lies in the certitude of man's salvation in his direct relationship with God through Christ. A broad foundation for this freedom was laid in Luther's sermon *On good works,* written in the early part of 1520, Those only are good works which are commanded by God; only those acts which He has forbidden are sins. The first and noblest of good works is faith, without which prayers, fasts, pious foundations and all outer acts, are vain. With faith every daily act of life and business is good; and everyone knows when he does right by the inner confidence that his act is pleasing to God. Any work done without faith might be done by Turk or heathen, Jew or sinner. Faith is not to be classed with other works, since it alone makes all other works good, and brings with it love, peace, joy, hope. In faith, distinctions between works fall away, and all works are equally good, since they are good and pleasing to God not in themselves but through faith in His word. Doubt leads the Christian to distinguish between works and question which is better. Only faith comforts us in our works, sorrows, and disappointments and dispels the thought that God has forsaken us, even when we stand in prospect of death and fear of hell.

Works without faith justify no one in the sight of God. Our works are praiseworthy only through our faith that they are pleasing to Him. Had every one faith, no laws would be needed. All things and works are free to a Christian through his faith; but because others do not yet believe, he works with them, and suffers them, freely, knowing that this pleases God. Thus the freedom of faith is no freedom to do evil, harmful acts. And Luther proceeds to set forth in detail that excellence of living which comes with faith in Christ and accords with the commands of God.

Such is the foundation of the freedom which Luther sought for himself and for every man. But in the tract upon the "Freedom of the Christian Man" written also in 1520, Luther completes the structure of this freedom, and indicates the way his mind had reached it; as Paul set forth in the Epistle to the Galatians the way of freedom which he had found, and now declared to them.

Miltitz, a gentleman of the world as well as a papal agent, seeing the dangers involved in the Lutheran revolt, sought a means of truce. He tried to persuade Luther into some sort of submission to the pope, perhaps unaware as yet of the vast truculence of Luther's nature. In the autumn of 1520 when Luther in fact was under excommunication, Miltitz asked him to write a letter to the pope and dedicate a conciliatory work to him. The request bore other fruit! Luther wrote a letter and prefixed it to *The Freedom of the Christian Man,* which was nearly through the press, antedating both the letter and the treatise, that they might not seem to have been written under the pressure of the ban. Indeed they scarcely would have given that impression. The letter was written in Latin and German, while the treatise was written in German, but was shortly followed by a Latin translation bearing the title *Tractatus de libertate Christiana.* [4]

[4] The German Title "Von der Freiheit eines Christenmenschen" is usu-

Luther begins his letter with an elaborate protestation that he has never said a word against His Holiness, and has always spoken of him with the respect felt by all. Indeed he had called Leo a Daniel in Babylon! He had, to be sure, attacked certain impious doctrines, and those who maintained them. Yet he will be found pliable and yielding, except as to the word of God, by which he must stand. True it is, continues Luther, that I have attacked your Chair, which is called the Curia; but no one knows better than yourself that its state is worse than Sodom or Gomorrah or Babylon! And I am grieved that in your name and that of the Roman Church, they have betrayed and robbed the poor throughout the world. I will stand against that! None is better aware than you, that for years nothing but corruption of body, soul, and estate has come out of Rome: all the people see that the once holy Roman church has become a den of cutthroats and a house of shame, of death and damnation! And you, Holy Father, sit as a sheep among wolves!

The writer goes on, pouring the vials of his wrath upon the papacy, with revilings not unlike those in the letter which Hutten prefixed to Valla's book on the forged "Donation of Constantine." "It is for you and your cardinals to cure this woe. But the disease laughs at the physic. . . . This is why I am sad, you pious Leo, to see you pope, for you are worthy of being pope in better times. The Roman chair is not fit for such as you: the evil spirit ought to be pope. . . . Would to God, you would resign this honor, as your spiteful enemies call it. . . . O thou most unhappy Leo, seated on the most perilous of chairs! . . ."

"See, my lord Father, this is why I have struck at this pestilential chair so violently. I had hoped to have earned your thanks. I thought it would be a blessing to you and many others to rouse intelligent and learned men against the ruinous disorder of your court. They who

ally rendered into English, as "the freedom of a Christian man," perhaps the best rendering, if one will bear in mind that *Mensch* means human being. Both versions of the letter are given in De Wette, Vol I, pp. 497 sqq.

attack such a Curia do the work which you should do; they honor Christ who put that court to shame." In fine, those are good Christians who are bad Romans! — And for me, when I had thought to keep silence, and had said 'Adieu! sweet Rome, stink on'; then the devil set on his servant Eck to drag me to a disputation! But that I should recant, and submit to be ruled in the interpretation of God's word, which is freedom,— never! As for thee, trust not those who would exalt thee as its sole interpreter; but honor those who would bring thee down. I, who cannot flatter, am forced to come to thy aid, and not with empty hands, but with a little book.— and Luther presents him *The Freedom of a Christian Man.*

The letter to Leo was written as a letter to Leo; but the little book which Luther as an afterthought presented him, was written to set forth for himself and those who might hold with him, the moving convictions of his spiritual freedom. The soul of Paul lives in this German sixteenth century book, which opens with a lofty Pauline paradox: "A Christian is a free lord over all things, and subject to no man. A Christian is a bounden servant to all things, and subject to everyone."

The solid reasoning of Luther's argument will best be brought out by following it point by point, on to its veritable attainment.

A Christian is both spirit and body. After the first he is a spiritual, new, and inner man; according to flesh and blood, he is a corporeal, old, outer man. Hence the scripture paradox, that he is both bond and free.

In so far as he is a spiritual inner man, no outer thing can make him pious and free. For piety and freedom, or their opposites, are not of the outer man. That the body is free and satisfied, or the reverse, neither helps nor hurts the soul.

The soul is not helped when the body puts on holy garb, frequents churches, prays, fasts, or does any good work; for an evil man can do all this. Nor is the soul injured when the body abstains from all this.

The soul needs only the holy Gospel, the word of God

preached by Christ; she has food and joy and light and truth, wisdom and freedom in that.

In that word thou shalt hear thy God telling thee that thy life and works are nothing in God's sight, but must eternally perish (ewiglich verderben). Believing in thy guiltiness, thou must despair of thyself, and with firm faith give thyself to God's dear Son and trust in him. Then thy sins will be forgiven thee through faith, thy destruction (verderben) vanquished, and thou wilt be righteous, at peace, with all commands fulfilled, and free from all things, as St. Paul says (Rom. 1, 17; 10, 4).

Therefore the true work and practice for Christians lies in building up Christ and the word within them, and in constantly strengthening their faith.

Faith alone, without works, makes righteous. Scripture consists in commands and promises. The former belong to the Old Testament, and bring no strength to fulfil them, which we cannot do.

Then the man despairs. But the divine promise assures him; if thou wilt fulfil all, and be free from sin and from desire of evil, believe on Christ in whom I promise thee grace and righteousness, peace and freedom. Believing, thou hast; unbelieving, thou hast not. God alone commands; and God alone fulfils. The promises are God's words in the New Testament.

" These and all words of God are holy, true, righteous, peaceful, free, and full of all good things; therefore, whosoever cleaves to them in right faith, his soul is so entirely united with them, that all the virtues of the word become the soul's, and through faith the soul is by God's word holy, righteous, peaceful, free and full of all good things, a true child of God. . . . No good work cleaves to God's word like faith, nor can be in the soul, where only the word and faith can reign. What the word is, that the soul becomes through the word, as iron becomes glowing red as the fire, through union with it. Hence one sees faith is sufficient for the Christian; he needs no work in order to be righteous. If then he needs no work, he is assuredly loosed from all commands and laws."[5]

To believe in God is to honor Him: to disbelieve is to dishonor Him. When God sees the soul thus honoring Him, He honors the soul, and holds it righteous.

Faith joins the soul to Christ, as bride to bridegroom. They become one. All the good things of Christ becomes the soul's, and the sins and negligences of the soul become Christ's. All sins are swallowed up in Christ's invincible righteousness.

Faith fulfils all commands, and makes righteous; for it fulfils the First Commandment, to honor God, and that fulfils them all. "But works are dead things, which cannot honor and praise God, though they may be done in His honor. Here we seek not that which is done like the works, but the doer and workman who honors God and does the works. That is none other than the heart's faith, which is the head and entire being of piety. (Frömmigkeit.) Therefore it is a dangerous dark saying, when one exhorts to fulfil the commands of God with works, since the fulfilment must take place through faith before all works; and the works follow the fulfilment, as we shall hear."

In the Old Testament, God reserved the first born male of man and beast, and gave him lordship and priesthood. This was a symbol of Christ, to whom is given the spiritual priesthood and kingship; which he shares with all who believe on him. Hence spiritually we are lords over all things, not as bodily possessing them, but as spiritually made free regarding them.

Through faith all believers are priests and intercessors, and lords of all, through God's power, who does their will; and we need nothing, and have abundance — spiritually. We lose it by thinking to achieve it by good works, and not through faith.

In Christendom, priests are distinguished from laity

[5] I use quotation marks here, because I have translated this passage in full. Elsewhere I have usually condensed the substance of the tract.

merely as ministers of the word and servers, with no further privilege over other Christians.

It is not enough for the preacher to tell the story of Christ; he must make plain all that Christ is to us; through whom we are kings and priests, with lordship over all things, and freed from the works of the Law, our sins taken by Christ, and his righteousness ours through faith.

But men are not all spirit; not altogether the inner man. We are also bodies. Thus the Christian is the servant of all, and bound to the service of all. Let us see.

Though we are "inner" men, justified through faith, yet we continue in this bodily life, associating with other men. Here works begin; and the body must be practised in good works, that it may conform to faith and the inner man, and not cause him to stumble. The inner man is one with God, and joyful in the doing of Christ's will in love freely; but he finds a contrary will in his own flesh, willing the lusts of the world, which faith cannot endure as Paul saith.

Works must not be done in the thought that they make the man righteous before God; but voluntarily, and freely, to please God; as Adam did what pleased God, while still righteous in Eden.

Thus it is truly said, just works do not make a just man; but a just man does just works. Nor do evil works make an evil man; but an evil man does evil works.

Conversely, good works will not save one who is without faith; nor will evil works bring him to perdition, but his unbelief. So it is vain and damnable to rely on works, or preach them uncoupled with faith.

As toward men, our works must be done in love. My God has given to me, utterly worthless and damned, righteousness and salvation through Christ, *so that henceforth I need only to believe that this is so.* I will act toward my neighbor likewise. So the Virgin, after Christ's birth, went to the Temple for her purification; not that she was impure, but did it freely out of love, so as to show no contempt for other women. And so Paul circumcised Timothy. On like grounds, we should be subject to the authorities.

Thus no work is good, unless its end is to serve another. Few cloisters, churches, masses, have been founded or endowed from love, but rather, vainly, to cure the founder's sins. Freely must the good things of God flow from one to another of us.

" From all this, the conclusion follows that a Christian does not live unto himself, but in Christ and his neighbor: in Christ through faith, in his neighbor through love. Through faith he ascends above himself in God, and through love passes out from God again beneath himself, yet abides always in God and godlike love. . . . Behold, that is the true, spiritual Christian freedom which frees the heart from all sins, laws and commands, which surpasses all other freedom as the heaven the earth. This may God give us truly to understand and keep. Amen."

So love and service of one's neighbor are made the criterion and sanctification of all the Christian's acts. His conduct shall not be hampered and harassed by anxieties regarding his sinlessness, holiness, aloofness from the dross of life. He does not need the safeguard of monastic vows: let him marry and beget children, or bear them if the Christian be a woman. Let the two take part in the business of life, plant and hoe and cook unpestered with vows and fasts and pilgrimages, so long as their lives are useful and do not cause their neighbor to stumble. Righteousness needs no other guaranty than faith, and the motive of useful service springing from it.

The incidents of Luther's life, which have been mentioned and the writings that have been analyzed, indicate the progress of his convictions until the time of his revolt and excommunication. To recapitulate: we know little of the experiences of his mind during his years at school and at the Erfurt university. But we know that from the time of his apparently sudden conversion he felt acute anxiousness over his sinfulness and consequent perdition. Life in the Augustinian convent consisted in conformity to a moral and religious code, in the observance of monastic rules, and the performance of incidental or occasional duties. Luther found that he could not clear his conscience and assure himself of salvation by the strictest fulfilment of these requirements, any more than Paul could satisfy his mind and justify himself by his efforts to do the work of the Law. Spiritual certitude was an imperative need with both. Paul, perhaps in that spiritually fruitful sojourn in Arabia (Gal. I, 17) cast off the saving agency of works and ensconced himself in the principle of faith in Christ Jesus. Luther in the early years of his professorship at Wittenberg (1512-16) following the example and the doctrine of Paul, accepted faith in Christ as the sole means and principle of salvation. It was a saving grace flowing directly from the Saviour to the sinner, without the intervention of any pope or priest, who to Luther's mind were prescribers of the outer act, the good work, the work of the Law, and were guarantors of its efficacy, which Luther had disproved in himself. So in accepting faith as the sole principle of salvation, he virtually freed himself both from the need of the visible church and from its authority.

He had accomplished this for himself, and had imparted some of the freedom of his faith to his associates and pupils, by the year 1516 or 1517. Then Tetzel came with his indulgences. Luther was aroused to a protest pregnant with defiance and revolt, by the abominable nature of this bartered and sold salvation, and by the realization that it directly countered salvation through faith, which he had reached by grace and not through money. Had there been no abuse, Luther would not have been stung to an open attack first upon the abuse and then upon the doctrine; but might have kept on quietly teaching salvation through faith. The sale of indulgences, which was his call to action, made clear to him his strength and independence. The posting of his Theses, and their astounding reception, impressed him with his rôle and duty to act for his Germans too.

The angry controversy which followed served to clear his thoughts, expand his arguments, and demonstrate the need to abandon other practices and tenets of the papal church. Moreover, the war against indulgences pushed on this very willing man to champion the cause of his Germans against Rome; and as the fray progressed he carried them along with him, from point to point, to ever clearer opposition to the papal church. He frees them, as he frees himself, from subjection to the papal hierarchy, and from the system of salvation which depends on priestly mediation and consists so largely in the performance of acts prescribed by priestly authority. Thus from denunciation of the abuse he advances to emphatic opposition to the institution from which the abuse had emanated, and emancipates his people, all stirred with German wrath against Rome, from Papal authority, and leads them on into that freedom of the Christian which is through faith alone. As a result, the imperial unity of the Roman Catholic church is broken, and the way laid open to other kinds of intellectual freedom with which Luther might have had scant sympathy.

III

The dynamic quality of religion is exhaustless. Man's conception of relationship to the divine Might, on Which or Whom his life and eternal destinies depend, constantly renews and manifests itself in all his faculties; it moulds his purposes and inspires his action. It seems to be the energy of God in man. It was so in Paul, so in Augustine, in Anselm, Bernard, Francis. It was so in Luther. There was a rebirth of Christianity in all these men. Luther had no more doubt than Paul that a personal revelation of God had come to him, and a divine call; and that Christ was actually reborn in him. The last thought might have come to him from the *Theologia Deutsch* as well as from his greatest teacher, Paul, who in another than a mystic sense was likewise reborn in Luther. Once more the power of the Gospel was shown, energizing and directing the nature and faculties of Luther, and spending its surplus force in the picturesque doings of Anabaptists for example, and the Peasants' War, where it worked along with other causes.

Luther was guided more directly by Paul than by the Sermon on the Mount. Yet he deemed himself to be following all the Scriptures, assuredly the Ten Commandments, assuredly the passion of the Psalmist, assuredly the teachings of his Lord in the four Gospels. Besides his almost superhuman grasp of Paul, he continued the strain of Gospel piety which appears in mediaeval saints. He says substantially in his *Table Talk:* Let no one stumble over the simple tales in Scripture; they are the very words and works and judgments of God. This is the book that makes fools of little wiselings. Thou shalt find in it the angels who guided the shepherds and the swaddling clothes and cradle in which Jesus lay: mean and wretched, but how precious the treasure, Christ, which lies in them. These phrases might be Bernard's as well as Luther's, and so might be many passages in Luther's letters. Do we not almost hear Bernard in the following to Spalatin, written in 1519: Quicumque velit salubriter de Deo cogitare aut speculari, prorsus omnia postponat praeter humanitatem Christi. Hanc autem vel agentem vel patientem sibi praefigat, donec dulcescat ejus benignitas.[6] Again: thou shalt find peace only in Him, through faithful despairing of thyself and thy work — per fiducialem desperationem tui et operum tuorum.[7] One notes that this sweet piety, whether of Francis, Bernard, or Luther, is filled with faith.

In his study of the Bible, Luther sought the veritable meaning of the text. The downrightness of his nature would have led him to this, even if he had not been influenced by the comments of Nicholas de Lyra and Johann Wessel.[8] More and more he was repelled by the strained and twisted applications which were made to support those teachings, practices, or institutions of the papal church which he found himself revolting from.

[6] De Wette's Edition, Vol. I, p. 226.

[7] To Spenlein, ib. p. 17; Cf. to Scheurl, ib. p. 49. Letters of 1516 and 1517.

[8] Ante, p. 189–191.

Yet no more than Erasmus did he give over the allegorical interpretation of the Old Testament, or even of the New. But he looked in the New Testament for confirmation of allegorical interpretations of words and statements in the Old.[9] He makes fewer references to allegorical meanings in his later writings, referring to himself as early as December, 1522, as "being already less curious regarding allegories."[10] To be sure, like any student of the Scriptures, in any age, with doctrines to uphold, Luther could bend the meaning to his own support.

Inevitably Luther judged the different books of the Bible by their bearing on the Gospel of faith in Christ, as he grasped it. Paul's Epistles were his chief armory. In the preface to his New Testament of 1522 he puts John's Gospel and Paul's Epistles, especially to the Romans, above Matthew, Mark, and Luke, which tell of Christ's *works*. In comparison James's Epistle is dry fodder, "eine rechte stroherne Epistel."[11] In the preface to *Romans* in the same edition, he says "Diese Epistel ist das rechte Hauptstück des Neuen Testaments, und das allerlauteste Evangelium." It was for him the great exposition of faith, which he thus characterizes in the same preface: "Faith is a divine work in us that changes and regenerates us as from God, and kills the old Adam, and makes us into different men . . . and brings the Holy Spirit with it."

The Psalter moved him strongly. In his Preface to it (1528) he holds it as the mirror of the Church and of the storm-tost Christian soul driven by anxiety and fear. Every soul can find apt counsel in the Psalter; can there find itself expressed: "In fine, if thou wouldst see the Holy Christian Church painted in living form and color . . . take the Psalter, and thou hast a clear pure mirror showing thee Christendom. Thou wilt also see thyself

[9] See generally the argumentation in *Vom Päpstthum zu Rom, etc.* (1520).

[10] Letter to Spalatin, De Wette, II, p. 267. Cf. to the same, ib. II, 356.

[11] This preface was omitted from later editions. In the preface to James's Epistle, he said it was not the work of an Apostle.

therein, and find the true 'know thyself' and God and all Creatures."

Later in life, in his *Table Talk* he says that the Psalms, St. John's Gospel and Paul's Epistles are the best to preach from when opposing heretics; but for the ordinary man and for young people, Matthew, Mark and Luke are best. Luther grasped the Scriptures very humanly, with all sides and faculties of his nature. Says he, also in his *Table Talk,* one must not attempt to weigh and understand them through our reason alone; but meditate upon them diligently with prayer. He had read the Bible through twice each year, for many years, and, as if it were a tree, had shaken each one of its branches and twigs, and every time some apples or pears had fallen to him. He felt the exhaustlessness of meaning in the Lord's Prayer.

In his address to his Augustines at Wittenberg on the *Misuse of the Mass,* Luther said, "Scripture cannot err, and who believes it cannot sin in his life." But while he held this large view of its inerrancy, and especially of its infallible presentation of the Gospel of faith, he did not hold meticulously to the inerrancy of the letter of every statement in it.

The authority of the pope was the real point at issue between Luther and the papal church. He writes of his Leipzig disputation, "if only I would not deny the power of the pope, they would readily have come to an accord with me." [12] But even he who was coming to the realization that he feared no man, felt the strain and danger of his situation. He implores the Emperor not to condemn him unheard [13] and exclaims to his friend Spalatin: "It is hard to dissent from all prelates and princes; but there is no other way to escape hell and the divine wrath." [14] After much thought and ample notice to his friends, he burnt the papal bull against him, and the Canon Law as well, before the city church of Wittenberg on the tenth of

[12] To Spalatin, 1519, De Wette, I, p. 287.
[13] Jan'y, 1520. De Wette, I, p. 393.
[14] Nov., 1520, ib. I, p. 521.

December, 1520. As he wrote to Staupitz, he did it in "trembling and prayer, but afterwards felt better over it than over any act in all my life." [15]

He was and always remained, opposed to resisting authority with arms [16]; but he had become convinced that he and every one who would be saved must fight to the last — though not with arms — against the papal laws. Though fearing no man, he stood in awe before the beliefs in which he had been educated, abandoning portions of them only under the compulsion of his reason, his conscience, and his circumstances; and still he felt anxious over what he had done, as appears in paragraphs intended to fortify the consciences of his Wittenberg Augustines placed at the beginning of his tract upon the *Misuse of the Mass,* written at the Wartburg in 1521. It is nothing that the world and all the priests of Baal dub us heretics and cry out on us, says he in substance; but we hear the cry of our own consciences, stricken with fear of God's judgment lest we be leading men astray. Even I was in doubt and fear. Could I alone be right, and all the rest of the world mistaken? Till God strengthened me, and made my heart as a rock against which the waves of apprehension beat in vain.

He had need of all his strength for his journey to Worms and his defense before the Emperor and the princes and prelates of Germany. A papal sentence, of death in this world and damnation afterwards, lay on him; and the Emperor Charles who sent him a safe-conduct commanded the burning of his books. John Huss had been burnt at Constance, whither he had gone under an emperor's safe-conduct. The Church held no faith with a condemned heretic. Luther had cause to tremble. His natural anxieties resulted in repeated illness. Yet his resolve and faith were unshaken; and he assured the Elector that he would go if he had to be carried. His journey in fact was made in a covered wagon. Cities

[15] De Wette, I, p. 542.
[16] See e.g. to Spalatin, 1521, De Wette, I, p. 543.

along the route received him with acclaim. He was a hero, and the pope was hated. He writes ahead from Frankfort:

> "We are coming, my Spalatin, although Satan has tried to stop me with more than one illness. All the way from Eisenach I have been ailing, and am still ailing, in ways quite new to me. And Charles's mandate [against his books], I know, has been published to frighten me. But Christ lives, and we will enter Worms in spite of all the gates of hell and powers of the air. I send a copy of the Emperor's letter. It seems best to write no more letters till, on my arrival, I see what should be done, lest we puff up Satan, whom my purpose is rather to terrify and contemn. Therefore arrange a lodging. Farewell." [17]

The papal legate, Aleander, tells of Luther's arrival at the city gates, sitting in a wagon with three companions, and protected by a hundred horsemen. As he alighted at his lodging near the Saxon Elector, he looked round with those demon eyes of his, and said "God be with me." A priest ecstatically threw his arms about him. He was soon visited by many personages, and people ran to see him. So far, in substance, Aleander.

On appearing before the Diet on the first day Luther seems to have hesitated in the presence of so august and largely hostile an assembly; but the next day he made a well ordered argument and spoke courageously in defense of his books and his convictions, to the wrath of the papal legates who protested that an excommunicated heretic had no right to defend his heresies. As for the Emperor, his face was against Luther whatever might be his own relations with the pope. For in his office Charles, equally with the pope, was heir to the Roman tradition of imperial unity. To one as to the other, Luther could only be a rebel; and the Emperor, an intense Catholic, was already started on his career of arch exterminator of heretics, in his dominions in the Low Countries, where he had the power that he lacked in German lands. He and the papal party would quickly have put an end to Luther's words and life, if Luther had

[17] April 14, 1521, De Wette, I, p. 586.

not had the protection of the Saxon Elector and the support of a large proportion of all classes in Germany.

In spite of commands, exhortations and persuasion, within the Diet and without, Luther refused to recant, or materially to retract his statements. He left Worms as he had entered it, an excommunicated heretic. The Emperor's ban followed quickly, proclaiming him an outlaw. But from these cumulative dangers he was spirited away, out of the sight and ken of enemies and friends alike, to a benignant confinement at the Wartburg, the historic castle, then belonging to the Saxon Elector. There he stayed for eight months, translating the New Testament, writing letters and tracts to exhort trembling or over-zealous friends, fighting the devil as well as mortal enemies, and advancing in his faith from strength to strength.

It was irksome to be confined, and bodily withheld from the strife. Half humorously, half lugubriously, Luther dates his letters, "in the region of the birds," "on my Patmos," "from my hermitage." Vehemently he works; or, again, the perturbations of his soul and body prostrate his energies. "Now for a week, I do neither write, nor pray, nor study, vexed with temptations of the flesh and other ills," he writes Melanchthon.[18] His words had already become a power with his friends, a terror to others. Albrecht, archbishop of Mainz, to relieve whose impecuniousness Tetzel had sold indulgences, now bethought him to do a little business quietly in that line at Halle. The Elector had no wish to make an enemy of the princely primate of Germany, and knowing that Luther was breathing forth threatenings, asked him to keep silence. Neither then, nor ever afterwards, did Luther hold his peace when speech was called for; and the vigor of his threats of public attack, made in a private letter to the archbishop,[19] caused the latter to stop the sale and excuse himself to Luther in a letter.

[18] De Wette, II, p. 22.
[19] De Wette, II, pp. 112–114. So Luther did not publish his *Against the Idol at Halle.*

In fact while at the Wartburg, as before and afterwards through his life, Luther worked and wrote torrentially. There were years when his productions monopolized the presses of Germany. At the Wartburg he seems first to have completed a little writing which showed how dearly he still loved the teachings and traditions of the Church. It was a charming piece for the Elector, *On the Song of Praise of the holy Virgin Mary, called the Magnificat.* He honors her sinlessness, and almost prays to her, saying at the beginning, " May the same gentle Mother procure me the spirit to interpret her song aright," and at the end, " This may Christ grant us through the intercession of his dear Mother Mary."

Paying this tribute to the clinging sentiments of religious habit, Luther proceeded none the less manfully to disembarrass his mind of matters which more loudly demanded discarding. He wrote a tract *On the power of the pope to compel Confession,* which he sent with an inspiring letter to a doughty patron and protector of his, the great swashbuckler knight Von Sickingen.[20] He then took up the marriage of priests, on which Carlstadt and Melanchthon had already taken a radical stand. Luther fundamentally agreeing with them, still wished to test their grounds more thoroughly. Next he undertook to settle the burning question whether monastic vows were binding. He sent his *Opinion* to his own father, who had so bitterly opposed his purpose to become a monk, and with it a telling letter,[21] in which he recalls the anxieties and the sudden fear that drove him into the convent, and his father's doubt whether it was not a crazed delusion: — and now, dear father, " wilt thou still drag me out? For still art thou father, and I am son, and all vows mean nothing. . . . But the Lord has forestalled thee, and has himself delivered me. For what signifies it, whether I wear the cowl or lay it off? Cowl and ton-

[20] De Wette, II, 13.

[21] De Wette, II, 100 sqq.— also printed as a preface to Luther's *Urtheil über die Mönchsgelübde.*

sure do not make the monk. 'All is yours,' says Paul, 'and you are Christ's'; and why should I be the cowl's and not the cowl rather be mine? My conscience has become free, which means that I have become free. So I am a monk and yet no monk, a new creature, not the pope's, but Christ's." Satan foresaw what great scathe he was to suffer from me, and attempted my ruin. But from this book "thou mayest see through what signs and wonders Christ has loosed me from the monk's vow and given me such freedom that, while he has made me the servant of all, I am subject to none but him alone. For he is my bishop, directly over me, my abbot, prior, lord, father and teacher. Henceforth I recognize none other."

In this tract, which was written in Latin, Luther maintains that the monk's vow is opposed to God and scripture; for whatever goes beyond the words of Christ is man's invention. To turn that which was at most a counsel in the Gospel into a command, is to go beyond and against the Gospel. The monastic vow is opposed to faith, and to the freedom wherein faith makes us free from all things. It infringes the gospel freedom set by God, which is no less a sin than to break any other commandment. It is opposed to love of neighbor, to obedience to parents, and to natural reason. "Those who make their vows intending to become good and blessed through this way of life, to blot out their sins and gain riches through good works, are as godless Jews fallen from faith."

At the same time Luther made ready another tract, *On the Misuse of the Mass,* from which certain opening reflections have already been taken. It presented Luther's conception of the priesthood and the sacrament of the body and blood of Christ, maintaining that this sacrament is not a sacrifice offered to God in propitiation for our sins, but is received from Him in token of His free forgiveness. There is one priest, who is Christ; the New Testament ordains no visible priesthood beside him; but all Christians are priests with Christ. Consequently the papal priesthood is nothing, their acts and laws are nothing; and the Mass which they call a sacrifice is sheer idolatry, a fabrication added to God's Testament.

It is hard for weak consciences to think that so many people have been damned in this idolatry, despite all the churches and cloisters where myriad daily masses are said; and they are tempted to believe the mass is instituted by God because it has been instituted by the Church. But the Church did not institute it, since the Church ordains nothing beyond God's word; and whatever body makes the attempt is no Church. Let us have done with the pope's priesthood and their mass; and to the argument that ordained power has authority to command, make reply: Go and take counsel with the blasphemers of those Gomorrahs, Paris and Louvain; we maintain with the power of the Gospel, that when ye rule without God's word, ye are the devil's priests, and your office and priesthood is the work of the devil to crush out the Spirit and Word of God.

The time was at hand when Luther no longer could endure to write and fight from his retreat. Disturbances among his own Wittenbergers demanded his presence and his voice. His more radically minded followers — whom Luther declared hurt him more than all his enemies and all the devils too [22] — had rudely gone to work; and fanatics were come from Zwickau, who would overthrow all things. Wittenberg was becoming a scandal; the town council petitioned him to return. The Elector, himself troubled by many thorny questions, felt still greater anxiety lest Luther's return should embroil him with the Emperor and endanger the reformer's life: demands would be made for his surrender, to his certain death. So at least it seemed to the Elector, and he wrote asking Luther not to come. Luther did not tarry at the Wartburg to reply, but answered from the road to Wittenberg. His letter respectfully explained the urgency of the situation, and then proceeded: " As for my own fate, most

[22] De Wette, II, p. 165.

gracious Lord, I answer thus: Your Electoral Grace knows, or if not, will be informed by this, that I have received the Gospel not from men, but solely from Heaven, through our Lord Jesus Christ, and well might and henceforth will declare and subscribe myself a servant and evangelist. If I have submitted to be heard and judged, it has been through no doubt of this, but from over-humility in order to win others. Now I see my humility bringing the Gospel into contempt, and that the devil will take the whole place, where I intended to give him but a palm; so my conscience compels me to act otherwise."

"I have done enough for your Electoral Grace by retiring for a year, obediently. For the devil knows that I have not done this from cowardice. He saw it in my heart, as I entered Worms, that had there been as many devils there as tiles on the roofs, I would have sprung into their midst gladly. Duke George[23] is not the equal of a single devil. And since the Father of all mercies has through his Gospel made us glad lords over all the devils and death, so that we may call him our own dear Father, your Grace will see what shame we should put on Him if we did not trust Him to make us lords over the anger of Duke George. . . .

"These things I have written to your Grace so that your Grace may know that I come to Wittenberg under a higher guard than that of the Prince Elector. Nor do I propose to seek that protection of your Electoral Grace. Rather it is I that would protect you. Indeed if I knew that your Grace could and would protect me, I would not come. In this business the sword should not and cannot either advise or aid; God must do all by Himself. Therefore he who has most faith will best protect. And since I perceive your Electoral Grace to be still weak in faith, I cannot find in you the man who could protect or save me."

The letter proceeds further to absolve the Elector from responsibility for Luther's safety; and begs him not to oppose the carrying out of any imperial edict. For himself, Christ has not so taught him that he should be a burden to another Christian. "Herewith I commend your princely Electoral Grace to the grace of God. . . .

[23] Duke George, ruler over the other parts of Saxony, an earnest Catholic, and Luther's enemy.

If your Grace believed, you would see the glory of God; since you do not yet believe, you have seen nothing." [24]

So Luther made his way to Wittenberg. The Elector, better than his protest, continued his protection. If Luther's word had first unchained the tempest which so rudely was throwing down the old forms and ceremonies of worship, his word and presence now restored peace. Mightily had he grasped for himself, and set forth for others, Paul's great doctrine of justification by faith. Now with equal power and effect he set forth another side of the great apostle's teaching, that it is not the Christian's part to cause his weaker brother to stumble. He preached sermons on eight successive days, and cast a spell of order and toleration over the city.

In the first sermon he pointed out to his hearers, who thronged the large city church, that each Christian must answer and fight for himself against the devil and death. Each should know the tenets of his faith. We are all children of wrath; our acts and thoughts are sinful and as nothing in the sight of God. But God gave his Son; and at this point the preacher briefly recalled the substance of Christ's gospel. To benefit by it faith is needed; then love of one another, in which his auditors seemed to have failed. Patience also is required, and forbearance. Each shall not insist upon his own way, but yield so as to win those who are without. No one should so use his freedom as to give offense to those who are weak in faith. You have surely the pure word of God; act then soberly and considerately. Our warfare is with the devil, who has many wiles. Those have erred who have inconsiderately swept away the mass, without advising with me — with me, who was called to preach, not by my will, but against it. Suppose your taunts to have driven some brother, against his conscience, to eat meat on Friday, and in the hour of death he is seized with fear; — on whose head falls the blame?

So speaks Luther's broad human and Pauline forbear-

[24] This, perhaps the most famous of all Luther's letters, is printed in De Wette, II, 137 sqq., and elsewhere very often.

ance. His rock-ribbed intolerance will elsewhere strike us. The second sermon opens with the avowal that the popish sacrificial mass is an abomination; but it is not for us to tear it out by the hair; leave it to God. Why? Because *I* do not hold men's hearts as clay in my hand; I can speak to the ear, but cannot force my words into their hearts. Let our words work free; but use no force. We preach the truth; let that work. Paul came to Athens, and saw the altars of idolatry. Did he rush to kick them over with his foot? Let faith be free. I will preach against the mass; but will not cast it out by force. I spoke against indulgences, gently, with the word of God, raising no tumult; and so I weakened the papacy more than the Kaiser ever did. Blood might have been poured out, had I done differently.

Monks' vows are null, affirms the next sermon; as null as if I had vowed to strike my father in the face. Yet to hurry out of convents and marry, is not yet for all. It should be left to the conscience of each. So images are useless; but do ye leave each man free to keep or reject them. Only one must not pray to them. Let us preach that images are vanities, but that no outer thing can injure faith.

The remaining sermons consider points of contention: taking the Sacrament into the communicant's hands; insistence upon both the bread and wine; the question of confession. Also the fruit of the Sacrament which is love.

The incidents of Luther's life so far referred to, with his words and writings, tempt us to further efforts to place him in proper categories of appreciation and form some estimate of him. At all events, he calls for emphatic statements. One must not approach him mincingly, nor be overnice. To be misled or repelled by certain of his qualities would be to hesitate over the immaterial and tarry with the impertinent. If we find contradictions in the man as well as in his doctrines, we should seek their harmony in the reaches of his nature and the reasonings which there had their home. We may find the contradictions bound together, as by the grace of God, into a mighty personality speaking always to one high argument.

In a letter to Melanchthon,[25] Luther says that his opponents to show their smartness gather contradictions from his books. "How can those asses judge the contradictions in our doctrine, who understand neither of the contradictories? For what else can our doctrines be in the eyes of the wicked than sheer contradiction, since it both requires and condemns works, abolishes and restores ritual, honors and reproves the magistrates, asserts and denies sin?"

"I am a peasant's son," says Luther, "my father, grandfather, and forebears, were *echte Bauern.* My father when young was a poor miner; my mother carried the wood on her back: and so they brought us up." Luther was a peasant too. The rank and ready coarseness of the peasant was an obvious element of his nature to the end. It crops out through his talk and writing in language absolutely unquotable even for purposes of illustration. It should not be compared with the expressions of many an Italian humanist; for such men were themselves contaminate, while Luther's soul, even as his life, was pure. A juster comparison lies with the great-natured Rabelais; but the latter's obscenity is a thing of imaginative art. Luther's coarseness is never for its own sake. Sudden, and uncalled for as it sometimes seems to us, it was with him a natural mode of speech, the ready weapon of anger and denunciation.

For Luther was a man of wrath, of violent and cyclopean indignation. He did not restrain it; but poured it out on the offense, as the wrath of God, given him to deliver. If he felt that the occasion called for tolerance and love, he was persuasive and compelling in these qualities, as when he calmed the Wittenberg disorders. But anger naturally nerved him to combat; he says in his *Table Talk* that people had warned him at the outset not to attack

[25] July, 1530, De Wette, IV, p. 103.

the pope: "but when I was angry, I went at it like a blindfold horse." That was human or animal; but he was also convinced of the divine sanction of his wrath: "The anger of my mouth is not my anger, but God's anger," he cried to a papal legate. And there could not be enough of it. "I have never satisfied myself and the enormousness of my anger against the papal monster; nor do I think I shall ever be able to satisfy it."[26] Luther was a German, and understood the gospel of hate as well as love.[27] As the years passed, neither his hate nor his language became mollified. In his tract of 1545, *Against the Roman papacy founded by the devil,* the pope instead of the allerheiligster (most holy) has become the allerhöllischte (most hellish) father, Sanctus Paulus Tertius. That pope, forsooth, has written to the Kaiser, angrily maintaining that the pope alone may call a council — which shall meet at Trent. Against such a council, whose decrees may be given, changed or nullified by the "abominable abomination at Rome calling himself the pope," Luther protests with vigorous wrath, addressing the pope always as "your hellishness." "*I* mock the pope!" he exclaims. "Good God, I am too slight a thing to mock that which has mocked the world to its perdition for six hundred years."

His convinced wrath was directed not only against Rome and her partisans; but against any one whom he thought was falsifying God's doctrine. "My one sole glory," he writes to Melanchthon, "is that I have delivered the pure and unadulterated word of God. . . . I believe that Zwingli is deserving of holy hate for his obstinate wickedness against the holy word of God."[28] Thus he delivered himself because of the Swiss reformer's view of the Sacrament of the Lord's Supper. Luther abom-

[26] Aug., 1545, De Wette, V, p. 754.

[27] It seems to me that in spirit the recent German war harks back to Luther, even to his tract upon the Freedom of a Christian man: each man outwardly subject to the powers that be, bounden in outward obedience; but inwardly free, and even finding in his inward freedom a certain detachment from responsibility for the nature of his outward acts, commanded by the powers that be.

[28] Oct., 1527, De Wette, III, 215.

inated transubstantiation; but on no point of doctrine did he insist more violently than on the real presence of the body and blood of Christ. This was the rock of controversy on which he and Zwingli wrecked the cause of Protestant unity two years later, at the Marburg colloquy, when Luther sat him at the conference table and wrote on it in chalk the words "This is my body," — from which he would not swerve. He and Zwingli reached an agreement on other points; but on this they parted.

The German Bucer, an early admirer of Luther, who was destined to carry on so excellently the work of the Reform at Strassburg, held views like Zwingli's. Having him in mind, Luther wrote: "Satan is angry, and perhaps feels that the Day of Christ is at hand. Therefore he rages so cruelly and will deprive us of the Saviour Jesus Christ through his trickery. Under the papacy he was sheer flesh, making out that even monks' cowls were holy. Now will he be sheer spirit, making out that the flesh and word of Christ are nothing." [29]

The vehemence of Luther's speech, the violence of his convictions, alike were needed for the doing of the work he did. Millions of protests had been wasted on the mighty mammon of the Church. Soft words and gentle persuasions would still have been futile. Even the rapier satire of Erasmus did not pierce the monster. No reform could be achieved by anyone so long as the authority of the pope remained unimpeached, and the unity of the Roman Catholic Church unbroken. Vituperation, revolt, attack, were needed. It may be, as men have thought, that Luther's breach with Rome not only underlay the spiritual remaking of the lands which became Protestant, but compelled the Roman Catholic Church to redeem itself from its overgrowth of abuse and corruption.

One may also argue for the need of Luther's firm, not to say violent, insistence upon certain doctrines, that of the Real Presence, for example. For the man was preaching no Erasmian piety, or ethics, of the obvious ra-

[29] De Wette, III, 206.

tional type, which men might accept and remain unmoved. He was preaching religion; he was delivering doctrine, not rationalism, to his followers: the doctrines which he held to be those of the true Christian faith and necessary for salvation. "Men still doubt that my preaching is God's word: that the true body and blood of Christ is received in the Sacrament, or that in baptism sins are washed away by the blood of Christ. But that I teach and preach the veritable word of God, I will pledge my soul and will die for it. . . . If thou believest this thou art blessed; if thou dost not, thou art damned." (*Table Talk.*)

The Protestant religion needed to be as stiff and staunch in doctrine as the Catholic, and as imperative. The world was not yet interested in liberalism and tolerance. It wanted sure salvation. Luther fought for and established his way of salvation, and disproved the Roman system, showed its falsity, its inefficiency. He who followed the Roman way would be damned just as surely, according to the Lutheran conviction, as in Catholic eyes men would be damned for following Luther. Who would have cared for Luther's faith had he taught or admitted that men could just as well be saved in the bosom of the Catholic Church? It did not irk Luther and his followers, any more than it did the Calvinists or the Catholics, or the Mohammedans for that matter, to think of many damned.

Luther wrote a book of *Fourteen Consolations for the Downcast and Oppressed,* and more especially for the Elector, sick and weary in the year 1519. In this work of reasonable Christian comfort, after reviewing the ills of life and the pains of hell, he remarks: "How many thousand are in hell's eternal damnation who have scarcely a thousandth part of our sins? How many young girls and boys are there, and, as we say, 'innocent children'? How many monks, priests, married people, who seemed to serve God all their lives, and now are eternally punished perhaps for a single sin? For . . . the same justice of God does its office on each sin, hating and damning it in whomsoever found." So, argues Luther, we realize the boundless pity of God in not damning us, and may well be thankful. He agrees with Augustine that he would not willingly live his life again, with its pains and anxieties. He speaks of the seven ills and seven compensations, or *goods,* such as a glad heart, and the goods of the mind, the sense of the glory of God, and the good things promised us through Christ hereafter, which include satisfaction from the punishment of sin in the damned, while through love we make the joys and sorrows of the saints our own.

Wonderful have been human consolations and convictions! Without earnest, sincere, terrible convictions the world might have stayed still; they are also among the plagues which have fallen upon men, driving those obsessed by them to blood and pious rapine.

So many elements, so many potent antecedents came to effective combination and living actuality in Luther. In the vortex of his nature, the *vivida vis* of living life made them all to live again. He was altogether alive, and put life into whatever he thought or said or wrote. His personality lives in every sentence, one is tempted to say, from the beginning to the end at last of the enormous array of his writings. He was a superman in power, in energy, in fertile facility. His reason does not work alone, nor does he ever act by impulse merely: his faculties act together spontaneously — with a spontaneity not always calculable for other men. No man was like him. Not another one of the reformers in his time or after him was spontaneous and alive as Luther was alive, not Zwingli, not Calvin.

The strength of Luther's faith, and the firm and violent convictions of which we have been speaking, owed something to his aliveness and vital imagination, and to his sensitive perception and realization of the intimacies of life about him, and the immeasurable reaches of existence which were as assured as the stars above his head. If Duke George was not the equal of a single devil, what was he then compared with the power of God shown in the rose which Luther holds in his hand, while he wonders at God's workmanship in the budding of trees in the spring, and in the functions of the human body. Consciousness of nature's marvels is a stay and comfort in times of trial, and how surely such for one who knows them to be creatures of Him who holds alike the faithful man and all his enemies in the hollow of His hand! Luther likewise loved his own children intimately and imaginatively. He saw them as God's best gifts, and let his mind play around their child natures, so ready for love and faith. Such love of children is another stay and comfort.

Wonderful illustrations of the calm and happy assurance thus given him lie in letters written from the Elector's castle of Coburg in the year 1530. It was an anxious time. The imperial diet was sitting at Augsburg, with the hostile Emperor at its head. The Saxon Elector John [30] was there, with Melanchthon and other theologians, who were to draw up the presentation of their faith known as the Augsburg Confession. But Luther was left at Coburg, a hundred and thirty miles away, on the Saxon border. Being under the imperial ban, he could not appear before the Emperor; and his presence would have excited animosity when the Lutherans desired concord. So Luther abode those anxious months at Coburg, while others fought the fight that was his. A restless, anxious state was that of this sequestered leader, restricted to reports of the battle, and to his letters of exhortation and admonishment in return. As all men knew, he would have yielded nothing, and could not have tipped his speech with velvet, or "walked as softly" as Melanchthon. He approved of the "Confession," if only they would leave off dallying with compromises and quit the diet. Quivering with impatience, he writes to them in July to leave, since they had spoken: "Igitur absolvo vos in nomine Domini ab isto conventu. Immer wieder heim, immer heim!!" [31] Constantly and most directly,

[30] Who had succeeded the Elector Frederick in 1525.

[31] De Wette, IV, 96. Luther often mingles Latin and German in his letters, as the one or the other tongue best expresses him.

he comforts himself with his trust in God, for himself and for his cause, as we read in many a letter to Melanchthon and to others. He assures Melanchthon that the troubles which seem to master the latter are huge only through his lack of faith. It is his learning that bothers him — as if anything could be accomplished through useless solicitudes. He is his own direct foe, armed by the devil against himself. "Christ died once for our sins, but for justice and truth he does not die, but lives and reigns. If this is true, what fear then for the truth, if he reigns? But, do you say, it will be overthrown by the anger of God? Let us be overthrown with it, but not through ourselves." [32] And again: "If we shall fall, Christ falls with us, to wit, he, the ruler of the world! So be it: if he shall fall, I had rather fall with Christ than stand with Caesar." [33] Later in the summer, he writes comforting a certain Jonas: "Gratiam et pacem in Christo. Ego, mi Jonas, nostram causam Christo commendavi serio (earnestly), et is promisit mihi . . . suam hanc causam esse et fore: [34] *And he has promised me that our cause is His and shall be!"*

Such were his direct self-heartenings. The more subtle serenity reflected in his mind from God's creation is illustrated by a letter written in lighter vein to those who lived with him at Wittenberg:

"To my dear table-companions, Peter and Jerome Weller, and Henry Schneidewin, and others at Wittenberg, severally and jointly: Grace and peace in Christ Jesus, dear sirs and friends. I have received the letter you all wrote and have learned how everything is going. That you may hear in turn how we are doing, I would have you know that we, namely, I, Master Veit, and Cyriac, did not go to the diet at Augsburg, but have come to another diet instead.

"There is a grove just under our windows like a small forest.

[32] June 27, 1530, De Wette, IV, p. 49.

[33] June 30, 1530, ib. p. 62.

[34] De Wette, IV, p. 157. I leave this sentence in the Latin. Luther's Latin letters are as direct and forcible as his German. Perhaps he never wrote a finer body of letters than those written from Coburg, from April to October, 1530. They make the first two hundred pages of De Wette's fourth volume.

There the jackdaws and crows are holding a diet. They ride in and out, and keep up a racket day and night without ceasing, as if they were all crazy-drunk. Young and old chatter together in such a fashion that I wonder voice and breath hold out. I should like to know whether there are any such knights and warriors still left with you. It seems as if they must have gathered here from all the world.

"I have not yet seen their emperor; but the nobility and bigwigs constantly flit and gad about before our eyes, not very expensively clothed, but simply, in one color, all alike black, and all alike gray-eyed. They all sing the same song, but there is an agreeable contrast between young and old, great and small. They care nothing for grand palaces and halls, for their hall is vaulted with the beautiful, broad sky, its floor is paved with lovely green branches, and its walls are as wide as the world. They do not ask for horses or armor; they have feathered chariots to escape the hunters. They are high and mighty lords, but I don't yet know what they are deciding. So far as I have been able to learn from an interpreter, they plan a great war against wheat, barley, oats, malt, and all sorts of grain, and many a one will show himself a hero and do valiant deeds.

"So we sit here in the diet, listening and looking on with great pleasure, as the princes and lords with the other estates of the realm so merrily sing and feast. It gives us special delight to see in how knightly a fashion they strut about, polish their bills, and fall upon the defense that they may conquer and acquit themselves honorably against corn and malt. We wish them fortune and health, that they may all be impaled on a spit together.

"Methinks they are none other than the sophists and papists with their preaching and writing. All of them I must have in a crowd before me that I may hear their lovely voices and sermons, and see how useful a tribe they are, destroying everything on earth, and for a change chattering to kill time.

"To-day we heard the first nightingale, for she was afraid to trust our April. We have had lovely weather and no rain except a little yesterday. It is perhaps otherwise with you. God bless you! Take good care of the house.

"From the *Diet of the Malt-Robbers,* April 28, 1530.

"MARTIN LUTHER, *Doctor.*" [35]

Two or three months later Luther wrote to Brück, the Elector's chancellor, a letter of wonderful comforting in-

[35] I have taken this translation from the excellent book of A. C. McGiffert, *Martin Luther, the Man and his Work.* The original is in De Wette, IV, p. 8. Luther was so amused with his idea of a Reichstag (diet) of rooks and daws, that he repeated it in several letters.

dicative of the peace which he drew from the sublimities of nature. He speaks of anxieties common to them both, and his trust in God who listens to their prayers, and will forget them never, and then says:

"I have lately seen two miracles. I looked out of the window, I saw the stars in heaven and the whole great vault of God, and saw nowhere any pillars on which the Master had set it. Yet the heavens fell not, and the vault stands fast. Now there are some who look for such pillars, and gladly would feel and grasp them. Because they cannot, they worry and tremble, as if the heavens would fall in, just because they cannot see and grasp the pillars. If they could grasp them, the heaven would stand fast!

"Again, I saw great thick clouds sweeping over us, so heavy that they seemed like a great sea; and I saw no footing for them and nothing to constrain them. Yet they did not fall on us, but greeted us with a sour face, and flew away. When they were gone the rainbow shone forth, as floor and roof, above us, which had held them — a weak thin little floor and roof, vanishing in the clouds, and more like a ray shining through painted glass than a strong floor. . . . Yet it upheld the weight of water and protected us. Still there are those who fearfully regard the weight of the cloud masses, rather than this thin small ray. They would gladly feel and make sure of its strength, and since they cannot, they fear that the clouds will bring an eternal Deluge (Sündfluth).

"So much I write to your Honor in friendly jest, and yet not in jest; since I learn with joy of your Honor's steadfast and trustful courage in this our trial. I had hoped that at least political peace could be maintained; but God's thoughts are above ours . . . and if He were to grant us peace from the Kaiser, the Kaiser and not He might have the glory. . . . Our rainbow is weak; their [the enemies'] clouds are mighty; but in the end it will appear whose is the thunderbolt." [36]

But there were catastrophes in Luther's life more dire than any arising from the attack of enemies. Against direct attack his courage was invincible and his faith a shield. The tragedies of his life were those conditions or events which seemed to show the futility or the evil results of what he had taught and worked for. Among such positive ill results from Luther's point of view might be set the obstreperous spiritual anarchy, as of Zwickau

[36] Aug., 1530, De Wette, IV, 127 sqq.

prophets and Anabaptists, which went so far beyond the orderly conservative religious revolution that was Luther's plan. Yet his enemies alleged, and Luther feared, that the fervor of his own teachings had loosed the misguided energies and entered the abominable opinions of intellectual radicals like Carlstadt and fanatic anarchists like Münzer.

Carlstadt was a keenly reasoning, radically minded man. He had been Luther's associate in the Leipzig debate against Eck in 1521. But while Luther was in the Wartburg, Carlstadt became moved with desire to set aside every religious practice and convention for which he could not find direct authority in Scripture. He was as radical in handling Holy Writ, and disposed to attack everybody's prejudices and acceptances in his insistence upon his new evangelical way of living and worshipping. Luther had become to him a time-server and a tyrant; while on his part he became an active thorn in Luther's flesh. Münzer was an evangelical anarchist, preaching the Gospel of God's fiery word resounding within the individual soul. Its dictates were to be made good not merely by persuasion, but with fire and sword, as Münzer demonstrated by taking up the peasants' cause, and urging them to blood. He was akin to the Anabaptists, as various anarchistic sects were called who were for throwing down the social structure altogether, and agreed in little beyond denying the validity of infant baptism and demanding adult immersion, for the full cleansing of sin. They too took to the sword, and largely perished by it too, when the forces of the established order, as well as the power of religious intolerance, were driven against them. But they spread far and wide in the sixteenth century, in Germany, the Low Countries, Switzerland, even France; the proper Lutherans in Germany were just as anxious as Calvin and the French adherents of the Reform, to clear their skirts of all connection with the Anabaptist anarchy.

The Peasants' War (1525-6) was worst of all. Its distressful causes broke out repeatedly in blood before

Luther's day. But now unquestionably his doctrine of Christian liberty was bearing fruit beyond his purpose and intent. Relief from oppression was the spiritual freedom which the peasants sought, and formulated in their Articles. These seem to us quite reasonable, but in 1525 they meant drastic change. The harsh rejection of them by the princes, the bloody dispersal of the peasants' gatherings, aroused fiercer passions in the sufferers, and drew Münzer and other preachers into a joint tumultuous movement for a manhood equality set on the prior massacre of magistrates and rulers. Of course Luther was appealed to, and his writings quoted, to support these aims. His first reply was *An Exhortation to Peace, in response to the Twelve Articles of the Swabian Peasants.* He admonished them to present their grievances in an orderly and peaceful way, and reminded the princes too that there had been injustice and oppression to justify the peasants' discontent. But he was staunch against mob violence, maintaining, as he always maintained, that the rulers alone could use the sword divinely committed to them. Let not the peasants invoke Christ's Gospel which had not to do with such affairs. If they were followers of Christ, they would drop their arms and take to prayer. Earthly society is built on inequalities; the Christian's liberty touches them not, but exists and serves in the midst of them.

Thus Luther was on the side of Christian freedom and the divine authority of rulers. He had spoken moderately, so far, but the outrages and riots witnessed by him soon after, and the appeal to his teaching to justify them, drove him mad. In his pamphlet, *Against the Murderous and Robbing Mobs of Peasants,* he turned on them with fury. He likened them to mad dogs; all the devils of hell must have entered into them. He urged the princes not to hesitate for conscience's sake, but to slay them without mercy; if a ruler fighting in this war himself was slain, it was a martyr's death.

Luther was a peasant's son; yet, before this insurrection, he held a low opinion of the common man's intelligence. The spiritual disturbance, which outran so wildly the respectability of his own reforms, confirmed his contempt for the common people who were led so easily beyond decency and reason and the correct understanding of Christ's Gospel. He expressed this contempt in his diatribe, *Against the heavenly prophets* (1524-1525), saying that the Common herd — *Herr Omnes* — must be made to behave by the sword and the constraint of law, as wild beasts are held in chains and cages. Although Luther was the most steadfast of men, and with a mighty faith in God, he and his reformed religion were in fact protected and preserved by the favor of the princely rulers of the land. In return, Luther and his state-protected Church were on the side of law and order and authority; and the spokesmen of that church, even though unconsciously, were influenced by social and political considerations.

As was shown in the matter of the fatal bigamy of Landgrave Philip of Hesse. The political fortunes of Lutheran Protestantism were at their zenith in 1540 when Philip, the ablest of the Protestant princes, feeling a resistless desire to marry a lady-in-waiting, wedded her secretly, but with the consent of his still living though not in all respects satisfactory consort. It was bigamy, and a crime by the laws of the Empire. The Landgrave appealed to Luther and Melanchthon to assuage his conscience, for he was a zealous Protestant, and had long felt qualms at the immoralities to which the vigor of his body impelled him.

Before this, the example of the Patriarchs had led some of the Anabaptists to declare for polygamy. Luther himself said in his *Babylonian Captivity of the Church* that bigamy was better than divorce. He had elsewhere written that he found no Scripture authority barring plurality of wives, but he hoped the custom would not be introduced among Christians; and some years before 1540 he so advised the Landgrave. But now moved by the Landgrave's urgent appeal and presentation of his scruples, Luther, Melanchthon and Bucer formally excused and sanctioned his bigamy, but as an exceptional case, not to be made a precedent, and if possible to be kept a secret.

This weak and baneful decision brought discredit and disaster on the Protestants. In connection, however, with this failure of Luther in firmness and foresight, one may add that he was a man by nature sympathetic with the stress of bodily desire. His own life was absolutely free from reproach, save, of course, that his marriage was a deadly sin in Catholic eyes. He was forty-two years old in 1525 when it took place; and if he was moved by natural need and impulse, he had given long and earnest doctrinal consideration to the question, and for several years had held all men free to marry or abstain. There is no evidence that personal desire to marry influenced his acts or doctrines. When he did marry, he made a faithful husband and a loving father. He was also a true lover of his friends, a hater of his enemies. His speech was mostly of religion; but he could be a jovial companion, eating and drinking like a German, and delighting in song.

To the Peasants' War and the Landgrave's bigamy, events which proved so tragic for the life and work of Luther, may be added disappointment over the result of his teaching and great labors. He had held high hopes that when men had been shown the Gospel truth, and accepted it, their lives would correspond; and there would be a regeneration of the nation. None such took place. Lutherans remained much as they had been before; while through Lutheran lands worship and education deteriorated, because the old compulsory ordinances were weakened or disturbed, and men were slack and negligent.

Luther declared that had he foreseen the toil and danger to come to him, wild horses would not have dragged him into the struggle. He had thought men sinned from ignorance, and only needed to be shown the right way! He had not supposed that the world would continue evil, when the true gospel had been preached. He had no idea how men, especially the clergy, despised God's Word in their hearts. Before the gospel was preached, men's hearts were hidden. Christ is the revealer of hearts; and now we know that princes, bishops, nobles, burghers, peasants, all are a lot of devils!

So Luther spoke in disappointment and depression. A little over a year before his death, when plagued by the course of events, by sickness in his family and his own bodily ills, he writes to a friend from out of even blacker depths: " Grace and peace in the Lord. I write briefly, my Jacob, lest I should write nothing at all, as if forgetful of thee. I am dull, tired, feeble, a useless old man. I have finished my course; it remains that the Lord should gather me to my fathers, and that worms and corruption should have their due. I have lived enough, if it is to be called life. Do thou pray for me, that the hour of my passing may be pleasing to God and salutary to myself. I care nothing for Caesar and the whole empire, except to commend them in my prayers to God. The world also seems to me to have come to the hour of its passing away, and to have waxed old like a garment, as the Psalm says, and soon to suffer change. Amen. There is no heroic virtue left in the princes, but only incurable hatred and dissension, avarice and the cupidity of profit. So the State is without strength, and the head runs the full course of Isaiah third. Wherefore no good can be hoped for, unless that the day of the glory of the great God and our redemption be revealed." [37]

But Luther had always assaulted vigorously those evils which were the chief ground of his depression. Thus in October, 1525, he informed the new Elector John of the wretched state of the parish priests: " No one gives, no one pays. Offerings have ceased, and parish incomes diminished. The common man has no regard for either preacher or pastor. Unless your Electoral Grace establishes order and support for them, the clergy will have no homes, and there will be neither schools nor scholars; and God's Word and service will fall to the ground." [38]

The Elector appointed a commission to visit the par-

[37] To Jacob Probst, Dec., 1544, De Wette, V, p. 7703.
[38] Oct. 31, 1525, De Wette, III, p. 39.

ishes and take action. There was need. For if the Roman clergy, as Luther said, had shamefully neglected church worship and religious instruction, the condition of the churches had since become worse, especially in the country, where the peasants seemed to have lost all religion. Gradually, however, as may be read, the tide of demoralization was checked in Saxony; and following the example of the Elector, the Lutheran princes of Germany established reformed state churches in their domains, conserving as much as seemed feasible of the old ecclesiastical order.[39]

Sometime after returning from his visitation of the Saxon churches, Luther composed the *Shorter* and the *Longer* catechisms to remedy the ignorance of pastors as well as flocks. Catholic primers existed, as well as manuals of preparation for confession and the Communion.[40] These may have afforded him suggestion. But in his hands and under his direction the Catechism became a most important means of instruction in the Lutheran faith, as well as an expository declaration of its principles and substance. The *Shorter Catechism* opened with an exhortation to pastors and preachers and a cry to God: Hilf! lieber Gott! in this ignorance so abominable that many pastors do not know the Lord's Prayer or the Creed or the Ten Commandments. The pastors were then instructed as to their duties, and admonished that those among their flocks who refused to learn should be kept from the land. Afterwards comes the substance of the Catechism, that which every good householder should impress upon his household. The Ten Commandments are given and briefly and piously explained; likewise the Apostles' Creed and the Lord's Prayer, in telling words. Next a brief explanation of the sacraments of baptism and the communion; also short forms of confession, of private prayer and grace at table; and forms for pastors to use in marrying and baptising.

The *Longer Catechism* expands the matter. Great

[39] See chap. XXI. of McGiffert's *Martin Luther.*

[40] See Jannsen, *Ges. des deutschen Volkes,* I, pp. 46 sqq. (18th edition).

stress is laid upon the Ten Commandments, which are so taken and expounded as to include the compass of Christian piety. "So we have the Ten Commandments as a pattern of the divine doctrine, what we shall do that our whole life be pleasing to God, and the true spring and conduit in which must flow everything that is to be a good work: so that beyond the Ten Commandments no work or thing can be good and pleasing to God, however great and precious it may be before the world." The Creed, the Lord's Prayer, the sacraments of baptism and communion, with other matters, are then given with lengthy comment. These two Catechisms became the vehicle of Christian instruction in the Lutheran churches, a function likewise to be fulfilled by Calvin's Catechisms in the churches following the Geneva Reform.

Luther likewise energetically met the need to re-establish education, in the tract *To the Burgermasters and Councillors of the Cities,* written in 1524. He speaks of the general admission that in German lands the high-schools are declining and the convent schools falling to pieces: — well enough that the latter should go down and that people should refuse to send their children to such nests of the devil. Now, raging at the fall of convents, where he was wont to trap young souls, he aims at the destruction of all schools, to the further ensnaring of the young. Alas! men give gulden for the war against the Turks, but do not see that they should give a hundred times as much to make their children Christians. I beg you, dear friends, to realize how much it profits Christ and all of us, to help the young.

So Luther speaks of the need of education in order that young men and women may understand their faith. The tract proceeds: if every burgher now, through God's mercy, has been released from iniquitous payments for indulgences, masses, monks, pilgrimages and the like, let him give part of this for schools, where boys now may learn more in three years than as heretofore in forty, when they became asses and blocks in the cloisters. Never before has Germany heard God's word as it is now heard. Let us then seize upon that word, lest it leave us as it left the Jews. There is no greater sin against God than not to teach the children. Do you say that this is the business of parents, not of town councils? But what if the parents do not do it: shall it then be neglected, and the authorities not have to answer? Often the parents are unfit, or have no time; and there are orphans. What is to become of city government if children are not educated? The business of a town is not merely to lay up wealth, but to bring up its citizens properly.

But someone says, why learn Latin, Greek and Hebrew, when we can have the Scriptures in German? So we Germans will ever be beasts, as other people call us. We would have foreign wares, and yet despise the foreign tongues and learning which might ennoble us! This is to continue German fools and beasts! We should accept the gift which God has given us, not without a purpose. He put his Scriptures in Hebrew and Greek: they are holy tongues. "Let us not think to hold the Gospel unless we hold the tongues." And, besides losing the Gospel from ignorance of the tongues, we should become unable to write Latin or German properly. A dreadful example is afforded by those schools and cloisters where they not only have mislearned the Gospel, but have fallen into a rotten Latin and German, like beasts. After apostolic times, as Greek and Hebrew disappeared, the Gospel, the Faith, Christendom, all declined, till they sank beneath a pope. Now the resurrection of the tongues has brought such light, that the world wonders at the purity of our gospel knowledge.

Here Luther points out that even Augustine erred in the interpretation of the Scripture through ignorance of the tongues; while that greatest of teachers, St. Bernard, is often carried beyond the true meaning. From lack of the tongues, the good Fathers encumbered the text with comment quite beside the point. "For as the sun is to the shadow, so is the tongue to all the Fathers' glosses." They would have been happy if only they could have learned as we can.

Luther proceeds further: though there were neither soul, nor heaven, nor hell, the government requires the education of boys and girls, in order that excellent and capable men may govern the land, and the women may manage their households. By pleasant methods children should be taught the tongues and liberal arts, with history, mathematics and music. "I only wish I had read more history and poetry myself." In fine, educated people are needed for worldly as well as spiritual functions. There should be libraries for books, from which we may well omit the Commentaries of the Jurists on the Law and of the theologians on the Sentences, as well as *Quaestiones* and monks' sermons. Have the Holy Scriptures first of all, in Latin, Greek, Hebrew and German, and if need be, other languages; with the best interpreters. The libraries should also contain books which aid linguistic studies; and the poets and orators, heathen and Christian, Greek and Latin. One learns grammar from them. Also text-books of the liberal arts, of law and medicine; with chronicles and histories, which preserve good tales.

It behoved Luther to urge the reinstatement of education. For the Lutheran revolt, reformation, awakening, however one may call it, troubled the universities, which needed troubling then as always, to keep their waters fresh; it also distracted the attention of students from their humane studies, and drew their spirits into the maelstrom of religious disturbance and revival, to the temporary dislocation of all other intellectual interests. Erasmus was not alone in saying, "Wherever Lutheranism reigns, there is an end to letters. Yet these men have been nourished and helped by letters."

Luther's revolt from papal authority and his reformed faith did not spring from humanism and arise in humanistic circles as clearly, or to the same degree, as the Reform in France. Nevertheless Erfurt with its university, where Luther received much of his education, was humane and liberal; and there he associated with as ardent humanists as Germany afforded. He was moderately read in the classics; but such classical allusions as may be found through his writings seem largely taken from the *Adagia* of Erasmus. Yet even in France, the Reformed religion, as it became more sternly conscious of its principles and aims, drew apart from humanism, naturally, since humanism in the main was pagan, or at least of this world, and the Reform was bent on Christian salvation. Likewise, Luther, with the impulses, energies, purposes of his dominantly religious nature set upon the proof and vindication of his faith, could not possibly be interested in classical studies for their own sake. Nor was he a man that was likely to maintain intimate and trusted relations with those whose aims and interests were quite different from his own. On their side, the humanists discovered that Luther's ways and Luther's interests were not theirs. They were free-minded men and patriotic Germans, who disliked the papal church as unfriendly to liberal studies and oppressive to Germany. The most typical production of these humanists was the book of *Letters of Obscure Men,* indicted in the Reuchlin controversy, a controversy which was altogether theirs.[41]

But Germans who were devoted to liberal studies were not alike in other respects, nor moved by the same motives. Beyond this common taste, there was little likeness between Ulrich von Hutten and Mutianus. When Luther had posted his Theses, and afterwards defied Rome both as a German and a true believing and enlightened Christian, his cause attracted the sympathies of humane scholars and roused the truculent enthusiasm of such a one as Hutten. Hutten lived long enough to quarrel with Erasmus, but his violent anti-papal soul found no reason to draw back from Luther, and would rather have urged the Wittenberger on to bloodier war against the Roman tyrant. Other humane scholars, Melanchthon, chief among them, merged themselves enthusiastically in the Lutheran movement, or kept manfully by its side. But quite as many, caring for letters above all things, and fearing to imperil their temporal fortunes and eternal souls in warfare with the Church, drew back from

[41] Ante, Chapter VI.

the Reformer, choosing to remain in the bosom of the mother who had nourished their souls, and might either clothe or castigate their tender bodies.

The body of Erasmus was extremely tender, and its wants insistent. Nor was he inclined toward strenuous defense of any cause save that of liberal thought and study. Our observation of him in a previous chapter has disclosed how impossible it was for an Erasmus to march hand in hand with Luther. The parting of their ways typified the incompatibility between devotion to letters and absorption in an enthusiastic evangelical agitation. It remains to see what Luther thought of Erasmus.

Early in March, 1517, Luther writes: "I am reading our Erasmus, and day by day my estimation of him lessens. It pleases me how learnedly he convicts monks and priests of their inveterate and sleepy ignorance;[42] but I fear that he does not sufficiently emphasize Christ and God's grace, wherein he is much more ignorant than Lefèvre of Ètaples.[43] Human considerations outweigh the divine with him."[44] Thus from the first, Luther discerned rational ethics rather than religious unction in Erasmus's attitude toward religion and Scripture.

In September 1521, Luther will not listen to a suggestion coming from Erasmus that he should show himself more moderate. "His opinion has not the slightest weight with me. . . . when I see him far from a knowledge of grace, and in all his writings looking to peace rather than to the cross of Christ. He thinks all these matters should be handled politely and gently; but Behemoth cares not for that, nor will emendment come of it. I remember, in his preface to the New Testament, that he says, referring to himself, that a Christian easily despises glory. But, O Erasmus, I fear, you err. Magna res est gloriam contemnere!"[45]

So he closes with a pious but quite human gibe. Three years later when Luther's friends no longer spared Eras-

[42] Seems to refer to reliance on ritual, etc.
[43] See post, Chapter XVII, 1.
[44] De Wette, I, p. 52.
[45] De Wette, II, p. 49–50.

mus, and that gifted man was also dipping his pen in gall, Luther wrote directly to him, asking that there might be at least a friendly truce between them.[46] Later, however, for the benefit of his son John, he characterized Erasmus as the "enemy of all religions and especially hostile to that of Christ, a perfect exemplar and type of Epicurus and Lucian."[47] Finally in 1534 Luther wrote to his friend Amsdorff, lengthily criticising the man Erasmus, his pernicious views of religion, and his erroneous understanding of Scripture. The letter leaves very little of him uncondemned, and ends with the wish that his works might be excluded from the schools, since even when harmless they are useless.[48]

Long before this, these two protagonists, the one of religion the other of humane piety, sacred and profane, had crossed arguments on the weighty matter of human free will and God's fore-ordainment. Erasmus, fretted by the stress of many subtle as well as palpable compulsions to declare against Luther, could refrain no longer. Had he selected purgatory, pilgrimages or indulgences, as the topic of his polemic, his argument must have stultified his real agreement with Luther upon such matters. But as a humanist in the broadest sense, he could not but uphold human liberty and the freedom of the will. This topic fell in with the scope and temper of his intellectual life; and as a subject of philosophy suited his position in the eyes of men. He treated it rationally and humanly, as a subject of discussion and opinion, yet adduced the support of scriptural passages.

The topic was vital to Luther's conception of God and man and the nexus of creatorship and creaturehood between them. For years he had devoted study and earnest consideration to it, and as early as 1516 had composed in

[46] De Wette, II, p. 498; April, 1524. Erasmus was already writing his *De libero arbitrio* against Luther.

[47] De Wette, IV, 497.

[48] De Wette, IV, pp. 507–520. Cf. another letter to Amsdorff, De Wette, IV, p. 545. There is a good deal in Luther's *Table Talk* on Erasmus's foolishness as a theologian, and his utter failure to recognize the function and meaning of Christ. See e.g. Preger, *Tischreden Luthers* (Leipzig 1888) nos. 357, 365.

scholastic fashion a searching *Quaestio de viribus et voluntate hominis sine gratia.*[49] With him it was a question of Christian faith, of salvation or damnation. Naturally, in 1525, as he wrote his *de servo arbitrio* in confutation of Erasmus's *de libero arbitrio,* he condemned his opponent's attitude in treating the subject as a matter of philosophical opinion and probability. "The Holy Ghost is no sceptic, and has not written dubious opinions in our hearts, but solid certitudes, — more solid and assured than life and all experiences."

You say, Erasmus, continues Luther warming to his argument, that all things in Scripture are not necessary for faith, and that some matters in it are obscure, and you cite Romans XI, 33, "O the depth of the riches both of the wisdom and knowledge of God! how unsearchable are his judgments, and his ways past tracing out." But I say: "God and God's scripture are two things; just as the Creator and the creation are two things. No one doubts that much is hidden in God that we do not know. . . . But that anything in Scripture is confused and not plain and clear, is a notion spread abroad by the godless sophists, with whose mouth thou speakest, Erasmus; but they have never brought forward an article, nor can they, through which this madness of theirs could be established."

To be sure, continues Luther, to one ignorant of the language and grammar of Scripture, much may be hidden; but not because of the height or difficulty of the substance. All is written for our instruction, and any seeming obscurity is due to the blindness of the reader. It is not to be endured that you put this matter of free will among those which are needless. On the contrary, we must know what the will can do and how it stands in relation to God's grace. We must distinguish surely between what is God's work and what is ours, if we would be righteous. "It is also necessary and salutary for Christians to know that God foreknows nothing casually and conditionally; but

[49] Stange, *Quellenschriften zur Ges. des Protestantismus* I. (Leipzig 1904).

that He foreknows, preordains and accomplishes all through His unchanging and eternal and unfailing will. This principle like a lightning stroke, strikes to earth and crushes out free will."

After some folios of Christian argument, these sentences are amplified as follows in Luther's final conclusions:

> " For if we believe that God foreknows and foreordains all things, and in his foreknowledge and foreordainment can neither be deceived nor hindered, then nothing can take place that He does not Himself will. Reason must admit this, while itself bears witness that there is no free will in men or angels or in any creature. So if we believe Satan to be the Prince of the World, who fights against the Kingdom of God in order that bounden men may not be loosed, and that he is overcome through the divine strength of the Spirit, it is again clear that there can be no free will. Likewise, if we believe that original sin has vitiated us . . . there is nothing left that can turn to good, but only to evil. . . . In fine, if we believe that Christ has saved men through his blood, we must acknowledge that the whole man was lost; otherwise we shall make Christ unnecessary, or into a Saviour of the most worthless part. This were blasphemous and sacrilegious."

The modern man is loosed quite otherwise from this particular predestination controversy, — or perhaps drawn to it by other chains. Luther's whole soul and faith were in it, and to his comfort. As he says substantially in his *Table Talk:* " when I think of the ineffable benefits God has prepared for me in Christ, then predestination becomes full of comfort: remove Christ, and all is shattered." The whole temperament of Luther is speaking and the sum of his convictions: the evangelical religious temperament, and the faith which it included.

Luther's faith was justified by its prodigious doctrinal effectiveness. His adamantine conservatism made his doctrines solid and tangible as rocks; they had body; they could be grasped and held to; and they had the sanction of divine authority. They were not presented as novelties, but were restored to men. Luther gave men what they had already, or might have had at any time from Scripture. And the doctrine which he had to offer, the Pauline Christian Gospel, was in itself so good, so comforting and assuring, so saving in this present troubled life, as well as for that to come.

Thus not only from logical necessity, but actually, Luther's clinging religious and social conservatism was an integral element of his reforms. These present a course of enforced surrender and substitution: the enforced surrender of one intolerable belief after another, and the substitution of the Scriptural doctrine or principle as he understood it. He kept what he could of the religion in which he had been reared, adhering to every belief, practice, or function of the contemporary Roman Catholic Church that the progress of his Scriptural faith and the logic and exigencies of his polemic state permitted him to retain.

His primal sources of strength and confidence lay in his mighty appropriation of the Pauline doctrine of justification by faith. It became the main criterion of his retentions and rejections. Another pillar of his strength was his conception of a Church universal, in which the papacy was but an incident and an evil one. He threw aside the hierarchical papal monarchy[50] for the older Pauline and Augustinian conception of a communion of true believers. Thus, with certain differences, Wyclif had done before him; and so should Calvin and other succeeding reformers do.[51]

[50] Cf. Harnack, *Dogmengeschichte,* III, pp. 410 sqq. Third edition.

[51] Luther gives his conception in the third part of his elaborate tract *upon Councils and Churches* written in 1539. He says that the Church according to the Creed is "a communion of the saints, a company or assembly of such people as are Christians and holy; that is, a Christian, holy, company or church. . . . The holy Christian Church is holy Christendom or the entire Christendom. In the Old Testament it is called the people of God." It is a pity, says he, that we have not kept that unequivocal expression "the holy Christian people of God"; for that is what the Church is. This Church, this holy Christian people of God, is recognized by the following works: It possesses God's Word; uses the sacraments of baptism and the Communion. It holds the *Keys* and uses them openly

Justification by faith, a universal church of believers, the freedom of the Christian man, not in his own will but God's: here was enough to stay a strong brave man against the papal dragon. Luther purged religion, even made those purge it who hated him. Yet one queries whether his teaching held as much of Christianity as did that great age-long institution of the Roman Catholic Church. It would have been hard for one man to be as universal as the Roman Catholic Church, which was built upon man as well as upon God. Lutheranism has changed and subdivided. And the Catholic Church in spite of its monarch pope, its vain absolutions, its excommunications and its interdicts, lives on. In spite of its mammon of abuses and corruption? Rather, because of it! For the Roman Catholic Church rests upon the imperfections and corruptions, as well as on the common needs, of man. It still has many saints; yet neither now, nor in Luther's time or before him, does its Catholicism point to truth for truth's sake, or to righteousness for the sake of righteousness. Its soul looks to the loaves and fishes, if not of this world, then of Heaven. Never could the Roman Church be supplanted by that mighty swashbuckler of the spirit, Martin Luther, though he was himself as much and as many things as a man could be; everything from a foul-mouthed German peasant to the mightiest of religious seers, and withal the greatest German we have known.

so that when a Christian sins, he shall be punished, and if not bettered, shall be cast out, bound in his sins. It selects and calls its servants, to wit, its bishops, pastors, preachers, who administer its holy things or offices, named above. God's people are also recognized by their public prayer and singing of psalms and spiritual songs; and by their holy cross of (a) enduring the persecution of the world, the flesh, and the devil, and (b) obeying the authorities. Such are the constituents of Christian holiness; and there are besides the outer signs of good conduct in all things according to the Commandments of God. The devil has aped God's holy Church in the papacy and its institutions and ceremonies through which papists think they will be saved. Yet beware, on the other hand, of those who cry Spirit! spirit! and decry all outer observances.

In closing, he says that the school is needed to educate true preachers; next, the household to provide scholars, then the Rathhaus to protect the citizens. The Church, God's own house and city, draws its protection from the city, and its members from the household. So the three orders are household, city, Church.

APPENDIX TO CHAPTER IX

MELANCHTHON AND ZWINGLI

THERE were two men very different from each other in their characters and careers, who when they met, met as partial opponents, and were not permitted to agree by the masterful Luther who held them apart: Melanchthon and Zwingli. With respect to their inclinations and functions they may also be regarded as people working at some half way station between Luther and Erasmus, a position more apparent with Melanchthon than with the vigorous and independent Swiss reformer.

In the Lutheran movement Melanchthon is second only to his chief in importance and effect; his is the one name besides Luther's which has survived in popular fame. There was reverence and affection between the two, which continued unbroken to the end, though sometimes strained. Melanchthon worked under Luther's leadership though not altogether under his dominance; and Luther held him to be far more gifted than himself. The tutelary deity of Melanchthon's youth was Reuchlin, his great-uncle, who saw to his university education and advancement and in 1518 obtained a call for him from the Elector to teach Greek at Wittenberg, when Melanchthon was only twenty-one years old. He was indeed a youthful prodigy in his studies and intellectual development; nor did his faculties weaken with the advance of years and knowledge. His attainments drew the admiration of Erasmus, with whom he remained on good terms; for he was a man inclined to stay at peace with all. Humanist, scholar, educator, promotor of the classical languages and thought, Melanchthon would gladly have devoted himself to Greek, and might have preferred it to theology. But as he clove at once to Luther, his labors, like his destinies, were cast in the fields of the great conflict.

Next to Luther himself, Melanchthon became par excellence the champion, the expounder, and the formulator of Lutheranism. He defended his chief in an Apology directed against the "Furious decree of the Paris Theologasters," the Sorbonne to wit, who had declared Luther an arch-heretic. Like his leader, he wrote against the murderous peasants, and after the deed, he approved the burning of Servetus in Geneva. He was, however, more conciliatory, and given to dreams of pace where Luther saw there could be none, as at the Augsburg diet. The Augsburg Confession and Apology were his masterpieces of Protestant formulation.

His chief work of theological exposition was of course the *Loci Communes theologici,* which emerging from an embryonic *Adumbratio,* proceeded onward through a first and second and third *Aetas* to its final bulk and form. Even as Calvin's *Institute.* And it is a matter of no slight interest to note that as Melanchthon's work and Calvin's reached their final form, they followed more closely the arrangement of the Lombard's *Sentences* and the *Summa* of Aquinas. The fact was that for the Lombard and Aquinas, as for Augustine before them, and later for Calvin and Melanchthon, Scripture itself furnished the arrangement of a work that should comprehend Scriptural doctrine. Says Melanchthon at the beginning of his *Secunda Aetas:* "Habet ipsa scriptura suam quandam methodum et quidem artificiosam. Series enim dogmatum ab ipso ordine historiae aptissime sumi potest. Initio de creatione, de peccato hominis, de promissionibus loquitur, postea tradit legem, deinde docit Evangelium de Christo:—" most aptly we arrange our matter after the order of Scriptural history; creation, man's sin, the promises, the law, and finally the Gospel.[1]

In this excellent work Melanchthon draws away from *scholasticae nugae;* and likewise from the *Aristotelicae argutiae,* although philosophically he held a profound

[1] Melanchthon's *Loci Communes* occupy Vols. XXI and XXII of the *Corpus Reformatorum,* where the work is printed in its three stages, of 1521, 1535 and 1543. The passage quoted is from col. 254 of Vol. XXI; compare with it col. 341 of the same volume.

respect for the Stagirite, and deemed his system salutary as a barrier against the *philosophical* disorder of the age. But the statements and arguments of the *Loci Communes* in the main are based on Scripture, and much more directly than those for instance of the *Summa* of Aquinas. For unlike the *Summa,* the *Loci Communes* does not move and find its substance in Aristotelian categories of thought. Melanchthon rather intended it as an ordered *Summa* of the Scriptural *Testimonia.* The new learning is present throughout the smooth Latin exposition of this master of clarity; and the work is humanistically flavored with Greek words and classical allusions. For the author was first and last a scholar, loving classical scholarship for its own sake. He also liked to find the analogues to scriptural truth in the lives and precepts of pagan philosophers; as one sees so clearly in those paragraphs where he arranges the precepts of the Law of Nature in correspondence with the Decalogue.[2] His liberal humanistic inclinations drew him toward Erasmus's side instead of Luther's in the controversy upon the freedom of the human will, which is evident in the *Secunda Aetas* of his *Loci* of 1535 and becomes even more pronounced in the corresponding sections of the *Tertia Aetas* of 1543.[3]

Confidence in the best in classical literature and philosophy, respect for the *lumen naturale* which the Fall of man darkened, but did not destroy, and recognition of the *lex naturae*, worked together to strengthen the moral quality of Melanchthon's theology, and broadened its consideration of natural reason and the conscience of mankind. All this tended to moralize his theology, as his tempered exclusion of Aristotelian arguments tended to simplify it. Again, it was his natural reason and moral conscience that insisted on the freedom of the human will, and afforded an independent testimony in favor of the soul's immortality.

Melanchthon was a moral theologian, and a moral

[2] *Loci Com. De lege naturae.* Third *Aetas* Vol. XXI, *Corp. Ref.* Col. 711 sqq.

[3] Vol. XXI, *Corp. Ref.* Col. 274 sqq. and col. 652 sqq.

philosopher, and in all his labors for education never lost sight of the moral betterment which should result from learning. He strove so to enlarge and complete the plan of education that it might embrace all revealed or tested truth. To that end he was wont to use the pagan elements to fill out the Christian scheme. His study of antiquity was Catholic. He admired Plato, yet followed Aristotle; and as was natural for a sixteenth century humanist, he found moral and philosophic discussions adapted to his taste and comprehension in the works of the eclectic Cicero. Following Aristotle, imbibing Cicero, he produced manuals of Dialectic, Physics, Ethics, or edited the Aristotelian treatises on these topics; and composed Greek and Latin grammars, and other books for the schools. This great array of admirable text books, which carried far and wide his stimulating personal instructions, earned for him the honored title of *Praeceptor Germaniae,* which more than one educational worthy had borne before him.

Zwingli was never a follower of Luther, but rather an opponent, though holding some of the same doctrines. He was bred to an utterly different social and political régime; his convictions did not come from Wittenberg, although their development appears to have been influenced by Luther's writings. The two men were of independent and rather opposite temperaments, and, when they met, parted in confirmed disagreement. Zwingli is supposed to have been jealous of Luther's power, and Luther always disapproved both of Zwingli and his views, and thought at last that his fate rightly came on him in the battle of Kappel; for, having taken the sword, he perished by it; and if God received him into blessedness He did it *extra regulam!* [4]— which is to say, acting not strictly in accord with Luther's ideas.

Zwingli was born in 1484 in the Toggenburg valley, dominion over which was disputed by Zurich and Schwyz.

[4] Preger, *Luthers Tischreden,* no. 218, cf. no. 509.

In 1518 he was elected priest and preacher for the great Zurich Minster; and thenceforth guided that city's political as well as religious destinies, in a way that anticipated the career of Calvin at Geneva. For Zwingli was a Swiss civic personality and politician before he became a reformer. From a certain teacher at Basel named Wyttenbach, he early took the principle of justification by faith, learned to look to Scripture as the Christian authority, and also to disapprove of papal indulgences. His education was mainly humanistic, and drawn from various masters. He professed to admire and follow Erasmus. But he was taken by the writings of Pico della Mirandula; and he drew from the Classics much that entered his life and affected the development of his convictions. He was a Greek scholar, and a student of the New Testament, who preferred the text to the commentators. He was also a reader of the Church Fathers. The Church was less powerful in Switzerland than in other countries, less well organized and correspondingly infected with looseness of conduct. But the papacy was tenderly disposed toward the people of the little mountain land, where its pay drew unequalled soldiers, of which the present papal guard is the last survival. Although he had profited from it, Zwingli declared himself opposed to this mercenary service and to the papal pensions which corrupted Swiss politics and people. He was rather antipapal from the beginning; and readily yielded to his developing protestantism to disavow the pope's authority. He was a preacher and a priest; yet his life was rather loose, and in 1524 he married.

By this time a general change in the forms of worship had been effected at Zurich, Zwingli leading the movement. The church there was made civic and democratic; its offices were reformed and translated into German; images were discarded, and the Mass abolished (April, 1525); the monasteries were secularized, and their incomes devoted to charity or education. A struggle followed with the Anabaptists, who were for the most part expelled.

The further course of Zwingli's life was involved in a tangle of politics, connected with the progress or blocking of the Reform in Switzerland.

Zwingli's formulation of a Christian faith was not as important as Luther's on the one hand, or as Calvin's on the other. If it was not carried through with the originative religious power of the one, or the insistent logic of the other, it was reasonable and genial. Politician, man of action, as he was, Zwingli was also a reader and a student. And, as is common with able busy men, who are also great readers, he assembled thoughts from many quarters, worked them into his convictions or philosophy, but had neither the slow meditative leisure nor the inner power to transform the matter of his reading into a seamless system. Yet he grasped with energy the Pauline Augustinian justification through faith, and genially and humanely enlarged his religious conceptions with thoughts drawn from Seneca's eclectic but predominantly Stoic store, or from the undigested mass of borrowed and yet temperamentalized ideas offered by the works of Pico. Through them, and independently of them, he gleaned from many minds thoughts which served his working faith. Withal, and this is a vital point, inasmuch as he was a man of action, a man of working faith, and a reformer of religious practice and doctrine, he did not fail to vitalize his teachings and endue them with qualities of power, by which men might live and endure, or fight.

With Seneca, philosophy was a way to virtue. It was a religion with him; and it became an integral part of the religion of Zwingli. Seneca expressed as much trust in God as was felt by a Paul or an Augustine. He had also said: "We are born in a kingdom; liberty is to obey God." God has the qualities of a Father, and is also the *summum bonum* for all. Zwingli adds the thought that believers are his willing instruments, working along with him for their only good, and for the glory which is in the fulfilment of the divine purpose: a mighty thought.

Zwingli advanced still further in his eclectic stoicism

and Augustinianism, following his own impulse too, and found God to be the sum total of good, that is of being: "unum ac solum infinitum . . . praeter hoc nihil esse." Universal being, (esse rerum universarum) is the being of God, (esse numinis).[5] Hence God includes all finite beings, who are part of Him and his universal plan. He is the founder, ruler, administrator of the universe. Man alone shall not stand without the scope of God's all-determining purpose. Zwingli brings the full stoical conception of *providence* into the Christian scheme of election.[6]

God reveals himself in the consciousness and consciences of men; and creates faith within them. That faith is true which directs itself solely to God; superstition consists in reliance upon other things.[7] He revealed himself to the minds of the chosen heathen, as well as to the flock of Christ. So with Zwingli, the outer revelation ceased to be all important; and incidents and observances became of no importance. He was disposed to discard the special miracle and intervention: why demand the particular supernatural manifestation when God is the sole first cause, and works all things in all, to the exclusion of secondary causes. Surely he who finds God working everywhere will need no special miracles. So Zwingli would admit no miracle in the Eucharist, no miraculous real presence such as Luther held to. For him, the sacrament was a memorial and a sign.

The outer ceremony may be negligible, indifferent. But there is a highest visible manifestation of the will and law of God, which men may bring to pass, working in faith: it is the Christian community or State, founded on the observance of God's law as well as on the promise of His Gospel. Here was again the mighty thought with which Calvin should build, Knox preach, and Cromwell smite, all of them willing instruments of God. No

[5] For these citations and more besides, I am indebted to Dilthey, *Auffassung etc des Menschen in 15. und 16. Jahrhundert.*
[6] In Zwingli's *De providentia.*
[7] Zwingli, *De vera et falsa religione.*

Lutheran church formed under the protection of an autocratic prince, and obediently adapting at least its outer self to the existent institutions and policy of a secular state, could even entertain such an ideal.

BOOK III

THE FRENCH MIND

CHAPTER X

THE UNLETTERED WIT OF LOUIS XI, COMMYNES AND VILLON

THERE were analogies of human endeavor and intent in the intellectual advance of France and Italy in the fifteenth and sixteenth centuries. In both countries the same fundamental humanity was somehow pushing on, struggling and manoevering for possessions, also seeking knowledge, truth, and beauty. Divergencies at the same time appear, due partly to ancient differences of racial trait, and assuredly to the different histories of the two countries. The resulting Gallic-French temperament was not as the Italian; and the French mind seemingly sought other goals. Obviously, moreover, in the period before us, the opportunities, possibilities, exigencies of the two lands were very different. The intellectual product, the finished self-expression of the French in the sixteenth century, will not resemble the Italian, except when directly imitating it.

Caesar's conquest of Gaul did not result in any such indelible Romanization of its people as to preclude a marked originality of growth through the mediaeval period. Yet the quick, susceptible Gallic faculties lent themselves happily to the discipline of the Roman order; and this people seem to have gained from it permanent qualities of clarity and logic. To the west and north, Gauls and Belgi shaded into Teutons, while the Teutonic conquests of the fifth and succeeding centuries set a strong German graft upon the Celtic stock. This resulting French race, fundamentally Celtic, yet with Teutonic strains, was akin on the one side to the Irish, and on the other to the Germans across the Rhine. Neither the Irish nor the Germans were subjected to the discipline of the Roman order; and in quite different ways were to betray through all the centuries the lack of this initial disciplinary period.

The progress of the fifteenth and sixteenth centuries in France would proceed from the equipment and faculties of the better people, be guided by their tastes, and depend upon their opportunities and the energy with which they should master further knowledge, and appropriate or develop new elements of life. French faculties and desires might in some respects show German and English affinities, rather than Italian; and Germany and the Low Countries furnished many of the new intellectual stimuli. Incentive and aid to better classical studies came not from Italy alone — Erasmus was an influence in Paris; the art of printing was introduced from Germany, while the style and method of Flemish painting extended through the lands of Burgundy and France. In philosophy, the influence of the German Nicholas of Cusa rivalled that of Ficino's Platonic translations; while many a new idea in terrestrial and celestial physics had its first home elsewhere than in Italy. With Frenchmen, love of formal beauty did not lead directly to the composition of classical centos and empty imitations. And, clearest difference of all, religious revolt, with its intended reform and reconstruction, which was but sporadic in Italy during these two centuries, in France, in Germany and Flanders, and in England, became the most drastic issue.

The fourteenth century, which for France was stamped by the ravages of the Hundred Years' War, was also marked by the partial disintegration of the social, political and religious conceptions which had sustained the mediaeval organism. France was still far from the attainment of political nationality. Much territory was distributed in dukedoms and count-doms, the lords of which gave little more than homage to the Valois Kings, who succeeded to the direct Capetian line in 1328. This lack of unity issued in civil war when Burgundy allied herself with the English enemies of France, and the kingdom seemed shattered past recovery. Yet there was vitality in the

French monarchy, which at last came into its own when Burgundy was joined to the royal domain by Louis XI, on the death of Charles the Bold (1477).

The contest of wits and arms between Louis and Charles is famous in history and story through the dramatic contrast between the two protagonists. It was a last phase of the conflict between feudalism and the monarchic principle, and was directly due to the custom of bestowing huge fiefs as appanages, upon the younger sons of the royal house. Philip le Hardi, the brother of Charles V of France, held Burgundy in 1364. Through the death of his father-in-law in 1381 he became also Count of Flanders, a year after the death of his brother the King. The King's son, Charles VI, a weakling from birth, became in the course of time an intermittent madman. Hostility between his brother Louis, Duke of Orleans, and his uncle Philip of Burgundy divided the realm till Philip's death in 1404. Philip's son and successor John took up the quarrel, and in 1407 had his cousin of Orleans assassinated. On his avowal of the deed, civil war broke out, each faction struggling to control the person of the King. John, a man of turnings and tergiversations, allied himself with the invader, Henry V of England, and brought to pass the temporary ruin of the realm. Upon his murder in 1419, Philip "the Good" came to the ducal throne. He had little regard either for France or England. But, deciding to make peace with Charles VII of France, he abandoned the waning fortunes of the English, and through apt measures for his own aggrandizement, succeeded in doubling his already enormous patrimony.

There could be little love between the rulers of Burgundy and France, and in the end Philip was pleased to foster trouble for the King by encouraging the latter's graceless son and dauphin, Louis, in his rebellion. He received, and for some years magnificently entertained him against the King's protest, who said: "Mon cousin de Bourgogne nourrit le renard qui mangera ses poules." At the Burgundian Court, Louis became the god-parent (parrain) of the heavy-fated Marie, daughter of Philip's son, the future Charles the Bold.

Philip excelled his liege sovereign in wealth and power; — only he was not a King! War was imminent between them, when the death of Charles made way for Louis in 1461. He was crowned at Rheims under the patronage and at the expense of the great Duke, whose splendor fastened all men's eyes. So it was in Paris too, till the Duke began to perceive that not he, but Louis, was the King.

The Duke was ageing; and his own far from dutiful son Charles (these Burgundian dukes were much too choleric) became reconciled to his father in order to direct the power of Burgundy against Louis whom he hated. He was soon heading the feudatory league, absurdly called the "Public Good"; and a critical time for the King followed the ill-fought and indecisive battle of Montlhéry, near Paris. Thenceforth through truce or peace, or declared hostilities, the warfare of intrigue and arms did not cease between them. This long and intricate story had its striking episodes, as that of Louis venturing almost fatally for him into Charles's Court and the mutually mistrustful potentates joining in an attack on Liége. The end of the story came through the perverse embroilment of Charles with the hard-hitting Swiss, which, after two disastrous defeats, led to his shameful death in flight. He was a foolish leader in war, and in diplomacy lacked patience and understanding.

The character and mental quality of the time appear in the *Mémoires* of Commynes,[1] the chief narrator of this story. Through his aid we realize how Louis netted Charles, being so much less foolish than his rival, so much more patient and self-restrained. Allowing for differences of temperament, the King was no more dishonorable than that futile man who with such folly and so little steadfast courage, dashed his choleric head against impossibilities. Indeed, Louis XI was no more of a liar and betrayer than other princes of his time; but he could hold

[1] Born in 1447, died in 1511.

to his purposes. Commynes while admitting in his Prologue that there will be found in his *Mémoires* matters not to the King's credit, says: "I dare affirm in his praise that I have known no prince with fewer vices (moins de vices) everything considered." He has just been remarking that princes are men like ourselves —"To God alone belongs perfection; but in a prince so long as his virtue and good qualities outweigh his vices, he is worthy of remembrance and praise."

The writer was a man of wide experience and tolerance; a true exponent of his world. His own record required indulgence. For his father had placed him at the Burgundian Court, and he was the servant of Charles before he chose to yield to the solicitations of his rival, whose diplomatic minister he became. He preferred to serve a wise prince, who had knowledge of affairs and took part in them and did not do everything through others. With such a master there is surer chance of recognition and reward. Of course one has to live under those who are over him, — and our whole hope ought to be in God. [2] It was part of the intelligence of the grasping and prudent King that he rewarded munificently those who served him well: "Among all the princes I have known, the King our master knew best how to act, and how to honor people of worth." This remark comes toward the end of a digressive chapter in which Commynes has been speaking of the advantage to princes of a knowledge of history; since life is so short that one cannot learn enough by experience, and should therefore make use of history's teachings.

Princes should understand men, and how, or at least when, to treat them well. Commynes brings in these sentiments when telling how an able Burgundian envoy, the lord of Humbercourt, preserved his own life and so handled the people of Liége that they decided to yield their city to the Duke when he could not have captured it. Humbercourt gained his end largely through his judicious treatment of certain hostages from the townspeople, sending them freely to negotiate with their fellow towns-

[2] Livre I, ch. 16.

men. The writer points to the ill-judgment of those princes who repent them of kindness or of generosity in pardoning. There will be some ingrates; but because of such, one should not forego the chance of doing well by others when opportunity offers. Commynes will not believe that any "personne saige" would prove ungrateful for benefits conferred. But princes deceive themselves in their choice of persons; to attach a fool to oneself will never profit long. A lord can show no greater sense than in gaining the attachment of worthy people—"gens vertueux et honnestes"; for men will judge him by those whom he surrounds himself with. And to conclude, says Commynes, "it seems to me that one should never tire of treating people well (jamais lasser de bien faire). For a single and the least one of those whom one has ever benefited, will perchance render such service and show such gratitude, as to atone for all the base and evil conduct of the rest."

According to the ideas of Commynes and King Louis, and of later times as well, the prince may wisely bestow gifts on the servants of other princes. Louis did this all his life with discretion and success. Commynes is capable of treating the matter with cynical humor, as when at a late period of Louis's career, after the death of Charles, he tells how Louis pensioned the great lords of England, to keep them friendly to his wishes, and prevent their interfering with his designs upon the lands of the Burgundian heiress. By paying Edward IV fifty thousand crowns a year, he closed his ears to the remonstrances at home or from abroad: "L'avarice de ces cinquante mil escuz, renduz tous les ans en son chasteau de Londres, luy amollissoit le cueur." Louis's ambassadors were always well entertained, while they beguiled Edward with talk of a marriage between his daughter and the dauphin. Yet certain members of Edward's council, or his Parliament, thought differently, "saiges personnaiges" they were, "who looked ahead, and had received no pensions like the others."

This King Edward was a valiant leader, as Commynes

says, and had won seven or eight great battles in England, himself fighting always on foot, which was greatly to his praise. But he was not as clever as King Louis, as men had good reason to think from the peace which Louis made with him when he had invaded France in aid of Charles. Louis obtained a truce, and sent the English three hundred chariots of the best wine, and afterwards made them still more royally drunk in Amiens.[3]

These happy ways of Louis did not include all his statecraft. Beyond other men, he knew how to sow dissensions. As Commynes says: "Que le roy Loys nostre maistre a mieulx seu entendre cest art de separer les gens, que nul aultre prince que j'aye jamais veu ne congneu; et n'espargnoit l'argent ne ses biens ne sa peine, non point seullement envers les maistres, mais aussi bien envers les serviteurs."[4] And if Commynes has shown how Louis could reward profusely, and even decide to trust, he shows that none could be more prudent and suspicious, as one had need to be amid the network of mutual treason and betrayal which made up the politics of Burgundy, France and England, the last country being then engaged in the Wars of the Roses. Speaking of how a clever Englishwoman won the Duke of Clarence away from the arch intriguer Warwick and deceived the best wits, our author remarks "that there is nothing shameful in being suspicious, and keeping one's eye on those who come and go; but it is a disgrace to be deceived, and lose through one's blunder. However, to be over-suspicious is not well."

King Louis was an adept at discoveries and espials, and kept himself informed of the intentions of friends and enemies. Usually he succeeded in laying his plots and counterplots a little deeper than theirs, and when the explosion came, it was not his trench that flew into the air. That was what the Count of St. Pol discovered, or rather failed to discover: a man who hoped by double or triple dealing to escape being ground between England, France and Burgundy. He would trick them all. The

[3] Livre VI, 1; IV, 9.
[4] Livre II, 1.

King's counter-wile was St. Pol's undoing when the latter sent his envoys with excuses. Louis concealed a trusted counsellor of the Duke's behind the curtain of the audience chamber, and then drew the envoys on to tell their master's mind touching the Duke, even alleging a slight deafness of his own, in order to induce them to speak louder. The enraged Burgundian counsellor reported what was said; and thereafter when St. Pol in person came to the Duke, on the latter's safe-conduct, he was seized, and handed over for final execution to King Louis, who, after trial, cut his head off.

Commynes was no Don Quixote. He viewed intrigue as he did war, of which he said, " qui a le prouffit de la guerre, il en a d'honneur." But there was a background of honesty in him, and much fear, or superstition, as to the anger of God descending upon flagrant injustice and the pride that puffeth up. He saw God's wrath coming on the Duke for giving all the glory to himself, and none to God, and especially for his treachery in delivering up St. Pol. Profoundly his narrative shows Charles a fatal fool, a man of rage and weakness, whom in the end God or his own fitting fate would not fail to destroy.

If the drama ended fitly as to Charles, it ended as fitly with the King. He was no man to be so foolishly undone as the potentate whom he deftly helped Fortune undo. Yet his ambition might vault too eagerly. In the matter of the Burgundian succession after Charles's death, all that Louis had been scheming and fighting for throughout his reign seemed within his reach. He was then unwisely grasping. Although he got the land of Burgundy, it would have been better not to have driven the Duke's daughter, with all her rich Flanders towns, to the arms and wedlock of Austria. Commynes seems to think that God had rather darkened the King's mind. He suffered, to be sure, no outward overthrow; yet he declined through many months of premature old age, consumed with lust of power which was slipping from his senile hands, and tortured with fears of surely approaching death. Through his whole life of scheming greed, Louis was beset with superstition. He practised astrology continually, and grovelled before graven images, and that chief graven image of a purchasable God! It is an impressive psychological picture that Commynes draws of the King's slow end — of his months and years of dying, his vacillations, yet tricking to the last his enemies, and sending them far and wide to other countries for horses and dogs so that his foreign rivals might suppose him strong enough to hunt; he never looked at these purchases when they had been brought. He held on to every thread of power and authority, the ruler in him outlasting his strength. He was maddened with desire for life, and paid incredible sums to his physician, besides sending far and wide for relics with healing virtues, and calling a famous hermit to come and restore him by his interposition. Profoundly unhappy, and profoundly foolish, he would not see the emptiness of the husks he clung to.

One might have preferred Charles's bloody death to Louis's bed-ridden end. Commynes is impartial in the long chapter on the small joys and the great pains that Louis had from being a tireless scheming King, and those which came to Charles from being a rich and powerful and consumingly ambitious Duke. From "l'enfance et l'innocence" Louis had every toil and trouble, with twenty days of travail and annoyance to one of pleasure. It had been the same with Charles —"toujours travail, sans nul plaisir. . . . car la gloire luy monta au cueur": — and the end was defeat and death. Nor were other rulers of the time much more fortunate. And Commynes concludes his disquisition:

"So you see the death of all these great men in so short a while, who labored for glory and to aggrandize themselves, and suffered such pains and passions, shortening their lives and imperilling their souls. Here I am not speaking of the Turk, who is lodged with his predecessors! As to our King, I have hope that our Lord has had pity on him, and on the others, if it please Him. But, humanly speaking, ... would it not have stood him in better stead, and the others too, and men of moderate estate as well, . . . to choose the middle path in these things? To worry and labor less, and undertake less; to have more fear of offending God, and persecuting the people and their neighbors by all the cruel means I have been speaking of, and to take ease through honest pleasures. Their lives would have been longer; sickness would not have come so soon; and their death would be more regretted and . . . less desired; and they would have less fear of death." [5]

One remembers that Commynes wrote in his later years, when he was sorely scratched by brambles; for at Louis's death, he fell from power, and was beset by foes, who wished to despoil him of part of the huge estates he had gained in Louis's service — honestly? That is no simple question. Commynes was a good manager, a quick accepter of emoluments; he cared for riches; and he was a man of piety, who feared God, and His way of upsetting the too flagrant and insolent wrong-doer. The iron had entered into Commynes's soul and into his view of life when he wrote.

This man of common sense and craft was a despiser of chivalry and its vain-glory; he believed in managing men, rather than fighting; diplomacy was his *métier;* worldly sagacity was what he admired. The seventeenth, eighteenth and nineteenth chapters in his fifth book give his views on public affairs. He has been telling how the men of Ghent, after Charles's death, executed certain of his noble ministers in spite of his daughter's protests, and of other doings of the people of this city — a city for which Commynes has little use!

"And I cannot think why God has so long preserved this city of Ghent, from which so many ills have come, and which is of so little utility for the land and the public interests of the land where it is situated, and much less for its Prince; and it is not like Bruges, which is a great gathering-place of merchandise and foreigners, where possibly more merchandise is handled than in any other city of Europe, and it would be an irreparable loss if it were destroyed."

Having delivered himself thus regarding Ghent, Commynes feels there may be other considerations. "Indeed it seems to me that God has created nothing in this world, neither men nor beasts, without making its contrary to

[5] Liv. VI, ch. 12.

keep it in fear and humility. And so this city of Ghent does very well where it is; for that country [Flanders] is the most given to pleasure . . . and pomps and lavish spending. They are good Christians, and God is well served and honored there.[6] It is not the only people to whom God has given a thorn." And he proceeds to speak of France as having England for an opposite, and England, as having Scotland, and so through the rest of Europe. These checks and thorns which God has set in every state and for every person are necessary:—"et de prime face, et parlant comme homme non lettré.[7] . . . principallement pour la bestialité de plusieurs princes, et aussi pour la mauvaistié d'aultres, qui ont sens assez et experience, mais ils en veulent mal user,"—and Commynes expresses the opinion that learning may make evil princes worse, but will improve the good. Yet knowledge can teach even an evil prince the fear of God and the limits to the power which God has given him over his subjects.

Commynes concludes that neither natural reason nor our common sense (nostre sens), nor the fear of God, nor the love of our neighbor, nor anything (riens) will keep us from doing violence to each other. And so God is constrained to beat us with many rods for our "bestialité" and "mauvaistié,"—and especially princes of whose ways Commynes gives a severe picture; their outrages upon neighbors, injustice toward the nobles serving them, and toward the common people whom they oppress with taxes and exactions. Commynes maintains that no prince has the right to make any levy on his subjects, without their consent, except within his own domain; and he admires England as the realm where least violence is done the people and the public weal is best cared for. The King of France has no excuse for asserting the privilege of levying on his subjects at his pleasure. His true praise lies in having good and loyal subjects that will refuse him

[6] He says the same of Venice. Liv. VII, ch. 18.

[7] One bears in mind that neither Commynes nor Louis nor Charles had part as yet in the new fashions of learning already prevalent in Italy. They are sheer French.

nothing. And Commynes praises the great loyalty of the French toward their young King, Charles VIII, to whom though but a child they humbly preferred their requests through the assembly of the Trois États held after his father's death; and this notwithstanding that the realm had been sore oppressed by the levies of the deceased King.

The greatest ills always come from the strongest! The little people and the poor find plenty who will punish them for cause or no cause; but there is none to punish princes except God. And for that reason God sets His judgments on them, that is to say on the bad ones — and there are few good! The ills they do proceed from the weakness of their belief in hell. Consider what a large ransom King John paid when taken captive by the Black Prince, pledging his lands and impoverishing his realm. That was to obtain release from prison! But how little he did to avoid the evils which brought this punishment upon him; and how little would a King do or pay to escape the pains of hell, which are many times worse than those of an earthly prison? The ill deeds of the great are due to their lack of faith.

Of course, Commynes has been compared with his younger Italian contemporary, Machiavelli, and one may throw the still younger Guicciardini into the comparison.[8] Commynes's protagonist, Louis, should be compared with Lorenzo dei Medici, rather than with Machiavelli's Cesare Borgia. In the first place these Frenchmen were Frenchmen, and these Italians, Italians: that carried some worlds of difference in the fifteenth and sixteenth centuries. Next obviously, as the Frenchmen were somewhat older, and as France was tardier than Italy in the new classical revival, and more especially as both Commynes and his master had " small Latin and no Greek," these two appear as primarily using their mother wit and their own political experience and knowledge of men and affairs. Their educational background was the ordinary schooling, the current literature, the Christianity and the

[8] Ante, chapter IV.

royal or feudal policies, which prevailed in France. To be sure, in the political education of France there had been such important foreign elements as the Civil Law and the *Politics* of Aristotle. But Lorenzo embodies the new classical culture of Italy; and Machiavelli bases his theorizing upon the wisdom contained in Roman History. He has more learning, and in the thoroughness of his political theory is as superior to Commynes as he is inferior to him in practical shrewdness and tact. Guicciardini also excels the Frenchman in his knowledge of the principles of politics, and may have been his equal in practical ability: but he is more utterly corrupt, being a creature of that political corruption which rendered Italian statecraft impotent. The politics of Commynes were more possible, embracing happy makeshifts of reasoning, such as a wholesome conviction that exceptional wickedness or pride would come to ruin, through God's punishments, — an idea as fundamentally sound as the Aeschylean conception of ὕβρις, the vain-glory of insolence, bringing the tyrant low. This thought was absent from the brains either of Machiavelli or Guicciardini. One queries whether it could be found in the conduct of Louis XI, who treated his God as purchasable. One notes that his addiction to astrology is not to be connected with the Italian classical revival, which strengthened this pseudo-science in fifteenth century Italy.

So France became a strong and united kingdom, whose forces could be used by its Kings in vain endeavors to extend their rule over other countries. The fact that the monarch had become the one source of land and gold and honors tended to renew the loyalty of the nobility in warlike devotion to the royal fortunes. Feudalism sank to a reactionary tradition, which might on occasions assert itself disastrously. And through the reigns of Louis's successors, royalty, following its caprice or taste, patronized learning and literature and art, and court life suggested the topics of art and literature, and affected their treatment.

Louis XI and Commynes, his expounder, were not affected by Italy and classical humanism. The forces of previous French development, those making for the fruits of this world and those incited by the luridly imagined next, still energized in their faculties, and led forward the society within which and upon which these two political personages worked so effectively. Agriculture and trade and the industrial crafts had laid the material foundation. Mechanical experimental methods contributed, proving themselves in many ways, for example in the effectiveness of the French artillery. A select few were interested in the more rational or theoretical physical sciences which had been developed from statements and premises of Aristotle, or by departing from them.[9] A still vigorous factor in thought and life was the scholastic theology whose home was the University of Paris. For literature, there was the mediaeval cumulation of *fabliaux, chansons,* Arthurian and antique romance, and such chronicles as those of Froissart, his predecessors and successors. The *Roman de la Rose,* composed of the allegorical idyl of De Lorris and the cynical encyclopaedia of De Meung, was popular and influential. The period was still mainly mediaeval in literary taste and theme; though the old *motifs* were breaking, and losing their vitality.

The fifteenth century writers of prose and verse manifest few distinctive qualities. Among them was the first of professional literary women, Christine de Pisan, a Venetian by birth, but living in France, and a good French patriot.[10] She wrote interminable verse, and in her old age greeted the glory of Jean d'Arc, dying shortly after 1429. Somewhat younger was Alain Chartier, a student of Sallust, Livy, Cicero, but more generally of Seneca. He was the author of tedious, moralizing poems, but used a prose which we may think his loyal heart, stung by his country's disasters, had helped to strengthen and

[9] See articles by Duhem, *La dynamique parisienne,* in *Bulletin Italien,* Vols. X, XI, XII, and XIII, and post, chapter XXXI.

[10] See sufficiently in Petit de Julleville, *Histoire de la langue et de la littérature française,* Vol. 2, pp. 357 sqq.

ennoble. He could not free himself from the mediaeval conventional setting of a dream even in those works of moving patriotism, where he adjured the nobility, the clergy, and the people of France to have pity on their mother's misery.[11] His mind revolved around the disaster of Agincourt and the defection of Burgundy. The lighter nature of Charles d'Orleans might have revolved about the same, since his father had been murdered by the Duke of Burgundy, and he had himself been taken prisoner at that battle, and not liberated until twenty-five years after, in 1440. Belonging to a race of Kings, he was an amateur of letters, and a clever maker of small poems. His faculty of verse was as a light skiff, which would have labored under heavy freight. Its usual theme was love, treated prettily, takingly, conventionally, and sometimes bitterly. Anything in his poetry might have been written and appreciated a hundred years before; and nothing in his cherished library indicated any taste different from that of the fourteenth century.[12] He died an old man in 1465, in the reign of Louis XI; about the same time that death put out the flame of François Villon.

It is difficult to speak of this thief and murderer, whose vivid gift of verse was rendered mordant by the bitterly insistent, hateful sense of death. Death pervaded his verse, making a mephitic atmosphere. This man of debauch and need execrated the cruelty which withheld from him gold and wine. Villain life would not keep him gratis in his lusts! It is the old false cry: had one his desire, he would do no crime! "Povre je suis de ma jeuness"— little had he through the heated years of youth, nor in "l'entrée de viellesse," in his thirtieth year! Prison had eaten body and soul. Villon saw that his end might not even be a filthy grave, but the gallows, to which he was once condemned, where he would be pecked by pies and crows till his skeleton rattled in the wind.

[11] In the *Quadrilogue,* see Petit de Julleville, o. c. 2, pp. 366 sqq. There is a monograph on *Alain Chartier* by D. Delaunay (Rennes 1876) in which examples of Chartier's passionate eloquence are given.

[12] See Pierre Champion, *La librairie de Charles d'Orleans* (Paris 1910): also *Poésies de Charles d'Orleans* ed. Guichard (Paris 1842).

> Ne soiez donc de nostre confrairie;
> Mais priex Dieu que tous nous vueille absouldre!

He had the common knowledge of the schools; but that scarcely affected a nature aflame with self. His verse was the utterance of this self, the cry of a thief and murderer, and yet the cry of a battered human soul, quivering with its ills. This cry was an envenomed melody of pain. No such vibrant lyric note had been heard in France.[13]

[13] The English reader may be referred to *Poems of François Villon,* translated by H. De V. Stackpoole (1914).

CHAPTER XI

SOME FRENCH HUMANISTS

In the France of the sixteenth century there took place a revival of classical studies, partly through suggestion and assistance from Italy, Germany and Flanders. The movement had power and volume and was to exceed all previous attainment. It even presents in vigorous acceleration the successive stages for which analogous phases of the study of antique thought had required a number of mediaeval centuries. That is to say, one sees a time of learning and appropriation, and then use is made of the new or increased material through constructive or imitative efforts in the fields of physical study and observation, imaginative and reflective literature, and the plastic arts.

Standing on the shoulders of the efficient past, sixteenth century France, vigorous, compact, brimming with life, reaches out for gain and adventure in military enterprise and distant exploration; reaches for pleasure in the intercourse of courts, in the grateful ennoblement of life through poetry and its luxurious adornment through architecture, sculpture and painting; reaches also for further fact and human values through classical studies, and through observation and reflection, and for a better verity in religion. The time's progressive energies may have equalled those of the twelfth and thirteenth French centuries, though their specific activities differed; and in the sixteenth century French development was more dependent on stimulus and aid from other countries. The classical scholarship of the twelfth century in France, the scholastic philosophy of that century and the next, and French Gothic cathedrals, were not due to suggestion and assistance from contemporary foreigners, although the masterful French culture might accept teachers as well as students from abroad. Paris was *par excellence* the productive centre of philosophy and theology in the thirteenth century; and if Albertus and Aquinas, Roger Bacon and Duns Scotus were born in other lands, they gravitated to Paris as of course.

With reference to the antecedents of the sixteenth century classical revival, one may remark that Petrarch's visit to the French Court in 1361, as the Visconti's ambassador, was not without its awakening influences. His ornate Latin orations were full of antique suggestions. Some of his Latin writings, and Boccaccio's also, were rendered into French, and then the *Decameron.*[1] Translations were made of Cicero's *de Senectute* and *de Amicitia,* and of the *Ethics* and *Politics* of Aristotle, the latter, of course, from Latin versions. The Roman history of Livy was translated too, which would serve to diffuse a different idea of Rome from that in the " Romans de Rome la grant." These works of translation and the classical studies of which they were the fruit, helped to develop the French language. Latin words pressed themselves into the rough and graceless verses of one considerable poet, Eustache Deschamps, in whom a national feeling is beginning to find voice.

The inchoate classical movement centres in the reign of Charles V (1364-1380), a king interested in letters and susceptible to their influence. He had assembled a large library, which naturally was quite mediaeval in its books. Among the king's counsellors was Nicholas Oresme, the principal translator of Aristotle. Through him Aristotle's ideas were brought to bear upon the royal government. A younger man than Oresme was devoted to humane letters more entirely for their own sake. Jean de Montreuil saw the light shortly after the middle of the fourteenth century, and perished in 1418 at the hands of the Burgundian faction. He was secretary to the unhappy Charles VI, and employed by him on diplomatic

[1] The *Decameron* was barbarously translated about 1414, and a good translation by Le Macon made about 1545. See Henri Hauvette, *Les plus anciennes traductions françaises de Boccaccio, Bulletin Italien,* Vols. VII, VIII and X.

missions. While on a mission to Italy in 1412, he met Coluccio and the younger humanists, Bruni and Niccolo Niccoli. Naturally, he admired his Italian friends, and revered the departed Petrarch, whose works seemed to him to rank with the classics themselves. His own taste had already made him a student of Cicero and Terence. He exerted himself and sought the aid of friends, to collect a library. In fine, he appears as an enthusiastic humanist. But when the Burgundians broke into Paris in 1418, and killed him with his like-minded friend, Gontier Col, there survived no one now known to fame blessed with a disinterested love of letters.

Classical studies were continued rather lifelessly under the grey reign of Louis XI. One Fichet printed a rhetoric at Paris, and his disciple Gaguin an *Ars Versificatoria.*[2] For printing was now established in the leading French cities, an incalculable potential gain. Yet the presses were busied mainly with what either was written or was used in the Middle Ages. For example, the *Doctrinale* of Alexandre Villedieu, most popular of mediaeval Latin grammars, was printed and reprinted. And the new books offered little novelty. The lifting of the spirit was very slow. It was vigorously stirred by Jacques Lefèvre of Ètaples, whose long life did not close till 1536. He was moved by a strong desire for verity, which led him to seek better methods of study and general education; to endeavor likewise for a surer knowledge of Aristotle, whom he deemed chief of philosophers and salutary to the Christian soul; and above all to search out a truer understanding of the religion of Christ. No more than Roger Bacon, does Lefèvre impress one as touched by the literary charm of the classics. And although he was an incitement to others in their quest for truth, he was not himself a good Greek scholar at a time when Greek was coming to be regarded as necessary for the best understanding of the word of God. Knowledge of

[2] Gaguin was an energetic scholar. On Gaguin, Lefèvre and others, see Tilley, *Dawn of the French Renaissance,* Chapters VI–VIII (1918). For Lefèvre see post, Chapter XVII, I.

the Greek language was established in France by the labors of Guillaume Budé.

Budé was born in Paris in 1468, of a substantial bourgeois family who for some generations had held positions in the royal administration. When a boy, he was sent to Orleans to study law. There he proved a slack and pleasure-loving student, and after returning to Paris continued his gay life. When twenty-three, as from some sudden change of heart, passing from youth to manhood, he gave himself earnestly to the Civil Law, studying at first the Commentators. He soon pushed back through them to the text of the Pandects. There he found himself with the veritable ancients, though still the Latins. The thirst for Greek came over him. Scarcely a Greek manuscript was to be had, and the one old Greek available as an instructor was incompetent. Budé's zeal and genius surmounted even such insurmountable obstacles. When a few years later Charles VIII brought with him from Italy the famous Grecian Lascaris, Budé, already a good Greek scholar, clave to him. Lascaris's stay in Paris was all too short; but he left his precious books with Budé, who had already proved his knowledge by producing more than one translation. He occupied a small post in a government office, and was twice included in an embassy to Italy, where he made acquaintance with men and books. Through the reigns of Charles VIII and Louis XII, he worked with zeal, neglecting the chances of emolument at Court, whither his reputation for learning had penetrated. Later he found a real patron of letters in Francis I, as he found a friend in the King's sister, Marguerite.

Budé became an enormous and universal scholar. He was the incarnation of the beginning of Greek studies in France; the incarnation too of the scholarship whose instinct is to penetrate to the source, as he showed in his *Annotationes* on the four and twenty books of the Pandects. The Bologna school of Jurists, working from the twelfth century onwards, had rescued and explained this great and veritable source of jurisprudence. But now that some centuries had passed, the commentaries of these *glossators* and their successors, especially the great commentaries of Accursius and Bartolus, were studied, rather than the original texts. Budé's work was again revolutionary, in that his *Annotationes* were directed to a renewed and better explanation of those texts, not rejecting the assistance of the Commentators. But his notes were interspersed with scornful attacks upon the wretched Accursians and Bartolists who in barbarous Latin blindly followed the Commentators even in their contradictions. Budé's work did more than represent a return to the methods of the best period of the Bologna school, for it proceeded with a clearer historical perspective and with the application of a philological erudition which they had not possessed. He sought to establish a better text, and to give truer explanations of its meaning. Nor did he stop there; but through an unprecedented knowledge of Roman history and institutions, he advanced to a broader explanation of those Roman customs and institutions, a knowledge of which was taken for granted by the juris-consults of the Pandects. He cast further light on matters of interest or difficulty through abundant Greek citations, which he always translated into Latin.

When the *Annotationes* had been published, and had aroused attention and applause, Budé undertook a work nominally upon Roman coinage, but in reality containing a store of information touching all antiquity. It appeared in 1515 under the title of *De Asse et partibus eius* and was greeted with acclaim, and some disparagement; its fame has not entirely passed away. Its author showed no care for methodical exposition, and may have lacked the gift. The main purpose of the work, if it had one, was to determine the weights and values of the ancient moneys and measures. To this end Budé subjected to review the ancient literature, comparing the innumerable passages bearing on the matter, and endeavoring to extract from them some certain data which might be expressed in the weights and measures of his time. He recognized the complexity of such problems, and his critical sense was not satisfied with plausible results, but weighed every atom of the confusing testimony, as he had actually weighed every ancient coin that he could find. He used his conclusions very intelligently to form estimates of the wealth and expenditures of the Romans. So enormous was the mass and variety of citations, that the work became a thesaurus of ancient literature. Budé introduced several long *digressiones,* in which he set forth his views on vital topics, showing in these personal opinions his French patriotism and his Christian piety. He denied the sole glory of Italy in scholarship — might not the air and soil of France produce as good? The trouble lay with the great, who deemed the arts of peace below their dignity. He also made it appear, what indeed had been evident throughout the treatise, that the ancient literary worthies occupied no unapproachable pinnacle in his mind; he could criticize their faults, moral and intellectual, and especially their failure to appreciate Christianity. [3]

Budé accomplished other feats of scholarship. Such was his *Commentarii Linguae Graecae,* published in 1529, a work of great use to younger scholars. Then in his dialogue *De Philologia,* he pleaded for the universal study of antique letters, as he did in the only French composition bearing his name: *De l'Institution du Prince.* As for his last large book, *De Transitu Hellenismi ad Christianismum* (1534) the title held implicitly the argument for Greek, which the body of the treatise expanded into an exposition of Greek philosophy as a preparation for Christianity. And he defended Greek from the imputation of heresy, cast upon it by the Sorbonne.

This great scholar's name has rightly gained honor from his efforts to prevail on Francis to establish chairs for " lecteurs royaux," who should teach letters and science for the ends of scholarship and knowledge, without regard to the demands of theology, — so insistent at the Sorbonne. These chairs of Greek and Hebrew, Latin and Mathematics, were the beginnings of the Royal College which in time became the " Collège de France."

Budè had his disciples and collaborators. Before his

[3] Thus far I have followed L. Delarnelle, *Guillaume Budé* (Paris 1907).

Commentaries of the Greek Language were published, French presses had printed two books of the *Iliad,* Plato's *Cratylus,* the *Tragedies* of Sophocles, and parts of Aristophanes. In 1539, Francis I commanded the casting of those beautiful Greek types which were to be the model for future Greek lettering, and in noble language appointed Conrad Neobar royal printer, confiding to him the printing of Greek books.[4] The royal patronage proved an incentive to Greek studies. Francis charged the French Ambassador at Venice with the purchase of manuscripts for his library at Fontainebleau, and assisted a scholar named Belon to undertake a voyage of discovery through Greece and Asia Minor.

The names of two young and exceedingly refractory scholars, poets, satirists, litterateurs, however one may characterize them, were Bonaventure des Periers and Estienne Dolet. They were born about the same time (1508 or 1509). The former died by his own hand in 1544, and two years later the latter was burnt in the Place Maubert for his obnoxious personality and opinions. He also may be said to have perished by his own violent will.

Des Periers was *valet de chambre,* or secretary, to Marguerite of Navarre. He held and expressed strong sympathies for the incipiently reformed religion, like Marguerite herself, or Marot and Lefèvre d'Étaples and Budé. But he passed on to a satirical scepticism about the year 1536, when Calvin published his *Institutio,* which was to bring Catholics, reformers, and we may add, humanists, to sharply opposed self-consciousness. Either a reaction against its tone and tenets, or other jarring or awakening influences, or his own clever carping soul, evoked from Des Periers those four allegorical satires in dialogue form, which he called the *Cymbalum Mundi en francoys.* As *dramatis personae* under mythical and fictitious Latin names, the Catholic church and its institutions, as well as Luther and Erasmus, were made ridiculous. Catholics and Reformers united to suppress both book and author. Marguerite had to dismiss him,

[4] See Egger, *L'Hellenisme en France,* Vol. I, Lec. 9.

and after two or three years of trouble and perhaps incipient insanity, he killed himself. He was a good storyteller, and a poet of sensitiveness and feeling, who held himself a disciple of Marot. He also made French translations from the classics, like his friend, Dolet.

Dolet was a youth of exaggerated self-conceit and intractable temper: precocious scholar, zealous worker, addicted to scurrilous depreciation of others, a captious, impossible young man. His importance is rather factitious, due to his insistence on himself, by which some of his friends took him at his own value. They spoke of him with that sort of excess of praise which marks the friendly utterances of Italian humanists.[5]

He was born in Orleans, and when twelve years old, went to study in Paris, where he seems to have imbibed his worship of Cicero. From his eighteenth to his twenty-first year, he studied at Padua. The university was then in great repute. The famous philosopher and teacher Pomponazzi, dying in 1525, had left behind him his arguments and influence, making for paganism and for disbelief in the personal Christian immortality. Bembo, at the height of his dignified reputation, made a home of lettered affluence in Padua from 1521 to 1539. Dolet studied under one Villanovanus, a great Ciceronian, and imbibed a love of Latin purity and the art of making orations out of Ciceronian phrases. Upon his teacher's death, he went to Venice as secretary to Jean de Langeac, bishop of Limoges, and after a year of study returned with the bishop to Toulouse where, yielding to persuasion, he began work on the civil law. His detestation of Toulouse the intolerant and superstitious, the archiepiscopal seat of the Inquisition and the scene of more burnings of Reformers than any other town in France save Paris, glares in his two orations of Ciceronian interpretation. In a letter to Budé, to whose greatness he had obtained an epistolary introduction, Dolet says

[5] Dolet's importance may have been enhanced by an interesting monograph on his time: *Etienne Dolet, the Martyr of the Renaissance*, by R. C. Christie (London 1899, 2nd Ed.). I am indebted to this work for my facts about Dolet.

that the Toulousans are more barbarous than Scythians. So he began his career of polemic abuse, which at the outset made him enemies influential enough to bring about his incarceration, from which only the influence of distinguished friends procured his release. So frequent were to be his subsequent imprisonments that someone spoke of jail as *patria Doleti.*

About this time a curious Italian impostor swims across Dolet's ken, whom he treats with proper scorn and ridicule. It was one Camillo, who through a life of laborious humbug, had elaborated a scheme of imparting to anyone a perfect knowledge of Greek and Latin, and the rest of human knowledge, in about three months. He devoted years to the perfecting of a sort of theatre of pigeon-holes, each labelled with some quality of the mind or division of knowledge. With what sort of key or handle or rotary movement he proposed to transfer their contents to the minds of his auditors is not clear. But he made important friends in Paris, as elsewhere, and Francis I subscribed five hundred ducats toward the theatre!

Dolet had found Toulouse too warm for him, and had withdrawn to the country, when he received news that the detested city had made an edict forbidding his return. It was in the summer of 1534, and he decided to set forth on a two hundred and fifty mile tramp for Lyons, where he had friends and introductions. Sick and exhausted he reached that city, the second in the realm, not merely for wealth and numbers, but for culture and learning, and where thought was freer than in Paris under the shadows of the Sorbonne. Lyons was filled with Italians, bankers, merchants, introducers of the silk industry, and indeed governors of the city in the able and liberal-minded family of the Trivulci. Rabelais, Marot, Servetus and Des Periers sojourned there, and there published their works, while other scholars were frequent visitors. The new art of printing had been introduced in 1472, and now flourished briskly at the presses of many master-printers, Sebastian Gryphius being the head of that scholarly profession. He had scholars (even the great Rabelais) as proof-readers. Among these Dolet was enrolled, and between him and the scholar-printer sprang up one of the few unbroken friendships of his life. Lyons remained his home until his death — when he was not fleeing or in prison, or visiting fatal Paris.

In 1528 Erasmus published his dialogue called *Ciceronianus* ridiculing the pedants who would use only the words and phrases, even the very tenses and cases, used by Cicero. The elder Scaliger brought himself into notoriety by a reply preposterously abusive, which Erasmus treated with irritating silence, and what was worse, supposed it to have been composed by another! Dolet saw fit to enter the fray with a clever Dialogue against Erasmus, which brought on him the censure of his friends for its intemperance, and also the wrath of Scaliger for presuming to write when he had written. A certain Odonus, in a letter to Erasmus's secretary, saw no reason why this fool Dolet should be answered according to his folly, least of all by the great Erasmus. The letter tells of his wretched mien, his squalor and premature old age, his monstrous conceit and scurrility. The picture is not more abusive than Dolet would have drawn of his reviler.

Dolet wrote this dialogue in Paris, when he was there in 1534 trying to obtain the royal permission for the publication of his *Commentaries*. The time was inopportune. That fatal tirade against the Mass, posted in an October night throughout the city, had driven the King to violent measures against heresy and enlightened thought. A year of persecution and burnings ensued, with edicts forbidding the printing of all books. If Dolet had influential friends, Budé among them, he had also active enemies, and he failed to obtain the permission. So he returned to Lyons and began the task of printing the huge work,— its first folio of seventeen hundred pages. About a year afterwards, Gryphius obtained the sought-for license, with exclusive right for four years, to print a book entitled *Commentaries on the Latin Tongue* by Estienne Dolet.

There was broader scholarship in Robert Estienne's

Latin *Thesaurus,* which was a huge dictionary alphabetically arranged. But Dolet classified his words according to the connection of their ideas, and commented upon their interrelated meanings. In this he claimed originality. His illustrative examples, especially in the first volume, were drawn almost exclusively from Cicero. As the work progressed, the writer indulged more frequently in digressions upon matters touching men and scholarship, his friends and enemies. In one of these, speaking of letters in the year 1535, he shows pleasure at the dignified position and flourishing state of literature,[6] but there are further sides to the picture:

> "Nothing is wanting save the ancient intellectual freedom and the prospect of acquiring distinction by the cultivation of the liberal arts. What the learned miss, is the affection, the liberality . . . of the powerful; the patronage of a Maecenas is needed. . . . Further, there is wanting to us an opportunity for the display of eloquence,— a Roman senate, a republic in which honour and due meed of praise would be awarded to it. . . . Instead of these inducements to the study of liberal arts, there is among many a contempt for literary culture . . . literary labour has to be pursued without any hope . . . of reward; the life of the student is passed without honour; the contempt of the multitude has to be endured; the tyranny and insolence of the powerful have to be borne; and danger to life itself is often the result of intellectual pursuits." [7]

The last, at all events, was true!

Pages might be filled with Dolet's labors, quarrels, intemperances and misfortunes through the remainder of his short life. He became hateful to the authorities at Paris, and after various imprisonments and releases, and renewed offenses, he was condemned to be burned in the Place Maubert, and there met his death in the year of grace 1546. Curiously, nothing contributed more directly to his final condemnation than the words *rien du tout* in his translation of a pseudo-Platonic dialogue, the

[6] Given by Christie, o. c. pp. 256–262. One recalls Rabelais's comparisons in the letter of Gargantua.

[7] Christie's translation. Dolet proceeds to speak of the war of the scholars with barbarism, and gives at length their names in Italy, Germany, France and England.

Axiochus. The questionable passage referred to the soul's immortality. Dolet's judges misquoted him as follows: *après la mort tu ne seras plus rien du tout.* This was the basis of the charge of blasphemy in that Dolet had falsely made Plato deny the immortality of the soul. It was joined with charges of sedition and the sale of forbidden books. His death is one of those many instances where the personality, rather than the specific acts and words of the freethinker, causes his temporal ruin; — an instance too of the sad unconquerable heart of man:

> Si au besoing le monde m'abandonne,
> Et si de Dieu la volonté n'ordonne
> Que liberté encores on me donne
> Selon mon vueil;
>
> Doits-je en mon cueur pour cela mener dueil,
> Et de regretz faire amas et recueil? . . .
>
> Sus donc, esprit, laissés la chair à part,
> Et devers Dieu qui tout bien nous départ
> Retirez vous . . .
>
> Sus, mon esprit, monstrés vous de tel cueur;
> Vostre asseurance au besoing soit cogneue:
> Tout gentil cueur, tout constant belliqueur,
> Jusque a la mort sa force a maintenue! [8]

The way for the full flowering of classical, and especially Greek studies, for France, was opened by the labors of the family of Estiennes (Stephens) who so grandly united the attributes of scholars, printers, and publishers. The first Henry Estienne printed a Latin abridgement of Aristotle's *Ethics,* with an introduction by Lefèvre d'Étaples, in the year 1502. He maintained a scholarly press with learned proof-readers. Of his three sons, printers and scholars all, Robert, born in 1503, dying at Geneva in 1559, was the most notable. This talented youth profited from the scholars who were his father's friends. Like his father, he was an ardent adherent of the reformed religion. In 1523 he printed a Latin New Testament, and a Greek New Testament in

[8] A poem written by Dolet in the Conciergerie of Paris shortly before his death; given at length by Christie, o. c. pp. 469–470.

1546. He made a biblical *Concordance,* in eleven hundred pages of four columns. He printed a number of the pagan classics, some for the first time, and in the course of years produced his prodigious Latin *Thesaurus,* and collected materials for a similar Treasury of Greek. But his scholarly publication of sacred as well as profane writings brought him into such conflict with the theological inhibitions of the Sorbonne that he left Paris for Geneva, where he continued his labors. At his death in 1559, he bequeathed his business and scholarly undertakings to his eldest son, Henry, his chief aid and consolation. But this testament bound Henry to Geneva, since it provided that his heritage should lapse if he changed his vocation, or forsook the Church of Calvin, a provision which the Genevan theocracy construed to mean that if he removed from Geneva, he should leave his books and types and presses behind him.

This great intractable son was to find the censorship of Geneva as galling as his father had found the Sorbonne. His indefatigable life was spent as a printer and productive scholar and vigorous polemic writer, and in scarcely intermittent struggle with the intolerable theocracy of Calvin's city. If Calvin died in 1564, revered even by Henri Estienne, his post mortem grip throttled liberal thought and studies in Geneva. The recalcitrant Estienne, save for occasional incarceration, might go and come, but not even the pointed suggestion of the French King (Henry III) or the influence of his ambassador could prevail upon the City Council to permit the removal of Estienne's presses to Paris, where also life and liberty might be endangered. Estienne, of course, belonged to the reformed religion. Else he could not have lived in Geneva. But that same fact imperilled him in Paris, in spite of the favor of the political weakling and patron of letters, Henry III. He was bringing out his great *Thesaurus* in Geneva when the massacre of St. Bartholomew's occurred, in 1572; the crime was due, he maintained, to Catherine of Medici and her Italian conspirators. Afterwards, between 1584 and 1589 he spent much time in

Paris until the assassination of Henry III made France too dangerous for him. Yet his dallyings with Catholic royalty in Paris roused the suspicion of Geneva, where he was otherwise disliked for his writings and rebellious temper. He was prone to print without previous submission to the censor, and after the censor's revision, was none too ready to insert or omit as directed. If his attacks or indiscretions were mainly levelled against Romanists, he cared not where he put his heel; and licentious freedom of speech made him seem to the Geneva Consistory like another Rabelais.

His French writings brought him the most trouble. Whatever the title or nominal topic, they were prone to prove polemic or satirical. His earliest important work, the *Apologie pour Hérodote,* bears an innocent title; the author professed to hope that the ministers of the Council would not trouble themselves to read his " little book " containing a defense of Herodotus. But they did, and found too many skits and funny stories reflecting on respectable people, and too great licentiousness of speech. They directed the excision of certain parts, and ordered Estienne to get back the copies which he had sent to Lyons. They were particular people, these ministers of the Council, having no taste for this hodge-podge of anecdote and satire; seeing no value in this *fatras* of arguments and funny tales.

It is easier for us to catch the point of Estienne's writings in defense of his beloved French tongue; which both defended its excellence, and urged its preservation from Italianisms and like foreign affectations, introduced by the Italianized Court of France and the writers who ministered to court tastes. Estienne sympathized with the *Defense et Illustration* of Du Bellay and Ronsard, though he deprecated their paganism, their " pindarisme " and lofty dithyrambic ways, their abuse of metaphors, their obscure images and comparisons. There was no condescension in his vindication of the French tongue, as there was with those who would defend it only when classicized and Pindarized. Estienne maintained the pre-excellence of French as actually written and spoken, and not merely when fashioned by a school of writers. This is the argument of his *Précellence du langage Français,* in which is shown the power and clarity of French, its convenience, its peculiar aptitude for diplomacy and statecraft. Perhaps he espoused its cause more academically, after the prevailing fancies among scholars, in his *Conformité du français avec le grec.* There he maintained that the Greek was the most perfect of all languages, and that the French resembled it most closely, and was therefore the next perfect. Thus he set French above the other Romance tongues and above the Latin, their common mother. His Greek Thesaurus showed in fact that often truer equivalents of the Greek could be found in French words than in Latin.[9]

Such were not unfruitful topics of discussion when the European languages seemed but crudely to answer to the needs of science and the higher forms of literature. Then a scholar might well set himself to build them out and perfect them, and render them more grammatically exact, impeccable, and, as it were, inevitable in their expression of the period's gradually clarifying thought.

The work of Henry Estienne in classical scholarship (which has not yet been touched on) was distinctive of the French accomplishment in this field as contrasted with the Italian. Among the French are not found those jejune exquisite works of Latin poetry and prose, which the Italian humanists took pride in. The efforts of French scholarship was rather to enlarge and solidify the knowledge of the Greek and Latin languages and literatures. Valla may be compared with the Frenchmen; otherwise Italy cannot match Budé's *De Asse* or his *Commentarii Linguae Grecae,* or the *Thesaurus Linguae Latinae* of Robert Estienne, who was so strenuously assembling materials for a Greek Thesaurus too. It was this that Henri Estienne brought to completion, and published in the year of St. Bartholomew, in five huge volumes, mak-

[9] For this I have drawn chiefly on Louis Clement, *Henri Estienne et son oeuvre française* (Paris 1899).

ing it the crown of French learning in the sixteenth century. The expense impoverished this redoubtable author and printer; yet did not prevent his increasing his fame and poverty by the publication of his splendid edition of Plato six years later.

Even this Plato was but one great classic among the many printed by Henry Estienne. For he travelled ceaselessly, searching for new classical matter, rewarding himself and the world with such discoveries as books of Diodorus Siculus and the " Anacreon " (what we call the " Anacreontea "), both of which he published for the first time, the latter to become a chief delight with Ronsard and his *Pléiade*. He is said to have published fifty-eight Latin and seventy-four Greek authors, among them eighteen first editions.[10] The texts of many of these publications were so excellent that they were scarcely improved upon for centuries. The man was great not merely in the tireless ardor of his scholarship, but in the force of his temperament and loyalty to the France which had driven him and his father forth, but to which he eagerly returned when the skies of persecution lifted. Estienne still represents the scholarship of the French Reform,— of the circle of Marguerite of Navarre, of Rabelais, of Budé and Lefèvre d'Étaples; the scholarship of a religious reform which loved classic learning, and had not submitted to the effective intolerance of Calvinism. This union of true scholarship with truth-seeking in religion, which found its exponent in Erasmus, still inspired Henri Estienne, fallen on times of persecution and religious conflict, when the mutual hate and military exigencies of the warring faiths left little sympathy for the tastes and labors of neutral scholars.

Without pausing with such admirable scholars as Turnebus and Lambinus, who were royal lecturers, a reference to two greater men of the following generation must close our brief and truncated consideration of French classical studies in the sixteenth century. Joseph

[10] Sandys, *Hist. of Classical Scholarship*, II, p. 175; who does not give his authority.

Scaliger (1540-1609) and Casauban (1559-1614) never saw each other, and yet became fast friends through correspondence and mutual respect. The former was the son of the learned and truculent Julius Caesar Scaliger, him of the abusive attack upon Erasmus — and on Cardanus too. The son, familiar with the classic tongues at an early age, and later studying with the best scholars at Paris, developed the qualities of a sound textual critic, and produced improved editions of a number of Latin authors. From textual criticism he passed on to profound comparative historical studies. The fruit appeared in his great work upon the reform of antique chronology, *De Emendatione temporum,* first published in 1583, and twice afterwards with improvements and additions in his lifetime. This work, and the principles of historical criticism exemplified by it, became the basis of later historical and chronological research. Scaliger was of Italian descent and belonged to the reformed religion. He spent his last fifteen years of life and learning at the University of Leyden.

Isaac Casaubon was born at Geneva of Huguenot parents, and became the son-in-law of Henri Estienne, who nevertheless would not let him use his library. He was called to Paris in 1599 by Henry IV, and after the King's assassination was subjected to well-nigh successful pressure to become a Catholic. He preferred, however, to accept an invitation to England, and was given a prebendal stall in Canterbury. He enjoyed the burdensome favor of King James, and the society of learned men; but he was unpopular as a foreigner, although he had been naturalized. Dying at the age of fifty-five, he was buried in Westminster Abbey. Among his contemporaries, his scholarship was reputed second only to that of Scaliger. His great merit as an editor sprang from his broad and accurate learning, his faculty of eliciting a true reading from a comparison of manuscripts, and the abundance of his illuminating commentary.[11]

[11] Good articles in the *Ency. Brit.* by Mark Pattison and Christie on these men. Pattison's *Life of Casaubon* is an authority.

CHAPTER XII

THE CIRCLE OF MARGUERITE OF NAVARRE

IN the broadening of French culture and the opening of the French mind to novel influences, a certain woman played a central rôle, through her station, her temperament and her intellectual gifts. Marguerite of Angoulême, the sister of King Francis, by marriage duchess of Alençon and later Queen of Navarre, was more than a patroness of the best spirits of the time. She was herself a moving agent in the diffusion of thought and feeling, tempering and rendering receptive the minds of those about her, of King Francis himself, who respected her, and whom she loved absorbingly.[1] Much of the period's spiritual history may be told in the careers of the men she at some time protected by her power, aided with her generosity, encouraged with her sympathetic understanding. Lefévre d'Étaples was among them, Budé, Clement Marot, Rabelais, Des Periers. Calvin was to prove recalcitrant to her influence and hostile to much she cared for. She was herself an incessant writer of letters without number, of poems which run on forever, of tales in prose with moralizings. Her thoughts and feelings could not keep themselves from ink and paper, either while she was staying at one of her residences, or while travelling in her litter, moving with her little court from place to place, as was her wont. Waiting and hoping for the coming of a messenger telling of her royal brother's recovery, she writes:

Quand nul ne voy, l'oeil j'abandonne
A pleurer; puis sur le papier
Un peu de ma douleur j'ordonne.

[1] Marguerite was two years older than Francis, and died two years after him. Their births fell in 1492 and 1494; their deaths in 1547 and 1549. Her grandson became Henry IV.

That was her way always. Her conversation must have been more influential than her writing, at least than her prolix and interminable verse, through which no enthusiasm for Marguerite will carry the reader.

Marguerite's breadth of intellectual interest was as admirable as her piety toward God and man; and the two will appear commensurate with her woman-faculty of loving. She and her court were the refuge and centre of that better scholarship and fuller humanism, and clearer-seeing piety, which characterized advancing thought in France, until Calvin so trenchantly severed goats from sheep. Marguerite and her friends, according to their several capacities, cherished the full gospel of man and God: the charm and lustiness of life; the antique philosophy and letters; and the truths of the Christian religion, more nakedly presented than the dominant Church approved. These people cared for these goods of life in whole or in part; and according to their several tempers fell in with or recoiled from the usages and beliefs of the Church.

Marguerite's ideal of life was humanly and religiously inclusive. She would unite the pleasure and excellence of this life with the Christian faith, and see life rise, stage upon stage, as it were from the flesh to the spirit, from man to God. The classics doubtless held the best of human learning. To them let there be added the book of the intricacy and sublimation of mortal love between man and woman. And as the last stage of life's completion let the whole world rise to God, human ambitions merging in the divine purpose, human loves melting in the love of God, human learning bowing down before the divine ineffableness. Marguerite found the method of this union in that loose and delectable "Platonism" which was the fashion of the Medicean circle at Florence. There Ficino had been chief expounder of Plato and Plotinus; and now, more especially in the decade from 1540 to 1550, his translations, his commentaries, and his own presentation of Platonic Christian thinking, had become known to Marguerite and her circle, and through their efforts or patronage had been made more accessible in republications and translations.

At an earlier period, however, Marguerite's first spiritual director, Briçonnet, had introduced her to the opinions of a greater than Ficino, to wit, Nicholas of Cusa, whose thought seemed destined to act as a universal solvent of case-hardened opinions, and as a suggestion and stimulant of larger views. As a churchman he had been liberal and earnest, and his opinions might incline men toward religious, as well as philosophic, reform. Specific traces of his influence appear in Marguerite's writings, and disclose the general effect of this great man upon her intellectual temper.[2]

It was in those years from 1540 to her death in 1549 that from the midst of her royal trials and disillusionment, and finally from the deep grief of Francis's death, Marguerite turned more completely to literature, philosophy, and religion. In the first years of this period she composed or collected most of the tales constituting the improperly notorious *Heptameron.* They are what they are, less amusing than those of Boccaccio, and with much the same sort of subject, though purporting to be true narratives of actual people. The real interest for one interested in Marguerite lies in the discussion which follows each story, and serves to moralize and uplift the tales, and prove them not to have been merely the pastimes of lubricity. These discussions relate to the various phases of love, its pain and pleasure, its good and evil, its brutalities and sublimities. Marguerite's thoughts, given to the speakers, especially to Dagoucin and Parlamente who seem to represent her, embrace Christianity, the new-vamped Platonism, and the preciosities of the mediaeval *amour courtois.* But the courteous love was affected by Castiglione's *Cortigiano,*

[2] See generally Abel Lefranc, *Le Platonisme et la littérature en France a l'Epoque de la Renaissance.* Rev. d'histoire litteraire de la France 1896, p. 1 sqq.; ib. Marguerite de Navarre et le Platonisme de la Renaissance, Bib. de l'École des Chartres, Vol. 58, p. 259, sqq. Vol. 59, p. 712, sqq. These essays have been reprinted in one volume: *Grands Écrivains Français de la Renaissance* (Paris, 1914).

the Platonism was that of Ficino, and the Christianity that of the dawning Reform, which was not Calvinism. These elements melted into each other. As a result, a scheme of human love rises through *precieuses* insistences and draughts of Plato's Symposium, to the love which, perfect and unshakable, is directed toward the utter good. On its way thither it will permit itself no dishonour. Replies Parlamente in the nineteenth tale:

"J'appelle parfaicts amans ceulx qui cherchent en ce qu'ilz aiment quelque perfection, soit beaulté, bonté ou bonne grace; tousjours tendans à la vertu, et qui ont le cueur si hault et si honneste qu'ilz ne veulent, pour mourir, mettre leur fin aux choses basses que l'honneur et la conscience réprouvent; car l'âme, qui n'est créée que pour retourner à son souverain Bien, ne faict, tant qu'elle est dedans ce corps, que désirer d'y parvenir. Mais à cause que les sens par lesquels elle en peut avoir nouvelles sont obscurs et charnels par le péche du premier père, ne luy peuvent monstrer que les choses visibles plus approchantes de la perfection, après quoi l'âme court, cuydans (thinking) trouver en une beaulté extérieure, en une grâce visible et aux vertus morales, la souveraine beaulté, grâce et vertu. Mais quand elle les a cherchez et expérimentez et elle n'y trouve point celuy qu'elle ayme, elle passe outre. . . ."

Throughout her life, Marguerite's dominant passion was to love, and think and talk about loving. It directed her studies, controlled her life, and moulded her religion to an emotional mysticism, in which this utter woman merged all her thoughts concerning man and God in love's desire and realization. Without change of theme, we pass from the discussion of love in the *Heptameron* to the philosophic-religious poem entitled *Prisons,*[3] which she wrote at the same time. Its first part has to do with human love, the first imprisoning illusion of the author's heart. When through force of will, the prisoner has freed himself from this embarricaded and fantastic tower, he sets forth at the opening of the second part to observe the world in all its grandeur and variety, the cities, the customs, and the conduct of mankind. He is stung by

[3] It fills pages 121 to 297 in Abel Lefranc's *Les dernières Poésies de Marguerite de Navarre* (Paris, 1896).

worldly ambition, is drawn toward the advantages of the Church, then to the Court. But an old man induces him to betake himself to study, since knowledge of the ancient philosophers, historians, and Scriptural authors will remove all ills. So he casts off ambition's chains, and builds himself, in the third and most elaborate part of the poem, a palace of knowledge; walls beyond walls, columns on columns, all learning's branches form this encyclopaedic structure of books, a prison as it is still to prove: poetry, law, mathematics, natural history, medicine, history, rhetoric, none is omitted, nor the name of any author; but Plato, St. Paul and Dante are the three our prisoner cares for most. Terrified by the pitfalls of error, and the danger of condemnation, he studies theology and Scripture, with watching, fasting, and prayer. From the prison of the letter, he is delivered by the divine Word: "I am that I am."

Clearly Marguerite is freed from her last prison through faith (the central principle of the Reform). She flings herself on Christ's universal redemptive power; in love she will fly to the All in Allness of God and revel in the antithesis of the All and the Nothing, *le Tout et le Rien,* which last is man. Marguerite loved to float amid sublimations and inflations of the thought of love. Well might Rabelais address her: "Esprit abstraict, ravy et estatic." She had proved a kind protector to him, and many a lesser man. And she herself represented the intellectual expansion of her land and time. She even represented that incipient and temperate religious Reform, which proceeded as much from the basis of the newly enlarged learning, and the accompanying clearer discrimination between fact and foolishness, as from disgust with the corruptions and superstitions of the Church. Religious reform, carried out in the spirit of Marguerite, would not have loosed the Furies upon France.

The poet, Clement Marot, wrote better verse than Marguerite, whose protégé he was, and whose views of religious reform he may have shared, though with different emphasis. If he had convictions, they were of the intellect; while Marguerite's represented the mysticism or metaphysics of religious intuition. The structure and substance of Marot's verse made no break with the previous, even the mediaeval, achievements of the French muse, which he absorbed. Still, he had read Boccaccio and Petrarch, as well as Virgil, Ovid and Catullus. Slightly and superficially he appears touched by the new humanism of Italy. For he was born in 1496, two years after Charles VIII invaded Italy; and he died in 1544, three years earlier than Francis I, and five years before Marguerite.

At Marguerite's court, at the court of Francis, Marot was of his entourage and livelihood, a court poet and a cleverer one than his father had been before him. His light and occasionally brilliant verse, his epigrams especially, had profited by the talk and badinage of a lively and superficially polished society. This did not always preclude the expression of delicate and sincere sentiment.[4] Personally he was gifted with a persistent gaiety, not to be quenched by dangers or imprisonment, but which might suffer from the ennui of a refuge sought in Ferrara and Geneva. Those places were as congenial to this fugitive libertine of the spirit, as the sanctuary to the sprightly murderer seeking safety at the altar.

No other work affected Marot as much as the *Roman de la Rose,* which he edited and modernized in prison.[5] Here he was of his generation, which still delighted in that famous allegory and pungent disquisition upon life. Only gradually he developed the individuality of his own gay personality and environment. Then if he continued to write *rondeaux,* he wrote also ballads, and gave his spirit play in the cleverest of epigrams and epistles in verse. He also translated a number of the Psalms at the command of Francis, strange to tell. These translations, made from the Vulgate, are rather flat and nerveless. But they gained vogue at the court, and formed

[4] Cf. A. LeFranc. Le Roman d'Amour de Clement Marot. (*Grands Écrivains* etc.).

[5] He edited Villon also.

the nucleus of the Psalter of the Reform. Naturally, they rendered their author obnoxious to the Sorbonne, and Francis was induced to forbid their further dissemination and dismiss their author.

Marot is an important personage in the history of French poetry. He is an effective predecessor not merely of Ronsard but of Malherbe; and La Fontaine recognized him as his master.[6] But this man had no temperamental affinity with the men of the Reform; he could not endure Calvin's city, nor would Geneva harbor him. Some of the tenets and practices of the Catholic hierarchy jarred upon the clarity of his intellectual perceptions, while the doctrines of the Reform appealed to his mind. Yet he was and remained essentially a court poet and a man who followed pleasure after the fashion of court society. He was not shocked by the *moeurs* of his time and place, and even his intellectual revolt against current religious opinion was not consistently serious.

[6] Cf. E. Faguet, *Seizième siècle, Études littéraires,* p. 73, sqq.

CHAPTER XIII

FRANÇOIS RABELAIS

THE people spoken of in the last few chapters open the ways. Their tendencies and tastes, studies and endeavors, their expression of themselves in their pursuits and writings, naturally precede the rounded thinking, the perfected utterance, the splendid and final modes of self-expression achieved by younger and greater men.

In a sense all intellectual labors and utterances endure in their results; for nothing that once is done and uttered fails of some effect. But the modes of self-expression of a Rabelais, a Montaigne, a Calvin, even an Amyot, not to speak of Ronsard and his friends, were great and finished utterances. These achieved self-expressions represent climaxes, finalities, inasmuch as in their kind they have not been surpassed. They endure not merely as influences carried on, but in themselves as entities, as perfected exemplars, always impressive, moving some men to imitation, others to avoidance; but in themselves forever notable.

There was one of these men whose nature included many surging desires of his people, woven in the warp of genius. He has been a much commented on puzzle ever since he lived and wrote that book which seems to hold all life from the cloaca to the heavens. Its author — only one of his own words will fit him — was Gargantuan in his self-expression. Never did a mortal pour forth himself, his huge, *ingens, informis,* sprawling self, in such torrential superabundance as Rabelais. He is the most prodigious expression of the French sixteenth century, voicing its life, its scholarships, its ideals, along with much that the Muse of Decency would leave unsung. Rabelais shouts it all forth in tumultuous delight. None will dare paint him; one may but follow his life, and put together bits of his Gargantuan self.

The intellectual currents of the times flowed into the capacious mind of François Rabelais, illuminating and expanding a nature that was itself an abundant spring of genial power and appetition. He had a Charybdean maw for life. Delighting in all knowledge, he ransacked the stores of learning available in the first half of the sixteenth century. He also delighted in every act and function of the human animal; it all made for life. Without sensitiveness, he wantoned with the lewd and disgusting. Feeling no repugnance toward any fact of human animality, he had no esthetic preference for the more obviously beautiful and ideal. Glowing with enormous tolerance and benignity for the natural man, his satisfaction went rollicking through the vast uncleaned halls of life. Every good thing was from God; and what was better than human nature? Unthwarted and untrammelled, it might be trusted in its brave carouse.

Rabelais's scorn and detestation were as tremendous as his approval and applause. Whatever was not life and knowledge, but a sham and lie, was a preposterous abomination; and likewise whatever broke life's currents and thwarted the joyful play of nature's functions was hateful and absurd — the work of charlatans and hypocrites, of prudes and pettifoggers. Monkish rules for diminishing joys and self-fulfilment were lewd hypocrisy usually, and, when observed, quite as pernicious. Rabelais was a supreme satirist, yet with little of the bitterness of hate. The usual way of his genial nature with the tricks and follies of besotted manikins was to smother them in obscene ridicule.

His works have called forth many interpretations. They and their author are touched with the mystery of the man endowed with an exceeding abundance of life; one whose work cannot be tabulated in categories of influence, or explained by conventions of allegory. These writings are alive, prodigiously. One sees in them the power of temperament,— which lies in the spontaneities of affinity and desire,— impelling the author's mental faculties to intellectual creation, supplying symbols and images. Yet this fecund temperament, so great a factor of the plastic faculty of this great student and artist, was not headstrong. It was amenable to worldly prudence, while the topics of its play might be suggested by the interests of the hour.

François Rabelais was born in Touraine, supposedly about the year 1494.[1] His father was a lawyer. When about seventeen, he entered the Franciscan convent at Fontenay, where not so much within as without its walls he enjoyed the society of a number of men of letters. The youth flung himself into his studies, learning Greek and laying the foundations of the encyclopaedic sort of knowledge shown in his writings. Later he will be found among the correspondents of both Budé and Erasmus. Before long he had himself transferred to the Benedictine Order, and became the secretary of his opulent and noble patron Geoffroy d'Estissac, a powerful bishop and a Benedictine prior. He found other noble friends, and knew many scholars, as he moved about and studied and observed. Monkhood sat lightly on this eager votary of life and letters. He would seem at some time to have studied medicine in Paris; and it is known that he finished his medical course at Montpellier in 1530. A year or two afterwards, he settled at Lyons, a great city, situated at a goodly distance from the sinister authority of the Sorbonne. In this town which sheltered Marot, Dolet, Des Periers, and Sainte-Marthe, church abuses were criticized, and many persons favored the Reform. Rabelais was appointed physician to the Hotel Dieu, and won the respect of the learned by editing sundry works of Galen, the *Aphorisms of Hippocrates,* and other medical and even legal texts. He was abreast of the best

[1] I am following Abel Lefranc in the Introduction to the critical edition of *Oeuvres de François Rabelais* (Paris, Champion, 1912–).

medical knowledge of his time, but appears not notably to have advanced it. Dissections are advised in Gargantua's letter to his son.

Toward the close of 1532 appeared his *Pantagruel,* and about the same time he wrote his famous letter to Erasmus, calling him his father and mother in learning, "the tutelary genius of letters, the invincible champion of truth." Two years later, after the *Pantagruel* had been condemned by the Sorbonne, its author went to Rome, as physician in the suite of the most distinguished of his patrons, Jean du Bellay, who was soon to be made Cardinal. This Roman journey over, Rabelais later in the same year, 1534, published his *Gargantua;* which told the life and deeds of Pantagruel's father. Apparently this book also was condemned by the Sorbonne, perhaps, like the *Pantagruel,* for its obscenity. At all events, its vituperative epithets and abuse of monkdom made it hateful to those theologians.

Almost at the moment of the publication of the *Gargantua,* the posting of the famous placards against the Mass, throughout Paris in the night of October seventeenth, turned the King from tolerance to persecution. Accord between the liberal minded of both parties was made impossible, and the next year the publication of Calvin's *Christian Institute* prepared the issue for the eventual arbitrament of the sword. Not long afterwards Rabelais left Lyons quietly, and accompanied Cardinal du Bellay to Italy and Rome. There he obtained a papal absolution for abandoning the Franciscans for the Benedictines and following the secular profession of medicine. Through the next years he led a life of study, medical practice, and — prudence. He expunged the most hostile passages of the *Gargantua,* and kept within the protection of his powerful friends, among whom was Queen Marguerite of Navarre. It was probably through her that in 1545 he obtained from the King the privilege to publish the third book of the *Heroic Deeds of Pantagruel,* and correct and republish the two previous books. The third book, in its Rabelaisean way, had mainly to do with the question of Panurge's marriage. Its matter was not unrelated to discussions then rife among the ladies. But the sunny weather gave way before some months of intolerant reaction, when Rabelais again found need to retire from Paris, and indeed from France. Several years later, in 1551, the Cardinal du Bellay gave him the cure of St-Martin-de-Meudon, which he held for two years, discharging its duties through a vicar. In January 1552 appeared the fourth and last certainly genuine book of the *Heroic Deeds and Sayings of Pantagruel,* with the author's name attached. It contained enormous satires on the papacy; but it appeared at a time when Rabelais had many protectors, and when the policy of Henry II was for the moment anti-papal. He saved himself from the reproach of Protestantism by calling Calvin the demoniac impostor of Geneva. Nevertheless this book was soon condemned by the Sorbonne, and the next year the author died.

Rabelais's omnivorous mind sought to engulf the entire learning and knowledge available in France — a France instructed by Italy as well as by Erasmus, a France which had its own Budé, who was becoming a colossal scholar when in 1500 the *Adages* of Erasmus threw the light of a penetrating intelligence over the classic literature. By the time of Rabelais's student years, the work of such scholars had made possible the study of Greek, and Rabelais gained a reading and writing knowledge of that tongue. Yet in his youth and early manhood, men still held to the educational matter of the prior time. In France, as in Italy, the mediaeval past was reviled rather than actually discarded; and the idea of the value of encyclopaedic conventional knowledge gained from books, with little independent thought or observation, still enveloped the mind of Rabelais. But he satirizes, somewhat imaginatively, the old curriculum and its stupefying effect upon the giant prince Gargantua, whose excellent parts had already been evinced in the dirtiest chapter of the book. He is instructed by a great doctor,[2] Master Tubal Holofernes, who spends five years with him on the alphabet, till he can recite it backwards; and keeps him for thirteen years, six months, and two weeks more on *Donatus* and other mediaeval school books, and then sixteen years on others, when the old fellow dies. Next, another old cougher (tousseux) takes him through other antiquated books, including the *Doctrinale,* a grammar which not all the scholars of that time disapproved.[3] In this way Gargantua was made stupider and stupider.

A neighboring prince comes to visit King Grangousier, having in his train a sprightly youth Eudemon. The latter exhibits his courtly accomplishments, and Grangousier is enraged over the futile education of his son. Gargantua is forthwith turned over to the care of Panocrates, the tutor of Eudemon, and sets forth in their company for Paris.[4] There, when the young giant has casually taken the bells of *Notre Dame* to string around his mare's neck, more ridicule is cast on current ways of speech and education in the person of the preposterous pedant who comes to plead for their return.

This picture of the old education and its teachers, and the effect on the pupil, is loud caricature and palpable misrepresentation. And when in the twenty-third and fourth chapters, Rabelais describes the new education of Gargantua,— after a draught of hellebore has purged his mind of the old stuff,— then we find a converse idealizing exaggeration, which befits this romance. Gargantua is instructed in all the learning of the time, and practiced in the martial exercises befitting a gentleman — the influence of Castiglione's *Courtier* is apparent. His studies are encyclopaedic, and, one may add, administered in ways similar to those prevailing for years or centuries in the colleges. Yet Rabelais introduces novel ideas. Gargantua's education is carried on through hours of repast,

[2] I, Chapter XIV, *Sophiste,* i. e. scholastic, in the more prudent editions of 1542; *docteur en théologie,* in the edition of 1535.

[3] Cf *The Mediaeval Mind,* Vol. II, pp. 152–154.

[4] It has been noted that the names of the representatives of the new learning are Greek.

repose, and recreation: he learns the stars in the wakeful hours of night, and the nature and qualities of the food he eats by hearing the ancient authorities read aloud at meals; and from tricks at cards he gains a taste for mathematics.[5] In rainy weather

> "they did recreate themselves in bottling up [bailing] of hay, in cleaving and sawing of wood, and in threshing sheaves of corn at the barn. Then they studied the art of painting or carving. . . . They went likewise to see the drawing of metals, or the casting of great ordnance; how the lapidaries did work; as also the goldsmiths and cutters of precious stones. Nor did they omit to visit the alchemists, money coiners, upholsterers, weavers, velvet-workers, watchmakers, looking-glass framers, printers, organists, and other such kind of artificers, and, everywhere giving them somewhat to drink, did learn and consider the industry and invention of the trades. They went also to hear the public lectures . . . the pleading of gentle lawyers, and sermons of evangelical preachers."[6]

Rabelais joins physical to intellectual training, regulates the hours of rising and repose, and advocates a diet suitable to periods of active exercise, or again to the indoor pursuits of rainy days.[7]

In the next generation, and the next book, (written two years before the first, however,) Gargantua's glorious son, Pantagruel, likewise goes to Paris for his education, but without the dead weight of a youth besotted with the pedantries of the past, as Rabelais would deem them. Pantagruel examines the library of St. Victor, and gives a list of books, filthy and ridiculous. The eighth chapter contains Gargantua's letter setting before his son the program of a truly liberal education, such as, indeed, he had himself received in part. It opens with thanks to God for permitting the writer to see his bald old age reflourish in his son's youth. But it would be small joy to see his body continued in his son, if the young prince's soul were degenerate. Not that he distrusts him, but would encourage him to advance from good to better.

[5] Cardanus (see post, Chapter XXXII) had this idea.
[6] I, Chapter XXIV, Urquhart's Translation (1653).
[7] Cf. Lefranc, Introduction, pp. XCIV, sqq.

"And that which I now write unto thee is not so much that thou should'st live in this virtuous course, as that thou should'st rejoice in so living and having lived. . . .

"But although my deceased father of happy memory, Grangousier, had bent his best endeavors to make me profit in all perfection and political knowledge, and my labour and study . . . went beyond his desire, nevertheless, as thou may'st well understand, the time then was not so proper and fit for learning as it is at present, neither had I plenty of such good masters as thou hast had. For that time was darksome, and savouring of the infelicity and calamity of the Goths, who had brought to destruction all good literature, which in my age hath by the divine goodness been restored unto its former light and dignity, and, that with such amendment and increase of the knowledge, that now hardly should I be admitted unto the first form of the little grammar-schoolboys, I who in my youthful days was, and that justly, reputed the most learned of that age. . . .

"Now all the Sciences (Disciplines) are restored; the languages are established, Greek, without which a man may be ashamed to account him a scholar, Hebrew, Chaldean (i. e. Syriac or Aramaic), Latin; and printed books are now in use, so elegant and correct, an invention of my age by divine inspiration, as artillery is a counter-invention through the suggestion of the devil. All the world is full of learned men, of most skilled preceptors, of vast libraries; and it appears to me a truth that neither in Plato's time, or Cicero's, or Papinian's, was there ever such opportunity for studying as we see to-day; and henceforth it behooves none to show himself in society who is not well polished in the shop of Minerva. . . . So much is this so, that I, at the age where I am, have been constrained to learn Greek, which I had not despised like Cato, but had no leisure to acquire in my youth. And willingly I delight in the reading of Plutarch's *Morals,* the admirable *Dialogues* of Plato, the *Monuments* of Pausanias, and the *Antiquities* of Athenaeus, in waiting on the hour when it shall please God, my Creator, to call and command me to depart from this earth.

"Wherefore, my son, I admonish thee to employ thy youth to good profit both in studies and the virtues. Thou art at Paris, where the laudable examples of many brave men may stir thy mind, and hast likewise thy preceptor Epistemon, who by his lively and vocal teaching may instruct thee.

"I intend and will have it that thou learn the languages perfectly,— first of all the Greek, as Quintilian will have it, secondly the Latin, and then the Hebrew for the Holy Scripture's sake, and the Chaldean likewise; and that thou form thy style as to Greek in imitation of Plato, as to Latin, upon Cicero. Let there be no history which thou shalt not have ready in thy memory; and to this end books of Cosmography will help thee much. Of the liberal arts of Geometry, Arithmetic and Music, I gave thee some taste when thou were yet little, about five or six years old. Follow them further, and of Astronomy learn all the laws; but I beg you to leave out the divinations of Astrology and the art of Lullius, as vanities and abuses. Of the Civil Law, I would have thee know the texts by heart and compare them with Philosophy.

"Now, in matter of the knowledge of the works of Nature, I would have thee apply thyself attentively; so that there be neither sea, river, or fountain, of which thou dost not know the fishes; all the birds of the air, all the several kinds of trees and shrubs whether in forests or orchards; all the herbs of the earth, all the metals hidden in the belly of the abyss, the precious stones of the Orient and the South: let nothing be unknown to thee.

"Then carefully peruse the books of the Greek, Arabian and Latin physicians, not despising the Talmudists and Cabalists, and by frequent anatomies get thee a perfect knowledge of the other world [the Microcosm] which is Man. And for some hours of the day pay your respects to (commence à visiter) the Scriptures, first the New Testament in Greek and the Epistles of the Apostles, and next the Old Testament in Hebrew.

"In fine, let me see a bottomless pit of knowledge; for when you grow up and are a man, you will have to leave this tranquillity and repose of study, and learn arms and chivalry in order to defend my house, and succour our friends in all their needs against the assaults of evil-doers. And shortly I would have you try how much you have profitted, which you cannot do better than by maintaining publicly Theses and Conclusiones [8] in every branch of knowledge against all comers, and by haunting the company of learned men.

"But, since, as the wise Solomon says, wisdom entereth not into an evil mind, and knowledge without conscience is but the ruin of the soul, it behooves thee to serve, love, and fear God, and in Him place all thy thoughts and all thy hope; and by Faith built up of charity be so linked to Him as never to be overthrown by sin. Suspect the abuses of the world. Set not thy heart on vanity, for this life passes, but the Word of God endureth forever. Be serviceable to all thy neighbors, and love them as thyself. Respect thy preceptors. Shun the company of people thou wouldst not resemble, and receive not in vain the graces which God has bestowed upon thee." [9]

Roger Bacon in the thirteenth century had no thought of forming his Greek and Latin styles on Plato and

[8] Compare those of Pico della Mirandola, post, Chapter XXX.
[9] Urquhart's translation with emendations.

Cicero; but for the rest he advocated and tried to realize a similar program of study and enlightenment. No man in the sixteenth century felt more deeply than he the need of an adequate knowledge of the original tongues. And his ideal of knowledge, for every scholar if one will, was encyclopaedic. He had as strong a hate as Rabelais for scholastic obfuscations, and was quite as eager for the advancement of the physical sciences. But living when the interests of theology were absorbing, he found scant sympathy or collaboration. Only a lack of literary feeling for the classics, a lack of this sort of humanism, marked the difference between this thirteenth century Franciscan and sixteenth century scholars, like Rabelais.

From these general approvals and disapprovals shared by Rabelais with others of his time, one turns to the convictions more peculiar to him, which he expressed with power and temperamental vividness. One may note these factors of his individuality, although one cannot analyze convincingly this abounding imaginative and rational genius, this insatiate man who would reject no positive element of life.

Indeed this would seem to be Rabelais's broadest principle: — that is to say, the nature of man is good; his desires, his concupiscent lusts, his natural actions, are good, and when unthwarted, make for life and joy. It is all from God. He recognized this with week-day devoutness. But he was utterly untheological; and had no faith in any dogma of original sin. For him no subtle poison pervaded natural desire, making it at best venially sinful. He worried not at all about sin. But he voided the excrements of his wrath upon every drivelling sham which extended its obscene tentacles across the path of life. Yes, yes, says he to the imaginary reader who might reproach him for the fooleries he writes: — you are as much to blame for reading them; but both of us are better deserving of pardon than that

"rabble of squint-minded fellows dissembling and counterfeit saints, demure lookers, hypocrites, pretended zealots, tough friars, buskin-monks, and other such sects of men, who disguise themselves like masquers to deceive the world. . . . Fly from these men, abhor and hate them as much as I do, and upon my faith you will find yourself the better for it. And if you desire to be good Pantagruelists, that is to say, *to live in peace, joy, health, making yourselves always merry,* never trust those men that always peep out through a little hole."

The heart and soul of Rabelais are in this last passage of the second book, given here mainly in the translation, with which Cavalier Urquhart whiled away his captivity in the Tower of London. Cast out this starveling mummery, ye who would be followers of the good Pantagruel, *and live in peace, joy, health, making always good cheer.* And this Pantagruelism is tolerant, kindly, and forgiving. For in all Pantagruelists there is that " by virtue whereof they will bear with anything that floweth from a good, free, and loyal heart." [10] There should be also the salt of Stoicism, as Rabelais puts it later in life, when he speaks of Pantagruelism as " a certain gaiety of spirit *cured* in contempt of chance and fortune." [11] With prodigious humor, wit, poetic imagination, Rabelais exemplified, illuminated, or befouled these principles, making them into an epic of royal giants, giants in the joy of mind and joy of lusty living, all one and whole and free from care and rancor. To this end he devotes his learning, his power of making borrowed stories live in a new pertinency; to this end he devotes his flood of words, and the images, the metaphors and similes, in which he thinks, and on which his theme moves as on pinions. No ideal beauty monopolizes any throne. Why not rather enthrone the belly — Gaster — whose voraciousness is the moving energy of life? Gaster is the master of arts, crafts and inventions, the mover of the progress of the world. Gaster indeed may symbolize this inspiring need and moving power as well as any other energy in that life whose first cry is Gargantua's: à boire! à boire! à boire! [12]

A gorgeous illustration of this benevolent love of joy-

[10] Bk. III Prologue, cf. an example of this tolerance Bk. III, Chapter II.
[11] Bk. IV, Author's prologue.
[12] Bk. I, Chapter VI. Cf. Bk. IV, Ch. LVII and XLI.

ous life, and contempt for whatever pinches or addles it, is the abbey of Theleme, with its name taken from the Greek θέλημα, meaning will or wish. The lusty monk who did such feats in the war against the tyrant Picrochole is to be rewarded by Gargantua. Sundry fat abbeys are offered him; he will have none of them, but will build one after his own mind. Gargantua bestows on him the country of Theleme by the river Loire; and the two kindred spirits found the new order upon the full contrary of all established rules of monkhood. There shall be no wall about the abbey, seeing that all others are walled about; nor shall there be any clock or dial, since what dotage is it for anyone to direct his courses by the sound of a bell, and not rather by his own discretion; beautiful women shall not be kept out, but only the ugly, nor shall any vow bind monk or nun to stay, when they choose to depart. Inasmuch as other Orders take the vows of chastity, poverty, and obedience, it was ordained that those who would should marry, and every one should be rich and live at liberty.

The abbey was built in grandeur and magnificence, with alabaster fountains and arcaded luxuries; with libraries in every tongue. Over its great gates were emblazoned verses forbidding bigots, hypocrites, dissemblers, attorneys, barristers, usurers, thieves, liars, drunkards, cannibals, to enter; but inviting all noble blades and brisk and handsome people, faithful expounders of the Scriptures, and lovely ladies, stately, proper, fair, and mirthful. The ladies had bowers and courts where they might bathe, shoot at the butts, and ride and fly their falcons, witness the tilting, and in fine, have every recreation suited to ladies of high birth. They slept in embroidered beds, their chambers hung with tapestry; perfumers waited on them in the mornings, and gave to each a casket of choice odours. They were apparelled to suit their pleasure, stockings of scarlet or crimson, slippers of red or violet, smocks of any color, coats of satin, damask, velvet, gowns of cloth of gold or satin: raiment to suit the seasons. The men were dressed as gallantly, and every morning received word of what the ladies were to wear, so that they might array themselves in harmony.

> "Their life was spent not in laws, statutes or rules, but at their own free will and pleasure. They rose from bed when they thought good, drank, ate, worked, slept, when the desire came to them. None did waken them, none constrained them either to drink or eat, nor to do any other thing: for so had Gargantua established it. The Rule of their order had but one clause: *Do what thou wilt.* Because persons that are free, well born, well educated, and accustomed to good company, have by nature an instinct and spur which prompts them to virtuous acts and withdraws them from vice. This they call honor. But the same people when they are oppressed and bound by base subjection and constraint, turn aside from the noble affections by which they were freely inclined to virtue, to shake off and break this bond of servitude. For we always attempt forbidden things, and covet what is denied us."

By this liberty, continues Rabelais, they entered into laudable emulation to do all of them what they saw did please one. So if one said let us drink, they would all drink, or let us go a-walking, they would all go, or a-hunting or a-hawking. So nobly were they taught that no man or woman of them but could read, write, sing, play upon musical instruments, speak five or six languages and compose verse and prose in them. Never were seen knights so brave and noble, or better skilled in fight on foot or horse; never ladies so proper and charming, or more apt in needle work and every act becoming a woman. And when it came to any man to leave the abbey, he took with him his ladylove and married her, and lived together in devoted love and happiness all the rest of their lives.

Rabelais's broad approvals and the butts of his satire and laughter bore not only on religion, but on the greedy or pettifogging affairs of men. Nothing could be funnier than his satire upon the windy irrelevancy of pleadings and arguments in court.[13] Yet what a creature his humor and toleration could build out of knavery, the character of Panurge will testify, as wonderful a creation as Falstaff. The broad happy acceptance of life includes the

[13] Bk. II, Chapter X–XIII.

cheerful scamp, let him but be clever and funny enough: and of course Rabelais's whole setting forth of life has always the permitted exaggerations of comedy and satire. But the comic does not exclude feeling which sometimes is as profound as it is large and beautiful. A Lilliputian may weep over a sparrow's death; but Pantagruel tells the tale of the strange announcement of the death of Pan, connects it with the tragedy on Calvary, and remains silent in contemplation. "A little while after we saw tears flowing from his eyes as big as ostrich eggs." Or again, one may find a seriousness in Rabelais's very comic picture of the underworld, where Emperors and Kings and Popes suffer ridiculous degradations, while philosophers foot it bravely. His own Kings, Grangousier and Gargantua, are humane in their statecraft, and long-suffering and forgiving, even when war is forced on them.

The religious or theological satire in the works of Rabelais raises the question whether he belonged to the Reform. We naturally tend to classify the incipiency of great movements by the clearer determinations of their maturity. Their vague beginnings may have carried little consciousness of the later purpose and resolve. Rabelais was no member of the Reform as its purport was stated by Calvin. The two men were repugnant and hostile. But Rabelais loved fact and verity; and as a penetrating scholar, he sought the source and despised the gloss. This was his way in studying the Civil Law, in which he was no tyro. He would cast aside the Commentators, and understand the *Pandects* for himself. So in religion, he was evangelical, looking back to the sure utterances of the Gospels and the contemporary testimony of the Epistles. His mind rejected the accretions of ecclesiasticism, which had no warrant in Christ's gospel. Greed and corruption were the working forces of this sacerdotal elaboration. Moreover, sacerdotal rules and prohibitions checked the flood and joyful play of life. Rabelais was a man of the sixteenth century, his pulses throbbing with its living currents and with the red blood of his own lusty nature. Continence, abstinence, any lessening of life's play, were in themselves as abominable as the false prerogatives and monstrous hypocrisy, which they did not even cloak. In accordance both with his nature and his rational principles, he hated the jealous, empty theologians of the Sorbonne, the monks with their rules and dirty lies, and the greed of Rome which fleeced the nations absurdly. All these detestable things were the monstrous offspring of *Antiphysis,* malignantly brought forth to spite the Beauty and Harmony, which Physis, that is to say, Nature, gave birth to in the beginning.

From such matter of Rabelaisean contempt and disapproval the Rabelaisean wit and phantasy produced the mordant, yet side-splitting, chapters of the fourth book. After Pantagruel and his ship's company have passed by the Island of Shrovetide and have had their adventures in the land of Silly Sausages, they come to the Island of the *Papefigues,* whose people have been set upon and enslaved for insulting an image of the Pope adored by the *Papemaniacs.* Sailing on, the next day they reach the blessed islands of these same Maniacal Papists, where they are treated with hospitality and veneration because one of their company, even Panurge, once had seen God, that is to say, the God on earth, to wit, the Pope. One reads and learns what, save by him, unspeakable ridicule Rabelais could heap on papist observances and superstitions, and on their foundation, to wit, Papal Decretals, Clementinae Extravagantes, and the rest, and the miracles wrought even by their parchment, perhaps the crowning miracle of all being their subtile power of drawing gold to Rome. And then, as the good company sail on, frozen words, wafted from the cries of men battling in hyperborean regions, are heard as they melt in warmer air. Once more a landing is made on the Island of Gaster, the great belly-master of all arts and sciences. Then the ship sails on, Pantagruel sleeping softly on his quarter deck with a Greek Heliodorus in his hand.

CHAPTER XIV

POETIC ENNOBLEMENT OF FRENCH THROUGH IMITATION OF THE CLASSICS

In the year 1549 appeared *La Défense et Illustration de la Langue Française,* a little book whose sails were filled with young enthusiasms. The author, Joachim du Bellay, " gentilhomme angevin," a youth of twenty-four, was aided and inspired by his friend Pierre de Ronsard, " gentilhomme vendomois," one year his senior. The two were destined to be the most memorable of the group of poets who dubbed themselves " La Pléiade." The name of Ronsard became as that of a prince in literature.

The *Défense* was a manifesto of a new school of French poetry; a precursory and necessarily rash attempt to set forth principles, if not a system. It contained inconsistencies, confusions, fallacies. Perhaps no critic has succeeded altogether in stating its doctrines for us. It was at all events a clarion pronunciamento in favor of French as the literary vehicle for Frenchmen. Rejecting the old forms of French verse, it defended the capacities of the mother tongue for the most glorious kinds of poetry. But the full resources of the mother tongue should be utilized, and above all, there was need to ennoble its literary forms through that veritable imitation of the Greek and Latin Classics which lay in appropriating the truth and nobility presented in them.[1]

The author, or authors, of the *Défense* seem to start from the idea that the weakness or excellence of languages depends on the arbitrary will of men. If some, having been " plus curieusement regleés," become richer than others, this is not due to any inherent felicity, but solely

[1] The modern, and especially the English, use of the word " Illustration " diverts attention from its meaning in the title to the *Défense,* where it means magnifying or rendering illustrious.

to the "artifice et industrie des hommes." Hence the folly of those scholars who think French unsuited to letters and erudition. If our own tongue is less copious than Greek, the fault lies not in it, but in the rudeness of our ancestors who chose to leave to posterity examples, rather than precepts, of excellence. But —

" Je n'estime pourtant nostre vulgaire, tel qu'il est maintenant, estre si vil et abject, comme le font ces ambitieux admirateurs des langues Greque et Latine. . . . Et qui voudra de bien pres y regarder, trouvera que nostre langue Francoise n'est si pauvre qu'elle ne puysse rendre fidelement ce qu'elle emprunte des autres; si infertile, qu'elle ne puysse produyre de soy quelque fruict de bonne invention, au moyen de l'industrie et diligence des cultiveurs d'icelle. . . ."

Translations will not suffice to raise our language. The Romans did not omit this labor: but chiefly they enriched their tongue " immitant les meilleurs aucteurs Grecz, se transformant en eux, les devorant, et apres les avoir bien digerez, les convertissant en sang et nourriture." And each selected the Greek author that best suited his own talents and the purpose which he had in view.

The chief point of art lies in this " imitation." Let him who would imitate understand that it is not so easy to copy (suivre) the virtues of a good author, and penetrate to his hidden qualities. It is profitless to imitate the old French authors; for that is but to present our language with what it has already. If Virgil and Cicero had been content to do this, Latin literature might have stopped with Ennius and Lucretius.

Yet translations are serviceable, especially of the science of the Greeks, so that all may study it, and not have to spend their time on the language. Indeed, that our men to-day are of less worth in science than the ancients, is chiefly owing to the study of the Greek and Latin. " For if the time which we consume in learning the said languages, had been devoted to the study of the Sciences, surely Nature is not become so sterile as not to have brought forth Platos and Aristotles in our own time." Of course Du Bellay had no thought of applying this rather two-edged argument to those who sought to excel in poetry and eloquence. He did not mean to depreciate the study of the ancient tongues; on the contrary, he maintains that no one can write well in French without a knowledge of Latin at least. But he pours ridicule on those " reblanchisseurs de murailles " who think to imitate the ancients in their own tongues, by copying their phrases, making poems on half lines of Virgil, and mouthing in Cicero's sentences. As if through such assembling one could rebuild an ancient edifice!

As for our old French poetry, continues Du Bellay in the second part of the *Défense,* William de Loris and Jean de Meun are worth reading " pour y voir quasi comme une premiere imaige de la langue Francoise, venerable pour son antiquité." Coming nearer our own times, Jean le Maire de Belges seems the first to have *illustré* our tongue, enriching it with poetic words and forms still in use. As for our very best poets after him, I would say " qu'ilz ont bien ecrit, qu'ilz ont illustré notre Langue, que la France leur est obligée; mais aussi diroy je bien qu'on pourroit trouver en nostre Langue . . . une forme de Poësie beaucoup plus exquise, laquele il faudroit chercher en ces vieux Grecz et Latins, non point és aucteurs Francoise."

To be sure, natural aptitude without learning can do more than " Doctrine sans le naturel." But learning is needed for the " amplification " of our tongue, which I am discussing, " and I advise those who aspire to this glory, to imitate the good authors, Greek and Roman, and indeed Italian, Spanish and others." Abandon the old French forms —" Rondeaux, Ballades, Vyrelaiz, Chantz Royaulx, Chansons, et autres telles episseries, qui corrumpent le goust de nostre Langue, et ne servent si non à porter temoinguaige de notre ignorance." Rather, imitate the epigrams of a Martial; the " pitoyables Elegies," of Ovid, or a Tibullus or Propertius, throwing in some of those ancient fables, which are no small ornament of poetry; —" chante moy ces Odes, incognues encor' de la Muse Francoyse. . . . Sonne moy ces beaux Sonnetz, non moins docte que plaisante invention Italienne." Adopt also into the " famille Francoyse " those tripping hendecasyllables, as of a Catullus or a Pontanus. Thus Du Bellay holds up for imitation those exquisite Italians, Petrarch, Sannazaro, Pontanus, even as he would Horace, Ovid, and still greater classic writers.

As for subjects, let our poet choose the noble ones — " quelque'un de ces beaux vieulx Romans Francoys, comme un Lancelot, un Tristan, ou autres; et en fay renaitre au monde un admirable Iliade, et laborieuse Eneide." Let him take fragments from our old French Chronicles as Livy did from ancient annals; and build therefrom a noble history, with harangues like those of Thucydides and Sallust. Would that our age had " des Mecenes et des Augustes " for honor nourishes art; and science will not flourish when despised by all. Antiquity testifies that heroes need poets for their fame —" à la verité, sans la divine Muse d'Homere, le mesme tumbeau qui couvroit le corps d'Achille eust aussi accablé son renom "— a sentiment expressed in the twelfth century by John of Salisbury in the Prologue to his *Policraticus*.[2]

But Du Bellay is not too proud to advise his poet (especially when he is at work upon a long narrative poem) to enlarge and enliven his language with the terms of artisans and mechanics, as well as of the learned: — let him keep company with " mariniers, fondeurs, peintres, engraveurs et autres, savoir leurs inventions, les noms des matieres, des outils, et les termes usités en leurs arts et métiers, pour tirer de là ces belles comparaisons et vives descriptions de toutes choses."

Du Bellay speaks of many other matters, of rhyme and rhythm, and the correct way of declaiming; and passes on to an eloquent appeal to Frenchmen to write in French; as Virgil and Cicero wrote in Latin, and Petrarch, Boccaccio and Bembo wrote in Italian, however well they wrote in Latin too. On, ye Frenchmen, finally

[2] The Mediaeval Mind, II, p. 141.

concludes the peroration: seize the antique treasures; make them your own. Recall the fashion of your Gallic Hercules, " tirant les peuples aprés lui par leurs oreilles avec une chaine attachée a sa langue! "

The precepts, the tone and temper, the general tenor, of the *Défense* are strengthened and illuminated in the prefaces of Ronsard to his hopeless epic *La Franciade*, and in his *Abregé de l'art poetique Francois*. These later proclamations from the prince of poets are as sonorous and striking as anything uttered in the first enthusiasm of the *Défense:* — " C'est un crime de lèse-majesté d'abandonner le language de son pays, vivant et florissant, pour vouloir déterrer [disinter] je ne sais quelle cendre des anciens." [3]

But the grand illustration of whatever principles the *Défense* intended to set forth was afforded by the poetic work of Ronsard and those starlets of the Pléiade whose lights paled in his effulgence. Their work, moreover, makes a fuller disclosure of the influence working in their manifesto, and of the fact that while they and all the world regarded them as innovating spirits, they had their definite antecedents. The genius of Alexandrianism worked in them, the genius of that school of epigonic Greek poetry that had made its home in the Alexandria of the Ptolemies, a school which was learned, meticulous and *precieux*, and openly made form its idol.[4] Their young talents were also inspired by another and a different daintiness, that of Petrarch, or perhaps that of his followers, the Petrarchists. Du Bellay began with the imitative sensibility and affectation of that school, and later declared his revolt from it. Ronsard also passed on and through its atmosphere.

Still nearer influences touched the Pléiade, from French poets scarcely older than themselves, whose home was the flourishing and many-minded city of Lyons. Among

[3] Printed in rather impossible small type in Laveaux's edition of the *Oeuvres de P. de Ronsard*, Tomes, III and VI.

[4] The very name *Pléiade* had been applied to a group of seven poets in Alexandrian times.

these was Maurice Scève, whose *Délie* appeared only in 1544; also Pontus de Tyard, no Lyonnais by birth, but closely connected with that city. He was himself to be numbered with the Pléiade; as was Daurat, the admirable classical scholar, who revealed Aeschylus and Pindar and Homer to Ronsard and Baïf.[5]

Of the Pléiade, Du Bellay early won note by his *Défense* and the *Olive,* a book of imitated or occasionally translated sonnets. He was a sensitive soul. If his *Olive* showed little beyond apt imitation, his own sentiments and feelings came to self-expression in his *Regrets,* a few years later. From his twenty-eighth to his thirty-third year, he lived in Rome, in the train of his relative, Cardinal Du Bellay. There this rather melancholy soul suffered from homesickness, and tended to withdraw into spiritual seclusion on account of the same affliction of deafness, which had so much to do with driving Ronsard from the life of a courtier to the life of letters. Du Bellay was also stung, if not afflicted, by the meanness and poltroonery of ecclesiastical court life at Rome. His disgust, put frankly in his volume of *Regrets* published on his return to France, nearly cost him the countenance of his noble relative, the Cardinal.

But his stay in Rome had done much for him, especially as he had loved a veritable Roman girl. It brought him close to the realization of his humanistic dreams of the loves and life of the good old world; perhaps it lured him, against his principles, to write Latin hendecasyllables like Catullus. At all events, with such waves of feeling as had risen in him, his tongue, indeed his self, was loosed; and found expression in sonnets, which draw us to one who was so touchingly sympathetic with himself and the human yearnings symbolized in his own sensibilities. Of the humanist poets of his time and race he was the most personal, the most impulsively and naturally expres-

[5] For these influences on the Pléiade see Brunetière, *Hist. de la Lit. Française classique,* T. I. pp. 233–261. Besides those already named, Étienne Jodelle and Rémy Belleau make up the seven. The names change, however.

sive.[6] This charming poet might have had much more to say had not death cut him short.

In the prodigious fame which was his while he lived the equal friend of kings, Ronsard was as fortunate as Petrarch. Their lots differed after death. For Petrarch then became the symbolic idol of the coming time; while Ronsard's fame was clipped by the unfriendly criticism of Malherbe. There was a curious coincidence in the failure of what each would like to have regarded as his master-piece; for the fame of Petrarch's *Africa* existed only in anticipation and for a factitious moment just after the poet's death; and *La Franciade* fell moribund from the press in spite of Ronsard's enormous fame in 1572, when it appeared.

The effect, if not the recognized influence of Ronsard, endured. He is still one of the greatest names in French literature; and while he lived, he was the prince of poets. Prodigies were connected with him. His birth, which he himself alleged to have taken place on September the eleventh, 1524, the day of the battle of Pavia when Francis I was taken prisoner, was thought a providential glory compensating France for the disaster of that day.[7]

Pierre de Ronsard came of good family, his father Louis having been so highly regarded by royalty that he was sent to Spain in charge of the two children of Francis I, who on the King's liberation were given as hostages for the performance of the Treaty of Madrid. Louis de Ronsard had some taste for letters, but esteeming a career at court more highly, he placed his son as page in the household of the dauphin, in 1536, when the lad was about eleven years old. Soon the dauphin died, and Ronsard was passed on to the service of his younger brother, Charles, Duke of Orleans. Next he was sent to

[6] On Joachim du Bellay see É. Faguet, *Seizième siècle;* as well as Brunetière, o. c. I, pp. 299–322.

[7] The poet may have been born on September 11th, 1524. The absurdity of the statement in the text, which goes back to Binet, his friend and biographer, lies in the fact that the battle of Pavia took place February 24th, 1525!! *La vie de P. de Ronsard* by Claude Binet (1586), is short and interesting. There is a critical edition by Paul Laumonier (Paris, 1909).

Scotland in the train of the King's daughter, married to James Stuart. She did not live long, and Ronsard, still little more than a child, returned to the service of the Duke. His biographers report that he soon excelled his fellows in courtly and martial accomplishments; and indeed he was a graceful, charming youth. He was already fond of poetry. Once more he was transferred to the service of another royal master, Henry, now the dauphin, and destined to become king as Henry II, and to die young, wounded by the lance of Montgomery in a tournament.

Sundry voyages completed the education and widened the horizon of the young page. But he became afflicted with deafness, which strengthened his plea to be allowed to devote himself to letters, or as his prudent father would have it, to the Church. The Church faded from Ronsard's view on his father's death in 1544, which removed the only obstacle to a literary life.

The young man had already found his teacher in Dorat (or Daurat) who soon was made head of the Collège de Coqueret. There Ronsard became fully and devotedly his scholar, along with Baïf, still a boy. Others who were to belong to the Pléiade came, among them Du Bellay, in 1549, whom Ronsard had met on a journey from Poictiers to Paris. Binet, Ronsard's later very humble friend and biographer, calls Dorat " la source de la fontaine," from which all this band of poets drank of the " eaux Pieriennes." Under him, (with some instruction from Tournèbe as well) Ronsard gained a penetrating knowledge of the classical Greek poetry, and equipped himself from the Latin arsenal as well. He studied Homer; he studied the great Greek tragedies; he gave himself to Pindar. With equal zest he studied the Alexandrians, Theocritus, Callimachus, Apollonius Rhodius, Aratus. When Henri Estienne published his *Anacreon* in 1554, Ronsard gave himself with delight to those sweet verses which we recognize as " Anacreontea," but not as the composition of the Teian master. The Pléiade of course accepted them as from him, and were delighted to find a classic so sweetly to their taste. Ronsard discovered that the torrents of Pindar were rather rough and difficult:

"Anacréon me plait, le doux Anacréon."

And he would seem to have turned from Pindar to these smoother forms of verse and feeling. Doubtless one influence and then another might thrust itself into his mood, and take form beneath his facile pen. His mind, his nature, was so thoroughly impregnated with classic reading, that only under drastic contemporary impulsion (as in his *Discours des Miseres de ce Temps*) could he write altogether from himself. Moreover, he changed and rearranged his poems so constantly throughout his life, that the critic moves on unsafe ground in attempting to arrange his work chronologically, and assign to one period the inspiration of one classic poet, and to another period the dominant influence of another. He absorbed the influence of the Latin poets quite as freely as the Greek, and rather more unconsciously. He owed great debts to Virgil always, and most dreadfully in *La Franciade*. Its first four books (all that he composed) so exhausted the episodes of the *Aeneid*, that one wonders with what material he could have carried his unhappy epic any further. Horace, and the Horatian forms also influenced him constantly; and perhaps it was from the good sense of Horace (which had kept *him* from essaying Pindaric strains) that Ronsard drew a like reluctance in the end.

The classics, Latin, Greek, including the Alexandrians, were not the only sources of his inspiration. Petrarch was an alluring mode and fashion. His lovely Italian sonnets and *canzoni* had almost classical authority. They furnished that attractive preciosity of love which fascinated these French poets of the sixteenth century. Ronsard copied Petrarch in sentiment and expression in his early "Amours à Cassandre." Afterwards he seems to have passed on and through his influence, as a more substantial body passes through a nebula.

He had devoted seven years to Greek and Latin, and to the composition of poems under classic inspiration, when in 1550 he published his first volume of *Odes*. At once his fame leaped heavenward. Friend and foe alike saw in him the chief of the band whose war cry had been the *Défense* of the year before. His fame and fortunes reached their zenith through the next ten years; and he could say to all other poets of the realm:

> Vous êtes mes sujets, et je suis votre roi.

So long as he lived, his royal place was not seriously threatened. If his material fortunes were less splendid than his reputation, they still enabled him to live in the enjoyment of courtly pleasures and the comforts of town and country, until his death in 1585. His art was the mistress of his most strenuous devotions. His towering consciousness of his position and deserts was chequered by touches of an inner humility. In fact, his nature was rather timid and retiring. Rarely he mingled in the strife of pens and swords, which was desolating France. To prove his orthodoxy and evince his patriotism, he wrote his *Discours des Miseres de ce temps,* against the reformed and now Calvinized religion; which his love of France, his love of pleasure, his love of letters, combined to impel him to detest. In him, humanism emphatically rejected the Reform. Catholic in his professions and beliefs, his life was pagan. He passed his days in the realization of pagan sentiments and the incidents of pagan mythology. But in his long last illness, he ended his life piously.

Ronsard's natural talents were large and various. His poetic accomplishment was diverse and immense. Much of it was of a high order. He accepted the practice of the ancients as the embodiment of poetic principles, which he would re-incorporate, and cause to live again, in French verse. At his best, he did most nobly reflect in his poetry the training and discipline, and the ennoblement of language, form, and conception, which classical studies graft upon a fine poetic talent. When not at his best, he imitated the classics stiffly and pedantically, deducing from their works principles having no living or universal application; and incorporating in his poetry classical material which had not been assimilated and recast in his own mind and temperament. He delighted to fill, or adorn, and *intriguer* his verse with obscure mythological allusions. He could be pedantic, prolix, and guilty of false emphasis. [8] Hating the commonplace, he strove, and often with brilliant success, to ennoble his French vehicle — verse, words, forms of expression, epithets. He loved splendid and striking images, despising those which were conventional and added nothing to the idea.

A marvellous artist in metre and rhythm, he remodelled and re-established the " Alexandrian " line of twelve or thirteen syllables. This mightiest of French lines was a creature of the Middle Ages; but had fallen into neglect. Under the influence of his classical training and the impregnation of his mind with the Greek and Latin hexameter, Ronsard perfected it, restored it to its place of primacy, and exemplified its adequacy.[9] He introduced as well a number of other verse-forms previously used by French poets, and fashioned others for himself. He would fain have composed the music for his verse, as Pindar did so naturally. Here he failed. But to find his equal in the abundance and variety of his verse, invention or adaptation, one must look back of French verse altogether, to the fecund genius for Latin verse-forms of an Adam of St. Victor or an Abaelard.[10] Ronsard had a fine sense of the harmony which should exist between rhythm and thought; a great talent for the adjustment of verse-forms to the thought and sentiment of the poem.

[8] In his occasional flattery, Ronsard may fall into bathos, as in his sonnet to Robert Garnier, "prince des tragiques," saying that if Bacchus should descend to Hades now, he would bring back with him, not Aeschylus, but Garnier. *Sonnets devers,* LXXXI, *Oeuvres,* Tome V, p. 354. Again, on the death of Charles IX (!!) he declared: "La France n'estoit pas ny digne de l'avoir, ny de porter ses pas." *Epitaphes, Oeuvres,* Tome VII, p. 170.

[9] "Les Alexandrins tiennent la place en nostre langue, telle que les vers heroïques entre les Grecs et Latins, lesquels sont composez de douze à treize syllabes, les masculins de douze, les foeminins de treize, et ont tousjours leur repos sur la sixiesme syllable." Ronsard, *Abregè de l'Art Poetique François.*

[10] Cf. The Mediaeval Mind, II, Chapter XXXIII.

Five books of *Odes,* manifold in theme, and following Pindaric, Horatian, or Anacreontic models; six or seven books of *Amours,* some eight thousand lines; two books of *Hymnes,* epic and lyric recitals; then other books of *Poèmes,* of *Elegies,* of *Epigrammes,* of *Epitaphes,* of *Mascarades,* of *Discours* over his Time's miseries, and a still-born Epic — was not this an unexampled mass for one man to have achieved?[11] Succeeding poets would scarcely go beyond either Ronsard's range of theme or formal modelling. And through it all, if there was endless borrowing, there was also much real expression of a master-poet's personality, of his own loves and feelings, even thoughts. He expressed a genuine love of nature, of the country, in his *Eclogues* and in his poems on his forest of Gâtine. Epic qualities were shown, not in his hopeless *Franciade,* but in many of his *Odes* and *Hymnes.* In the best of these last, his long discipline of "imitation" of the classics has become veritable assimilation, is transformed into power and inspiration of his own, — into the self-expression of a poet.[12]

The *Roman de la Rose,* especially that sophisticated longer portion written by De Meun, incorporated much substance from the antique philosophy and literature, but was little affected by classic form. It was not artistic quality that the author had sought in his reading. The Pléiade on the other hand — Ronsard above the rest — strove to gain artistic quality, beauty, ennoblement of form, from a more thorough and direct classical study. Especially they were keen Greek scholars; and had read Homer, Pindar, and the Tragedians, though they may have found the very beautiful Theocritus and other Alexandrians quite as congenial to their taste. A taste for

[11] See Brunetière, o. c., I, pp. 323, 396.

[12] For example in the Hymn to Death, the last in Bk. II, (*Oeuvres,* Tome IV, p. 364).

Ronsard has been so excellently analyzed and criticised by the French masters of criticism, that a foreigner who will always find difficulty in appreciating the finer points of French poetry, may leave to them the literary criticism of Ronsard. See particularly, Brunetière in his *Hist. de la Lit. franc. classique,* Vol. I; É. Faguet, in his Seizième Siècle, *Études littéraires;* and J. J. Jusserand's *Ronsard.*

Petrarch, for Sannazaro, for Bembo, and other Italian literati, who also cared for form supremely, further incited them to the study of form in these Alexandrians, or in Horace, Tibullus and Catullus; all of whom exemplified not merely form, but the palpable endeavor for it. Those Alexandrians and Latins cared for art, seeking even its highest *ars celare artem*.

So the Pléiade represent the love of artistic beauty very consciously. Not that there had been an utter neglect of it before them. What good workman lacks this love? But they emblazoned it, proclaimed it, felt it as an inspiration throughout their entire poetic consciousness. And more than all others who had preceded them, they left it as a rich legacy for future generations of French poets.

Ronsard had foolish friends and degenerate imitators. The over-learned Baïf pursued an impossible idea of his own, that of writing French metrically. The result was abhorrent; yet he was not alone in his idea. Another poet, Philippe Desportes, with charm and facile skill, was ignoble in thought and theme, — a sheer court poet. Perhaps Mathurin Regnier (1573-1613) was the best of these epigoni. On the other hand, there were adherents of the Reformed Religion, who were poets and looked on Ronsard as their chief. Among them, the tedious Du Bartas returned to sacred themes. His poetry gained vogue in Germany, where, later, Goethe admired it. He may possibly have influenced Milton.

Agrippa D'Aubigné (1551-1630) was a far more interesting personality. Learned in Latin, Greek and Hebrew, he was consecrated in boyhood by his father to the cause of the Reform, with maledictions on his head if he should ever blanch. There was no need of them. At the age of sixteen, after his father's death, he escaped by a window at night, barefooted, in his shirt, to hurry after a passing troop of horse. Thus he hurled himself into the wars of religion, and thereafter, in battles, sieges, skirmishes and single combats, fought wherever fighting could be had. Save when sick or wounded or in prison, his sword was rarely laid aside, till the conversion of his great master Henry IV to Catholicism forced peace upon this devoted and outspoken follower. He had always had the habit of writing; he was a pamphleteer as well as soldier, producing satires, diatribes, and poems constantly. He would not follow Henry into the Roman church, and retired to his government of Saintonge. Verses which he had composed, some of them literally in the saddle, some of them when in fever from wounds, he now put together in his still protesting, still militant *Tragiques*. He never gave up the cause of the Reform; and cursed his son for abandoning it. Long after Henry's death, always contending with words or arms, d'Aubigné found refuge in Geneva. Four times had he been condemned to death! Militant, active to the end, he induced Berne and other Swiss cities to construct mural fortifications which he himself designed. He remarried when over seventy, and died an octogenarian. He was the grandfather of Madame de Maintenon.

He left a mass of prose and verse; a *Histoire universelle* of his times; *Meditations* on the Psalms; satires in the form of elaborate prose fictions; political discourses; odes, sonnets, poems of gallantry; for like his master Henry, though less irrational in love, this Cavalier of the Reform sighed for the ladies not infrequently. But his chief work, *Les Tragiques* in angry Alexandrians, are a tableau of the miseries of the time. Into it he poured his wrath at the evil turn of things; while scriptural incident and mythological allusion jostled each other in the almost epic outcry of this Huguenot, swordsman, councillor, scholar, poet, indomitable soul.

CHAPTER XV

SELF-EXPRESSION THROUGH TRANSLATION AND APPROPRIATION: AMYOT, BODIN, MONTAIGNE

NOT only in Ronsard and his Pléiade, but in others who, like him, were scholars and also Frenchmen, one observes a dual interlocked phenomenon or process, very noticeable through the sixteenth century. It is this: imitation or appropriation of intellectual material from the antique culture combines with the ripening French mind and personality, promotes its development, and facilitates and enriches its self-expression. This dual process may present the appearance of conflict between the classical or antique influence and the native French faculties, which will also make use of contemporary foreign strains from Italy or Germany, and to some extent fall under their influence. Some Frenchmen will accept opinions and sentiments straight from the classics; but in general such was the organic power of sixteenth century life in France, that the antique influence becomes a contribution to its advance. The French mind and personality emerges, asserts itself, gains strength and even distinctness from the study and use and assimilation of the ancient material.

I

The Pléiade made a literary and stylistic use of the contents of Greek and Latin poems and of the lessons to be drawn from their form and manner of composition. It is interesting to consider other Frenchmen, publicists and moralists, who make a different use of different antique material, and would distil from it the wisdom of life which it so notably contained. One may observe in the first place the more impersonal phases of the appropriation of the antique by the genius or vigor of the French race or people, especially in that most palpable expression of the race, its language. This will illustrate plainly both sides of the dual process. There is the obvious competition between the French and Latin languages. French is used in daily life, also in poetry. But Latin is in possession of the sphere of university instruction and of all branches of learning, of theology and religion, of philosophy and mathematics, of law and medicine. French is supposed to be unfit for these higher branches. Yet the advocates of French not only assert its capabilities, but put their mother tongue to school; instructing and amplifying it from the example and resources of its own ancient mother, Latin, with some light as well from its newly adopted foster-father, Greek. Under classical tuition this same French tongue, far from becoming Latin, asserts itself with mounting energy and enlarging capacities, and presses its claims to universal use by Frenchmen, even for the highest literary and intellectual purposes.

For the victory of French, prejudice had to be overcome, and the rude tongue made fit for those higher uses. In the fourteenth century scholars introduced Latin words into the French vernacular; through the fifteenth, this was carried on diligently by greater numbers. Yet in the sixteenth century much had still to be done to enlarge and ennoble the French language. So thought Du Bellay and Ronsard as well as Henri Estienne and others who were none the less convinced that French was the true literary vehicle for Frenchmen. Along different paths, they directed their efforts to this common end.

In spite of men's devotion to the classics, the necessity of using French became more imperative. As the social and intellectual life of court and town progressed, ways of thinking and the contents of thought assumed distinctive character, and for that reason would less readily flow in the thought-forms of antiquity, less easily find expression in Latin. This difficulty was aggravated by the efforts of the stricter sort of scholars to purify contemporary Latin and bring it back to classical correctness. For thereby they made it still less suitable for current thinking.

One bears in mind that the Romance tongues orginally had not developed from the Latin of Cicero and Quintilian, but from the vulgar Latin of the people, especially the peoples of the Provinces. Hence classical Latin, with its suspended thought and different structural articulation, was always alien to the current expression of the current thought of the so-called "Latin Countries" of Europe.

The progress of thinking in the sixteenth century, continuing the like mediaeval tendency, could not but draw away from Latin. And whenever any branch of science advanced beyond the data supplied from ancient sources, it would tend to pass further from the antique, and would less naturally conform to the antique vehicle of expression: it would more vigorously demand expression in a vernacular language vitally corresponding with its own progressing ways of thinking. Still for a century or two, scholars, philosophers, physicists might write in Latin, deeming it a more satisfactory medium, or in order that their works might be read abroad. But how inevitably any such practice was doomed to cease, may be plainly seen by looking forward through the growth of the sciences in the eighteenth and nineteenth centuries, even to our own time. The different sciences still continue to derive or devise numberless special terms out of cuttings and combinations of Latin and Greek words. But it would now be a stupid *tour de force* to compose a scientific work in Latin; for the people who evolved that language as a living tongue did not have the conceptions or turns of thought which the modern author wishes to express. In the sixteenth century, the substance of all the sciences was largely drawn from the antique. Yet thought did not run in antique conduits; but already demanded more closely fitting forms of expression.

A far more obvious reason for using French was that it was the mother tongue, understood by all, and spontaneously used by all, and not learned through years of study. Reasons of State might also intervene, as when in 1539 a royal decree directed that henceforth all proceedings before magistrates should be in French, a decree which was enforced even in Provence. G. Tory in his *Champfleury* published in 1529, and before him, Claude de Seyssel in the preface to his translation of Justin, dedicated to Louis XII, spoke ardently for French, and made good use of the political arguments from the example of the Romans, who insisted on the official use of Latin throughout their conquered provinces. The crown was the pulse of France; and as was natural, its influence through the reigns of Louis XII, Francis I, and their successors was on the side of French.

Starting from the general fact that in the first part of the sixteenth century, Latin was used at the University (except in the primary classes), as well as in all the sciences and learned professions, one may observe the steps by which French intruded upon its stately mother, in one province after another.[1]

A plea for the use of French in education was made by the jurist, Jean Bodin, in 1559; but Ramus, boldest of educational innovators, was already using French effectively, though not exclusively, at his college in the Paris University. Yet Latin held its own tenaciously; and, if we turn from education to the Catholic Church, we find the liturgy in Latin even to our own day. As for the Scriptures, Erasmus had argued in favor of putting them before the people: and a few years later Luther followed with his powerful German translation (1522). The next year appeared Lefèvre's translation of the New Testament, approved by the delicate reformer Bishop Briçonnet and even by King Francis, but at once hateful to the Sorbonne. The more radical reformers, like the impetuous Farel, used French in writing and of course in preaching before the year 1541, when Calvin startled the theological rookeries by publishing the French translation of his *Institute*. One may say that from the middle of the century, French became the regular language of the Reformed Church wherever French was spoken; and in order to meet the reformers before the nobility and peo-

[1] For the following sketch I have relied on F. Brunot, "La langue au XVI Siècle," in Vol. III of Petit de Julleville. *Hist. de la langue et de la littérature Française.*

ple, Catholic advocates also resorted to the vernacular when necessary.

Looking to the sciences and professions, we find that, from the opening of the century, oral surgical instruction was given in French, because of the ignorance of the would-be practitioners. A number of French surgical treatises were in use when the great Parè [2] entered on his career of surgical practice and teaching. His instruction was carried on in French, and in French were written his *Methode de traicter les playes faictes par harquebutes* (1545), and his *Traité sur la peste* (1568). Likewise in spite of many conservative protests, treatises upon the art of medicine were largely written in French. Through the latter part of the century, with increasing frequency, French text-books were composed in Arithmetic, Geometry, Astronomy, Cosmography and Geography. Chemistry, or rather alchemy, and physics were followed rather in Latin treatises or translations from the Greek or Latin. But the genial observer of nature, Bernard Palissy, [3] troubled himself as little as possible with the learned tongues. He was born about 1510 and died in prison, a martyr to his religious convictions, about 1589. His observations upon the action of the sea, upon fossils, and his discoveries as to enamels as well as agriculture, he put in an individual and taking French. Naturally, as it were, the fruits of experiment and actual observation were put in the living language, a practice continued by Olivier de Serres, who in his *Théâtre d'agriculture et mesnage des champs* placed the translated precepts of ancient writers along with the results of his own experience.

Histories, usually composed with a moral or political purpose, were for the most part written in French; though unfortunately the chief historian of the second half of the century, De Thou, decided to write his *Historia mei temporis* in Latin. On the other hand Étienne Pasquier, as patriotic as he was erudite, stanchly advocated French, and wrote in that language his quite famous

[2] Post, Chapter XXXII.
[3] Post, Chapter XXXIII.

Recherches de la France. From history one passes over to rhetoric and poetry, where Du Bellay, in the *Défense,* spoken of in the last chapter, expresses in his way thoughts and hopes which men of his time or before him had either expressed or put in practice.

Along with the endeavor to use French for these higher purposes of education, science and literature, went the efforts of many to improve the language, as we have noticed for example with Robert and Henri Estienne, and with the Pléiade. Before them Jacques Dubois had made a sorry attempt to purify his mother tongue, which he regarded as a decayed Latin, by endeavoring to re-Latinize it. But saner and greater men, like the Estiennes, recognized the sovereign authority of usage. Montaigne pointed out that the "beaux espris" raise their mother tongue less by verbal inventions than through the noble uses to which they put the language, giving weight and dignity and further meaning to the words they find in it.[4]

II

From the close of the fifteenth century, the desire for access to the antique literature created a demand for translations; and the work of the translator becomes an important feature of the active-minded life of the time. Many Latin classics were translated, the popular Italian authors, as well as certain Spanish books. The translation of the Greek classics was undertaken, at first from Latin versions, since very few Frenchmen in the early decades of the sixteenth century knew enough Greek to translate directly. This was improved upon in the next generation, when Greek scholarship had made greater progress,— the generation of Henri Estienne, Danès, Dorat, Tournèbe and Ronsard, the generation also of Amyot, the translator of Plutarch's *Lives* and *Morals.*

Translations of the classics corresponded with a desire among tolerably educated people to read them. They implied a tacit recognition by the translator and his audi-

[4] *Essais,* Liv. III, 5.

ence that the French language was fit to express the antique thought. Making them was a quasi self-assertion, a claim of victory for the French tongue. The use of French to translate the round of ancient thought and circumstance enriched the language with new words and concepts, and gave it new flexibility and capacity. Moreover, the reading and enjoyment of the translations meant a more general reception of Greek and Roman thoughts; it meant the assimilation of such, their reapplication under sixteenth century conditions, and their partial transformation in the French temperament and acceptance of life. This is exemplified in the work of Amyot.

Born of lowly parentage, he was endowed with the desire and aptitude for learning, and with the faculty of making his learning acceptable in high places. Somehow he won his education, the best that Paris could give, under the royal professors Toussain and Danès. They recommended him to that tutelary goddess of learning, Marguerite of Navarre, who placed him in a chair of Greek and Latin at the University of Bourges. His translation of the Greek romances *Daphnis and Chloe* and *Theagenes and Chariclea* won the gift of a rich abbey from Francis I. Either the King, or Amyot's affinity with the old author, commanded him to translate Plutarch. The selection was a stroke of fortune or of genius. Blessed with an income and abundant leisure, he set forth on a delightful scholar's pilgrimage to Italy. The year may have been 1547, and he was about thirty-five. He made long stays in Venice and Rome, studying, searching for manuscripts, incidentally winning new patrons. In 1554 he published a translation of Diodorus Siculus, a manuscript of whose work he had discovered. Before then, however, he was living with Plutarch, translating his *Lives,* entering upon his *Morals,* which he translated afterwards. He lived in Plutarch, and Plutarch was to live again in him.

Plutarch was indeed a world, and a world wherein a Frenchman of the sixteenth century could readily find himself at home. For the man who amid the lengthening shadows of the antique world, passed his years between Chaeroneia and Rome, saw his ancient worthies through human cosmopolitan eyes, and presented them in human guise with human attributes; so that they could be admired and understood by humane-minded men in centuries to come. His writings were an encyclopaedia of antique humanity, affording instruction, precept, example, countenance or warning, for any man in any situation.

Homo sum; humani nil a me alienum puto — if Plutarch did not quote this Menander-Terence line, he exemplified it at its very best. For he found nothing alien from him in the human story, that could illumine and illustrate and teach. Amyot became his mirror, his *alter ego,* and yet remained a Frenchman of the sixteenth century. His translation even carried further the universalizing of the encyclopaedia of antique man. He was a true translator, who rendered his original truly. He did not change Plutarch's illustrious ones to sixteenth century Frenchmen, nor travesty the ancient world. But with penetrating sympathy he softened recalcitrant terms and in apt French phrase made the old names and incidents and situations live again.

This was necessarily a modernizing and universalizing. It was a presentation of Plutarch's heroes not as Frenchmen, but in such way that Frenchmen could understand them, and see the underlying human identity between Greeks and Romans and themselves. These personages did not cease to be Greeks and Romans because they were made to show palpably the same traits which Frenchmen possessed, by virtue of a common humanity. Nor did their setting cease to be antique because retouched with the likenesses or analogies pervading human circumstance.

Even here the splendid result was not Plutarch's alone — not alone the work of the man of Chaeroneia. It was also the product of Amyot's understanding of life, and of the capacities of the French language and Amyot's faculty of managing and expanding it so as to render the antique incidents and thoughts. Thus these translations marked Amyot's French assimilation and presentation of Plutarch's world, and became an expression of the translator's mind.

Amyot knew that he was presenting the universal human which was Plutarch. The expressions of his lengthy prefatory " aux lecteurs " are quite clear. Plutarch is history, and " l'histoire est à la verité le tresor de la vie humaine." It is the great school —" une regle et instruction certaine, qui par examples du passé nous enseigne à juger du present, et à prevoir l'advenir, à fin que nous sçachions ce que nous devons suyvre ou appeter, et qu'il nous faut fuir et eviter." As in a picture, it sets before our eyes

" les choses dignes de memoire, qu'anciennement ont faictes les puissants peuples, les roys, et princes magnanimes, les sages gouverneurs, et vaillans capitaines, et personnes marquées de quelque notable qualité, nous representant les moeurs des nations estrangeres, les loix et coustumes anciennes, les desseings des hommes particuliers, leurs conseils et enterprises, les moyens qu'ilz ont tenus pour parvenir, et leurs deportemens, quand ils sont parvenus aux plus hauts, on bien qu'ilz ont esté dejettez au plus bas degrez de la fortune."

The man who has read these histories will encounter no chance of peace or war in which he will not find their counsel apt and prudent, to guide his choice and action, moderate his elation in prosperity and sustain him in adversity. History with its examples is a better teacher than books of moral philosophy with their precepts.[5]

" Brief . . . la lecture des histoires est une eschole de prudence, que l'homme se forme en son entendement, en considerant meurement l'estat du monde qui a esté par le passé, et observant diligemment par quelles loix, quelles moeurs et quelle discipline, les empires, royaumes et seigneuries se sont jadis premierement establies, et depuis maintenues et grandies, ou au contraire changées, diminuées et perdues."

Such is history's obvious function; and most necessary for princes and people in high station, giving them in-

[5] The last thought is in Aquinas's *Summa,* and so is doubtless Aristotelian.

struction without flattery, which those they live with will not give them. Beyond this, what pleasure does it give us, moving with fear and hope and joy, through pains and dangers not our own! Happiness and wonder come upon us as we view in this eloquent picture "les cas humains representez au vif, et les variables accidens que le vieillesse du temps a produits dès et depuis l'origine du monde." A spectacle indeed, amazing and most intimate as well: *les cas humains,* the human incidents, which might have been and still may be ours: indeed which certainly are ours as well as theirs on whom they fell; for nothing that is human is not ours.

We may leave our Amyot with his Plutarch and ours. In him Plutarch lived again, delighting and expanding the natures of Frenchmen and Englishmen through generations. Montaigne seems to have become Montaigne through Amyot; from North's English version of him spring Shakespeare's *Coriolanus, Julius Caesar, Anthony and Cleopatra.* The fortunes of his book were wonderful; his own were prosperous and troubled. He was the preceptor of two princes, who became Charles IX and Henri III of France. He was made grand almoner of France, and bishop of Auxerre. Troubles came upon him from the clergy of his diocese. He was in danger of assassination; he may have been excommunicated; at least he was compelled to beg for absolution. He died in 1593 eighty years old, — loved by future generations.

III

How a French mind — that of a publicist —could make use of antique (and also mediaeval!) thought, and also express itself with vigor and originality, is shown in Jean Bodin, a native of Angers, born in 1530 and dying in 1596. Although living through the bitterest periods of the Wars of Religion, he rose above the atmosphere of strife, and viewed human institutions with admirable intelligence — sometimes.[6] His *Six livres de la Republique*

[6] "Jean Bodin est un bon autheur de nostre temps, et accompagné de

appeared in 1576. Their purpose was to bring the experience of mankind, shown by the histories of ancient and modern peoples, to bear upon the questions of the nature of the State and the best forms of government and law. Bodin would apply the argument of facts, of universal experience. "La philosophie mourrait d'inanition au milieu de ses preceptes, si elle ne les vivifiait par l'historie," he says in words recalling Amyot. Being a magistrate and jurist, he would also find in history, the principles of jurisprudence. For himself, he will decide his main problem in favor of a law-abiding but absolute hereditary monarchy.

The *Republique* was the fruit of enormous reading and assembling of evidence; its matter was well ordered to the purpose of the author's arguments. All parts of the organism of the State were presented more largely and systematically than by any previous writer, and so the sum of this great matter was laid before the reading French public. The work was translated at once into Latin, that it might reach an international audience. Ten years before, Bodin had composed in Latin a preliminary, but weighty work, entitled: *Methodus ad facilem historiarum cognitionem.*

The details of Bodin's argument are beyond the present purpose. Yet it is interesting to observe how his vigorous mind moved with apparent independence and at the same time was enthralled by its inheritance and environment. Bodin had read Plato's *Republic* and had studied the *Politics* of Aristotle. Yet in his conception of the State, he agrees with neither. For he conceives the State to consist in the control of a number of *ménages,* (households), and of that which is common to them (qui leur est commun), by the sovereign power. He reasons from the analogy of the family, which consists in the control by its head of what is common to its members.

Besides his encyclopaedic marshalling of evidence, perhaps his most striking contribution to a knowledge of the

beaucoup plus de jugement que la tourbe des escrivailleurs de son siècle, et merite qu'on le juge et considere." Montaigne, *Essais,* II, XXXII.

factors of the human story was his recognition of the effect of climate upon racial development, of the rôle of environment in the advance or retrogression of the faculties and fortunes of a people. In this and in other matters,[7] he was the forerunner of later publicists, above all of Montesquieu.

So Bodin could think with originality, handle masterfully the ancient thought, and accept or depart from it, for better or worse, according to the requirements of his argument. But,— and the " but " is a very large one — he had other sides. He was held by the current superstitions of his time, and even by its cruelty. He believed in sorcery, and wrote a book entitled *Démonomanie des Sorciers*. Again he supported himself upon experience! As a magistrate, he had conducted trials, and knew the facts, which had been judicially proved! He would stand by the decisions of tribunals, which condemned witch or sorcerer upon the facts! Alas! these facts were but a proof that this large-minded man was held by the superstitions of his own time, and of the prior centuries, including antiquity. His considerations upon the effect of climates were made half foolish by his acceptance of astrology, of planetary influence, beliefs which had renewed their vigor with the revival of antique letters! [8]

IV

The Essays of Montaigne [9] are the most striking example of the emergence of an ensemble of personal opinion, and still more personal expression, from its

[7] As in his protest against slavery, and his philosophic approval of religious toleration.

[8] One cannot blame Bodin. The great surgeon Ambroise Parè accepted sorcery on the same grounds as he. Belief in it was practically universal: only Montaigne did not accept the evidence. Cf. post, Chapter XXXII.

[9] *Les Essais de Montaigne* by Motheau and Jouast in seven small valumes (Paris, 1886), is a pleasant and convenient edition. It follows the text of 1588, and gives the additions of 1595,— a discrimination required by the intelligent reader. One need not refer to the enormous literature upon Montaigne. I have found Pierre Villey very useful: *Les Sources et l'evolution des Essais de Montaigne,* 2 vols. (Paris, 1908); Montaigne, *Textes choisis,* etc., (Bib. Française), Paris, 1912.

classical matrix. In them a French personality reached self-expression through assimilation and application of classical material, as well as through consideration of its own humanity and the ways of humanity at large. Yet this expression of a French personality does not cease to represent the humane moralizings of the later classical spirit. As Seneca was a moralist in his fashion and Plutarch in his, so was Montaigne in a manner which had drawn upon them both.

The classics did not make this close scrutinizer of life, opinion and belief; but they gave him matter for his scrutiny, and disciplinary instruction throughout the process. The *Essays* show the final stages of Montaigne's evolution, the stages of his final self-expression. They are the history of the man during the last twenty years of his life.

With the articulate development of his opinions, the expression of them, to wit, the Essay, takes form. It ceases to be a fagot of borrowed instances or opinions; and becomes a personal composition; cited instances and opinions are illustrations.

A virtuoso in egotism, Montaigne was an incomparable scrutinizer of himself. Self-scrutiny may have various motives and draw toward different ends; it may become the agent of intense, even inspired, purpose. In Montaigne it never won élan. But it possessed a large faculty of, as it were, reciprocal generalization, bringing this scrutinizer's consideration of the experience of mankind to bear upon his knowledge of himself, and in return presenting his self-knowledge in its universal bearing upon the knowledge of man.

The way in which Montaigne was reared and educated confirmed his natural disposition. Through honorable exertions his family had become wealthy and respected in Bordeaux. Within a generation or two an estate in the neighborhood had been acquired. Montaigne's father was a prudent man of affairs, and as a gentleman followed the profession of arms. He brought his son up carefully, perhaps too tenderly, certainly in a way to aggravate his physical and intellectual sensitiveness. The father was a Catholic; his wife, Montaigne's mother, is said to have been a Protestant and indeed a Jewess. At all events, the home atmosphere was one of religious tolerance. The boy, who was born in 1533, was taught Latin as his mother tongue, was sent to school and college, and in his early teens put to study law at Toulouse. Finishing his legal studies at the age of twenty-one, he was made a magistrate and, in a little while, counselor to the Parlement of Bordeaux. He retained this office till 1570, when, his father having died, he retired to his estate. He was already married and a father. In 1580 he published the first two books of his *Essays,* and travelled in Germany and Italy. While absent he was elected mayor of Bordeaux, an honorable position which he hesitatingly accepted. He was re-elected two years later. He would seem to have discharged this office satisfactorily, though without zeal, keeping away from the city when the plague raged there. Politically, through the difficult times in which he lived, Montaigne avoided partisanship. He was a moderate royalist, a conservative who distrusted change. He enjoyed health, but seems to have been lazy, and averse to severe physical exertions or prolonged mental application. At all events he says so. He published the third book of his *Essays* in 1588, and in 1592 he died. The *Essays* brought wide repute to this man of position, whose gentility nevertheless was not so ancient as to have lost its self-consciousness. Disliking tedious forms and ceremonies, he did not forget that he was Michel, Sieur de Montaigne, whose father had been mayor of Bordeaux, and who himself once held that office as the successor of one Marechal de France and the predecessor of another. For the rest, his temperament and mentality, as well as his opinions, disclose themselves in his *Essays*, which became an examination and a mirror of himself.

Of all sixteenth century Frenchmen, Montaigne most surely made a personal path through the teachings of antiquity, the practical teachings of its later phases of accumulated precept and blended moralizing philosophies. His affinities were with the late pagan centuries which immediately preceded and followed the opening of the Christian era, and were so practically or ethically concerned with human conduct and vicissitudes. Within this sphere, Montaigne's interest and curiosity appear universal; nothing that was human failed to prick him. But his mental activity does not reach beyond this round of domestic consideration; it never addresses itself to the heights of inhuman knowledge, nor is touched by cosmic problems or any matter of physics or natural science. He had not the detached interest of a Democritus, a Plato or an Aristotle in the knowledge which does not bear directly upon human life. His mental scope and entire self-expression lie within the sphere of humanism.

Accordingly it goes without saying that in his studies he had not mastered the successive systems of Greek philosophy, austere and difficult in their aloofness. He did not know the theories of early Eleatics and Atomists; nor had he penetrated the thought of Plato, having neither the temper nor the application. Yet in his later years he read the *Dialogues* in Ficino's Latin translation; for he was fascinated by the personality of Socrates, whose sayings he gathered also from Xenophon's *Memorabilia.* As for Aristotle, Montaigne had spent scant hours in his perusal. Epicureanism he had studied in Lucretius, and Stoicism mainly in Seneca. But he vitally mastered whatever he learned, absorbing the cosmopolitan tempers and blended philosophic moralizings of Cicero and Virgil, Horace and Seneca and Plutarch. He read and reread and never ceased to read the last, the *Illustrious Lives* and the *Morals* or philosophic pamphlets, all in the incomparable translations of Amyot, to whom he bears so warm a testimony of gratitude and admiration at the beginning of the fourth essay of his second book.

Montaigne also read widely in the Latin, French and Italian writers of his own and the preceding generations. They promoted the development of his sixteenth century personality; and helped him to lay an independent path through the opinions of the ancients. His own judgments are evolved as he proceeds through Stoicism and Epicureanism; then he is pricked by the Scepticism of Pyrrho. This also was a phase through which he passed on to the gentler questionings of the later Academy, which did not preclude the attainment of sufficiently pragmatic and positive opinions. Horace comes to his aid; and he expands the sinews of his moral nature with the experience and fortitude of Plutarch's men and the varied philosophic suggestions of Plutarch's moral and philosophic pamphlets. In the course of these studies and lucubrations, he turns from Cato, the finished Stoic, to Socrates, the ideal sage.

Attracted at the first by Stoicism, Montaigne can say: "La vertu ne veut estre suyvie que pour elle mesme; et si on emprunte parfois son masque pour autre occasion, elle nous l'arrache aussitost du visage." He eventually wearied of Stoicism, as the antique world wearied of it. One becomes ennuied with self-reliance and steeling oneself against life's trials and last catastrophe: one is bored with reading about Cato and learning how to die. An early Essay, composed in 1572 when Montaigne was, as he says in it, thirty-nine years old, bears the title: *Que philosopher c'est apprendre a mourir,* a tedious antique sentiment, which fortunately had not been exemplified either in the philosophy or the life of the ancient world. Montaigne takes it from Cicero. Study and contemplation serve this end of severing the soul from the body, and teaching us how to die. All are agreed that happiness is our aim, though men differ as to the means. We cannot be content, however, with the fear of death before our eyes; and so philosophies seek to instruct us to despise it.

In some such way, none too clearly, Montaigne chooses to moralize at the beginning of this Essay. He draws the conclusion: "Le but de nostre carrière c'est la mort: c'est l'object necessaire de nostre visée; si elle nous effraye, comme est il possible d'aller un pas avant sans fiebre? Le remede du vulgarire, c'est de n'y penser pas.

Mais de quelle brutale stupidité luy peut venir un si grossier aveuglement?" As the essay proceeds, the naturalness of death is made to appear; and a late addition points to the opinion that life and death are indifferent.

Naturally, Montaigne was more readily influenced by what he read in the first years of his retirement than when he had pondered longer upon the relative invalidity of human opinion. His earlier essays consist rather of excerpted incidents and sentiments illustrating some topic in his mind. Later he will not so quickly veer his helm to puffs of suggestion; his essays will embody his own thoughts more organically, and those thoughts have become more penetrating. He decided to make less of death: it ceased to be the *but* or final end, and becomes merely the *bout* or terminus, of life. To live happily, rather than to die happily is the great matter: "A mon advis, c'est 'le vivre heureusement,' non, comme disoit Antisthenes, 'le mourir heureusement,' qui faict l'humaine felicité." [10]

It may be that stupid peasants follow the better way, in bothering so little about their latter end. Preparation for death has tormented men more than the experience. "Nous troublons la vie par le soing de la mort; et la mort, par le soing de la vie: l'une nous ennuye; l'autre nous effraye. Ce n'est pas contre la mort que nous nous preparons, c'est chose trop momentanée; un quart d'heure de passion, sans consequance, sans nuisance, ne merite pas des praeceptes particuliers." [11]

Montaigne was not one utterly to abandon his earlier ways of thinking. Virtue might seem the better part of pleasure to him even in his last years.[12] He was always Epicurean. In the essay *De la Solitude,* moderate Stoicism and Epicureanism mingle in a tempered Horatian view of life. One needs the daily pleasures and occupations, but should not entangle one's liberty. "Il fault avoir femmes, enfants, biens, et surtout de la

[10] III, II, a passage subsequent to the edition of 1588.
[11] III, XII, about the middle of the Essay.
[12] See a passage appearing only in the 1595 edition, inserted in I, XIX; (pp. 110–111 in T. I. of Motheau and Jouast's edition).

santé, qui peult; mais non pas s'y attacher en maniere que nostre heur en despende: il se fault reserver une arriere boutique, toute nostre, toute franche, en laquelle nous establissions nostre vraye liberté et principal retraicte et solitude."

Although a man of ready social gifts as well as inclinations, Montaigne felt the value of solitude, especially for one who, having lived much in the world, would turn to that fine Horatian goal of belonging entirely to oneself: "La plus grande chose du monde, c'est de scavoir estre à soy." It is thus that one best may husband the pleasures that remain,— the intellectual most assuredly, but also "les commoditez corporelles," which nature bids us cherish. "J'estime pareille injustice prendre à contrecoeur les voluptez naturelles, que di les prendre trop à coeur." One should not belittle the element of pleasure: — to what other end do we pursue the Muses? Whoever thinks that this is to debase their office, "ne scait pas, comme moy, combien vault le plaisir, le jeu, et le passetemps." But self-content through mental pleasures and bodily comforts is not for any fool! Self may be found an empty refuge. "Retirez vous en vous; mais preparez vous premierement de vous y recevoir."

Montaigne was also as one quite unafraid, ready to confront any opinion with doubt and inquiry as to its validity. His was no metaphysical, but very practical scepticism touching the value of human judgments. Human ignorance and prejudice impressed him. Whatever men are wont to do and believe, they hold as incontrovertible and necessary for the welfare of man. It is easy to show that this opinion is unfounded. The habit of approach through doubting inquiry became part of Montaigne's mentality. For a period he cultivated scepticism by pursuing the reasonings of Pyrrho and other well-instructed doubters. His famous *Apologie de Raimond Sebond* (II, XII) discusses at rather interminable length the conflicting opinions of philosophers, and the variances and oppositions among human customs and convictions. It concludes that human reason is not to be relied on, nor can men penetrate the changing phantasmagoria surrounding them, or attain stable truth.

Should one think of Montaigne as passing through some sort of sceptical storm at any time? Did he seek partial shelter from it in some doctrine of practical probability, such as he might find in the teachings of the later Platonic Academy? He is so apt to utter whatever enters his mind, that generalizations as to his more abiding opinions and their sequence are hazardous. One may remember his own words: "touts jugemens en gros sont lasches et imparfaicts." Yet temperamental conservatism, the habit of weighing probabilities, and the honesty of his nature which knew its unfitness for the building of lofty certitudes, seem to have continued to give him some practical reliance on the instincts of his nature and the customary acceptances of his time. He would have been the last man to claim consistency for his temperate and partial convictions. His own reason, peccable as he recognized it to be, should also guide him always; restrain him, on the one hand, from following hurtful impulses, and on the other from accepting stupidly cruel practices and credences. So he condemned judicial torture, and rejected sorcery and witchcraft as unreasonable and unproved.

That Montaigne recognized himself as a bundle of inconsistencies, may be read where one will in his *Essays,* for example in the first of the second book, "De l'Inconstance de nos actions." Likewise his ideas and opinions; for they were but himself. The *Essays* as they expressed his opinions, were just as much an expression of himself, a study of himself, a mirror of himself. He very consciously recognized them as such; and declared many times that in them he intended above all to paint and portray himself, his "humeurs et opinions." Thus expressing himself for others, he painted himself more clearly for himself, greatly to his own benefit and instruction. He said late in life: "Je n'ay pas plus faict mon livre que mon livre m'a faict, livre consubstantiel à son autheur."

He had arrived at this idea and intention before 1580, when he published the first two books, and wrote his memorable preface to the reader. That spoke the truth in opening with the words: " C'est icy un livre de bonne foy, lecteur." But it may have had its deprecatory affectation in asserting that the book was intended for the use of his relatives and friends. Doubtless it spoke the truth again, or meant to, in saying that the author wished to disclose himself without artifice or veil. And of a surety the truth and kernel of the preface was in the words: " C'est moy que je peins."

The idea of portraying himself had taken form gradually with Montaigne; and only gradually was it clothed upon with the further idea of painting himself as the mirror of men. Autobiography was rife in the late sixteenth century. Montluc, D'Aubigny, had painted, had *narrated* themselves in their striking acts and sufferings. Montaigne's life did not afford such. It was always absorbed in its daily incident and experience, its observation and study, in its penetrating consideration of itself. All this would yield the material of self-portrayal. At first his tendency is to give the rather trivial outer incident or experience; then he goes deeper, painting the more inner Montaigne, consisting of thoughts and knowledge and opinions. " Je ne puis tenir registre de ma vie par mes actions . . . je le tiens par mes fantasies." He will make this psychological portraiture as penetrating and complete as possible. " Ce ne sont mes gestes que j'escris, c'est mon essence."

This mirror of self may be turned upon the nature and limitations of man: and justifiably; for I am the measure of all men. The idea that the individual exemplifies universal human quality seems to rationalize itself through one of the few bits of metaphysics to be found in the *Essays*. Montaigne uses the scholastic Aristotelian conception of the form or species contained in each individual, which is representative of the universal genus, in this case, man. Thus he argues: I present in my book a common, ordinary life; but it is all one: the whole matter of moral philosophy can be hung on such a life as well as on one of richer substance: " chasque homme porte la forme entiere de l'humaine condition." Montaigne wrote these words before 1588, and subsequently attached this further comment: " Les aucteurs se communiquent au peuple par quelque marque special et estrangiere; moy, le premier, *par mon estre universel;* comme Michel de Montaigne, non comme grammairien, ou poëte, ou jurisconsult."

Metaphysics was not his métier; and naturally he did not keep meticulously to his conception of *forme.* Yet he keeps near enough to it to preserve and simplify its illustrative value. It becomes, with him, the abiding character or nature within each individual. Those, says he substantially, further on in the same essay, who have essayed the rôle of reformers in my time, reform only the surface vices; " ceulx de l'essence," they do not trouble. Indeed the reform of these outer casual vices may pander to the satisfaction of vices " naturels, consubstantiels et intestins." No one who will listen to himself will fail to discover " en soy une forme sienne, une forme maistresse," which fights against the passions that are contrary to him. For myself, I am not commonly shaken by such shocks, and find myself always in my place, like a heavy body. " Mes desbauches ne m'emportent pas fort loing." The common trouble with men is that their retreat itself is befouled; the *idea* of their amendment is defaced, their penitence as faulty as their sin. " For myself," continues Montaigne one or two pages further on, " I can condemn and mislike *ma forme universelle,* et supplier Dieu pour mon entiere reformation, et pour l'excuse de ma foiblesse naturelle."

In the course of another thoughtful essay, Montaigne speaks of peculiar and retiring natures — " naturels particuliers, retirez et internes." *Ma forme essentielle,* on the contrary, is communicative and social. The phrase here means evidently Montaigne's underlying and relatively abiding nature. He also uses the word itself, nature, and in various senses, just as we do. This vaguely changeable, but reassuring, thought underlies his later more positive philosophy of life. He has adopted this ancient maxim, that we cannot err in following nature, and that the " souverain precepte, c'est de ' Se conformer à elle.' "

Although the illustrative value of the author and his knowledge of himself are universalized in these later essays, the intimate self-portrayal does not cease. Rather the author and his book — mon livre et moy — become more intimately in and of each other. All the world will recognize each in the other. The discussion of broad human topics is ever and anon brought back to the author through personal statements, which put Montaigne again visibly upon the stage. This is all illustrated by the closing essay of the third book, upon *Experience*. In this penetrating consideration of life, if anywhere, may be found the author's own conclusions,— his conclusions as to the best way of life, according to Nature.

The essay is intricate. Beginning with reflecting on man's natural desire for knowledge, it notes the many forms of reason, and the like diversity of experience — on what shall one lay hold? Philosophy is a maze; another is the multiplicity of law: comment upon comment, adding to obscurity; precedent upon precedent, obstructing justice. " I study myself more than any other subject: 'tis my metaphysics, 'tis my physics. . . . In this monstrous maze — en cette université — I let myself ignorantly and negligently be fashioned on the general law of the world. I shall know it well enough when I feel it; my knowledge will not make it change its course. . . . Philosophers rightly refer us to Nature's rules . . . but they falsify and sophisticate them. . . . The more simply one commits oneself to nature, the more wisely he commits himself. . . . From the experience I have of myself, I find enough to make me wise, were I a good scholar."

Through pages which follow, Montaigne has much to say of the physicians' ignorant interference with nature's ways, a favorite theme with him. As for his own diet, he has found that whatever disagrees with his palate, disagrees with his body. "Je n'ay jamais receu nuisance d'action qui m'eust esté bien plaisante." Moreover, as to bodily ills,—"il fault apprendre à souffrir ce qu'on ne peult eviter."

If modern readers have found Montaigne commonplace, it is because they have begun at the beginning and not at the end of the *Essays*. The third book contains the author's most penetrating and original consideration of life; and the concluding pages of its last essay (on which we continue to draw) are of Montaigne's very best. The thought of following nature underlies them. Elsewhere Montaigne has shown Socrates, antiquity's most complete sage, educing from his own nature through simple truth, his admirable way of life — not like Cato, "monté sur ses grands chevaux," but "d'un pas mol et ordinaire," delivering to us the most useful discourses, and addressing himself either to death or to the thorny traverses of life. Now Montaigne will speak directly, and give the results of his own observation.

"Nature has seen to it as a mother that the actions which she has enjoined for our needs, are also pleasurable; she invites us to them not only through our reason, but through our appetite; it is injustice to corrupt her rules. When I see Caesar and Alexander in the thick of their enterprises openly enjoying humane and corporal pleasures, I do not say that they slacken, but strengthen, their minds." "We are great fools" continues Montaigne in a passage inserted later,

> "'He has passed his life in idleness' we say: 'I have done nothing to-day.' What! have you not lived? That is not only the fundamental, but the noblest of your occupations. You would have shown what you could do, had great affairs been given to your charge? If you have known how to consider and manage your life, you have done the greatest of all. Nature has no need of fortune pour se montrer et exploicter. Avez vous su composer vos moeurs? Vous avez bien plus fait que celui qui a composé ses livres. Avez vous su prendre du repos? Vous avez plus fait que celui qui a pris des empires et des villes."

Le grand et glorieux chef d'oeuvre de l'homme, c'est vivre à propos,—

that is, to live humanly as a man should; all other matters, reigning, piling up treasure, are the merest accessories. I am pleased to see a general, at the foot of a breach which he is about to attack, give himself over altogether to his dinner with his friends; or to see Brutus, with heaven and earth conspiring against him and the liberty of Rome, snatch some hours of the night to devote to his abridgement of Polybius. It is for little souls, buried in the weight of affairs, to know not how to lay aside and take them up again.

O fortes, pejoraque passi
Mecum saepe viri! nunc vino pellite curas:
Cras ingens iterabimus aequor."

This, with plenty of antique suggestion, is Montaigne, either in his own words, or briefly translated, even to the summing up of his argument with his apt Horatian lines. And after further illustrations, he observes how men deceive themselves, failing to recognize how much easier are extremes than the broad middle path.

"The greatnesse of the minde is not so much to drawe up and hale forward, as to know how to range, direct and circumscribe itselfe. It holdeth for great whatsoever is sufficient. And sheweth her height in loving meane things better than eminent. There is nothing so goodly, so faire and so lawfull as to play the man well and duely; nor science so hard and difficult, as to know how to live this life well. And of all infirmities we have, the most savage is to despise our being." [13]

A little further on, he continues: "J'ordonne à mon âme de regarder et la douleur et la volupté, de vue pareillement réglée, et pareillement ferme; mais gaiement l'une, l'autre sévèrement. . . . Le voir sainement les biens tire après soi le voir sainement les maux" — a sane view of the good things of life brings a sane view of the evil.

[13] Florio's translation.

Montaigne says he has a way and a vocabulary of his own; he " passes the time " when it is bad, and holds to it when it is pleasant. Nature has put into our hands our time so well equipped — " garnie de telles circonstances et si favorables "— that it is our fault if it hangs heavy or escapes us unused. There is husbandry in life's enjoyment, especially in making the most of it when our days have become few.

He continues with a subtle passage in which he explains that he does not merely sense the sweetness of content and prosperity, as others do; he intellectualizes his feelings, associates his mind with his sensations, but does not entangle it in them. His mind (âme) amplifies its good fortune, and measures its indebtedness to God; with its conscience in repose and the body fulfilling natural and pleasant functions, it experiences a great calm. " As for me, then, I love life, and cultivate it just as it has pleased God to bestow it on us," including the natural pleasures of the senses. " J'accepte de bon coeur, et reconnaissant, ce que nature a fait pour moi. . . . On fait tort à ce grand et tout puissant Donneur, de refuser son don, l'annuler et desfigurer. Tout bon, il a fait tout bon: *omnia, quae secundum naturam sunt, aestimatione digna sunt.*

" Des opinions de la philosophie, j'embrasse plus volontiers celles qui sont les plus solides, c'est à dire les plus humaines et nostres. . . . Socrates . . . prise, comme il doit, la volupté corporelle; mais il préfère celle de l'esprit, comme ayant plus de force, de constance, de facilité, de varieté, de dignité. Cette-ci ne va seulement seule, selon lui (il n'est pas si fantastique), mais seulement première; pour lui, la tempérance est moderatrix, non adversaire des voluptés. Nature est un doux guide, mais non pas plus doux que prudent et juste." Montaigne would follow her track, simply and without sophistry, and make no divorce among the acts which her harmony has joined together. It is folly to praise the soul and despise the body; they are a joint gift from God. Rarely are men's fantasies worth a good ragout,— except for " ces ames vénérables élevées par ardeur de dévotion et religion à une constante . . . meditation des choses divines . . . c'est une étude privilégé. Entre nous, ce sont choses que j'ai toujours vues de singulier accord: les opinions supercélestes et les moeurs souterraines."

So Montaigne ends his paragraph with a note of sarcasm, which he does not leave unsounded as he closes his essay. He would show that there is time to spare for everything. "Die zeit ist unendlich lang," Goethe will say after him. It is folly to try to lift oneself out of human nature. "Ces humeurs transcendantes m'effraient, comme les lieux hautains et inaccessibles. . . . C'est une absolue perfection, et comme divine, de savoir jouir loyalement de son être. Nous cherchons d'autres conditions, pour n'entendre [from not understanding] l'usage des nôtres, et sortons hors de nous pour ne savoir [from not knowing] quel il y fait"— even when mounted on stilts we still walk upon our legs, and though placed on the highest throne in all the world, we sit upon what nature has given us. "Les plus belles vies sont, à mon gré, celles qui se rangent au modèle commun et humain, avec ordre, mais sans miracle, sans extravagance. Or, la vieillesse a un peu besoin d'être traitée plus tendrement. Recommandons-la à ce Dieu protecteur de santé et de sagesse, mais gaie et sociale:

> Frui paratis et valido mihi,
> Latoe, dones, et, precor, integra
> Cum mente; nec turpem senectam
> Degere, nec cithara carentem.

So he ends with a sentiment of Socrates and a verse from Horace.

Of all sixteenth century Frenchmen,— except Henry IV! — Montaigne is still the most universally read or considered, and written about. In his self-deprecation, he would not have claimed membership in the company of "les belles âmes . . . âmes universelles, ouvertes, et prestes à tout; si non instruictes, au moins instruisables." In contrast with such he points to his own ignorance and ineptitude; and somewhat further on in this essay (II,

XVII), suggests that his constant preoccupation with the antique temper, and those " riches âmes du temps passé," disgusts him with himself and his contemporaries. Yet there he is, in fact, if not the most " instruict," at all events the most " instruisable " mind of his epoch. How ceaseless has been his influence, how very close and personal with so many men! Reading Bacon's *Essays,* we see the mark of Montaigne; stepping on briskly through the centuries, we find our own Emerson soaked with his manner.

The purpose of these few pages has been to distinguish his place in the intellectual development of sixteenth century France. Incidents and characteristic details of his thought and disposition have been passed over. No attempt has been made to give a close and intimate picture of one who has proved just as curiously interesting to later generations as he was to himself. One may well refrain from attempting that which has been essayed time and again, and has been achieved by only one man, Montaigne himself. None can rival Montaigne in drawing Montaigne. It is irksome to string excerpt upon excerpt from one so well known; and to restate him is to lose his flavor.

Of course he is not always the same Montaigne; in which respect he is akin to all of us. We recognize him in his universal aspect, as a type of the wingless intelligence. His is a constant analytical consideration of life, with the habit of accepting what seemed the better part — but which was not quite the best! He even recognized some things (like the most honorable service of the public) as beyond his energies. If the complete art of life, life's full content and wisdom, lies in action as well as thought, Montaigne did not achieve it wholly.

Undoubtedly good reason for the impression which he has made upon all the generations after him, lies in the independence and originality of his consideration of life, unequalled, even unrivalled, in his time. This joins with the fact that he was such a wonderful writer, so easy, so affable, so picturesque. Hence an individuality, nay a personality, is presented in a book, engagingly, instructively, and in such way as to make plain for every reader the practical applicable lessons of its experiences and opinions. The *Essays* of Montaigne have been a perennial source of the wisdom of life. Their persuasive reason and convincing charm helped to impress a rational urbanity upon French methods of expression. The *Essays* became part of the French mind, a formative element in the French genius.

CHAPTER XVI

RAMUS

BEFORE speaking of the phase of sixteenth century progress and expression exemplified in the reformed religion of Calvin, a brief reference should be made to the work of intellectual and educational reform attempted by a certain independent and combative Pierre de la Ramée, commonly called Ramus.[1] He also belonged to the reformed religion, and sealed his faith, willy nilly, in the massacre of St. Bartholomew's. An Elizabethan playwright made his death the subject of a tragedy.

His is the story of one born in squalor, with an unquenchable desire for knowledge. At an incredible early age, he went in search of it in Paris, and continued resolute (this child!), and at the alleged age of twelve, in the year 1527, he became the servant of a rich student at the college of Navarre. He tried to work for his master by day and study for himself at night, till his eyes gave way. His spirit from the first was revolutionary. One of his early exasperations was at the current method of teaching logic and practicing it as a boisterous game of tripping up. He realized the uselessness of his years devoted to Aristotelian scholasticism, especially to the study of the *Organon*. His good angel led him to Plato, and he became fascinated with the Socratic method of reaching and testing truth. It occurred to him to apply it to the scholastic Aristotelian dialectic. With what result he made manifest when, in 1536, he sustained for an academic day against all comers the argument of his Master of Arts thesis *Quaecumque ab Aristotele dicta essent, commentitia esse,* that the works

[1] For Ramus, see Charles Waddington, *Ramus, sa vie, ses ecrits* etc. (Paris, 1855), (from whom I have chiefly drawn), F. P. Graves, *Peter Ramus and the Educational Reformation of the Sixteenth Century* (New York, 1912).

ascribed to Aristotle were not his, and were, moreover, full of error. This was to attack the scaffolding, if not the entire structure, of theology; and the noise of the conflict echoed through the universities, as far as Italy.

Although looked upon askance by the authorities, Ramus obtained an opportunity to teach in one of the colleges. Before long his lecture room was thronged, and to the end of his career he continued the most popular and effective of university lecturers. A classical scholar and lover of letters, French as well as classical, he introduced into his lectures apt illustrations from literature and life. His mind was throbbing with desire to cast off the futilities of his education, and in the place of smoke and noise, gain the verities and realities of knowledge. He pursued this aim in all branches of education, branches of educational reform, as they became with him.

In 1543 he published an elementary text book of logic, written in clear and excellent Latin, *Dialecticae partitiones,* and the same year his *Aristotelicae Animadversiones,* a work of a different sort. In that, with a violence afterward regretted, he accused Aristotle of sophistry, and reviled his followers for their barbaric Latin and sterile disputations. Naturally this polemic brought trouble to its author. The Sorbonne held Aristotle to be the orthodox philosopher *par excellence;* his philosophy was inseparably interlaced with the saving dogmas of the Church. To attack one was to question the other. The Sorbonne of the sixteenth century was in a state of such excited conservatism, that the questioning of any accepted way of thinking, or the opening of any new avenue of knowledge, appeared fraught with peril; a frame of mind not confined either to the Sorbonne or the sixteenth century. Those sixteenth century theologians were prone to impute " Lutheranism " or like baneful tendencies (often with reason) to all innovating scholars. They were more sensitive as to Aristotle than Thomas Aquinas or Albertus Magnus had been, who could admit that he was but a man, and might err. In the case of Ramus, the Sorbonne was right; for the same impulse for verity which drove him against logical conventions, alienated him from the Church, along with the better part of contemporary French scholarship.

The heads of the University were aroused. Process was instituted against the books, and against their author for corrupting the youth and disrupting authority. Such was the noise that Francis himself ordered the matter to be argued before his royal self and five arbiters, two appointed by each of the parties, and one by the King. The topics were as formal and academic as those disputed on about the year 1000 before the Emperor Otto II, by Gerbert, the future pope, and his German opponent Otric.[2] Ramus and his antagonist, each provided with a Greek Aristotle, disputed as to the object and divisions of logic, and whether a treatise on dialectic should start from a definition of the subject. The argument wound on, and Ramus finally obtained such damaging admissions from his enemy and had him so cleverly on the hip, that the three hostile arbitrators adjourned the court, and ordered the affair reargued from the beginning, with those admissions nullified. Ramus objected, but the three, having the King's authority behind them, condemned the book, Ramus's two friends registering their protest in favor of the freedom of philosophical discussion! The King issued a long sentence of condemnation, declaring that the said Ramus had been found *temeraire, arrogant et impudent d'avoir reprouvue et condamné le train et art de logicque receu de toutes nations.*[3] All men were forbidden to buy or sell or read either of the books, and the university authorities made an orgie of bonfires with them, regretting only that the author had not been condemned to the galleys.

Thus the aroused established system defended itself against innovation. But in a year or two, a pestilence having in the meanwhile scattered the university, one of its colleges, the *Collège de Presles,* invited the able innovator to re-establish its membership and add to its

[2] See *The Mediaeval Mind,* I, p. 291, sqq.
[3] The whole text is given in Waddington, *Ramus,* pp. 49–52.

prestige. Ramus became its head, and also gained the protection of the new King, Henry II, through the favor of the powerful Cardinal of Guise (later Cardinal of Lorraine) who had been a student with him at the college of Navarre. At the instance of this mighty friend — who twenty years afterwards threw Ramus to the assassins — the King founded a new Royal Lectureship of eloquence and philosophy, where Ramus would be safe from the persecution of his enemies in the University. But he was never to be free from their persecution, nor did he ever cease attacking current methods of university education, until he fell by the swords of assassins directed against him probably by his university colleagues.

We turn from the tale of these old rancors (a long one in the case of Ramus), to the labors of this eager and restless man, which were spent in simplifying the old methods, naturalizing and animating them, restating the educational matter, discarding the superfluous and absurd, and adding, as it were, a new-found quality of life. He fought to free education from vicious jugglery, to make it correspond with human nature and aid human accomplishment. In the reform of educational methods he seems to see ever and anon, a panacea for ignorance. In this he falls in with Roger Bacon long before him, and with Francis Bacon too, and others who imagined that all knowledge could be quickly gained through proper methods of approach. He had the dream that if men could but freely follow the light of reason, a century might suffice to bring the sciences to their goal.[4]

Ramus's chief grievance against Aristotle was that his logical system did not follow the natural inborn logic of the human mind. In true dialectic, as in other practical sciences, there is first the faculty of reason; next, the precepts for its right employment; and finally the practice through which precepts become habits, part of the normal play of the reasoning faculty. Conversely, one will observe that the practice of dialectic pre-supposes the art or science consisting in a body of precepts which, in turn,

[4] *Scholae in liberales artes,* cited by Waddington, *Ramus,* p. 343.

pre-suppose the reasoning faculty and the nature of reason, of which the body of precepts should be the accordant expression. Practice must conform to precept, and precept to the nature of that of which it is the precept or expression.

The end of dialectic is its practice or exercise in discourse, in accordance with right precepts, themselves in harmony with reason itself. These precepts are to be discovered from the practice of the best and most illuminating writers and philosophers of Rome and Greece, who exemplified the art of composing, of arguing and refuting, in their works. From their works we deduce the dialectical and rhetorical precepts, which have, in turn, proceeded from the rational natures of their great authors. With Ramus, dialectic is a close twin to rhetoric; and the two rest in scholarship and humanism, the study and love of classical letters. He makes clear that the true practice of this art must be real and living, serviceable in the affairs of life, in literature, and in the pursuit of truth. Let no fool think to attain it through the word play of the schools! And he illustrates his dialectic by a multitude of examples drawn from the best works of literature.

It was in this revivifying of dialectic, and then of other branches of education, that Ramus was creative. First, in dialectic, he attacked the matter truculently, shook it up, and worked it over resolutely, though not independently. For, of course, he could not free himself from Aristotle's system. His technical modifications were not as radical as perhaps he imagined.[5] His rather vainglorious and self-conscious boldness made him attribute undue novelty to his results. Great had been his travail, as in 1555 he writes in the preface to his *Dialectique* addressed to his Maecenas, Cardinal Charles of Lorraine. But it was worth the pains "to have dared enter the lists against all the philosophers who ever were, in order to wrest from them the prize of dialectic which

[5] Yet a fairly numerous school in various countries called themselves *Ramists* and professed to follow the precepts and practice of the master.

they had won by their great genius and diligence, and the prescription and judgment of centuries had confirmed to them."[6]

We turn to his well hated reforms in other fields. In a *Remonstrance au conseil privé*,[7] in 1567, against the appointment of his arch enemy Charpentier to a chair of mathematics, Ramus quotes his enemy's invective against himself, " que c'est un homme violent, importun, impérieux, qu'il avoit renversé la grammaire, rhétorique, logique, philosophie, mathématique, qu'il avoit faict tout un monde nouveau." " In which, gentlemen," says Ramus, " he spoke some truth." But Socrates had small repute at Athens till the Oracle declared him the wisest of men. " And one part of his admirable wisdom was his contention that the liberal arts should be kept related to human life, and help men to think and act well; but the schools teach subtilties useless in practice. . . .

" Gentlemen, when I came to Paris, I fell among the subtilties of the sophists, and they taught me the liberal arts through questions and disputings, without showing me any other advantage or use. When I had graduated as master of arts, I . . . decided that these disputes had brought me nothing but loss of time. Dismayed by this thought, led by some good angel, I chanced on Xenophon and then on Plato, and learned to know the Socratic philosophy."

Then when he had learned from this how silly the University professors were, to think to turn the liberal arts into sophistries, he spoke up and got himself in trouble,— as has already been shown. From which he was delivered by the good King Henry, and given a place among the royal lecturers.

" Ainsi doncques estant delivré, estant invité par pris et honneur royal, je me mis en tout diligence de traicter les disciplines à la socratique, en cherchant et démonstrant l'usage, en retranchant les superfluitez des regles et preceptes. En ceste laborieuse et pénible

[6] Given by Waddington, *Ramus*, pp. 401–407 — a characteristic piece of writing.

[7] Printed in Waddington, *Ramus*, pp. 411–417.

contention d'estude, j'ay travaillé jour et nuict à enseigner et mettre en meilleur ordre la grammaire grecque, latine, françoise, la rhétorique et surtout la logique, instrument singulier à manier et traicter tous discours. . . ."

Next he took up in order arithmetic and geometry, in which he is at present occupied.

This was a truthful picture of his labors. When the favor of King Henry and the Cardinal in 1551 made him a royal lecturer, in what was to be the Collège de France, he recognized as his the task of universal reform. The eyes of Paris were upon him. The youth thronged to his lectures, and he felt the responsibilities of a public man. His lectures on the classics, especially Cicero, were very popular. They were meant to illustrate his instruction in the seven liberal arts. These he taught with constant endeavor to keep their topics in correspondence with the practical needs of life and literature. He himself wrote grammars, of the Latin, Greek and French languages. In rhetoric he took up the warfare against the fashion of slavishly imitating Cicero or following Quintilian. Great was the fracas; Rabelais burlesqued it; Joachim du Bellay also satirized it. But Ramus kept sturdily on in the endeavor tc apply to all the liberal arts the principles of his natural and living dialectic; so as the better to make education conform to life. To this end also he translated Euclid, and wrote an arithmetic and a geometry, which like his other school books passed through numerous editions, and exerted influence in Germany and England as well as France. He was an ardent mathematician, and his text-books were better and clearer than those they superseded.

Ramus thought for himself in every field of education, testing all things boldly, discarding the useless, and reforming each topic along the lines of common sense. Strenuously in all things he endeavored to follow the light of his own reason. Three years before his death he wrote in a preface to his *Scolae in liberales artes:*

"Someone has written recently that Ramus teaches Plato's

method, and condemns that of Aristotle. The author, otherwise well instructed, has never read the Logic of Ramus; for there he would have seen it held that there is but one method, which was that of Plato and Aristotle as well as Hippocrates and Galen. . . . The same is found in Virgil and in Cicero, in Homer and in Demosthenes; it presides over mathematics, philosophy, and over the judgments and conduct of all men; it is not the invention of Aristotle or Ramus."

This was the method of man's inborn reason, which more men seek than find, and still more, perhaps, think they possess. With Ramus the struggle for it had been attainment. His real life's work, which told upon his world, lay in his endeavor to apply in every field of knowledge this method divinely implanted in man, and man alone, to which, as he thought, all true education, all valid knowledge, all human progress, must conform.

CHAPTER XVII

JOHN CALVIN

I. Humanist Reformers
II. Calvin's Formative Years
III. The Work at Geneva
IV. The "Christian Institute"

I

Reform of the generally accepted and practised Roman Catholic religion was certain to issue from the human growth and enlightenment which made some halting progress in France in the fifteenth century, and in the sixteenth advanced with broader energy. The Reform began almost unconsciously as a concomitant of the newly stimulated scholarship, which was winning a clearer impression of the past. Men were studying the Latin classics with the increasing insight of a larger knowledge, and were attempting Greek and Hebrew. The emboldened and deeply religious French scholarship naturally addressed itself to a like examination of the Bible, and began to compare what they found there with current ecclesiastical doctrines. This could not fail to show the lack of Scriptural authority for many teachings of the Church, as well as for much in its general complexion. If these awakening eyes perceived the Church to rest upon tradition and doctrine in part at least unsanctioned by Scripture, they would also see it standing upon practices which Scripture implicitly or explicitly condemned. Moreover, a new study of the Scriptures not improbably would lead to a constructive understanding of the Faith different from what the Church had taught for some centuries.

Lefèvre of Étaples, a coast town of Picardy, was the chief interpreter of these tentative beginnings of Reform, springing up in truth-seeking natures and issuing apparently from the habit of scholarly research. His was a gentle, earnestly religious, nature which was impelled to controversy by the love of truth. He is said to have been almost a centenarian when he died in 1536, and it is as an old man, at the end of a life of humane studies, that he comes forward as the exponent of a better truth in certain matters of the Faith. If he hoped to correct some baseless teachings, he had no thought of separation from the established church which held them. His mind was given to sacred study some time before 1509, when he published, in spite of his very imperfect knowledge of Greek and Hebrew, his *Quintuplex Psalterium,* saying in the preface: " For a long time I have been devoted to humane studies and have scarcely tasted of the studies which are divine, august, and not to be rashly approached. But from afar so brilliant a light has already broken on my sight that human learning seems darkness, compared with the sacred studies, while these seem to me to exhale a perfume unequalled for sweetness by anything on earth." [1]

The inchoate doctrinal reform that was in him becomes articulate in his *Commentary on the Epistles of St. Paul,* appearing in 1512. He puts the Scriptures as the one sure foundation of our religion. The doctrine of Christ is found in them; let us not follow the precepts and dogmas of men which have no foundation in the light from on high.

> " There are men to-day," says he, " who teach the people a silly piety instead of the doctrine of Christ. What profits it to observe new fasts and pay tithes? Why should I rely on prayers set by unknown men, and omit apostolic injunctions? Why die in a monk's frock, when one has all his life worn other clothes? Nothing of this sort is commanded by Christ. . . . The rest perhaps is superstitious rather than religious. . . . Let us cling to Christ alone, and to the apostolic teaching. That is enough, and is the chief thing for salvation."

He states the principle of justification by faith:

[1] Given by E. Doumergue, *Jean Calvin,* etc., I., p. 81 (Lausanne, 1899).

"It is most profane to speak of the merit of works, especially in the face of God. For a merit does not seem to ask a favor, but to demand what is due. To ascribe a merit to works is almost to hold the opinion of those who believe that we can be justified by works, the error for which the Jews are condemned. Let us keep silence over the merit of our works, which is little or nothing; and let us celebrate the grace of God which is all. One can attribute merit only to Christ, who has merited all for us; but, for ourselves, let us confess that we have no merit before God, and hope in His grace." Again: "Wilt thou say, has ever anyone been justified without the works of the law, written or natural? Yes, innumerable people." [2]

Works alone will justify no one. Neither will mere belief; — the devils believe. God alone justifies. Evidently Lefèvre has not elaborated his position. But he makes other steps in the direction of that Reform which was to acquire the name of Lutheran, Calvinist, Protestant. For him the waters of baptism are losing their magic quality, the Eucharist is ceasing to be a priest-made sacrifice, and becoming a memorial; though he does not reject the "real presence." He disparages fasts, and priestly celibacy leading to loose incontinence, and objects to the Latin liturgy, which is not understood by the laity who take part in its prayers.

Lefèvre plants himself upon the Bible against which no human doctrinal authority, no custom or tradition of the Church, can prevail. He set to work upon a translation of the Vulgate into French. This brought him into conflict with the Sorbonne (the theological faculty of the university) who would not have the Bible thus presented to the people. His antagonist was the fanatical Beda, the head of the college of Montaigu. Incidentally a bitter dispute arose over the "three Maries," as Lefèvre would prove them to be from Scripture, one and the same as the Church held them to be, and the Sorbonne again officially affirmed; — another instance of ecclesiastic fearfulness lest light be let in on some of the untenable positions of the Church. Francis, influenced by his sister Marguerite, kept Lefèvre from prison and the stake.

[2] Passages given in Doumergue, o. c. pp. 81–83.

But Paris was no longer safe from him and he eventually closed his eyes at Nerac, in Aquitaine, protected and comforted by Marguerite. His influence had been considerable; a number of able men had been his disciples, some of whom saw fit later to purge themselves of their Reform. But among them was Guillaume Farel, the fiery exhorter of Calvin.

One may assume that a University whose most powerful faculty fanatically opposed the acceptance of anything out of harmony with church tradition, would in other matters offer but an inferior and hide-bound instruction. All evidence shows this to have been the fact at Paris in the first half of the sixteenth century. It is also clear that the efforts to improve instruction came from men who were inclined to the Reform or known to be adherents of it. Budé and Ramus are examples. Mathurin Cordier was another. He had been converted in 1528 by his friend Robert Estienne, and was Calvin's first teacher at Paris. Known as the author of certain repeatedly printed *Colloquies,* he taught in Calvin's academy at Geneva, and died at the age of eighty-five, in 1564, the same year with his great pupil.

Besides these pronounced reformers, both in education and religion, there were scholars, poets, ecclesiastics, men of the world, who approved of the Reform, but fled from persecution, or escaped it by restraint of speech or, sometimes, by recantation. Their protector was the Platonically inclined Marguerite of Navarre, who declared (à propos of evangelical preaching) that no one should fear to hear the word of God. Among them was Briçonnet, bishop of Meaux, who loved Plato and advocated the Reform, till he was frightened back from it; and Clichtove, a pupil of Lefèvre, who also recanted. There was Clement Marot, court-poet and translator of the Psalms; and Rabelais, greatest of all. Marot shows a clear, if moderately instructed, intelligence alienated by the beliefs and practices of the Church. Rabelais's capacious mind, filled with the best learning of the time, despised the silly stories of the *theologastres* — belly theologians — of the Sorbonne, vain talkers, " sophistes sorbillans, sorbonagres, sorbonigenes " and so forth; and just as vehemently he despised the futile pedantry of the education which his youth had been subjected to. Such a man, of course, and Marot too, would be repelled by the later ways of the Reform under Calvin's dominance. For they combined love of the world and love of letters, with some subordinated rational desire for a religion freed from palpable untruth and follies.

The reform of education as well as the Reformed religion represented intellectual advance. It meant much to brush the encrustations from logic, and improve the study of grammar, rhetoric, and arithmetic. Whatever value the old crudities once had, to discard them now meant a truer and larger view of what was useful and what was useless in education, knowledge, life. Likewise, a more scholarly perception in matters of the Faith brought clearer understanding of the foundation of Christianity, and a rejection of some baseless traditions, of some conceptions more appropriate to magic, and some superstitious practices. The contemporaneous study of the Roman Law was penetrating through the accumulation of gloss and commentary to the text of the Digest. So now this new religious scholarship would pierce the once living spells of mediaeval symbolism, custom, and tradition, to the sure records of the pristine Faith, read them with fresh eyes, and re-interpret them according to their evident meaning, rather than follow traditional acceptances. The final systematized and ordered culmination of the Reform, which came through Calvin, represents still further intellectual or logical advance. But the austerity of Calvinism narrowed the fullness of interest in life embraced by the prior humanistic generation of French reformers. Yet his system was a product of a French mind, working itself out as soul and body in the Calvinist Church and State.

II

One may observe the environment of genius, and note the pabulum on which it has fed. But it presents a larger mystery than the capacities and limitations of common men. John Calvin was a man of power; the *vivida vis* of his nature entered his deeds and words, and made his *Christian Institute* a living sword. He was the incarnation of the power of reliance upon Scripture. He spoke in the assurance that he was the spokesman of God's truth. He lived in the conviction of God's perfect worth and sufficiency for men, his energies consecrated to God's glory. This lifted him above any selfish and meticulous interest in his own salvation, and made the inspiration of his leadership.

His *Christian Institute* [3] was the expression of himself. But this mighty self-expression of Calvin was emphatic re-expression. He belongs to the second generation of Reformers, and stands on Luther's shoulders. He is an interpreter of Paul and Augustine. He still speaks with the mouths of the great mediaeval schoolmen. His Institute is a *Somme,* a *summa* of Christian doctrine, only somewhat less inclusive and universal than the *Summa Theologiae* of Thomas Aquinas.

The arguments of this great book held themselves erect in Calvin's time and for the generations of his followers. But it was not merely the contents and the matter of the argument that made the book's enduring influence. Its consummate language and power of expression penetrated and held fast in the consciousness of men. The first Latin draft overwhelmed the ardent preacher Farel with its power, and a conviction of the god-given genius of the author. Here was the man to declare and organize the Church of God. And Farel had been right. This was in 1536: five years later Calvin's French version became a sword of flame in the vernacular. Its words and

[3] There is no ground in the Latin and French originals for the plural title "Institutes," used by all English translators of Calvin's great work, and followed, so far as I know, by English writers upon Calvin.

phrases transmitted themselves as a rich legacy to the advancing French language, carrying new disclosures of clarity and force.

One may mention the apparently formative facts of Calvin's life, until his final establishment at Geneva.[4] He was born at Noyon in Picardy in 1509. His father, a man of law and business, employed by the clergy and influential families of the neighborhood, was much interested in the education and worldly welfare of his son, whom he destined for the church. The town was not especially bigoted or religious; nor were its ecclesiastical affairs edifying. A powerful family held the bishopric as by hereditary right, and there were quarrels between the bishop and the chapter, and controversies touching the forgery of relics; with all of which John Calvin as his father's son must have been acquainted. His boyhood was little impressed with reverence for the Church; nor was his respect likely to increase when at the age of fourteen he set forth to carry on his education at the Paris University, which gave instruction in the elementary as well as the higher branches. There Calvin was first taught by Mathurin Cordier, and under him progressed from the barbarous Latin smattering prevailing among the half-educated youth, toward an ample and effective command of Latin. His intellect was rapidly developing, his memory was prodigious, and he was an indefatigable student. Hence the extraordinary attainments of his first ten years after reaching Paris.

As Cordier did not teach the higher courses, Calvin was transferred to the dirty old reactionary college of Montaigu, where the students' lives were passed in toil and squalor. Its principal was the most fanatical spirit of the Sorbonne, the intolerable Noël Beda, "not the Venerable," as his enemies remarked. There was war between him and the really venerable Lefèvre during these student years of Calvin; and one cannot doubt to which

[4] For them see finally E. Doumergue, *Jean Calvin,* etc. (Lausanne 1899, etc.); more conveniently, Willeston Walker, *John Calvin, the Organizer of Reformed Protestantism* (N. Y., 1906, Putnam's). H. Bossert, *Calvin* (Les grands ecrivains français) — and innumerable other books!

side Calvin had inclined when he left Paris in 1528. This young man, who had already been given sundry small benefices, and was destined for the Church, now proceeded to Orleans to study the Civil Law. His vacant place in the college of Montaigu, one may almost say, was taken by a slightly older man, by name Ignatius Loyola!

After some months at Orleans, Calvin was drawn to Bourges by the fame of the jurist Alciat. Bourges was the city of Marguerite, who protected many truth-seeking scholars there. Among them was Melchior Wolmar, a Lutheran who taught Calvin Greek, and became his friend for life. At his house Calvin associated with "God-fearing" men, and advanced in his religious convictions and the knowledge in which they were rooted. He met there also the little Theodore de Béze, ten years his junior, who was to become his adoring friend, biographer and successor.

After Bourges, Calvin is found again in Paris, studying more Greek under Danès, a highly reputed Royal Reader. Loyola and Rabelais may have listened with him to this Greek professor, perhaps, in the year 1531. The fruit of Calvin's classical studies soon appeared in his first work, in April 1532, a commentary upon Seneca's *De Clementia,* erudite and philological, and perhaps showing the moral tendencies of his mind.

But henceforth classical scholarship was to be the humble handmaid to the Reformed theology, with Calvin. He went again to Orleans, where at the University he was the "procureur" or representative, of the "nation" of Picardy. But by October 1533, he was back in a Paris excited by an attack upon Queen Marguerite in a comedy acted by the students of the college of Navarre, and by the Sorbonne's animadversions on a book known to have been written by her. The Rector of the University was Calvin's friend Nicholas Cop. He had spoken already in the Queen's defense, and is supposed to have asked Calvin to prepare for him the annual Rector's discourse before the University. Either Cop or Calvin, or the two together, prepared this fateful manifesto of the Reform.

Men's passions, already aroused, became enflamed. Cop fled to Basel, and Calvin left Paris. For a while he lived at Angoulême, then at Nerac, Marguerite's residence after she became the Queen of Navarre, and where dwelt the good old Lefèvre. After a while Calvin returned to Noyon, apparently was imprisoned there, and resigned his benefices! He went to Poictiers; then the Affair of the Placards drove him to flight in earnest; and he too went to Basel, and there composed in 1535 the first draft of his *Institute*.

The occasion of its rapid completion and publication was the need to defend the Reform from the accusations of lawlessness and anarchy, which the violence of Anabaptist bands had provoked, and Catholic hate had quickly seized upon. The first Latin draft, with its powerful epistle to King Francis, was published at Basel in March 1536. But the date of the letter to the King is August 1535. It opens with the statement that the writer had had no thought of addressing His Majesty when he first set himself to write his book. His only purpose was "d'enseigner quelques rudimens; par lesquelz, ceux qui seroient touchez d'aucune bonne affection de Dieu, feussent instruictz à vrai pieté." [5] But "seeing that the rage of certain of the wicked had so risen in thy realm as to leave no place for sound doctrine, I thought it better to make this book serve both as instruction to those whom I had intended to teach and as a confession of Faith to thee, that thou mightest know what is the doctrine against which those so furiously rage who are troubling thy realm to-day with fire and sword."

He had felt no shame to present a "somme" [6] of this same doctrine, which they think should be punished by imprisonment or exile, or the fire; and he knows with what horrible reports the King's ears have been filled, and the false calumnies by which this doctrine has been

[5] From Calvin's French translation of 1541. It is almost impiety to translate Calvin's mighty French. Where it seems quite clear, I have not tried to.

[6] The Latin, of course, is *summam,* which takes us back to Thomas Aquinas. See post p. 404 sqq.

defamed. He has no thought of making a personal defense, which might again open France to him. " Mais j'entreprens la cause comme de tous les fideles, et mesme celle de Christ." We have no reason to glory, save in the pity of God, through which with no merit of our own, we are saved. But our doctrine is above the glory and power of this world; " car elle n'est pas nostre: mais de Dieu vivant et de son Christ." Calvin refutes the charge that it is new and dubious and unconfirmed by miracles, which are not needed by those who forge no new Gospel, but can claim the miracles of Christ and his apostles for their re-assertion of Christ's truth. He shows that the Church Fathers are not against him; and as for *custom,* it were sheer iniquity to yield to it, since the better things rarely please the majority. So particular vices attain to a common vicious consent:—" mauvaise coustume n'est autre chose qu'une peste publique." As to which is the true Church, he has also much to say. And again, he begs the King not to be moved by false charges of sedition brought against those who live simple, peaceable lives, who even when driven from their homes do not cease to pray for the prosperity of the King and his realm. " They have not so ill profited from the Gospel that their lives are not examples to their defamers, of chastity, mercy, temperance, patience and modesty. Surely the truth itself testifies for us that we fear and honor God, when by our life and by our death we wish to sanctify His name."

Thus this letter reads as an early Christian " Apology " to a Roman Emperor, using similar arguments. It closes with a veiled threat. If their just pleas will not be heard, but are answered only with prison, blows, and burnings, then truly, as sheep led to the slaughter, they are reduced to extremity. " Tellement neantmoins, qu'en nostre patience nous possederons noz ames, et attendrons la main forte du Seigneur: laquelle, sans doubte, se monstrera en saison, et apparoistra armée, tant pour delivrer les povres de leur affliction, que pour punir les contempteurs."

" Le Seigneur Roy des Roys vueille establir ton

Throsne en justice, et ton Siege en equité, Tresfort et Tresillustre Roy."

One should read this epistle to King Francis to feel its power. The author was twenty-six years old. Before taking up the contents of his *Institute,* we may follow for a while the man himself.

Having published his book, Calvin left Basel for Ferrara, perhaps to counsel its Duchess, Renée of France, who led an anxious life as an adherent of the Reform. He exhorted her to steadfastness, and composed writings against papist rites and superstitions, the Mass, the worship of the wafer, indulgences, and the use of holy water. He evidently detested Italy, declaring, as Béze reports, that he entered it only that he might leave it.

From Ferrara, by various circuities of route, with Strasbourg in his mind, Calvin came to Geneva. The town had already cast out its objectionable bishops, and with the aid of Berne, had freed itself from their domination and the over-lordship of the dukes of Savoy. Through troubles and disturbances, it had organized itself democratically after the model of other towns in the Swiss Confederacy. The General Council of all the citizens elected the four syndics and the Lieutenant de la Justice. Sixteen citizens, also chosen by the General Council, with the four Syndics of the current year and the four of the year before, made the Little Council, usually called simply the Council. In emergencies, it could add thirty-five leading citizens to itself, and thus become the Council of Sixty. In imitation of Berne, a council of Two Hundred also was inaugurated, chosen by the Little Council. Under the exhortations of the fiery preacher Farel, and with the support of Berne, Geneva had declared itself "for the holy law of the Gospel and the word of God. . . . abandoning all masses and other rites and papal abuses, images and idols." It voted also to establish schools. In this action the Councils represented Church and State. They adopted the strict discipline of manners obtaining in other reformed Swiss cities, which represented the reaction of the French and Swiss Reform against the current looseness of morals. At this time, Geneva had about fifteen thousand inhabitants; and its violent quarrels were merely stifled for the moment, when Calvin arrived in July 1536 *en route* for Strasbourg.

Farel was the most influential leader of the Geneva Church — and State. He had published a brief " Sommaire " of the Reformed Faith. But on the appearance of Calvin's *Institute,* this fiery enthusiast declared his own book useless, so much more abundantly did the celestial water flow in Calvin's work. He accosted Calvin at the inn, and did not stop with gentle persuasion in his endeavor to change Calvin's plan to proceed to Strasbourg, and lead a life of study. He swore that God would curse him and his retired life if he drew back and refused to aid the Genevan Church in its necessities. Calvin was as if struck from heaven; he recognized the call of God, and overcoming his timidity and reserve, agreed to stay.[7]

III

Under Farel's aegis, Calvin entered upon a career destined to create a Reformed Church, with a Reformed dogma, liturgy, and ethics, and political institutions in harmony. It was in Geneva that he brought the Calvinistic Church-State into most complete existence; not without setbacks, revolts, and many troubles. At times, when his influence was great in Europe, a city election (1553) might go against him, or the Council might withhold its consent to the publication of one of his books! One thinks of Innocent III lording it over the kingdoms of the earth, when his unruly Romans had driven him to take refuge in Viterbo.

The first labor of Calvin, and those with whom he worked, and later dominated, was to bring about the organization, one might say, the formulation of a godly community. The fact and its expression lay in the Articles, the Catechism, and the Confession of Faith, and

[7] The scene is described in the writings of both Calvin and Farel.

their sworn acceptance by the city. The Articles — Articuli de regimine Ecclesiae — were presented with a written statement in the name of Farel and " other preachers "; and were approved in January 1537. They declared that the Communion of the Lord's Supper should take place every Sunday, in view of the consolation received from it by the faithful, and seeing that Jesus did not institute it for commemoration once or twice a year, but as a frequent exercise of our faith and charity. Those of evil life should be excluded, so that the sacrament might not be polluted and profaned. " Pour ceste cause, nostre Seigneur a mise en son Esglise la correction et discipline d'excommunication. . . ." To carry out this " discipline " good men were to be chosen from the different quarters of the city whose duty was to report evil doers to the ministers, for admonishment or exclusion from the Supper, but not from the preaching, since it might please the Lord to touch their hearts.[8] Whoever was thus excluded from the Supper was no longer in the Communion of the Church, and should not be permitted to remain within the community of the faithful, to wit, the City. Calvin was as adamant in his insistence upon the right of the Church to excommunicate, untrammelled by any authority beyond itself. And here, as often in the promulgation of the Reform, one is reminded of the organization of the early churches in the Roman Empire.

For the instruction of the rude and ignorant, Calvin composed the first catechism of the church of Geneva; in which the teaching of his *Institute* was put concisely.[9] It was an advance in religious instruction. Like the *Institute* which it summarized, this " Instruction " was not novel in substance, but new in its function and its efficacy. From its opening sentence —" Que tous hommes sont nez pour cognoistre Dieu "— in simple, dignified language, it moves with force and even sweetness in the power of its reason:

[8] The Articles provided also for church singing, the religious instruction of children, and marriage.

[9] It was not till 1541 that he composed the *Little Catechism,* in dialogue form.

"Il nous fault penser, nous qui faisons profession de pieté que ceste vie caduque, et qui bientost finera, ne doibt estre autre chose qu'une meditation d'immortalité. Or, on ne peult trouver nulle parte vie éternelle et immortelle, sinon en Dieu. Il fault doncques que la principale cure et solicitude de nostre vie soit de chercher Dieu et aspirer à luy de toute affection de cueur et ne reposer ailleurs qu'en luy seul."

Present needs demanded a declaration or *Confession* of the Faith, which "tous bourgeois et habitans de Genève et subjectz du pays doyvent jurer de garder et tenir." The Councils approved the measure. The difficulty was to make all the people take the oath, which should be administered through the local assemblies of the "dizaines," in which the city was divided. Objections came from many kinds of people. There were soon two parties, "jurants" and "non-jurants." In the main the oaths were sworn at last. But the next election was unfavorable. The preachers were requested by decree to abstain from politics and devote themselves to preaching. The powerful reformed city of Berne supported certain forms of worship, and after a conference with the Bernese representatives, the government of Geneva demanded of Farel and Calvin that they administer the Communion in the manner agreed upon with Berne. Calvin was no stickler as to such minutiae; but was a rock against interference. Hence a refusal. Banishment was pronounced against them. And Calvin made his way to Strasbourg, upon the strenuous invitation of Sturm, the great Reform educator, and others. The year was 1538.

In Strasbourg, Calvin taught and preached, gained much from intercourse with Sturm and Bucer, revised his *Institute,* and composed his reply to Cardinal Sadoletus, through which the godly minded of Geneva saw that there was none like him. The affairs of Geneva did not proceed securely. There were party tumults. The strenuously religious faction, friends of Farel and Calvin, were called *Guillermins,* after Farel's Christian name: later one said Calvinists. Farel counselled charity; Calvin for a while abstained from action. When he spoke, it was to express his love for Geneva, and point out that the enemy of his people was not their fellow citizens, but Satan.[10] The new preachers lacked Calvin's power of moral austerity. The College, the Hospital, the morals of the town, deteriorated. A Catholic reaction made some progress, fostered by the persuasive letter of the Cardinal. Berne menaced Geneva's liberties. The City could not safely appeal for succor from without. Solidarity, inner strength was needed, that it might take its free and independent place by the side of the other Reformed cantons. That could come through reorganization, regeneration; for which Calvin was the only fitting instrument. The decision was taken to recall him. He had scruples, felt distrustful of Geneva and of his own timid nature (of which no one else accused him!). He had many interests elsewhere; at Strasbourg where his influence was growing, in his studies, in the colloquy at Worms, which he attended, as he did the adjourned colloquy in Ratisbonne. His decision wavered; but again a letter from Farel turned him toward Geneva. His disinterested friends in Strasbourg, and also the pastors of Zurich, exhorted him to undertake the charge, urging that Geneva, situated at the confines of France, Germany, and Italy, might be the hearth from which the Gospel was destined to spread, for the enlargement of the Kingdom of Christ. So the event proved. Through the genius of Calvin, Geneva became the capital city of the Reform, radiating energy and inspiration.

Calvin returned to Geneva in September 1541, and entered on his task. At his request the Council immediately selected six of its members to act with him. Three days later he wrote: "After offering my services to the Council, I declared that the church could not maintain itself unless a constitution were established modelled on the word of God and the practice of the primitive church. I sketched the chief features, that I might be understood." His object was to secure the self-government of the

[10] Ep. to the Church of Geneva — Bonnet, *Lettres de Jean Calvin,* I, p. 13 (Paris, 1854).

Church, and give it sufficient disciplinary powers to keep its members in right belief and conduct. The *Ordonnances* as finally passed, somewhat modified from Calvin's draft, declared that Christ had instituted in his Church the four "offices" of pastor, doctor (or teacher), elder and deacon. Pastors (or ministers) were to be examined and chosen by the body of pastors in office, and confirmed by the Council; the elders were chosen by the Council, on consultation with the ministers. The ministers' duty was to preach, admonish and reprove, in public or private, and administer the Sacraments. It was for the teachers, through the school, to instruct in sound doctrine and in the "sciences humaines." The deacons were entrusted with the distribution of alms and the management of the hospitals, which were open to the indigent as well as to the sick. Begging was prohibited. An exceeding abundance of sermons was prescribed, not on Sunday alone. The Communion was to be administered four times a year. All the ministers were required to meet weekly for discussion, and every three months for criticism of one another; if there was contention among them, the elders should be called in; and when no decision could be reached upon grave matters of doctrine or conduct, recourse was to be had to the magistrates. Under the circumstances, the body of ministers obtained great influence in affairs. But the central organ of spiritual government and discipline was the *Consistory,* composed of members of the ministry and of twelve elders. It could summon before it for examination, censure, or ultimate excommunication, whoever offended in doctrine or conduct, or failed in church attendance. As the functions of the Consistory might impinge upon the powers of the Council to maintain order and punish for crime, the following significant provision was inserted:

"That all this [discipline] shall be done in such fashion that the ministers shall have no civil jurisdiction, and shall use none but the spiritual sword of the Word of God as St. Paul directs them; and that the authority of the government and of ordinary justice shall in no way be diminished by the Consistory, but that civil authority shall remain unimpaired. And, in particular, where it shall be necessary to inflict some punishment or restrain the parties, the ministers with the Consistory, having heard the parties and made remonstrances and admonitions as shall be fitting, shall report all to the Council, which shall deliberate on their report and order and render judgment according to the merits of the case." [11]

These provisions for the exercise of discipline by the body of ministers or by the Consistory made the primary Calvinist solution of the problem of maintaining the independence and disciplinary power of the Church in harmony with the authority of the civil government. Calvin set himself to uphold the Church in this relationship of independence and coöperation. The struggle was long, and in moments doubtful. Calvin, although minister, held no position in the city government, and was not even made a burgess till 1559. Yet he had become Geneva's autocrat, "the boss," in the language of American politics; and that in civil as well as church affairs. Although he felt the conflict to be repugnant to his timid and retiring nature, he must have known his ability and fitness for it. With vividness and tenacity he beheld as set in principle the import of seemingly small matters; and the power of his logic and passionate insistence was not to be withstood. All effective opposition to him ceased in 1555, when the Councils by a vote to abide by the *Ordonnances,* finally secured to the Consistory the right of excommunication.[12] Shortly afterwards the foolish violence of Calvin's opponents brought upon them cruel measures of banishment and death. Calvin approved and aided in the prosecution, and saw the hand of God in the tortures which forced questionable admissions from the victims. With Calvin the spread of Christ's Kingdom and the word of God hallowed every measure. One may add that his influence in Geneva had been strengthened through the admission to citizenship of numerous Frenchmen,

[11] From Walker's *John Calvin,* p. 273.

[12] See Walker's *John Calvin,* Chapters VIII–XIII for the story of these conflicts. Also, "Calvin's Programme for a Puritan State in Geneva," H. D. Foster, *Harvard Theological Rev.,* Oct., 1908.

exiles for their faith, men of education and intelligence, devoted to the cause of the Reform.

In accord with the spirit of the *Ordonnances,* Calvin formed an Academy combining elementary and university instruction. It was inaugurated in 1559 under the rectorship of Beza, the master's most devoted disciple. Distinguished teachers were installed, and students drew together from all countries. It became a power for the spread of Calvinism, as it sent forth convinced and instructed disciples to teach and preach in France, England, Scotland and the Lowlands.

Calvin continued in the Academy the courses of theological lectures which he had given unremittingly for years. They formed the nucleus of his Commentaries on the books of Scripture. To the task of commentator he had brought wide reading, an exceptional knowledge of the tongues, and a new and personal insight into the meaning of the sacred writers. They were the inspired enunciators of God's words. Calvin divined that these words of God had definite and single meaning, to be derived from the text. His exegesis, following upon the work of Luther, measurably freed itself from allegorical and mystical interpretations. His Commentaries have always exerted enormous influence.

The struggle and victory in Geneva, and the lectures in its Academy, were the fulcrum of Calvin's active influence upon western Europe, and most directly upon France. Thither passed innumerable letters from Geneva, strengthening and sharpening the convictions of the faithful, heartening the wavering, insisting upon order and organization. From Lausanne and Strasbourg, as well as from Geneva, travelled preachers, impressed with the thoughts and words and the formative ideas of Calvin; — "daring all things boldly for the word of God, of which they are made the ministers." The Reformed churches of France organized themselves along the lines which Calvin set — a band of communicants, one or more ministers, a Consistory, with regular preaching and administration of the sacraments.[13] But from lack of a co-operating civil government, the Genevan model could not be wholly followed in these French churches. The minister was chosen by the elders and deacons, who were elected by the body of the church. Ministers, elders, and deacons constituted the governing Consistory. The mode of worship, with the Catechism, came also from Geneva, where Calvin had fixed the liturgy of the Reform. In 1559 a small synod of French churches met in Paris to formulate a Confession of Faith and a general plan of organization. Calvin's teaching and methods were embodied in the result, although he had doubted the wisdom of the meeting.[14]

IV

Calvin's sweep of purpose made for the greatness of his *Christian Institute*. All the discipline of his study and all the wisdom of his experience rendered this book of many revisions a complete expression of his personality.

The first draft was completed in 1535, when Calvin was twenty-six. The strenuously systematized religious thinking which characterized it must have been gaining form in the young man's mind through the preceding years, overarching his classical and legal studies with a consecrating purpose. Great was the disciplinary value of these studies. What could have been more suggestive to the man who was to pierce through church tradition to the rock of Scripture, than the new training in the Civil Law, from which gifted students gained the faculty of penetrating through the maze of gloss and commentary to the text of the *Digest*?

His education, his tense purpose, and his conviction that he was the spokesman of God's truth, contributed to his style of power. He wrote Latin admirably; and his French, for lucidity and force, has never been excelled.

[13] Cf. Lemonnier, in *Hist. de France* (ed. by Lavisse), Vol. V,[2] p. 219, sqq.

[14] In 1557 Calvin put in the form of a letter "To the King of France," an admirable "Confession des Eglises de France." Bonnet, II, p. 151, sqq.

He is one of the great creators, and is often called the "father," of modern French. Pascal and Bossuet, in whatsoever they may have equalled or surpassed him, "stand upon his shoulders." [15] His unequalled talent for argument and effective presentation was early shown in the "Reply to the Letter of Cardinal Sadoleto." He took great pains with the arrangement of topics. The repeated revisions of the *Institute* brought some new matter and further elaboration; but most clearly they evince the author's constant effort to perfect the arrangement, the general lucid composition of the work.

The power of argument, the power of style, both were the man; the moving energies were a sense of the overwhelming primacy of God, faith in God's purposes, and a conviction of the loving nature of those purposes as to the elect, among whom of a surety was this vessel of divine truth, John Calvin. The power which reliance upon God has imparted to chosen men, becomes irresistible when increased through the devoted religious sense that the ineffable Will is enough for man — yea, though He slay me! Assurance of his own salvation may steel the martyr's heart, or the soldier's arm. But conviction of God's absolute worth and sufficiency for men, devotion to His Honor and His glory, rather than interest in the individual's salvation, is needful for the inspired religious leader. This devotion was possessed by Calvin, who felt and knew that the chief end of man was not his soul's salvation, but to know and glorify God.[16]

These were perhaps the most personal and intimate elements of the power entering the composition of the *Institute*. Around and about and behind them was the fund of the opinions, knowledge, and convictions belonging to the Reformers in France and Germany and Switzerland. There was no part of Calvin and his work that was not affected and made possible by this fund of antecedent Protestant knowledge and opinion.

[15] See generally all French works upon the literature of this period, e.g., Lanson, Brunetière, Faguet.

[16] Again, see the *Reply to Sadoleto;* and Bonnet, o. c. II. pp. 164 and 203.

Of the great books which have exerted enormous influence, the *Christian Institute* of Calvin contains a minimum of strictly speaking original thought. In a way, all books of Christian theology are based on Scripture interpreted reasonably or fantastically. The *Institute* was founded on Scripture rationally and acutely interpreted. But here, less learnedly, Luther preceded Calvin. Doctrinally the mighty antecedent of the *Christian Institute* was that man of prodigious doctrinal originality, the Apostle Paul. Augustine, in his further elaborations, is the next antecedent of Calvin's book. The *Christian Institute* is Paul and Augustine absorbed by a man of living power, and re-endowed with life through restatement and adaptation to the sixteenth century. Calvin added little to Paul and Augustine doctrinally, but much institutionally as it were, through his constructive faculty of civic and church organization.

The *Institute* is indebted to other Fathers of the Church, and may draw on them by name. Naturally it has absorbed the Nicene formulation of dogma; and is thus fundamentally orthodox. Its debt to the mediaeval schoolmen is less evident, less conscious. But Calvin knew Peter Lombard, Bernard and Aquinas; Duns Scotus affects his conception of the will as the primary element of the divine nature. The *Christian Institute* is by no means an unscholastic work. Calvin and other great reformers of his epoch strove to re-establish what they conceived to be the teaching of the New Testament and the early Church; but they had neither the will nor the power to shake themselves out of the assumptions, the modes of thinking and argumentation, which constituted a large part of their normal mental processes.

The very idea of the *Institute* as a summary of Christian doctrine reverts to the *Sentences* of the Lombard and the *Summa Theologiae* of Aquinas. But as the name *Institute* implies and as Calvin says explicitly,[17] it was a work of elementary instruction, " une clef et ouverture

[17] E.g. at the opening of the Epistle to the King in the " Argument " to the French edition of 1541.

pour donner accès à tous enfans de Dieu, à bien et droictement entendre l'Escriture saincte," and not a comprehensive Summa of whatever could be enfolded beneath the wings of *sacra doctrina.* Calvin's work has nothing to do with the "ancillary sciences," and so far as possible eschews the metaphysics of theology, all of which were dear to Thomas, and had place in his great *Summa.*

It is interesting to compare the arrangement of the two books. The *Summa* of Aquinas follows what one may regard as the natural order of presentation of the Christian matter, which had practically been followed by Peter Lombard, and is indicated in Augustine's Commentary on Genesis: i. e. God, His unity and trinity, the creation of the world, man, his fall, the Incarnation as the restoring means of his salvation, the Sacraments and the final Judgment.[18] To a considerable extent, especially in his final edition of 1559, Calvin follows the same order.[19] Thus in Book I of that edition, he treats of God, and of the nature of Christ and the Holy Spirit, and so of the doctrine of the Trinity, in substantially the order of Thomas; and, in the same order, he takes up the Angels and the creation of man, body and soul. With Book II comes the Fall of Man and the Incarnation, and, in fine, the saving work of Christ. This matter is continued through Books III and IV, concluding with a treatment of the Church and Sacraments.[20] Thus the order which Calvin

[18] Cf. *The Mediaeval Mind,* Vol. II, p. 352 sqq.

[19] It will not be necessary, either for this or for our other purposes, to discuss the numerous editions of the *Institute* as revised by the author and published in his lifetime. Suffice it to say that in 1539 he published a revised and somewhat enlarged edition, and in 1541 what was substantially a French translation of the same; it is this edition of 1541 that should be read as a monument of French. Calvin continued to revise and republish until, in 1559, he published what must be taken as the final and standard edition, divided into four books, in which the work was rearranged and much enlarged. In 1560 this edition appeared in a French translation made by Calvin or under his direction. See the *Prolegomena* to Vol. I and the *Introduction* to Vol. III of the Strasbourg edition of the *Opera* (1863 sqq.) and the *Introduction* by A. Lefranc to the French edition of 1541 (École des Hautes Études, 176–177). Among the Reformers, Calvin's *Institute* had been preceded by Melanchthon's *Loci Communes,* by Zwingli's *Commentaries,* and Farel's *Sommaire brieve,* all designed as Compendia of the reformed religion.

[20] There is one last chapter on Civil Government.

adopted in his final revision was, in skeleton, the order followed in the *Summa.* The resemblance becomes less obvious when perusing the substance of the work, because of the different stress laid by Calvin on his topics. Where he finds himself in harmony with the Church of all the centuries, he speaks briefly. Thus in treating the fundamental dogma of the Trinity, he avoids its metaphysics, gives a plain discussion of the Scriptural testimony to its truth, and reaches an orthodox conclusion.[21] On the other hand, in treating of the redemptive work of Christ and the believer's faith in Him, in Book III, he greatly enlarges the controversial topics of justification by faith and the divine election to salvation or damnation; while in Book IV, his treatment of the Church and its Sacraments, though falling in its proper order, becomes largely a polemic against the Papacy and the Mass, which naturally had no place in the *Summa* of Aquinas.

Like the personality of which it was the expression, the *Christian Institute* grew and developed, and yet in many respects remained the same from the first to the last edition. Its temper, its point of view, its attitude toward God and man, its human quality, was unchanged; but its doctrinal expositions were elaborated and made more sheer and ineluctable; while the author's accumulations of experience as well as learning, Christian and profane, contributed to swell the book. Calvin's personality seems to project most saliently from the French edition of 1541. That, with the Latin of 1539 on which it was based, had been thoughtfully revised from the first draft of 1536, but was not yet overlaid with the learned argumentation which serves to veil the man Calvin from the would-be twentieth century appreciator. We have already drawn upon that powerful French version for his letter to the King, and may advantageously continue with it for the body of the book, still giving brief extracts in Calvin's nervous French, so far as they seem readily comprehensible.

The prefatory Argument points out that although Holy

[21] It is in Chapter IV of the 1541 edition, say pp. 217–234. It is somewhat enlarged in the 1559 edition, where it makes Chapter XIII of Book I.

Scripture contains "une doctrine parfaicte, à laquelle on ne peut rien adjouster [ajouter], nevertheless the untrained man needs guidance through it; those who have received "plus ample lumiere de Dieu," may lend the hand "pour les conduire et les ayder à trouver la somme de ce que Dieu nous a voula enseigner en sa parolle." One notes here a point in Calvin's position: the Bible is for all, but there is need of guidance from those who have received more light from God: "à ceste fin j'ay composé ce present livre," which shall be a key to a right understanding of Scripture for all the children of God. And since we should recognize that all truth proceeds from God,— "j'oseray hardiment protester, en simplicité, ce que je pense de cest oeuvre, le recognoissant estre de Dieu, plus que mien." Let God have the praise, for His is the work, this work of Calvin's which he does not hesitate to exhort everyone to read diligently if they would have "une somme de la doctrine Chrestienne, puis une entrée a bien proffiter en la lecture tant du vieil que du nouveau Testament." Having done that, they will know "par experience" that I have spoken advisedly. "Si quelqu'un ne peut comprendre tout le contenu, il ne fault pas qu'il se desespere pourtant: mais qu'il marche tousjours oultre, esperant qu'un passage luy donnera plus familierement exposition de l'autre. Sur toutes choses, il fauldra avoir en recommandation, de recourir à l'Escriture, pour considerer les tesmoignages que j'en allegue."

Here is a further disclosure of Calvin's attitude: Let all read his book for guidance, and prove it, each for himself, from the passages of Scripture which it cites. This indeed is Calvinism, or individual judgment exercised under wise, i. e., Calvin's direction. Independence and guidance are not easy to reconcile, yet they must be joined by those who would escape the Charybdis of Romanism and the Scylla of the Anabaptists.[22]

[22] As to the limits to a proper consideration of the profundities of Scripture, Calvin says that we should keep to the statements of the text, and not probe unrevealed mysteries, and should also study Scripture for our edification and not to satisfy curiosity. Bk. I, 14, 4, of 1559 edition, the passage practically the same as in prior editions.

What would I know, cries Augustine, but God and the Soul? — quite enough! Says Calvin, opening his treatise:[23] The sum of all our wisdom falls into two parts, knowledge of God and of ourselves. The first shows that there is one God whom all should honor and worship, "la fonteine de toute verité, sapience, bonté, justice, jugement, misericorde, puissance, et saincteté,"— from whom we should expect and ask all these things. The second, by showing us our weakness, misery and wickedness, brings us to mistrust and hate ourselves, and kindles in us a desire to seek God, since all our good (bien) lies in him, while in ourselves we find a world of misery.

Augustine echoes through the opening of the *Institute;* which passes on to point out the correlations between knowledge of God and of ourselves: through the consciousness of our vanity and wretchedness, we recognize His truth and wisdom, and every excellence we lack. We are thus drawn and as it were led by the hand to find Him.[24] On the other hand, man comes to a true abasement and knowledge of himself only through contemplation of the wisdom and might and purity of God. And in order that no one may plead a pretended ignorance, some perception of divinity is implanted in the mind through natural inclination.

Calvin's emphasis is upon the greatness and righteousness and the sovereignty of God. Nothing has been said thus far of love between God and man. Man's life should be unbroken obedience to God's will, since men are His creatures, and He is the source of every good. Instead, the perversity of man seeks to appease Him with "quelques petites satisfactions. Au lieu qu'il luy faillot complaire en saincteté et innocence de coeur, nous forgeons je ne scay quelz fatras et ceremonies de neant, esperant l'amuser."

How much of Calvin and of the gist of his indictment

[23] When not quoting the French, I do not translate Calvin in full, but abbreviate the substance.

[24] The French is "mené par la main à le trouver," while the Latin text of 1539 has "quasi manu ducitur,"— the verb *manuducere* so frequent in Aquinas.

of the Roman Church is in this sentence! Oh! let man beware of that misknowledge of God which comes from fashioning Him after our image; which the "coeur fidele" will not do, but will be content to have Him such as He manifests Himself, beholding Him upon His throne as a just Judge, "lequel fera une fois rude vengeance sur tous transgresseurs," and to the good, will give eternal life. This faithful heart will be moved not by fear alone to keep from sin: "mais d'autant qu'il l'ayme et revere comme son pere, et le craint comme son Seigneur, mesmes quand il n'y auroit nul enfer, si ha-il horreur de l'offencer." This is true religion, faith joined with that fear of God which includes delight in the righteousness of His law and reverence freely offered to His majesty. Since we are all born to know God, and the knowledge which lacks such delight and reverence is vain, manifestly those who do not address to this end the thoughts and actions of their lives, fall away from the purpose of their creation.

So Calvin makes his point and clinches it, and then confirms it with testimony from pagan philosophers. He declares in fitting, but not novel terms, that God has graven upon "chacun de ses oeuvres certains signes de sa majesté, par lesquelz il se donne à cognoistre à nous selon nostre petite capacité." Thus, though His essence remain hidden, we perceive His virtue in His works. Nor did He omit to communicate by word and vision with His chosen people. And though new oracles no longer come to us from heaven, we have Scripture "en laquelle il a pleu à Dieu de coucher sa verité à eternelle memoire." We must consider this question, why Scripture has "mesme authorité envers les fideles, que pourroit avoir la voix ouye de la propre bouche de Dieu." Whereupon Calvin begins his argument to show that Scripture rather than the Church is the final authority for Christians. Some ask how we could know that Scripture is from God, unless the Church declared it? On the contrary, the authority of Scripture is founded on the "tesmoinage interieur du Sainct Esprit. Car jacoit [quoique] qu'en sa propre majesté elle [Scripture] ait assez dequoy estre reverée, neantmoins elle nous commence lors à nous vrayement toucher, quand elle est séellée en noz coeurs par le Sainct Esprit." Thus enlightened, we do not rely on the judgment of ourselves or others for the assurance that Scripture is from God; " mais par dessus tout jugement humain nous arrestons indubitablement, qu'elle nous a esté donnée de la propre bouche de Dieu, par le ministre des hommes: tout ainsi que si nous contemplions à l'oeil l'Essence de Dieu en icelle."

Strong words! This is the height of Calvin's argument for his assured reliance upon Scripture — the testimony of the Holy Spirit in our hearts. In the light of that, the excellences of Scripture reveal themselves more strongly in corroboration; for instance, its divine simplicity which uses no artifice beyond truth, so different from Demosthenes or Cicero or Plato, as to whom, says Calvin, " je confesse bien qu'ilz attireront mervielleusement, et delecteront, et esmouveront jusques à ravir mesmes l'esprit."

On the other hand, the consensus of the Church " n'est pas sans importance "; and the witness of so many holy men who have given the testimony of their blood. Beware of such as would lead astray with individual imaginings and alleged inspirations. It is not the office of the Holy Spirit " de songer nouvelles revelations . . . ou forger nouvelle espece de doctrine, pour nous retirer de la doctrine de l'Evangile, apres l'avoir une fois receu. Mais plustost de séeler . . . en noz coeurs la doctrine qui nous est dispensée par l'Evangile. . . ." Thus would Calvin warn off vagaries (as of the Anabaptists if one will) and bring all men back to the sure foundation of the Gospel truly and simply understood, as by Calvin.

The second chapter of the French edition of 1541 opens with a reference to an ancient proverb advising man to know himself — indeed the lack of self-knowledge is disgraceful. But the old philosophers wrongly sought through self-knowledge to enhance the dignity of man; we should seek it that we may humbly realize our misery and weakness. Gladly men hear good of themselves, and would fain believe in their ability to live well and happily. The more modest concede something to God, while retaining for themselves the better part of wisdom and virtue. Whoever will exalt human nature is most welcome everywhere. All this is fatal self-deception.

Although God's truth and human judgments agree that our best wisdom is self-knowledge, they differ as to the way of knowing. After the opinion of the flesh, man seems to know himself when, relying on his understanding and virtue, he sets out to do his duty. But he who looks to the standard of God's judgment finds in himself no hope, nor anything by which to order his life. There is indeed some seed of nobility in our nature, for we cannot think of our origin or end and not be spurred to consider and desire the immortality of the Kingdom of God. But this should humiliate us. For what is our origin but that from which we have fallen? And what is our end but that from which we have turned away? There is nothing but to groan and sigh for our lost dignity.

It is well to know how man was first created, before we consider his vices; lest we be led to impute them to the Author of his nature. So Calvin sets himself to this great factitious problem of Christian doctrine. And what sentences he contributes, contending against this slander upon God: —

> "Attendu donc que nous voyons la chair desirer tous eschappatoires, [loopholes] par lesquelz elle pense la coulpe de ses vices pouvoir estre transferée allieurs: il fault obvier à ceste malice. Il est donc besoing de traicter tellement la calamité du genre humain, que nous couppions la broche à toutes tergiversations de nostre chair; et que la justice du Seigneur soit delivrée, non seulement d'accusation, mais aussi de toute reproche et murmure. Neant moins que cela se face en telle sorte, que nous ne declinions point de la pure verité."

It is certain that our father Adam was created a participant in the divine wisdom, righteousness, virtue, holiness and truth. By his ingratitude he effaced the divine image which he bore; and ignorance, weakness, filth, vanity and injustice took the place of those qualities in him and in his descendants, born like unto him, infected with his pollution. Here Calvin pauses, with Augustine, to thrash the beastly Pelagians who held that this original sin was transmitted by imitation, and not through generation. It is enough for us to know, that as God set good gifts in Adam not for himself alone, but for all human nature; so when Adam lost them, he lost them for us all. And with clear conviction Calvin declared original sin to be "une corruption et perversité hereditaire de nostre nature, laquelle nous faict coulpables, premierement de l'ire de Dieu, puis apres produit en nous les oeuvres, que l'Escriture appelle oeuvres de la chair: . . . adultaires, paillardises, larcins, haynes, meutres, et gourmandises,"— the list taken from Paul. With gathering power of demonstration, following the good Augustine, he shows this corruption penetrating our entire nature, becoming our very selves:

> "nostre nature n'est seulement vuide et destitutée de tous biens; mais elle est tellement fertille en tout espece de mal, qu'elle ne peut estre oysive . . . C'est que toutes les parties de l'homme, depuis l'entendement jusques à la volunté, depuis l'ame jusques à la chair, sont souillées et du tout remplies de cette concupiscence, ou bien, pour le faire plus court, que l'homme n'est aultre chose de soymesme que corruption."

Having thus delivered himself, Calvin considers how far there may remain in man, "environné de misere et necessité," some spark of freedom and desire for good; a topic which leads (as in the *Summa* of Aquinas) to a discussion of the human faculties, according to the philosophers and the Doctors of the Church. With them, the Lombard is cited, and St. Bernard. At the end, Calvin abides in the conviction that the will and understanding are bound in sin and impotence, requiring the "remede de la grace de Dieu, par laquelle nostre nature vicieuse est corrigée." Grace is not bestowed on all men, nor, when given to one, is it bestowed because of the merit of his will, but through the free gift of God, whose justice may also withhold it. And Calvin agrees with Augustine "que la volunté humaine n'obtient point grace par sa liberté, mais obtient liberté par la grace de Dieu." He follows the great Father's presentation of the further offices of grace in reforming and strengthening the will; discusses points of view from which grace may be regarded, and with much argument shows the falsity of the Pelagian view of human liberty and merit, and upholds the position of Augustine. In opposition to an adverse interpretation of the parable of the man who fell among thieves, he makes the sound remark touching allegorical interpretation: "Les alegories ne doibvent estre receuës, si non d'autant qu'elles sont fondées en l'Escriture." For himself he will admit that the human soul has some knowledge of good and evil, and some notion that there is a God, though it does not know him aright. Nothing impugns the conclusions of Saint Augustine:

> "C'est que les dons gratuitz, qui appartennent à salut, on esté ostez à l'homme apres sa cheute; que les dons naturelz, qui ne le peuvent conduire à salut, ont esté corrompus et pollus . . . que l'entendement de l'homme est tellement du tout aliené de la justice de Dieu, qu'il ne peut rièn imaginer, concevoir, ne comprendre, sinon toute meschanceté, iniquité, et corruption. Semblablement que son coeur est tant envenimé de peché, qu'il ne peut produire que toute perversité. Et s'il advient qu'il en sorte quelque chose, qui ait apparence de bien, neantmoins que l'entendement demeure tousjours envelopé en vanité, le coeur adonné à tante malice."

Chapter III is devoted to God's "Loy escrite," given as a more certain witness to what had become obscured in the "loy naturelle." In this law God discloses Himself as a God of righteousness. "Mais le Seigneur, non content d'avoir monstré, en quelle reverence nous devons avoir sa justice, à fin aussi d'adonner noz coeurs à l'amour d'icelle [righteousness] et haine d'iniquité, il adjoinct des promesses et menaces." By threats and promises, God incites love of righteousness in the hearts of the faithful — according to Calvin.

Passing over this chapter, in which the Ten Commandments are treated at length, we come to chapter IV, *De la Foy, où le Symbole des Apostres est explicqué.* Calvin accepts the Pauline view; since we cannot fulfill the Law, our only way to escape rejection is through God's compassion, which we must receive in firm Faith, and rely upon in certain hope. He will consider the nature of the Faith through which *the chosen children* of God enter His Kingdom. It is not the " credulité vulgaire " with which one assents to the statements of the Gospel. That such suffices is a pernicious opinion taught by the " Sophistes et Sorbonistes," who also add " je ne scay quelle distinction frivole de la foy formée et informe," a distinction, by the way, not lightly treated by the great Aquinas, whom Calvin does not mention here. For faith we must turn to the Word of God, which is faith's end and object, the mirror where it beholds and contemplates God, and seeks and trusts His will, gaining a knowledge of His compassion, in which the heart of man, touched by grace, may indubitably repose. And Calvin gives as the " pleine " definition of faith: " une ferme et certaine cognoissance de la bonne volunté de Dieu envers nous: laquelle estant fondée sur la promesse gratuite donnée en Jesus Christ, est revelée à nostre entendement, et scellée en nostre coeur par le Sainct Esprit." If Calvin had not thus kept his discussion austere and intellectual, carefully avoiding the word " love," he would have come closer to the *fides formata* of Aquinas.[25] Calvin's faith is an intellectual certitude. " Certes la Foy ne gist point en ignorance; mais en cognoissance "; and it does not lie in reverence for the Church. He passes on to discuss each phrase of his definition, and next takes up the successive clauses of the Apostles' Creed.

In the fifth chapter Calvin turns to the subject of *Penitence,* which not only " est conjoincte á la Foy, mais aussi en est engendrée." He is scandalized at " the fasts and other things " by which the monks and schoolmen, with Peter Lombard, their captain, have stuffed their books.

[25] Cf. *The Mediaeval Mind,* Vol. II, p. 510.

And he launches a grand attack on the likewise time-honored Purgatory, which is but a fiction of Satan, built of blasphemies against the full and sufficient sacrifice made by Christ. Other reformers had been silent here;

"Mais quand la purgation des pechéz se cerche aillieurs qu'en Christ, quand la satisfaction est transferrée autre part, qu' à luy, il est dangereux de se taire. Il fault donc cryer à haulte voix, que purgatoire est une fiction pernicieuse de Sathan; laquelle faict un opprobre trop grand à la misericorde de Dieu, aneantit la croix de Christ, dissipe et subvertit nostre foy. Car qu'est-ce que leur est purgatoire, sinon une peine que souffrent les ames des trespassez, en satisfaction de leur pechez? Tellement que si on oste la phantasie de satisfaire, leur purgatoire s'en va bas. Or si de ce que nous avons par cy devant disputé, il est faict plus que manifeste que le sang de Christ est une seule purgation, oblation, et satisfaction pour les pechez de fideles, que reste-il plus sinon que le purgatoire soit un pur et horrible blasphesme contre Jesus Christ?"

Perhaps Calvin never showed more boldly his clear consistency of reason than in this hazardous attack upon the doctrine of Purgatory, so dear and so natural to the stumbling faith of those who know themselves unfit for heaven.

The sixth chapter takes up the cardinal topic, Justification by Faith and the merits of works, " le principal article de la religion Chrestienne." We need not follow Calvin through his elaboration of the favorite theme of the Reform. His position is defined in an opening sentence: Since most men imagine a mixed righteousness of faith and works — " imaginent une justice meslée de la Foy et des oeuvres, monstrons aussi, devant que passer oultre, que la justice de Foy [the righteousness of or through Faith] differe tellement de celle des oeuvres, que si l'une est establie, l'autre est renversée." This assuredly is Paul, and this is Calvin. And at the end of the long chapter we note the conclusion of the argument whereby one who has been guilty of the breach of any one command is worthy of death,—" entant qu'il a offensé la majesté de Dieu," he is guilty of them all. The righteousness by works — " la justice des oeuvres est une parfaicte obeyssance de la

Loy . . . une observation entiere et consommée de la volunte de Dieu." Obviously impossible: hence there can be no righteousness, no justification, through works. This is the Pauline conclusion, not easy for every stomach to digest.

Passing over the next chapter, in which polemically, and with scholastic narrowness, Calvin discusses the difference between the Old and New Testaments, we reach another pillar of his system, Predestination, a doctrine in its twofold terror unto salvation or damnation, necessitated by God's foreknowledge of the Fall of Man with its entailment of corruption, and the justification, through Faith, of the elect.[26] So long as election unto salvation, with Paul, with Augustine, was accepted, to flinch before the converse election of the rest of men to hell was but an amiable weakness unjustified by the logic of the situation. And to-day in an age when science will not blench before the grim facts of the natural world, and recognizes the equal grimness of human social fact, we need not stammer over this theology, which seems to reflect the ways of nature, and present a divine analogue to the teeth and fangs of life. And even as to election, predestination, why go back to Eden and the Fall of Man? We see election in ourselves and those about us, rich and poor, the gifted and degenerate, saints and criminals. Did they make their characters, their faculties, their circumstances, which raise or damn them? Is there not a surfeit of election here? And of the double predestination to heaven and hell, so far as concerns this world? Yet — here we stammer — the good man or the wise man steers his life through perils which are seen and through others utterly unseen by him. Whether his barque is wrecked or not, seems chance; and yet somehow he steers.

Calvin did not stammer; but, with unamiable logic, accepted the double predestination of mankind to heaven and hell, according to the good pleasure and righteous will

[26] One queries just when this doctrine of the double predestination seized upon Calvin. There is next to nothing about it in the *Institute* of 1536, while it is full fledged in the editions of 1539 and 1541.

of God. He acknowledged predestination to be a difficult matter, easily obscured. Let faithful inquirers be admonished, and first of all remember that when they " enquierent de la predestination, ils entrent au Sanctuaire de la sagesse divine." The overbold and curious will find it a labyrinth with no escape. " Les secretz de sa [God's] volunté, qu'il a pensé estre bon de nous communiquer, il nous les a testifiez en sa parolle — la voye unique, la seule lumiere " to conduct us through what it is allowed us to discern of this deep matter: " sortiz des limites de l'Escriture, nous cheminerons hors du chemin et en tenebres." We need have no shame " d'ignorer quelque chose en ceste matiere, où il y a quelque ignorance plus docte que le scavoir "— the last phrase reminiscent of Nicholas of Cusa. But, continues Calvin very finely,

> " Il fault donc garder, d'empescher les fideles d'enquerir ce qui est contenu en l'Escriture, de la predestination à fin qu'il ne semble, ou que nous les veuillions frauder du bien que Dieu leur communiqué, ou que nous veuillions arguer le sainct Esprit, comme s'il avoit publié les choses, qu'il estoit bon de supprimer. Permettons donc à l'homme Chrestien d'ouvrir les aureilles et l'entendement à toute la doctrine qui luy est addressée de Dieu; moyennant qu'il garde tousjours ceste temperance, que quand il voirra la sacrée bouche de Dieu fermée, il se ferme aussi le chemin d'enquerir."

And much more follows which in its power and narrowness may recall Milton: — even as in his language this same Calvin reminds us of his stylistic child Pascal: " La vie humaine est environnée, et quasi assiegée de miseres infinies." Might that not have fallen from the immortal *Pensées*?

He excels in definitions in this chapter. For instance: " nous appelons Predestination le conseil eternel de Dieu par lequel il a determiné ce qu'il vouloit faire d'un chascun homme. Car il ne les créé pas tous en pareille condition: mais ordonne les uns à vie eternelle les autres à eternelle damnation. Ainsi selon la fin à laquelle est créé l'homme, nous disons qu'il est predestiné à mort ou à vie." Naturally, his argument follows Augustine; and he passes through the deep waters of God's will covering murder and rapine, and wrestles with the equally difficult problem, why men should plan and pray and strive, seeing that everything in their lives is predestined. Even Calvin cannot make this quite clear;— there are limits to the consistency of every thinker. But practically and religiously, he transforms predestination into trust in God; which indeed had been Calvin's rock before he laid hold upon predestination. To him and his followers had come the power of those who know that no harm can break the guard of God's protection. Their courage, their energy, their strength, were doubled through faith in God's purposes with them,— and with their evil enemies! The Lord is my helper! True it is, as Calvin says, and ought to know, that the doctrine of predestination neither shakes nor troubles faith, but strengthens it, at least, for men of faith and power.

This is abundantly confirmed by the next chapter upon Prayer. Beautifully the opening paragraph declares that, knowing his own impotence, man if he would have succour in his need, should seek it beyond himself. How generously has God given us of Himself in his son Jesus Christ; through him offering us happiness for our misery, and riches for our poverty: to the end that our Faith shall look to His dear Son, and our strength and hope repose in Him. "Ceste est une secrete, occulte, et cachée philosophie, laquelle ne se peut entendre par syllogismes; mais ceux là comprennent ausquelz nostre Seigneur a ouvert les yeux, à fin que en sa lumiere, ilz voyent clairement." Calvin's heart had its arcana, where logic did not enter: though logic is present with him when in this same chapter he shows that prayer should not be offered to the saints.

The following chapter on the Sacraments is incisive. Only baptism is recognized and the Lord's Supper. A Sacrament is defined as "un signe exterieur, par lequel nostre Seigneur nous represente et testifie sa bonne volunté envers nous, pour soustenir et confermer l'imbecillité de nostre Foy." Calvin goes very far toward utterly rejecting the magic-mystery element, which from the time of the early Church had made the sacraments into life-giving miracles, regularly administered. He teaches that in the Lord's Supper we are spiritually fed with the body and blood of our Lord, and assured that his body once given for us is ours forever, and that we possess Christ crucified. As for the thorny question, *how* we possess him,— " pensons premierement que c'est une chose spirituelle que la Sacrement; par lequel nostre Seigneur n'a pas voulu repaistre noz ventres, mais noz ames. . . . En somme contentons-nous de l'avoir spirituellement." Calvin rejects transubstantiation, and the actual physical presence of the body of Christ,— thus, advancing beyond Luther. Mightily he thunders against the Mass as a sacrifice and oblation: the Saviour offered once and for all a sacrifice upon the cross, the efficacy of which endures forever.

We come to the fourteenth chapter, which Calvin in the edition of 1559 transferred to his discussion of predestination (Book III, ch. XXIV). It sets forth the freedom of the Christian from the servitude of the Law: first, in that the assurance of his Justification rises above the Law and its righteousness; secondly, in that his conscience is not bound by the Law, but, having been delivered from its yoke, freely obeys the will of God; thirdly, in that he will not make external things a matter of conscience before God.

> " Or il fault diligement considerer que la liberté Chrestienne en toutes ces parties, est une chose spirituelle: de laquelle toute la force gist à pacifier envers Dieu les consciences timides, soit qu'elles travaillent en doubtant de la remission de leurs pechez, soit qu'elles soient en solicitude et crainte, à scavoir si leurs oeuvres, imparfaictes et souillées des macules de leur chair, sont aggreables à Dieu, soit qu'elles soient incertaines de l'usage des choses indifferentes. Pourtant elle est mal prinse de ceux, ou qui en veulent colorer leur cupidité charnelle pour abuser des dons de Dieu à leur volupté; ou qui pensent ne l'avoir point, s'ilz ne l'usurpent devant les hommes; et pourtant en l'usage d'icelle ilz n'ont nul esgard à leurs freres infirmes."

All of which is excellent Pauline teaching.

Such freedom would seem to be made vain by subjection

to men. Yet to set ourselves above human laws would cause much evil. One must therefore distinguish between what is spiritual, belonging to the things of God, and what is political or civil; the first pertaining to the life of the soul, the second to the present life, enabling men to live justly and decently, and having to do with "meurs exterieures." Such are the respective functions of these two, "l'une Royaume spirituel, et l'autre Civil on politicq."

Calvin argued doughtily throughout his life upon the distinctness of Church and State; yet his policy sought to unite them in the common service of God. He drew something from the constitution and history of Geneva, where bishopric and town had the same boundaries, and the functions of one and the other overlapped. But in maintaining the liberty of the Church, he tended to superimpose its authority upon the State. If both Church and State unite in their object of right belief and conduct, and both have God as their lawgiver and sovereign, the Church, being concerned with the immortal soul, is superior to the State, which more immediately administers temporal affairs. Thus the Calvinistic religious element tends, if not to dominate politics, at all events to direct them. At the same time the possibly opposing presence of two organisms exerted reciprocal restraint, and tended to prevent the tyranny of either. In their righteous union of purpose, and restraint upon the abuses or usurpations on the part of either, the Calvinistic Church and State promoted the development of civic liberty and function in those who were members as much of one as of the other. The weapon of the Church was disapproval, censure, excommunication in the end, which cut off the recalcitrant civilian from all that he respected. On the other hand, the actual application of physical punishment, constraint, or banishment or death, was with the State, and might be brought to bear even upon the too intolerable ministers of the Word.

Calvin conceived the Church to consist of all the elect of God, the dead, the living and the yet unborn. It is one, inasmuch as Christ cannot be divided; and no one is saved who is not a member of it. It implies "the Communion of the Saints," inasmuch as those who are one in the fellowship of Christ, impart to each other the divers spiritual gifts bestowed on them by God. The marks of the Church are the preaching of the Word of God and the administration of the Sacraments through its ministers, and the mode of life, *vitae exemplum,* shown by those who are truly its members. Its visible and efficient union is preserved by its chosen ministers, whose election properly issues from the people and is sanctioned by the approval of those who are already ministers. Visibly organized in this manner, each church has charge over the conduct of its members, and authority to reprove and excommunicate, whereby it warns the member of his final condemnation before God. The purpose of excommunication is that those who lead scandalous and wicked lives shall not be counted among Christians, and corrupt the good; but rather that they be turned to repentance.

This true and universal church exercising its due authority, is to be distinguished from the Papacy and its corruption of ecclesiastical power; which Calvin characterizes in his fifteenth chapter, *De la Puissance Ecclesiastique.*[27] The usurpations of the Roman Church would "imposer necessité aux consciences, ez choses desquelles elles sont affranchies par Jesus Christ." That Church has succeeded to the tyranny of the Law. "Il fault qu'elles [the consciences of Christians] recongnoissent pour leur Roy un seul Christ leur Liberateur et qu'elles soyent gouvernées par la seule Loy de liberté, qui est la sacré parolle de l'Evangile, si elles veulent retenir la grace qu'elles ont une fois obtenue en Jesus Christ. Et qu'elles ne soyent assubjecties à servitude aucune." So Calvin would hold his church and people free from those burdens which St. Paul said should not be laid on men's consciences. He would reject "toutes les constitutions qui sont aujourd'huy nommées ecclesias-

[27] Here we return to the French edition of 1541. In the last two or three pages we have drawn from the edition of 1559.

tiques." Authority is granted to the Church as St. Paul says, for edification, not for destruction. And Calvin denounces the usurpations of power to make new articles of faith and assert for the Church and its tradition an authority equal or superior to Scripture. The tyranny of human traditions lays such inventions falsely on the Church, and causes it to transgress the command of God.

In chapter XVI, *Du Gouvernement Civil,* Calvin turns to that authority whose function is the administration of civil justice, decency and order. There are those who when they hear of a liberty assured in Christ, think they have no fruit of it so long as they see any authority set over them; they would alter the world, and abolish laws and magistrates, by whom they deem their liberty impugned. " Mais celui qui scaura discerner entre le corps et l'ame, entre ceste presente vie transitoire, et la vie advenir, qui est eternelle, il entendra pareillement assez clairement, que le Royaume spirituel de Christ, et l'ordonnance civile, sont choses fort differentes." The latter has nothing to do with the Kingdom of Heaven, and would be needless there. Its purpose — " le but de ce regime temporel est, de nous fere conformer à la campaignie des hommes, pour le temps qu'avons à vivre entre les hommes; d'instituer noz meurs à une justice civile; de nous accorder les uns avec les autres; d'entretenir et conserver une paix et tranquilité commune." Therefore, following the example of Christ, we should have respect for magistrates, who are made protectors of public tranquillity and decency, and the common peace and safety. Further, the tributes and imposts set by princes are their legitimate revenue, which they should use for the maintenance of the State. We should obey the laws, and recognize even wicked kings and rulers, and obey them so long as we do not thereby disobey God. The Lord is King of Kings: " Nous devons puis après estre subjectz aux hommes qui ont preeminence sur nous; mais non autrement sinon en luy [Christ]." An enormous and elastic reservation this, as the Roman world had learned from the early Church, and as the sixteenth and seventeenth centuries were also to learn, with much spilling of blood.[28]

In his last chapter, *De la Vie Chrestienne,* Calvin sets the general rule, that we should imitate Christ, and show forth his image in our lives. If we cannot be perfect, we should strive to " tendre à la perfection que Dieu nous commande." It is a chapter of Christian morals and piety, suited to a time of stress and tribulation. At the close a special emphasis is laid upon *vocation,* which God has commanded us to regard in all the acts of life and to keep our own " estatz et manieres de vivre." One should not exceed or go beyond: for example, it is not for a private man to presume to kill a tyrant. But there also lay in this conception of vocation the power of the call of God, which in this man Calvin spoke masterfully to kings and princes, and moulded a religious revolution.

We leave the *Institute,* to view Calvin's work more generally. Out of the small distracted city of Geneva, he created a model church-state, in which the morals, beliefs and energies of the people were held at the pitch of efficiency. If pleasure-lovers sharply were restrained, and impediments set upon the free intellectual action of individuals, at least it was done by the will of the people, effectuated through this dual communal organism. Yet, while he lived, Calvin's masterful genius could not but make him autocratic; and his direction of affairs promoted the welfare of the town. He lent the acumen of his mind and legal training to a codification of the city's laws, and to the best adjustment of its taxes. He taught that it was not usury to accept reasonable interest upon money loaned; an economic recognition greatly to the commercial

[28] Paul F. M. Mealy, *Les Publicists de la Réforme* (Paris, 1903), gives the political ideas of the French reformers after Calvin, showing their departure from his quasi-pacific doctrines. After the massacre of St. Bartholomew (1572), Hotman, de Béze and Marnay turned to the idea that authority is from the people, who can revoke it when abused. Under God, the people are sovereign, and from them a delegated authority passes to King and magistrates. They perceived the importance of the representative assembly; and their ideas influenced Englishmen.

advantage of the Reformed. The city's health was the better for his aid in the construction of sewers and the erection of hospitals. He concerned himself with methods of heating and protection against fires; through him the weaving industry was revived. His latest years brought the establishment of an Academy, through whose eager scholars his influence and the fame of Geneva were spread through France and England. It is hard to say what the city did not in some way owe to her illustrious minister.

Looking from Geneva to France, we see in Calvin a second Paul, taking on himself the care of all the churches. It is he who organizes them; who moulds and formulates their beliefs; regulates their conduct,[29] who mediates their differences; who upholds their courage under persecution. His letters to the French martyrs take us back to exhortations from the persecuted churches of the second century, whose situation was reproduced in the decimated, but ever growing, reformed churches of France.[30] Or again in his letters one might think to hear St. Bernard speaking in the case of some little monk whose parents would not have him so robustly fight for Christ. To a cautious friend who unobtrusively favored the Reform, and would have his more ardent son act with like prudence, Calvin, almost in Bernard's words, writes " si vous estes froid et tardif à sortir de l'abysme où vous estes plongé, pour le moins ne portez pas envie à vous enfans si Dieu les en délivre . . . . Vous ne debvez estre marri [disturbed] que l'authorité de Dieu soit preferée à vostre contentment." [31]

It was wonderful how sure he was that he was right, in the spirit of those who from all Christian times have been ready to die for their faith, and to glorify God. It seems also wonderful to us, (as if we again were listening to Augustine answering queries) what remarkable things this sixteenth century man of God conceived himself to know. He writes in a letter, " Aux cinq prisonniers de

[29] See e.g. Bonnet, *Lettres de Jean Calvin,* I, p. 213, II, p. 311–320, " Aux fideles de France."

[30] See Bonnet, *Lettres de Jean Calvin,* II, pp. 182, 298, 301.

[31] Bonnet, o. c. II, p. 285. Compare *The Mediaeval Mind,* I, p. 415.

Lyon," who had reason to inquire of such matters: "Touchant de la nature d'un corps glorifié, vray est que les qualitez sont changées, mais non pas toutes." [32]

Calvin had developed his system under German influence at Strasbourg; it came to its full flower only in Geneva, where it could work itself out actually, soul and body, Calvinistic Church and State. But it was a product of the French mind, of the French faculty of undeviating logical thinking and expression. Yet it was not to prove permanently suited to the French character, or adaptable to French institutions. In France, it showed capacity for organization in the face of persecution, comparable to that of the early Church in the Roman Empire, and also amazing fighting energy against overwhelming power. But there it could never reach that full dual church-and-state development which it attained under Calvinistic governments, as in Scotland, and for a time in England. Only under such concurring conditions could all its possibilities be actualized.[33]

[32] Bonnet, o. c. I, p. 343.

[33] To pass beyond the boundaries of France, and her wars of religion, and follow the influence of Calvin in the Low Countries, in Scotland and in England, would require a history of the second half of the sixteenth century, and a history of the seventeenth in the New World as well as in the Old. Calvin "knit the forces of non-Lutheran Protestantism into a real spiritual communion animated by similar ideals and dominated by one view of the Christian life. The ill-related Reformation movements of France, of the Netherlands, of Scotland, to a less degree of Poland and Hungary, found in him their unifying force. He gave them creed, discipline, and organisation. He formulated their theology. He inspired their martyr-courage. He taught them how best to oppose Rome. He trained many of their leaders, provided them a city of refuge in persecution, and an example of a disciplined Christian community which attracted their admiration and imitation. Over all this vast region he exercised an unofficial but far-reaching episcopate. By constant correspondence, by personal acquaintance and appeal to those whom he never met face to face, by the labours of those who had been his pupils and reproduced his spirit, he moulded the growth and determined the form of the Reformation movement to a degree comparable with the work of no other among the reformers save Luther. But for him the story of the Reformation outside of the land of its birth would have been vastly different. . . . [His] authority was not due to office or peculiar advantage of station. It was purely one of mind over mind. But it was all the more real and long enduring. Calvin so impressed his interpretation of Christian truth and of the Christian life upon men that they thought his thoughts after him, and his ideas became part of the mental fabric of a large portion of the inhabitants of central and western Europe, and ultimately of North America.

Nevertheless in France, as well as in Great Britain and Massachusetts Bay, Calvinism was an educational discipline, teaching men to know the Bible, training them to think straight and true, and giving them courage to apply their logic to religion, to government and to society. It carried tremendous educational value as a discipline and sharpening of the mind. Further; it represented a heightening and an increase of the effective validity of thought. If its specific tenets are no longer held by enlightened people, it was in its time a most specific enlightenment in religion, piercing through superstitions and the distortions of the glosses of tradition, to the text and significance of Scripture. It was a way out from the pit. Intellectual advance may relate directly to religion and to ultimate conceptions of the relationship between God and man. It need not be directly concerned with secular temporalities, with physical science, or with *belles lettres*. Yet Calvin himself, in the entire compass of his knowledge, might perhaps be held the most notable scholar of his age, surpassing all men in the keenness of his knowledge of the Bible, and with splendid training in law and in classical scholarship. So far as relates to this large compass of his learning, he was a humanist; though never a humanist in the sense of regarding the humanities as in themselves an end. Instead, he was a Deist; his end was God, and the glory of God, reflected downward through restoring grace freely given to obedient and adoring men, that is to the elect. In the otherwise ineradicable corruption of man's nature, there was no good thing, save what came with this freely imparted saving grace of God.

Rabelais and Calvin, those two greatest of contemporary Frenchmen, peers in knowledge and in mental grasp;

"The influence of Calvinism, for more than a century after the death of the Genevan reformer, was the most potent force in Western Europe in the development of civil liberty. What the modern world owes to it is almost incalculable. Yet Calvin was never by intention a political reformer. His interests were always overwhelmingly religious; and the results of Calvinism in the cause of religious freedom were the indirect and unexpected, rather than the anticipated consequences of his work. They were the effect of the logic of Calvin's principles, rather than any conscious part of his reformatory aim." W. Walker, *John Calvin,* pp. 402–404.

in their different ways both set against the superstitions and corruptions of the Church;— is it not interesting to observe their far more fundamental and universal opposition? The understanding and acceptance of life by Rabelais and by Calvin were in mortal conflict. The one held all human life, including every positive element of it, to be good and utterly desirable; the other held humanity to be vile and diseased, until restored and changed by the injection of what was not human, but from God. Rabelais was as comprehensive and tolerant in his temperament as in his mind. Calvin subordinated life to service, and though abominating monkish vows and like formal renunciations, had but casual consideration for any happiness or pleasure which did not make for the glorifying of the Creator and Monarch of the World, the Creator and restorer of the Saints.

THE END OF VOL. I